I0797053

SLAVERY, SEGREGATION, and the SECOND FOUNDING of RICE UNIVERSITY

SLAVERY, SEGREGATION, and the SECOND FOUNDING of RICE UNIVERSITY

Alexander X. Byrd
and W. Caleb McDaniel

Foreword by Ruth J. Simmons

LOUISIANA STATE UNIVERSITY PRESS  BATON ROUGE

Published with the assistance of Rice University

Published by Louisiana State University Press
lsupress.org

Manufactured in the United States of America
First printing

DESIGNER: Michelle A. Neustrom
TYPEFACES: Whitman, text; Futura PT, display
PRINTER AND BINDER: Sheridan Books, Inc.

All photographs appear courtesy of Rice University.

Jacket illustration: Jacqueline McCauley at Rice University, September 1965. Courtesy Rice University.

LIBRARY OF CONGRESS CATALOGING-IN-PUBLICATION DATA

Names: Byrd, Alexander X., 1968– author. | McDaniel, W. Caleb (William Caleb), 1979– author.
Title: Slavery, segregation, and the second founding of Rice University / Alexander X. Byrd and W. Caleb McDaniel.
Description: Baton Rouge : Louisiana State University Press, [2025] | Includes bibliographical references and index.
Identifiers: LCCN 2025018347 (print) | ISBN 978-0-8071-8442-4 (cloth) | ISBN 978-0-8071-8551-3 (epub) | ISBN 978-0-8071-8552-0 (pdf)
Subjects: LCSH: Rice University—History—20th century. | William M. Rice Institute—History. | School integration—Texas—Houston—History—20th century. | African Americans—Texas—Houston—History. | Segregation in education. | Slavery—Texas—Houston—History. | Houston (Tex.)—Race relations—History.
Classification: LCC LD6053 .B97 2025 (print) | LCC LD6053 (ebook) | DDC 378.764/141—dc23/eng/20250617
LC record available at https://lccn.loc.gov/2025018347
LC ebook record available at https://lccn.loc.gov/2025018348

In memory of Edward L. Cox (1943–2024),
mentor, colleague, and friend

Contents

Illustrations

MAPS

FIGURES

Foreword

Almost twenty years ago, in the summer of 2005, I was invited to speak at Gettysburg, a site emblazoned on my intellectual and emotional landscape as the place symbolizing the heroic battles that delivered my great-grandparents from slavery, transforming the lives of my family and giving me the freedom to claim my future. That visit stirred me to reflect on the postwar reconciliation between the North and the South and led me to consider the many ways in which we are obliged to reconcile historical legacies with our current needs, aspirations, and opportunities. Contrasting our idealized "emancipation vision of Civil War memory"[1] with the exacting and jagged work of healing and reconciliation, I wondered how I might, as president of Brown University, apply the lessons of the war's aftermath to our university's examination of the links between Brown's founders and the transatlantic slave trade.

It is no secret that a university is avowedly a place where strong positions arise and collide and where passion and loyalty enflame and deepen those positions. Campus combatants often lack the advantage of established rules of engagement, making the revision of long-held heroic university narratives fraught. Yet, just as intentional efforts across time helped the nation survive and thrive following a civil war, thoughtfully designed truth-telling and reconciliation efforts are important to fulfilling our founding ideals.

The founding of Rice University offers an unusually and helpfully striking example of how this process can be wholesomely and productively undertaken as society grapples with issues that could not have been foreseen by previous adherents. When endowed by William Marsh Rice, the university was imagined as a place for young white men and women (but especially men) who would be leaders in a city the donor recognized as needing a high level of knowledge and expertise. I am reminded of John Adams, who, in his time, worried about whether there were enough men sufficiently "fit" to satisfy the needs of an aspiring nation. That such founders considered the preparation of those who would come to lead in subsequent times is a testament to the thoughtfulness and seriousness of purpose of Rice and his founding trustees. That they were unable to acknowledge fully the Black Texans already leading their communities and to imagine how the city and nation would change, bringing other groups into full participation, is to be understood as altogether typical for the historical moment in which they were moved to act. But if one might forgive them their inability to see a future that included an immense diversity of individuals and abilities in the service of their goals, one must also celebrate the fact that every era has the opportunity to examine the suitability of extant parameters and purposes, judge their applicability to future needs, and reenvision a more relevant direction. Thus, we should see this natural process of reimagining past actions in the context of what is needed today as implicit in every institution's responsibilities.

The task of revisiting a founding purpose should, I believe, fall to those with the knowledge and skills to be judicious in the way they look back on history, particularly if that history has been challenged as discriminatory, excluding what we would recognize today as groups that fully warrant inclusion. To proclaim that we must always hold to the original founding principle or design is problematic for two reasons: first, because, if we acknowledge that the world is ever changing, we will acknowledge that today's needs may differ significantly and, second, we must also allow that institutions that resolve to remain the same at any cost may ultimately fail. Thus, one need not fear a careful review of how the mission or purpose has evolved or reject a considered questioning of whether adjustments are in order. For what can be more uplifting to the ultimate purpose for which an institution was formed than to understand the degree to which that underlying purpose can be made even more salient today?

The Rice University Task Force on Slavery, Segregation, and Racial Injustice began its discussion of the history of Rice University with an examination of its founder and namesake's connections to slavery and his activities during the Civil War, as required not only by its official charge but also by the imperative duty of a university to tell the truth. The task force continued to follow that charge by then turning to examine the university's early history, from its chartering in 1891 and opening in 1912 through the half-century following, during which Blacks were denied admission. Task force members wrestled with how to tell the story of the evolution of this practice in a way that might help the Rice community understand its costs and consequences. At the same time, the lengthy and inclusive process encouraged the community to understand the benefits of embracing the manifold changes that have occurred since the university's first founding. Both aspects of this story are important to the full understanding of where the university sits today as well as to its prospects in the future. There is no question that the first founders were prescient in understanding the importance of an excellent university to the development of a great city. There is also no question of the importance of an intentionally and robustly diverse university to a city that has become not only one of the most populous and important in the United States but also one of the most internationally diverse in the world. Anyone able to apprehend the power of William Marsh Rice's original idea for developing the city must also see and, I trust, rejoice in the powerful rationale for a robustly integrated university in the service of the city that Houston has become.

This volume is rich in details about the environment at the time of William Marsh Rice's arrival in Texas and the founding of the William M. Marsh Institute, adding names, entities, events, and data that directly and indirectly influenced the unfolding of events up to the period when the university initiated desegregation and admitted its first Black student in 1964, the year after I graduated from a Houston high school. Richly populating the history with these details, Alexander X. Byrd and W. Caleb McDaniel masterfully document the elements of the period, bringing to life for today's readers a fuller understanding of those times. One particularly notable element of this history gives long-overdue visibility to those previously deemed lesser actors who nonetheless bore much of the credit for enabling and assisting in "the second founding" of Rice as a more modern university.

Lovers of history will appreciate the details. From the survey of the original Rice property to the struggle with nearby Black landowners who defended their property rights against an encroaching university, the painstaking disclosure of long-forgotten or obscured elements of the struggle to open casts light on some of the more unseemly elements of the founding. Some details will be unsettling to those unfamiliar with facts such as the proximity of "Freedmen's Town" in the city's Fourth Ward, which had also housed the Gregory Institute for Black students. Further, revelations about the early white students of Rice Institute permit us to imagine the climate for Black workers who preceded Black students on campus. White students in the early days of Rice were also victims of the bigotry of the times, and learning that some were members of the Ku Klux Klan should not surprise. The authors bring needed balance to these unsavory revelations, being careful to point out that there were in fact Rice students who advocated for the admission of Black students prior to the university's endorsing integration of the student body.

Most moving to many will be the invaluable accounts of Black men and women who joined Rice as workers in an oppressive environment in which their humanity and dignity were not fully recognized. Figures like the trainer Jack Shelton rightly deserve to be a part of the history of the university for, though often caricatured in typical racial tropes, they were the vanguard for the transition to an integrated university where equal access and equal rights were to be implicit even though not initially acknowledged.

The high point of this rich account, however, is the years during which the legal impediment to integration gave way to the admission of the first Black students. Those early enrollments, not surprisingly, were fraught; indeed, neither of the first two undergraduate enrollees graduated. The students who followed them would have a difficult adjustment. From some whites not wanting a Black roommate to the overwhelming loneliness that students reported about those years, much of what we learn about how Black students experienced Rice is very moving. Yet, one can appreciate the effort the authors make to render the campus environment in its fullest context. For example, while citing the lack of support for early Black enrollees, the authors assert that all students at Rice in that period faced a lack of proper "support structure."

It is fitting that the authors recall the 2023 Black Excellence Gala, at which Velma McAfee Williams was recognized for her contributions to Rice. In many ways, relating this recognition is emblematic of the need to bring many elements of Rice's history into fuller relief. How did Rice become the place that so many love and admire today? It was by dint of courageous individuals who were willing to teach Rice something about what it was and what it could ultimately be. Without their willingness to do so, the university would be but a footnote in the history of the great universities of the world. That Rice is firmly and undeniably among the top universities in the world today, with the potential to become ever more prominent, rests in large part on the willingness of so many to undertake and follow the perilous journey from segregation to full integration and inclusion. The story of that journey, as told so ably by the authors, is not only important to the integration narrative of Rice but is also vital inspiration for future faculty, administrators, and students who will hold Rice accountable for honorably living up to its founding ideals.

Ruth J. Simmons, President Emerita
Brown University
Houston, October 2024

Preface

In 2019, Rice University's then-president, David Leebron, commissioned the Task Force on Slavery, Segregation, and Racial Injustice and appointed us as cochairs. The task force was charged with investigating Rice University's past with respect to slavery, segregation, and racial injustice; encouraging frank and honest discussion about that past; and identifying suggestions for Rice's future. This book is one of the products of that work.

Rice's task force followed a trail blazed by many other universities that had already undertaken the hard work of reckoning with institutional histories of slavery and racism. Particularly important was the pioneering example of Brown University and its Steering Committee on Slavery and Justice, commissioned in 2003 by Brown's then-president, Dr. Ruth J. Simmons, who later served as a member of the Rice University Board of Trustees and as president of Prairie View A&M University, a historically Black university just outside of Houston. When our task force joined a consortium of similar projects, known as the Universities Studying Slavery, Rice University became the sixty-third school to join the group, which as of this writing has more than one hundred members. Our task force, which convened a steering committee of faculty members, students, alumni, and staff, benefited greatly from our review of similar projects at other colleges and universities.

These projects have collectively led to a powerful new understanding of the roles that slavery and racial injustice played in the histories of colleges and universities, as well as the roles that colleges and universities played in the histories of slavery and racial injustice. Yet no two of these projects have been exactly alike. Each reflects the distinctive past of a particular institution and the specific present in which the project began.

In our case, the history of Rice University (chartered in 1891 by its founder and namesake, William Marsh Rice, but not opened for classes until 1912, after his death) raised a particular set of questions. Whereas many other projects had focused either on the roles of institutions during slavery, or on the later history of segregation, or on questions about equity and belonging in the present, Rice's history offered us an opportunity to think about linkages across typical chronological divides. How was a university that was not opened until the twentieth century connected to the history of slavery? Conversely, how did the histories of slavery and segregation continue to shape a university even after integration had begun?

From 2019 to 2023, our task force wrestled with such questions over a four-year period of historic change for both the university and the nation. Yet the mission of research universities like ours remained a fixed star by which to navigate. As we noted in a final message from our task force to the Rice community in 2023, universities aim "to pursue knowledge freely for the betterment of the world, and to follow evidence wherever it leads—even when new evidence challenges conventional wisdom, and especially when the evidence exposes a university's own errors." At their best, universities also provide models for collaborative and democratic decision-making and governance.

In that spirit, our steering committee met more than two dozen times over four years, including multiple day-long retreats as well as numerous smaller gatherings of subcommittees and working groups. Through intensive discussions, the committee arrived at twelve key recommendations for the university, published with our final report in 2023 and reproduced here as an appendix. In addition, we organized a wide-ranging series of public programs featuring invited speakers and panels.

As cochairs tasked with producing a narrative about our historical research, we also hosted a total of forty-nine public, one-hour webinars known as "Doc Talks" between 2020 and 2023. In these webinars, we shared documents from our ongoing research with each other, discussed their significance, and invited feedback from guests and audience members, who contributed greatly to the work by sharing their own research, refining our interpretations, and pointing us in new directions. These programs served as the building blocks for the three research reports released by the task force and for this book.

In the summer of 2021, the task force released two interim updates. One discussed our research to date on slavery. The other focused on the history of a statue of William Marsh Rice that sat at the center of a campus quadrangle and that had become a focus of protest and discussion on campus in the summer of 2020. Then, in the fall of 2023, we released a final report with our recommendations and a lengthy additional narrative entitled "Constraints of Race: A History of Rice University and Black Texans from Segregation to Second Founding."

The present book brings significantly revised and updated versions of these three reports together for the first time in one volume. We have solidified some conclusions that were advanced provisionally in our interim research updates from 2021, and we have modified others in light of some new evidence. For example, in 2024, after the release of our final report, additional research uncovered a document that no previous history of the university had discussed: a will and last testament written by William Marsh Rice that discussed his plans for a school for "poor white children" in 1868—more than ten years earlier than the documents previously believed to record Rice's first thinking along these lines. (We have included an annotated transcription of the will as an appendix.)

That discovery in particular contributed to a substantial revision of what appears here as chapter 2, but other new archival material appears throughout the book. An entirely new section, chapter 9, treats the context in which the task force began its work. And to make space for such additions, some passages in the reports are not reproduced here.

Interested readers can still find all three of the original reports, which contain fuller summaries of the work of the task force, online and in the collections of the Woodson Research Center at Rice's Fondren Library. We extend a special thanks to the archivists there for their sustaining support over many years. The reports also document the work of countless people who supported and joined in this work from the beginning, especially the members of the steering committee listed in this book's appendix. For feedback on parts of this new volume, we are indebted to Randal Hall. Bruno De Castro Sousa and Matt Drwenski produced the maps, and we gratefully acknowledge the work of Farès el-Dahdah on the historical data underlying the campus map. Louisiana State University Press's peer-review and editorial processes greatly improved the whole. We are grateful to President David Leebron for entrusting us with this work and to President Reginald DesRoches for supporting this book's publication. For our families, who have held us up in love over the past five years, words alone are not enough to express our thanks. Above all, we thank the many Rice Owls, in the past, present, and future, who have worked, are working, and will continue to work on fulfilling the promise of the second founding.

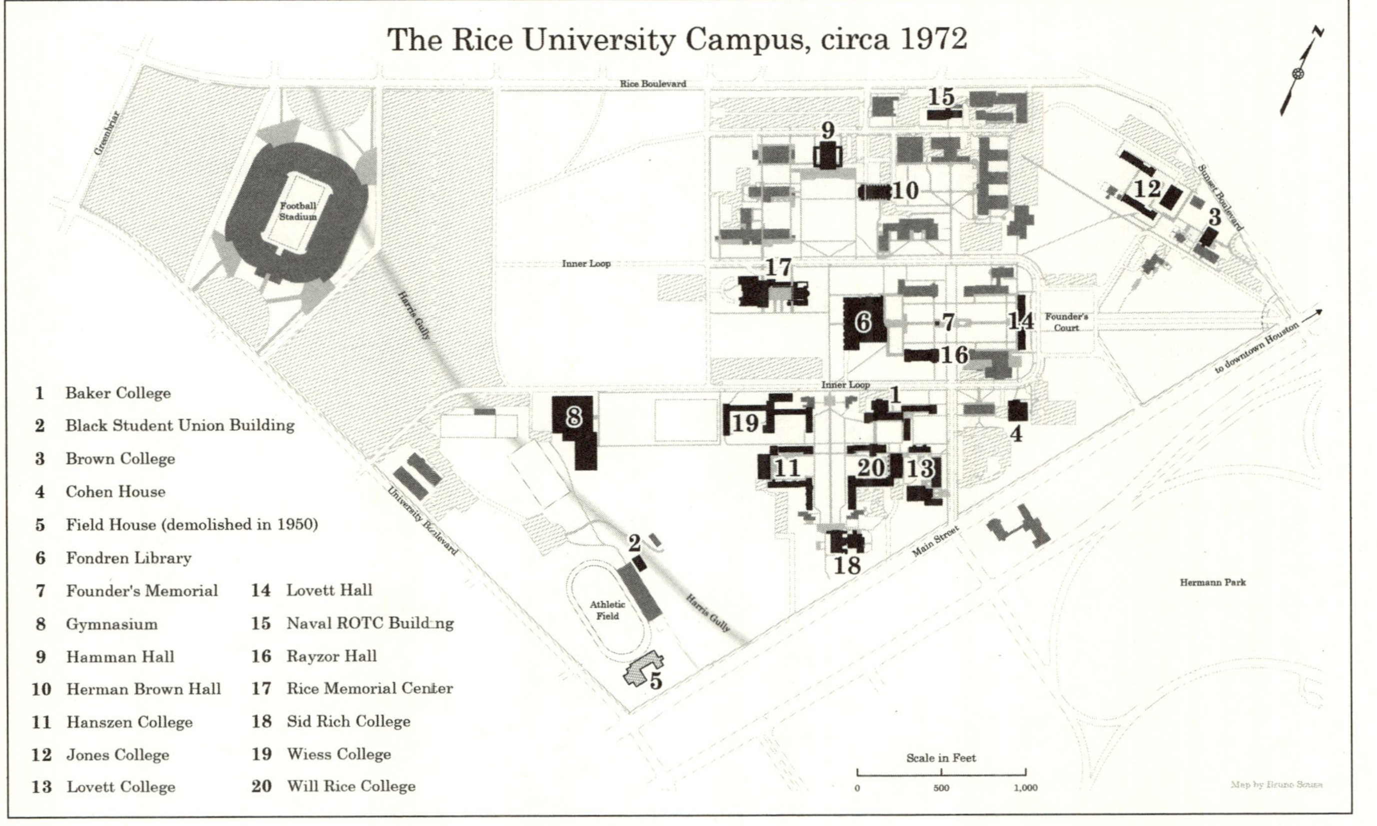

The Rice University Campus, circa 1972
Rice Boulevard
Greenbriar
Football Stadium
Harris Gully
Inner Loop
Sunset Boulevard
Founder's Court
to downtown Houston
Athletic Field
University Boulevard
Main Street
Hermann Park
Scale in Feet
0
500
1,000
Map by Bruno Sousa
1 Baker College
2 Black Student Union Building
3 Brown College
4 Cohen House
5 Field House (demolished in 1950)
6 Fondren Library
7 Founder's Memorial
8 Gymnasium
9 Hamman Hall
10 Herman Brown Hall
11 Hanszen College
12 Jones College
13 Lovett College
14 Lovett Hall
15 Naval ROTC Building
16 Rayzor Hall
17 Rice Memorial Center
18 Sid Rich College
19 Wiess College
20 Will Rice College

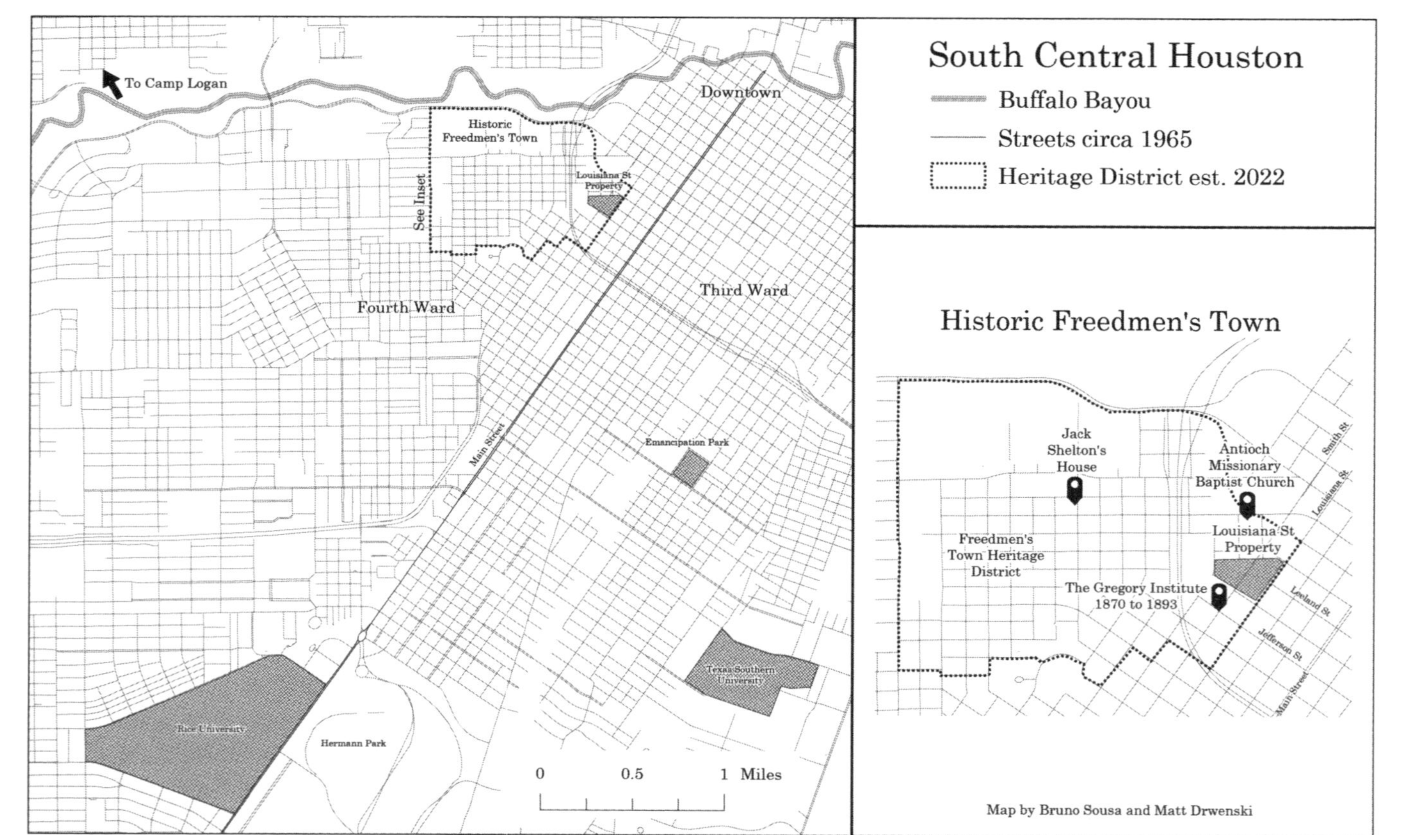

South Central Houston
Buffalo Bayou
Streets circa 1965
Heritage District est. 2022
To Camp Logan
Downtown
Historic Freedmen's Town
Louisiana St Property
See Inset
Third Ward
Fourth Ward
Main Street
Emancipation Park
Texas Southern University
Rice University
Hermann Park
0
0.5
1 Miles
Historic Freedmen's Town
Jack Shelton's House
Antioch Missionary Baptist Church
Smith St
Louisiana St
Louisiana St Property
Freedmen's Town Heritage District
The Gregory Institute 1870 to 1893
Leeland St
Jefferson St
Main Street
Map by Bruno Sousa and Matt Drwenski

SLAVERY, SEGREGATION, and the SECOND FOUNDING of RICE UNIVERSITY

INTRODUCTION

Waco, 1967

On a stormy Wednesday at the end of May in 1967, Dr. Earl W. Rand, professor of education at Texas Southern University in Houston, traveled up the road to Waco, Texas. He had come to deliver the commencement address for A. J. Moore High School.

Moore High was a proud, historic Waco institution, with roots stretching back to the final years of Reconstruction in Texas. Its founder, African American educator Alexander James Moore, had come to Waco not long after slavery's abolition to be a professor at Paul Quinn College, established in 1872 by circuit preachers in the African Methodist Episcopal Church. While there, Moore had begun teaching the children of freedpeople in his home, and the classes quickly grew until they had to be moved to a small wooden building with four rooms. Moore served as that school's first principal, and in 1923, Waco city officials moved the now officially segregated school into a larger brick structure. The new institution, which would graduate thousands of Black students before its closure in 1971, was named after A. J. Moore.[1]

In 1967, near the end of that school's storied history, Earl W. Rand was a fitting choice as Moore's commencement speaker. A native of east Texas, Rand had graduated from Jarvis Christian College, a private school that opened in 1912 with few funds but powerful human resources in the form of Black students like Rand, who would later serve as Jarvis's president in the 1930s. Now he served as head of the Division of Education at Texas Southern University (TSU), the chronically under-resourced, minority-serving public university in Houston's predominantly Black Third Ward. In short, Rand was a seasoned veteran of the century-old struggle to provide higher education options to Black Texans after slavery.[2]

Rand had titled his speech to the Class of 1967, "Education Pays Dividends—Invest Wisely." But as he looked out over the crowd of 160 graduates and their families that day, the professor decided to set his prepared remarks aside. He then asked for the audience's "indulgence" while he suggested some causes for concern about the moment they were living through.[3]

A "new era" was beginning in Texas, he noted. Elite, historically segregated institutions, including schools and universities, had started to open their doors to a select group of African Americans. Sounding a refrain familiar to the generation of Black teenagers who sat before him, Rand advised the Moore graduates that to "compete" in this new "market," they would have to "be better" and do even more than their white counterparts to prove they belonged.

Their task would not be easy, said Rand. "A people who have been left out of the main stream of life in a culture" shaped by "300 years of 'slavery and second class citizenship'" might find it disorienting to join the institutions that had so recently, and for so long, barred them from entry. Using an illustration that his central Texas audience could readily understand, Rand argued that people who had learned to swim in calm backwoods streams would not have an easy time swimming in the deep Brazos River. "Right now," however, "in many situations, Negroes are being asked not only to swim in the Brazos but to swim upstream."

That was one reason why Rand preached the continued importance of historically Black educational institutions, which were perpetually under threat and would face increased pressures in the "new era" of integration. Perhaps Rand could not help but think of the crisis then facing his own university. Only two weeks earlier, civil rights protests on the campus of Texas Southern University had ended with Houston police officers firing thousands of rounds into a student dormitory, leading to the death of one officer by another officer's stray bullet and the arrest of nearly five hundred Black students. In the wave of recriminations that followed, some outraged white Texans called for the closure of TSU.[4]

"We need to think long and hard, study and make appraisals," Rand warned, "before we conclude that the shortcomings of Negroes or Negro students result from the Negro schools rather than the combined effects of second class citizenship and all of the resultant effects coming therefrom." After centuries of slavery and segregation, what Black schools and students needed was "the provision of all the conditions which promote equality," Rand said, a goal that he predicted would take at least three or four more generations to achieve.[5]

Racial injustice was complex and "must be attacked on all fronts," Rand argued. There were many uncertainties on the horizon. Of one thing, though, he was sure: "the mere opening of the doors of formerly all-white schools will not solve all of the problems." So Rand believed; what his listeners thought is unknown. But as the professor took his seat, and the graduates readied themselves for the awarding of diplomas, at least one student in the crowd might well have wondered if Rand's remarks were addressed directly to her.

For, in only a few months, Gloria Darlene Oliver, valedictorian of the A. J. Moore High School Class of 1967, would be on her way to Houston, where that fall she became perhaps the fifth Black undergraduate to enroll at William Marsh Rice University.[6]

* * *

The history of Rice University and racial segregation, as it has most often been told, is a story with familiar beginnings, endings, and names. The oft-told story goes like this: William Marsh Rice was a businessman who came from Massachusetts to Texas in the 1830s, made a fortune there, and returned to the North after the Civil War, settling first in New Jersey and then in New York. In 1891, he made plans to leave his considerable wealth to a group of trustees who were directed to build an educational institute in Houston, chartered that year as the William M. Rice Institute for the Advancement of Literature, Science, and Art. Rice stipulated that the school would be free for students, but in keeping with the conventions of the South at that time, he restricted the institute to white people in its founding charter.

In 1900, the school had yet to be built when scandal struck: Rice was murdered in New York City by a con man who had forged a will naming himself as William Marsh Rice's legatee. Captain James A. Baker, Rice's longtime Houston lawyer and chairman of his school-to-be, exposed that brazen scheme in court, proving that Rice had actually directed his multi-million-dollar estate to the Rice Institute. In 1912, more than twenty years after it was chartered, the school opened for classes under the leadership of its first president, Edgar Odell

Lovett, a mathematician and astronomer from Princeton, who spent the next three decades building a dynamic, coeducational university that was progressive in most respects, save one. Finally, in 1963, with leadership from President Kenneth Pitzer and facing the loss of federal grants that the institution (now renamed William Marsh Rice University) needed to expand, its board initiated a lawsuit to change its charter and admit its first Black students, some of whose names are now well known: Raymond Johnson, Charles Edward Freeman III, Jacqueline McCauley, Theodore Henderson, and Linda Faye Williams.

Given that familiar narrative of Rice's beginnings, it may seem jarring to start a new history of the university in Waco in 1967, with a speech at a historically Black high school by a professor from a historically Black university in Houston. We make that choice deliberately, however, because it reflects a central thesis of the pages that follow.

Put simply, to understand the history of Rice University, we must attend carefully to the history of Black Texans who were excluded from Rice's academic community for its first five decades, including some who never joined the Rice community at all. Each of the chapters of this book will begin with the story of one such African American whose vantage on and role in the history of the university deserves to be better known. What does the history of Rice University look like, and how does our understanding of it change, if we include less familiar names, starting points, and perspectives in the narrative? What happens to the narrative when people like A. J. Moore, Earl W. Rand, or Gloria Darlene Oliver—and schools like Paul Quinn College or Texas Southern University—are taken into account?

Even the brief story outlined above suggests some initial answers. First, looking back at 1891 from the stage of A. J. Moore High, it is possible to see William Marsh Rice's founding vision in a broader historical context. Rice was not the only person to envision planting institutions of higher learning in Texas in the late nineteenth century. Black Texans had begun to build schools in their earliest years of freedom. In fact, the founding of public land-grant universities in Texas owed much to the work of the state's first Black legislators in Reconstruction, and Black Texans also dreamed up bold plans for private colleges and universities.[7]

A primary difference between these plans and Rice's, besides the latter's provision for racial exclusion, was the disparity in resources available to support them. William Marsh Rice's enormous fortune gave the men who were charged with building and managing his institute an enviable power to execute their visions; to lobby for public policies and private deals that benefited the institute's further growth; and to retain the services of leaders, architects, and faculty from other well-endowed universities around the world. Rice's largesse allowed the Rice Institute to survive without having to charge tuition for its first fifty years, providing a free, racially restricted benefit to several generations of students who enrolled. In contrast, the Black visionaries who founded schools like Paul Quinn College had far fewer material resources at their disposal from the start.

These disparities in institutional wealth compounded as time passed, but their origins can be traced back to the history of slavery. In Texas, the forced labor of enslaved Africans and their descendants created wealth that enriched the owners of cotton and sugar plantations, as well as the myriad businessmen and investors connected to their operations, all while plundering the families of enslaved Black men and women whose financial value increased over the course of the antebellum period.

Within this racialized economic system, William Marsh Rice himself rose to become a member of the most elite class of white Texans: those with the power to buy enslaved people themselves and leverage that property to acquire even more wealth. Though slavery was long passed over in the stories told at the university about its institutional origins, the personal fortune that the university's founder made in antebellum Houston was unimaginable apart from the role that slavery played in the economy of Texas in general and in Rice's businesses in particular. Among Houston residents, fewer than a dozen people owned more enslaved people than Rice in 1860, and his brother and business partner enslaved dozens more on a plantation in nearby Fort Bend County.

By 1861, as secessionists prepared to go to war in defense of human property, William Marsh Rice was among those who abetted calls for secession in Houston, despite the erroneous depiction of him as a Unionist in many accounts of his life. During the American Civil War, Rice moved to Mexico to better protect his interests, and he returned to Texas after the war with much of his fortune intact. Other former slaveholders likewise drew on social capital and private reserves of wealth to rebound quickly from defeat. Five of the seven trustees named in the Rice Institute's founding charter, signed in 1891, had either owned enslaved people before the war or been born into households that did.

The end of the Civil War and the abolition of slavery created new opportunities for Black Texans, too, especially in the early years of Reconstruction. But those gains were soon slowed by disenfranchisement, racial violence, new forms of economic coercion, and the rise of Jim Crow, a legal regime that consigned Black Texans not only to second-class citizenship, but also to a lower economic class. From the outset, segregation was a system of both social control and economic stratification, one in which, for example, Black Houstonians could be paid cheaply to construct campus buildings for the Rice Institute into which, once completed, they would not be allowed to step, except under circumstances severely restricted by race.

The wealth created by slavery and segregation was never distributed equally, even among white Texans; the poorest white southerners also lost ground under the antidemocratic rule of the elites who constructed the Jim Crow political order. But racist ideas about white supremacy—preached from newspapers, law books, lecterns, pulpits, textbooks, monuments, and theaters, as well as enacted through brutal violence and the rhythms of daily life—did double duty as justifications for the status quo. Anti-Black racism rationalized wealth gaps across the color line while reassuring poor white southerners that there were rights, privileges, and even special duties conferred upon them by race.

The William M. Rice Institute was built, its foundations laid, within this broader culture of segregation and white supremacy, a culture that it, in turn, helped to build and perpetuate—all with fateful consequences for the history of the institution that followed. From the beginning, though, Black Texans resisted all of this, fighting against slavery, segregation, and racial injustice, and that story too would have consequences for the history of Rice University. As Lovett, Baker, and the architects of the Rice Institute worked to realize William Marsh Rice's vision, Black Texans were working to realize the visions of men like A. J. Moore and E. W. Rand. Making "bricks without straw," they built schools, churches, communities, and institutions in the midst of segregation of which they were justifiably proud, and for which the modern denizens of Rice University have reason to give thanks.[8]

Looking beyond familiar names and landmarks allows a second theme to emerge: the persistence of Black people and institutions in challenging the narrowness of the vision that birthed the Rice Institute. At key stages in Rice's history—and especially at the moment of its "second founding" as a modern, desegregating university—Black men and women played vital roles in educating Rice students, faculty, and administrators about the ways that race worked to structure their shared world, even if the lessons imparted were not always welcomed or applied. Eventually, once Rice's process of desegregation began in the mid-1960s, administrators at the university would also depend on Black colleges and universities like TSU to stop the gaps that integration exposed in Rice's curriculum, faculty, and personnel. But only when increasing numbers of Black students were admitted and enrolled at the university did the full extent of Rice's debt to the vision and labors of Black Americans under segregation became clear. And this is because, as often as not, it was the alumni and staff of institutions like Paul Quinn College and A. J. Moore High who would raise up and prepare the first generations of Black students at Rice University—teenagers such as Gloria Darlene Oliver of Waco—to walk bravely onto its spacious, tree-lined campus and claim their place inside its hedges.

* * *

Oliver's name returns us to the scene where we commenced, while pointing ahead to a third important argument of this book. When it finally began, desegregation at Rice (and elsewhere) was not a single, triumphant moment. It was a long, jagged, and ongoing process that has contained tragedy, too. "Desegregation in the 1960s represented progress," as two recent historians of the University of South Carolina note, but "such progress did not come without cost for the African American students involved."[9]

Before she became a Rice Owl, Gloria Darlene Oliver had clearly been taught and nurtured well by the dedicated community of Texas Black educators whose history stretched from Moore to Rand. Named an "outstanding junior" in her 1966 Moore High yearbook, she had been selected to participate in a six-week summer program in biology at Prairie View A&M University. That same year, she was voted "Most Scholarly Girl" by her classmates, whose yearbooks featured a picture of Oliver in a stylish pose, perusing a book in the library. The next spring, as the studious senior received her diploma at the head of her class, with a grade point average above 4.0 and an award from a local essay contest in hand, it must have been clear to many in the audience, and dearly hoped by the rest, that if anyone could meet the challenges ahead, she could.[10]

University archives do not record what Oliver might have felt as she arrived on the Rice campus in Houston that autumn and found her first classes. Lovett Hall and its iconic arch, the Sallyport, towered above the school's historic quadrangle. At the center of that quad sat an elevated statue of William Marsh Rice, placed there in 1930. Known formally as the Founder's Memorial and informally as "Willy," it was impossible to miss as visitors and new students processed through the Sallyport. "Quiet, scholarly, and handsome as its archways allow it to be," the Rice campus sat serenely at the center of the "rushing" city, wrote the editors of the 1968 yearbook, the *Campanile*. "And Willie presides over it all." The smiling portrait of Oliver in that same yearbook does not reveal much of her own hopes or fears (common feelings for any young person venturing off to college) but she must have been eager to get her career at Rice well underway.[11]

Midway through her second year, however, Gloria Oliver withdrew from Rice, a quick departure that was not unusual among the earliest Black students at the university. On the contrary, out of the first five Black undergraduate students the university enrolled, Rice lost three after only three semesters. The other two who had left were already gone when Oliver arrived. And at least two Black graduate students would also soon depart without degrees.

Although each of these departures came with its own story, private struggles, and unique contributing factors, a worrying pattern was unmistakable at the time, and it was magnified by the small number of Black students Rice admitted and enrolled. An early review of the university's experience with integration, conducted as part of a self-study in 1974, concluded that Rice had made a "dismal beginning," one that called into question how committed the institution really was to transformative change.[12]

Today, some fifty years after that report, the university is more committed to change than that "dismal beginning" might have foretold. Still, the second founding of the university remains unfinished business, and the stories of many of the "second founders" responsible for the university's transformations remain unknown, under told, or underappreciated. The process of desegregation, which began half a century after the Rice Institute opened, required changes so fundamental that they amounted to a refounding of the university. Yet change began slowly, even in comparison to other southern universities with similar histories of racial exclusion. Progress since has been hard-won, contested, and incomplete.

Why, after desegregation had begun, did the second founding of Rice have such a slow and troubled start? In the end, Earl W. Rand's comment to Oliver's graduating high-school class proved prescient: the "mere opening of the doors of formerly all-white schools" did not "solve all of the problems." And as Rand had foreseen, the problems were difficult to solve—could not be solved only by dropping a racial bar—because the problems arose from ideas and conditions that had long promoted inequality.[13]

Understanding the sources of inequality requires going even further back in time, not only to the first founding of the university as a segregated institution, but also to the histories of slavery that came before then and shaped the foundations on which the university was built. We begin, therefore, with a detailed examination of the founder's extensive connections to slavery and his actions before, during, and after the Civil War, which include his earliest expressions, in 1868, of an intention to endow an educational institution for the "poor white children" of Harris County, Texas.

That early idea would eventually be realized—on a scale grander than the original plan in some ways, but just as narrow in others—with the chartering of the William M. Rice Institute in 1891. More than seventy years would pass before the first Black students would be admitted into Rice University in 1964 and 1965. Yet only by starting the story before those dates, and even before 1868, does it become possible to understand the perspective of Earl W. Rand in his commencement address at A. J. Moore High School.

Speaking barely a century after the abolition of slavery, and nearly one hundred years since William Marsh Rice's first imaginings of a school to which he could devote his wealth, Rand understood that racial injustice stemmed from a long and violent history of unequal treatment. It would have to be "attacked on all fronts," he said, until it had been replaced by "all the conditions which promote equality" instead. In 1967, Rand predicted that this work would fall to generations then unborn as much as it would to the Black high-school graduates who sat before him on that May commencement day, when Gloria Darlene

Oliver walked across the stage in Waco and into an uncertain future. The desegregating work that their generation began now belongs to a new generation to continue and complete. But to move forward requires that we also look back, seeking a fuller understanding of how—and where—Rice University began.

I

BEFORE THE FOUNDING

1 | RICE AND SLAVERY

On February 27, 1856, the following paid advertisement appeared in the Houston *Weekly Telegraph:*

> Ranaway
>
> From the subscriber on or about the 1st of January a negro woman named Merinda; she is about 30 years old, dark complexion, slender built, and has a slight hesitancy in speech. She is probably lurking about town. I will pay a liberal reward for her apprehension and delivery to me.
>
> W. M. Rice

As with many documents about slavery, questions abound in this fragment from the past: Who was Merinda, where was she from, and where was she going? Who were her parents, and what other kin or communities did she claim? Whom did she love; who loved her? In what way, and why, did she hesitate in speech? And what had immediately preceded her apparent decision to flee? The knowledge of what slavery could entail for Black women in general can provide a kind of answer to some of those questions. But the specifics of Merinda's life remain unknown. No other record documenting her story has been found.[1]

More—much more, by comparison—is known about "W. M. Rice," the man who offered a "liberal reward" for Merinda's capture. Born in Massachusetts in 1816, William Marsh Rice had come to Texas in 1838, quickly succeeding as a merchant and entrepreneur in Houston. A civic booster, a city alderman, and a vestryman in the local Episcopal Church, he invested in real estate, railroads, and steamboats in the city. In 1850 he married Margaret Bremond, the daughter of a fellow northerner and railroad executive. And by 1856 he was already a very wealthy man, with the seeds of a fortune that later endowed the university bearing his name. But long before he became known to most as a generous philanthropist, the woman known only to us as Merinda knew him as something else.

The making of Rice's fortune in antebellum Texas was inexplicable apart from the history of slavery. At the end of the Civil War, Rice himself would summarize his career in Houston by saying that he had "acquired by extensive and laborious commercial pursuits for a long period of years before the Rebellion considerable property consisting of real estate, merchandise, bills receivable, lands, [and] slaves." "Slaves" were at the foundation of the political economy in Rice's adopted state, where "commercial pursuits" like his were not separable from the labor of enslaved people. The "considerable property" that Rice amassed in prewar Texas—along with the social capital it created—therefore cannot be disentangled from Rice's postwar fortune and philanthropy, including his establishment of the William M. Rice Institute for the Advancement of Literature, Science, and Art. The point bears repeating: *Rice's fortune is inexplicable apart from the history of slavery.* This much we may suppose that Merinda knew.[2]

For most of the institute's first one hundred years, Rice's early history with slavery was little understood and seldom acknowledged at the school he endowed. In a 1912 address, Rice's first president, Edgar Odell Lovett, described the founder as "a man in a million, an inspired millionaire. . . . With no resources other than soundness of body and strength of will, from a New England home of English and Welsh forebears, he came to Texas in his youth to make his fortune" and succeeded by "temperate habits of industry and thrift." In 1918, biology professor Julian Huxley noted more simply, "How [Rice] made his money does not concern us. Money was to be picked up then by enterprising men." Throughout the university's first century, the depiction of Rice as a "typical Yankee yeoman" and self-made "capitalist," a "shrewd business man as well as a good merchant," was repeatedly invoked whenever the institution's beginnings or its founder were discussed.[3]

This depiction of Rice was not altogether wrong, but it left a silence at the center of the university's origin stories, one that both mirrored and contributed to a wider reluctance among Americans to grapple fully and honestly with histories of slavery and racial injustice. The often mythic portrayal of the university's founder passed over his investments in slavery, which stretched back to his earliest years in Houston and continued through the Civil War. It did not sufficiently explain how slavery and its legacies had shaped the society in which the university was conceived. And like the segregated school that Rice later endowed, the prevailing story excluded Black people such as Merinda.[4]

On occasion, the silence was broken, though in ways that left the dominant story largely undisturbed. In the 1950s, alumnus and historian Andrew Forest Muir began writing a biography of the founder. His first drafts posited that Rice had "no slaves." Muir later revised that claim, writing in an unpublished paper that "Rice, in his mercantile pursuits at least, trafficked in human flesh." But he argued that "the bulky evidence reveals few such transactions for so large a mercantile establishment as his was" and speculated that Rice's actions belied his views: "Perhaps he actually objected to Negro slavery."[5]

Muir's published work on Rice either passed over slavery or argued that he had "no ambition to own either land or slaves." Much like Lovett, Muir saw Rice primarily as "an honest, honorable man who accumulated his fortune through constant and indefatigable application to business." So in 1952, when Muir published a brief biographical entry on Rice in the *Handbook of Texas*, an influential reference work, he did not mention slavery at all. Not until the handbook's 1996 edition was the entry revised to add that Rice was "a slaveowner . . . and served on the slave patrol for a year."[6]

Muir died in 1968 before finishing his book, but his research notes do contain his eventual findings about some, though not all, of the people Rice enslaved. Those notes formed the basis for the first full biography of William Marsh Rice, written in 1972 by Sylvia Stallings Morris, who was the first to acknowledge in print that Rice "was in fact a slaveowner." A new edition of her biography, edited by Randal Hall and published in 2012 to mark the university's centennial, further revised the earlier, incorrect view that Rice had little involvement with slavery.[7]

As these revisions demonstrate, documentary evidence has gradually helped to update what is known about Rice and slavery. But in the years since Muir, Morris, and Hall wrote, new evidence has come to light, including Rice's advertisement seeking Merinda. Archival collections that were not readily available to earlier biographers are available now.[8] And looking again at familiar sources has also revealed persistent errors that need correction. For example, the long-accepted claim that Rice enslaved *fifteen* people in 1860, first published in 1972 and repeated often ever since, is based on a misreading of the U.S. Census for that year. In fact, the census listed *eighteen* enslaved people in Rice's household in 1860, two of whom were working for him despite being owned by someone else. It is more accurate to say that Rice enslaved *at least sixteen* people on the eve of the Civil War, and benefited from the forced labor of countless others.[9]

This more accurate figure is still an incomplete measure of the many ways Rice profited from slavery. But even if the 1860 census were the only evidence of Rice's active participation in enslavement, it alone would serve as a telling measure of his complicity. Of all the Texas slaveholders listed in the 1860 census, fewer than 3 percent enslaved forty or more people. Only about 15 percent enslaved fifteen or more. In Houston, only about one out of every four households owned enslaved people at all in 1860, a ratio comparable to the state as a whole. And out of the nearly two hundred enslavers who resided in town, only twenty-five claimed more than ten slaves. Fewer than a dozen of those Houstonians had more enslaved people listed in their households than William Marsh Rice did.[10]

In short, while small in comparison to a large planter's slaveholdings or as a percentage of his overall wealth, the number of people Rice enslaved in 1860 placed him in an elite class, reflecting his status as perhaps the second richest man in Texas at the time, with combined assets of $750,000. If the class structure of antebellum Texas is pictured as a pyramid, Rice sat near the peak, high above even the vast majority of white Texans. Black women like Merinda, meanwhile, were held in an even more subordinate position, constrained by law to help build the pyramid without being able to climb it.[11]

William Marsh Rice continuously approved of and profited from this stratified racial order. His offer of a liberal reward for Merinda's return is only one of many signs that he viewed "negroes" as both valuable to him and far beneath him and others of his race and class. And when he later came to believe that he should give liberally from his wealth for the benefit of others, he would continue along these lines.[12]

"1842 or Thereabouts"

When William Marsh Rice decided in his early twenties to leave his home in Massachusetts and head to the South, the breakaway Republic of Texas had only recently established its independence from Mexico. Rice arrived in Houston in 1838, only two years after the victory of Texas general Sam Houston over Mexican president Santa Anna at the Battle of San Jacinto. By then, as the young arriviste certainly must have known, previous white settlers had already created a firm foothold for those determined to profit from chattel slavery in Texas.

In the 1820s, hoping to attract Anglo-American settlers into what was then northeastern Mexico to establish cotton plantations, the American *empresario* Stephen F. Austin had advocated the violent dispossession of Native American groups like the Karankawa and lobbied antislavery Mexican officials to permit slave labor in the region. After winning its independence in 1836, the new Republic of Texas continued Austin's policy by enshrining slavery in its constitution and offering generous land grants to entice white settlers. When white migrants from the southern United States flocked to Texas after an economic downturn known as the Panic of 1837, they brought thousands of slaves with them.[13]

Although the Republic of Texas did ban international slave trading, hoping in that way to win recognition of Texas's independence from the by-then antislavery British Empire, the fledgling nation could not control its own borders, and smugglers even brought African-born people into Houston's hinterlands for sale in the late 1830s. Recent survivors of the transatlantic Middle Passage thus formed a small but, in some counties, a substantial minority of the roughly twelve thousand Black people enslaved in Texas by 1840, most of whom had been born in the United States and brought west by their enslavers.[14]

This rapid expansion of slavery into Texas coincided with the rise of abolitionism in the northern United States. As a young man in Springfield, Massachusetts, the state where abolitionist William Lloyd Garrison had established his newspaper *The Liberator* in 1831, William Marsh Rice likely saw some of the many northern editorials that criticized Texas as an illegitimate slaveholders' republic and predicted (accurately, in the end) that white southerners would try to get it annexed as a slave state. Many northern journalists derided white

Texans' fight for independence from Mexico (which had abolished slavery after winning its own independence from Spain) as nothing but a fight for "the liberty to enslave their fellow beings." Debates about slavery also raged within the Methodist Church, to which Rice's Massachusetts family belonged. When he decided to move to Texas to seek his fortune, Rice could hardly have been ignorant of slavery's dynamic growth in the nascent southern republic.[15]

There was little disagreement about slavery among new white Texans. Nevertheless, a few Anglo-American settlers did envision a different future for the region. In 1843, a Houston lawyer named Stephen Pearl Andrews, who was born in Massachusetts four years before Rice and arrived in Texas around the same time as he did, was chased by an angry mob from Galveston, the republic's most important port, after he floated proposals for gradual emancipation in a speech. Later that year, Andrews would travel to an antislavery convention in London. But his exile made clear that abolitionists were not welcome in Texas.[16]

Slaveholders, on the other hand, were. By the time Texas was annexed by the United States in 1845, the enslaved Black population had doubled in five years to 24,400 people, and Texas had numerous laws designed to convince would-be cotton planters that their human property would be protected there. One provision made it illegal for any free Black person to remain in Texas without special application to the legislature. These conditions tightly circumscribed the lives of early Black Texans, even as economic opportunity beckoned to white newcomers. Like other white immigrants to Texas, William Marsh Rice collected a free grant of public land soon after his arrival.[17]

Instead of establishing a farm, Rice set up shop in Houston, Harris County, as a merchant. Before it could become the economically thriving slaveholding society that Stephen F. Austin and other early boosters had imagined for Texas, the region needed not only planters and the enslaved laborers they brought with them, but also town-builders, brokers, and merchants who could provide tools, goods, transportation, and financial services to the predominantly agricultural counties around them. Rice, who already had some experience as a shopkeeper in the north, threw himself into such work.[18]

By all accounts, he quickly prospered. According to tax records, Rice sold \$6,500 worth of merchandise in 1841.[19] That sum tripled by 1844, thanks partly to a mercantile partnership he had formed with Ebenezer B. Nichols. During

Texas's final few years as a nation-state, Rice and Nichols sold large amounts of groceries "*cheap for Cash*" and imported a wide array of goods from New Orleans and New York, from handsaws and skillets to stationery and hats. By 1846, Rice had also formed a new partnership with Charles W. Adams in nearby Galveston, where they sold "all kinds of Goods suitable for Plantation use."[20]

As that reference to "Plantation use" hints, slavery was at the source of many things that Texas merchants sold, reflecting the importance of unfree labor in local and global markets. Some groceries were produced in slave societies outside of North America, like coffee from Rio de Janeiro and sugar from Havana. Other goods catered especially to planters in the counties surrounding Houston: cottonseed for planting; spades and hoes for weeding; cotton gins, bagging, and rope for making bales. Rice and his partners sold all these items, as well as fine goods from the North.[21]

Above all, though, commerce in early Galveston and Houston depended on the success of cotton crops in Texas, and merchants promoted cotton's cultivation. In 1841, Rice was one of a group of businessmen who offered a silver trophy to the first farmer of the season to produce five bales, hoping to "encourage praiseworthy exertions on the part of the Planters." Unmentioned in the published notice of the prize were the exertions of the laborers forced to tend and pick that cotton, but tax records show that T. S. Howard of Washington County, the winner, enslaved at least eleven Black people that year.[22]

By the middle of the decade, Rice's growing wealth allowed him to offer planters something more valuable than a prize: credit. Like other merchants, he and his partners made interest-bearing loans to planters at the start of the growing season. In exchange, the planters gave merchants a lien on their crop and paid them a commission to transport and sell the finished bales. Rice and Adams explained these arrangements succinctly in one 1846 advertisement: "Liberal advances in cash will be made by us on Cotton or other produce consigned to our address." The following year, Rice, Nichols, and Adams announced that they would also act as agents for a cotton and commission merchant firm based in New Orleans.[23]

Such credit relationships between merchants and planters were vital to Texas's early cotton economy in part because, in the absence of good roads or railroads, bringing the crop to market remained costly in the early 1840s. Near the end of his life, William Marsh Rice remembered these conditions in a letter he wrote to a lawyer and old friend in the state. "I have been familiar [with] and handled more or less cotton for more than fifty years," Rice told his correspondent in 1900, while commenting on a recent slump in prices for the crop.[24]

"In 1842 or thereabouts," he recalled, "cotton was hauled from Bastrop to Houston by teams and sold for 4½ cents good cotton." In these conditions, profit margins were small. But planters who owned slaves already had distinct advantages. "Negro labor did not cost much," Rice claimed, "only to feed the Negroes and give them a coarse cotton suit which the Negroes made." Moreover, enslaved people were appreciable assets who, by law, could be bought, sold, and bequeathed to transfer wealth across generations. Cotton prices in 1850 could be two or occasionally three times higher than the price per pound that Rice remembered from 1842, even for cotton of average quality. And as cotton prices rose, prices for slaves rose apace. "In those days," Rice concluded in 1900, "raising Negroes was the most profitable."[25]

Rice was not alone in that judgment at the time. According to historian Randolph Campbell, white Texans "who owned a few slaves found them valuable in many ways and hoped to acquire more," while nonslaveholders, far from opposing slavery, generally "recognized that owning slaves was a measure of financial success and wanted to hold bondsmen themselves." Another historian has calculated that, by the 1850s, price trends enabled slaveowners to expect steady profits on the laborers they enslaved from "capital gains alone." The rising value of "Negro Property" proved so reliable that enslaved people were sometimes accepted in payment for real estate or as collateral for loans.[26]

Responding to these trends, in the 1840s some Houston merchants added sales of enslaved people to the services they provided. In 1846, the firm of Wade and Cruger advertised "A Likely Negro Woman" for sale in a Houston newspaper, right above its ad for imported coffee and mackerel. Two years later, H. S. and L. G. Bachelder advertised for sale not only the usual groceries and dry goods, but also "slaves of different ages and descriptions, low for cash."[27] Another notice offered "a Valuable Plantation on the Brazos, with negroes, stock, and inventory thereof." Interested buyers were told to contact Rice's fellow merchant, Benjamin A. Shepherd, future namesake of the Shepherd School of Music at Rice University.[28]

Shifting Conditions

Advertisements offering slaves for sale have not been found for any of William Marsh Rice's firms, but by the mid-1840s at least, he too had begun to participate directly in enslavement as a buyer, seller, and creditor. In some of these transactions, Rice acted alone; in most of them, one or more of his business partners was a joint party. In 1845, for example, Rice and Nichols bought "a slave for life" for $650. A deed recording the sale described the man in question only as "a certain black boy named John, age between 22 and 23 years height 5 feet 7."[29] The following year, the firm purchased a man called Tom for $775. The deed described him, too, as "a certain boy," a demeaning term applied by white Texans to Black men of all ages.[30]

The first available record to show that Rice purchased an enslaved person on his own dates from no later than 1849. For the sum of $550, Jesse McCreary transferred "a certain negro woman 'Ann' of a griff color aged about thirty years unto him the said Wm. M. Rice his heirs and assigns forever."[31] County records for 1849 assessed Rice for taxes on one enslaved person, appraised at $550, likely another reference to Ann, and the following year, an enumerator for the 1850 U.S. Census (the first to be taken in the new state of Texas) listed four enslaved people as part of Rice's household. The barely legible entry shows one woman aged twenty-five or twenty-eight, and three girls aged six, four, and two.[32]

The woman may have been Ann and the girls her daughters; it is impossible to know. Most of Rice's surviving private papers date from later periods, giving limited insight into his personal life prior to 1850, the year he also married his first wife, Margaret Bremond.[33] Given the typical conditions of urban slavery in this period, it is reasonable to assume that John and Tom performed heavy labor of various kinds for Rice and Nichols: from packing and hauling merchandise, to loading and unloading steamboats and wagons that carried cotton consigned to the firm. Ann probably did domestic labor for Rice—cooking, laundering, ironing, cleaning—but historians of Black women's experiences in slavery have also shown that working in the private spaces of a white home could be just as dangerous as working outside the house, or even more so. Heavy labor is, in many ways, an insufficient phrase for the experiences of John, Tom, and Ann.[34]

Meanwhile, other enslaved people served as collateral for some of the many loans that Rice extended in this period. In the absence of a banking system in antebellum Texas, interest-bearing promissory notes circulated like currency, and commission merchants served as crucial sources of credit. Merchants often insisted on security for their loans in advance, usually in the form of real estate, and they used the courts to collect unpaid debts. When a defaulter possessed enslaved people, they too could be lawfully seized to repay the lender.[35] Loaning money with interest is one of the principal ways Rice grew his own wealth in Houston, and he took a hard line on collecting payment when a debtor defaulted. In an 1887 letter to his brother, he described the approach to lending that had helped to make him rich forty years before: "Trust nobody without security in hand is the rule of successful men."[36]

A case from 1847 is an early example from Rice's experience. John M. Lewis, a Virginia-born planter in Montgomery County, Texas, was indebted to Rice and Nichols for the sum of $889.58. On June 5, he signed a note promising to pay back that amount in six months at 10 percent interest. To secure the debt, as well as any other loans or advances from Rice and Nichols, Lewis entered a legal agreement known as a deed of trust.[37]

In this agreement, Lewis first transferred his title in four enslaved men to a third-party trustee, William H. Fowler. The men were named Charles, London, John, and Umphry, ranging in age from twenty-three to twenty-seven. If Lewis defaulted, Fowler would sell the four men at public auction "to the highest bidder for ready money." As trustee, Fowler would then pay Rice and Nichols what they were owed from the proceeds of the sale, and return any remaining balance from the sale to Lewis. In the meantime, Lewis could retain possession of the four men and "take the profits" of their labor on his plantation. If he repaid his debts to Rice and Nichols on time with interest, he would regain full title to all four people.[38]

By such common arrangements in the antebellum South, Charles, London, John, and Umphry performed labor for one white man (Lewis), while securing a loan that generated revenue for two others (Rice and Nichols), all while being technically the property of a third who served solely as a trustee responsible for auctioning them in the event of default (Fowler).

In a similar deed from 1843, Rice played the role of trustee in an agreement between Charles W. Adams and James McKenzie, who was indebted to Adams. McKenzie transferred his title in a "negro slave named Isham aged about twenty two years" to Rice, who agreed that, in the event of a default, he would sell Isham at public auction and pay McKenzie's debt to Adams (Rice's own business partner) from the proceeds.[39]

In most cases where he loaned money, Rice appears to have accepted security in the form of land, whose value was often staked to its agricultural potential. But in antebellum Texas, practices like the ones described above could also expose enslaved people to sudden sale. Two other cases demonstrate what might happen to enslaved people when a debtor did default.[40]

In 1849, William Marsh Rice and Charles W. Adams, his Galveston partner, agreed to advance James Love and A. T. Burnley up to $4,000 to convert a plantation on Oyster Creek in Brazoria County from cotton to sugar production. Sugar plantations required especially high capital investment, and Love and Burnley planned to use the advances "for the purchase of machinery for making sugar to be propelled by horse power and of the necessary materials for the erection of a sugar house." Rice, Adams, and Company agreed to keep the plantation supplied with merchandise and groceries, and Love agreed that all of the crops would be consigned to them for sale. Charles W. Adams signed the agreement on behalf of himself and his partner, Rice.[41]

To secure repayment of the loan for sugar machinery, and an additional $624.85 that Love and Burnley already owed, Love agreed to put up as collateral "one undivided half" of a huge amount of property, including the whole plantation (some twenty-eight hundred acres), all of the livestock and tools used on it, and at least five dozen enslaved people, named within a deed of trust:

> Harey, Bancola, Bob, Ado, Ellick, George, [Itatie?], Toney, Cudjo, Coca, Dick, Tom, Adela, Yua, Daniel, Lewis, Jim, and Charles, all of whom are grown, together with all the women slaves on said place and their children to wit Rose, Eliza and Anthony her children, Equ, her children are Oscar, John, Frank, Jane and Judy, Tara her children, Caroline, Julan, Sally her children are Malinda and Besha, Nancy and her children Lushe and Oelta, Jenna and her children, Gulius and Love, Malinda her children Mary, Madie and Davie, Lucinda and her children, Abby and Henry, Sabine and her children, Polly and Carsai, Aliba and her children Bill, Kits, Jack, Emiline, Alice and Louis, Martha Jane, her children, Mary and her child Jane, Sally, Willow. . . .

In keeping with a legal principle dating to the seventeenth century that the children of enslaved women were also enslaved, this revealing document listed mothers and children together. The deed made explicit that Rice, Adams, and Company would be secured not only by the people living and working on the plantation at the time, but by the "increase of said slaves," a reference to any future offspring. It was because of such laws that Rice could later remember, in 1900, the profitability of "raising Negroes" in early Texas.[42]

The 1849 deed is significant for two additional reasons. First, the property it described on Oyster Creek, a plantation known as Chenango, was one of the places through which African-born slaves had been smuggled before Texas statehood. By some estimates, as many as one thousand African-born people lived in Brazoria County by 1840, the year before Love and Burnley took over the plantation. Some of the people listed in this deed may have been among them or their descendants.[43]

A second significant fact is that the people and property in the 1849 deed had already been provided as security for a separate loan. In 1846, Love and Burnley had mortgaged the premises and most of the property mentioned in the 1849 deed to a different creditor, Nathaniel A. Ware, whom they owed $15,531. Many of the people listed in the agreement with Rice and Adams were therefore twice mortgaged, putting them at even greater risk of sale by auction if Love and Burnley ever defaulted.[44]

A default on the loan eventually did occur, not long after Burnley sold out his half share of the plantation to William Sharpe. Ware foreclosed on Love and sold his half of the property to Sharpe in 1852, but the proceeds of that sale were less than what Ware was owed from Love, who was also, at the same time, thousands of dollars in debt to Rice, Adams, and Company.

When Rice's firm sued multiple parties, attempting to recover its debt, the complicated litigation eventually found its way to the Texas Supreme Court in 1857. In an appeal to the court, Love's onetime partner Alfred T. Burnley claimed that Love never informed him about the risky decision to cultivate sugar and argued that he was not responsible for paying Love's debts. But the court ruled against Burnley, affirming that partners like Love and Burnley were liable for each other's debts, even if one later claimed not to be aware of what the other was doing. It was the same legal principle that made Rice personally interested in an arrangement that had technically been signed in 1849 by his own partner, Adams. A partner was legally complicit in what his partner did.[45]

The published report of this case did not say what happened to the enslaved people who had been mortgaged to multiple parties, and whose labor had powered the calculations of all the white men who sought to profit from Chenango. It did not even list their names. The context suggests that at least some of them had been sold in the breakup of Love's business to satisfy his and his partner's debts, but it is not known for certain what happened to Henry and Bancola, or Malinda and Besha, or the many others enslaved on the plantation. Even so, the case shows clearly that William Marsh Rice and his partners would pursue their rights as creditors to the fullest extent of the law, and in ways that could be deeply consequential to Black families involved.

A different case that came before the Texas Supreme Court in the same year underlines the point. It concerned an enslaved woman named Eliza and involved Rice's partnership with Ebenezer B. Nichols. Some time earlier, the two men had foreclosed on a debt owed to them by a man named Sydney Cummins, and the matter landed in a Houston court, which decided in favor of Rice and Nichols. To collect the amount awarded in the judgment, Rice and his partner "levied execution upon a negro girl named Eliza, in possession of said Sydney."[46]

In response, Sydney's father, Uriah Cummins, filed a countersuit claiming that Eliza was his property, not his son's. On those grounds, he argued, Rice and Nichols could not seize her to satisfy Sydney's debt. A Harris County jury saw through the tactic and decided against Cummins, who moved for a new trial. When that motion was denied, Cummins appealed to the state Supreme Court, which upheld the jury's decision.

"The girl appears to have been kept in a somewhat shifting condition between Uriah S. Cummings [*sic*], the claimant, and his two sons, Sydney and William H.," the Supreme Court said. The judges did not consider what the experience of being passed back and forth between father and sons meant for Eliza, whose age was not even recorded. Did she know that her fate was being decided in the state's highest court? Either way, with the drop of a gavel, her "shifting condition" had shifted again. She became the joint, legal property of William Marsh Rice and E. B. Nichols. What happened to her next, including whether she ever worked under the direct control of Rice or Nichols, is unknown.[47]

Such documents about mortgages and lawsuits between white Texans offer far too little access to the experiences of enslaved persons. Nonetheless, such documents do illuminate the multifarious roles that slavery played in the economy of Texas and the reasons why enslaved people were so coveted as property. Slave labor powered the plantations that merchants like William Marsh Rice supplied with goods and credit. In the case of a sugar operation like Chenango, the labor performed by enslaved people was both highly skilled and dangerous; violence stalked their daily lives. Enslaved people and their "increase" were regularly exchanged as property. Sometimes they were shifted on paper long before they were moved between people or places. And if they were mortgaged, or conveyed to a firm, enslaved people could even end up legally "belonging" to more than one person at once.

Another deed involving William Marsh Rice makes the implications especially clear. In 1848, Rice and Nichols appeared before the Harris County Clerk of Court to record a kind of deed different from those discussed above: a "deed of gift" made to Nichols's young sons, Frank Rice Nichols and William Hamilton Nichols. Using the legal boilerplate common to such instruments, Rice swore that, "in consideration of the love and affection he has to said Frank Rice Nichols," he was granting to Frank and the boy's future heirs "the half interest owned by him in and to a certain negress slave named Ellen aged about 17 years and of light black color and also in and to her infant child named Louisa aged about one year and of yellow color."[48] The other "half interest" in Ellen and Louisa was owned by Ebenezer B. Nichols, who in the same deed gifted his half share in the young mother and her infant girl, along with their "future increase," to his other son, William Hamilton.[49]

Few documents better illustrate how slavery twisted the reproductive labor of Black women into wealth for white families. As the system was practiced in the antebellum United States, white men could legally turn a Black teenager and her future "increase" into an inheritance for white sons and their future "heirs." At the time of this gift, Frank Rice Nichols was no more than two years old. His brother William was five. Louisa was younger than either, yet all of her own future children were promised to them and their descendants.[50]

Even with all it contains, this deed of gift also raises more questions than it answers. How did Rice and Nichols come to have a split interest in Ellen and Louisa? Had they purchased the mother and child? Received them in payment of a debt? Seized them through litigation, as in Eliza's case? Who was Louisa's father? And why did the partners give one half interest in Ellen and Louisa to the young Frank Nichols and the other half to his brother?

Whatever the answers, the deed serves as a revealing endpoint to William Marsh Rice's first decade in Texas. By 1848, he had created new business networks and friendships in Texas. He had also accustomed himself to profiting from the enslavement, by himself and by others, of Black men, women, and children. And in the years that followed, his connections to this system of human commodification, like those of Texas writ large, did not lessen. They grew.

Boom Times for Slavery: The 1850s

The 1850s were economic boom times for white Texans. The state exported 431,000 cotton bales in 1860, an increase of almost 650 percent since 1850. The uptick in migration to Texas was equally dramatic, as new white settlers rushed into the state, hoping to strike it rich with cotton. As one newspaper editor in Matagorda County, south of Houston, boasted in 1858, a planter with twenty slaves could expect to double his number of slaves in three years "and in six years will be rich." It was better to have a plantation in Texas, this booster concluded, "than a gold mine at Pike's Peak."[51]

No wonder, then, that in the 1850s, an estimated 400,000 white people moved to the state, a population growth so rapid that four of every five Texans at the beginning of the Civil War had come since 1846. One of those who came was Frederick A. Rice, William Marsh Rice's younger brother. Frederick arrived from Massachusetts in 1850 and soon partnered with his brother in a firm known as William M. Rice and Company. Other newcomers poured into Texas from nearby cotton states, including James A. Baker Sr., father of the future first chairman of the Rice Institute. Born in Alabama, Baker Senior relocated to Huntsville, Texas, in 1852, not long after the death of his first wife. Soon he remarried and became administrator for the estate of his father-in-law, Hardy Hightower, a prominent planter and large slaveholder in Walker County. Baker built a successful law practice that often handled the Hightowers' business, and by 1861, he enslaved at least twelve people himself. His son Jimmie, later known as Captain James A. Baker and a key figure in the history of the Rice Institute, was born in 1857.[52]

Though not all of the newcomers started plantations, the growth of slavery both fueled and was fueled by the cotton and settlement booms. The population of enslaved people in Texas increased from around 58,000 at the beginning of the 1850s to about 182,500 ten years later. Several counties around Houston had Black majorities, and the population of enslaved people in Houston itself doubled over the decade.[53]

An increase in the number of people enslaved by William Marsh Rice—from four reported in the "slave schedule" for the 1850 census, to at least sixteen in the 1860 census—followed this upward trend. County tax records suggest that, for the decade in between, the number of people individually enslaved by Rice was usually closer to the 1850 total than the larger 1860 one, although tax assessments often undercounted total holdings. The jump in number from 1850 to 1860 is thus a notable spike. Rice clearly increased his investments in slavery toward the end of the decade, perhaps in response to a bullish market for slaves at the time.[54]

Indeed, according to one historian, "the number of Houston slave traders doubled in the 1850s in response to surging demand." One of them was Thomas S. Gresham, who in 1853 placed an advertisement in a Galveston newspaper for a new "Negro Mart" in Houston. It reported that Gresham had just received "direct from Virginia and Maryland 50 negroes from 10 to 25 years old—one of the most likely lots of negroes ever brought to Texas," and he promised to continually "have on hand a supply of men, women, and children, sufficient for the Texas market, of the best kind, at prices as low as they can be bought in New Orleans." Gresham concluded by listing several local merchants who could vouch for his reliability, including "B. A. Shepherd and W. M. Rice & Co., Houston."[55]

The ad suggests that both Shepherd and the Rices knew Gresham, either socially or from doing business together; they may or may not have knowingly allowed him to list their names as references for his "Negro Mart." Either way, seeing regular sales of people was generally unavoidable and probably unobjectionable for Houston businessmen. In 1857, Edward Riordan (who served three years later on the city council with Frederick A. Rice) began operating as a "Negro and Real Estate Broker" at the corner of Main and Congress streets, not far from William Marsh Rice's warehouse on Main Street between Congress and Franklin. A northern visitor to the city around the same time saw posters advertising slave sales hanging in many store windows "and on the doors and columns of the hotel" where he stayed.[56]

The growth of the urban slave population in Houston also facilitated "hiring out," a practice in which owners would collect wages from the labor that enslaved people did for someone else. William Marsh Rice's firm did this, too, advertising in a Houston newspaper that it was seeking "to hire four Negroes for whom good wages will be given," a number that would have doubled the size of the workforce the firm actually claimed as property at that time. And in addition to the sixteen enslaved persons listed as Rice's property in the 1860 census, there were two more listed as "employed" in this way by Rice; the census enumerator listed their owners as "not known."[57]

Rice and his partners "hired out" people they enslaved as well, participating in a system that gave even poorer white households some access to slave labor. In the spring of 1859, a couple named the Hurlbuds was preparing to reopen a hotel and restaurant called the Rusk House. Rice and Company first sold the Hurlbuds the tables, chairs, bedding, carpeting, wallpaper, and other supplies needed to furnish the place. Then, after the establishment opened, the firm started leasing to the inn the services of an enslaved man named William at the rate of $30 per month.[58]

The boom years for slavery in Houston had various effects on the experiences of enslaved people themselves. On the one hand, the slave trade brought many forced migrants to Texas who had experienced traumatic separations from family members and communities in distant states. In 1877, for example, Perry Wilmer described how the slave trade brought him to Houston before the Civil War and wrenched him away from his family. In an advertisement he published hoping to find his siblings, Wilmer wrote of how a man named John B. Bostic "brought us from Baltimore to Houston, Texas, where I was sold first to John Shackleford and then to a Mr. Craft." Twelve years after Juneteenth, Wilmer still had not seen his brothers Joe and Sam, his sister Maria, or his parents Perry and Minty.[59]

At the same time, the growing population of Houston and the spread of practices like "hiring out" facilitated the growth of new Black communities and families. African Americans in cities like Houston sometimes socialized at dances, worship services, and other gatherings in ways that city officials found difficult to control. And despite laws banning the residence of free Black people in Texas, some sold goods and arranged their own jobs, building lives similar to those of free Black southerners in other states.[60]

These realities may explain how an enslaved woman like Merinda was able to evade Rice's detection for some time after her disappearance around New Year's Day in 1856. He supposed that she was still "lurking" about the city, sheltered perhaps by other enslaved people and possibly finding some jobs on her own. Harris County did have a "slave patrol" assigned to police the enslaved population and catch runaways; Rice himself briefly served on the patrol in 1851. But the patrols were not always effective, and only a few months after Merinda's escape, the *Weekly Telegraph* complained that laws requiring slaves to carry written permission to move about the city were effectively a "dead letter" in Houston: "In certain quarters of the city there are large congregations of negroes, who hire their own time, and who live entirely free from the supervision of any white man."[61]

Even allowing for hyperbole, such lines hint at the communities that Black Houstonians were making among themselves, networks made possible in part by their growing numbers and the mobility of their work. In 1851, the March 14 edition of the *Telegraph* reported with alarm that a "negro man belonging to Messrs. Rice and Nichols, was brought to this city on Thursday last from Galveston," where the man had been exposed to smallpox while working under the supervision of an agent for the firm. Before his exposure was known, said the paper, "several of his fellow servants visited him."[62]

The last phrase offered a passing glance at the relationships among enslaved people in Houston, and the care they provided to each other, while obscuring the realities of slavery behind the euphemism "servants." Of more concern to the author was the fear of disease spreading. The *Telegraph* urged citizens to vaccinate the people they enslaved and criticized a doctor for allowing the infected man to return to Houston. The next week, the accused physician defended himself in a letter to the editor that revealed the patient's name as "Tom," perhaps the same man purchased by Rice and Nichols a few years before.[63]

Two years later, in 1853, an advertisement placed in the New Orleans *Daily Picayune* alerted readers to be on the lookout for another man likely enslaved by Rice's firm named John.

> Ran away from the steamship Louisiana on Tuesday, the 22d November about 3 o'clock, a black boy named JOHN, about 5 feet 6 inches high, 25 or 30 years old, large head, pock marked, full and fleshy face, stout and well built, was dressed in a red flannel shirt and copper colored pants with a wool hat. Had just arrived from Texas, and was without a pass. Masters of steamboats are requested to be on the look out for him. A suitable reward will be paid for him on his delivery in either of the guard houses or to Wm. M. Rice and Co., Houston Texas or E. J. Hart and Co., New Orleans.[64]

The "John" mentioned in this advertisement may have been the man purchased by Rice and Nichols eight years before, though he cannot be identified with certainty. Nonetheless, the ad casts more light on the growing commercial web that connected markets and merchants from Houston to New Orleans and beyond. By the 1850s, that web was shadowed by a world of Black relationships and movement, what historian Stephanie Camp called a "rival geography," that unsettled white observers. But the disparities in power between white and Black Texans remained stark. Black men like Tom or John and Black women like Merinda were subject to constant surveillance and suspicion, while white men like Rice continued to grow their fortunes in the South.[65]

"Negro Property"

As the notices about Tom, John, and Merinda make clear, slaveholders could never totally deny that enslaved persons were human beings, with their own communities, the capacity to suffer, and the creativity and courage to resist. Yet a substantial amount of wealth depended on an alternate reality: that slaves were a form of capital recognized by law.

By marking them with terms like "negro," "mulatto," "yellow," and "colored," white Texans also projected onto people of African descent a host of pernicious myths about racial inferiority, rendering them supposedly unworthy of the same regard and rights afforded to those marked as "white." These realities indelibly marked the archives of slavery, too, often frustrating the efforts of historians to learn more about specific enslaved people. Sometimes, it is only because of an episode of resistance or an exception to the everyday that an enslaved person's name survives in the archive at all.

One such episode occurred in January 1861, when an advertisement in the Houston press offered a $50 reward for the capture of a fugitive "named Tom, of yellow complexion, about 25 years of age." According to the ad, Tom (apparently a different man than the Tom who contracted smallpox ten years before) "was formerly owned by Dr. James M. Cox, of Fort Graham, Texas, and was sold by him about two years ago to Wm. M. Rice, of Houston." That spare information makes it possible to speculate that Tom was one of the men who appeared in the census of 1860 as enslaved by William Marsh Rice—perhaps the one whose age was given as twenty-four, and whose "color" was marked with an "M" for "mulatto."[66]

Another record about Tom may survive in the pages of a rare antebellum ledger kept by Rice's firm, one of three found and deposited in the collections of the Woodson Research Center at Rice University sometime in the late twentieth century. The second of these ledgers shows that James Cox had indeed transferred $1,600 worth of "Negro property" to Rice in April 1859. Though it did not name him, the transaction may have included the purchase of Tom, who might still have legally belonged to Rice when the 1861 runaway ad about him appeared.[67]

Occasionally, Rice's ledgers did give names for particular enslaved people. On June 25, 1855, he paid $1,050 to purchase a man named "Ben" from R. J. French, a partner with the firm in Washington County, north of Houston; on a separate page, a clerk kept track either of expenses for or exchanges with the enslaved man, amounting to $34 over three months, under the heading "Ben, belonging to W. M. Rice." In most cases, though, surviving records do not disclose even this much detail about the identities and histories of the people Rice and his peers regarded as their property. A more typical entry showed the firm's acquisition of an enslaved person for $600 from another merchant firm in May 1854. No name for this person was given.[68]

Another page in the same ledger was labeled only as "Negro Property" and appears to show that Rice and Company (by that time comprising William Marsh and his brother Frederick) participated in at least two sales of enslaved people that year. On one line, a clerk recorded a credit to the "Negro Property" account for $1,950 by William S. Day, a farmer and lawyer also in Washington County. On Day's account, that amount appears on the same date as a debit, but it is recorded as a note to be paid thirty days later. The accounting suggests that the firm offered the buyer thirty-day financing on either one or a small number of unnamed slaves.[69]

Other entries in this early ledger show Rice and Company receiving "Henry" as "Negro Property" from J. W. McCown for $792.99 and conveying "boy Lewis" to one of Rice's other partners, Abraham Groesbeeck. This last notation could record a sale, or it may suggest that the values of enslaved people were being shifted on paper from one part of Rice's business to another. It is difficult to know; only occasionally can such notations be connected to other sources that provide a longer look at the lives of particular people. One entry in Rice's ledgers simply attached a transaction involving slaves to the account for "sundries," a word usually reserved for general merchandise.[70]

What the ledgers do provide is a sense of how valuable property in people had become to white Texans by the end of the 1850s. In a book kept by Rice and Company from around 1858 to 1859, the account labeled "Negro Property" apparently showed transfers to the firm's credit totaling $13,300 over six months. In terms of 2022 dollars, that amount alone would be worth more than $480,000.[71]

Yet Rice's antebellum ledgers can offer only partial insight into his accounts. Each book contains hundreds of pages of detailed, often cryptic notations, covering everything from cotton bales to children's chairs and kegs of nails. All three books refer to other volumes that are no longer extant. The surviving books cover only a few years, spanning 1855–56 and 1858–62, with a few entries from 1863. Given that each volume contains pages describing "Negro Property," it is reasonable to assume that other books kept by the firms contained similar pages, but the surviving record does not enable a comprehensive survey of Rice's accounts over time.

The closest historians may come to such a survey lies in the files of R. G. Dun and Company, an early credit-reporting firm whose agents summarized the affairs of firms across the country. Its antebellum reports about William Marsh Rice suggest that a full audit of his businesses was difficult even then. In 1850, a Dun and Company agent estimated that Rice and Nichols did about $400,000 worth of business per year, primarily "on credit to country merchants," but he noted that the firm's solvency was hard to judge because the partners' records were "not well kept." The following year, a Dun and Company agent reported that, since the arrival of E. W. Taylor as a partner, "the books have been better managed." Still, the complexity of the firm's accounts was a recurrent theme. "Their affairs are greatly complicated," said an agent in 1856.[72]

The Dun reports concluded that Rice and his partners were "steady money making men" and one of Houston's most reliable firms. The credit agents did not mention Rice's human property in particular, but those holdings may not have struck them as remarkable or exceptionally large. Of the 263 Texans who were reported as owning at least $100,000 in property on the 1860 census, all but thirty owned slaves. The median size of that group's enslaved property was 38 people, placing Rice on the smaller end of this spectrum, though that was not surprising given his location in a city and the nature of his business.[73]

Contemporaries were nonetheless aware of the ways that a business like Rice's was dependent on slavery. Because his firms were engaged in the "country trade" (especially in the first half of the 1850s, when Dun and Company made its first reports on Rice), his bottom line depended on enslaved people whom he never saw or held title to himself. They labored, far from his house or storefront, on cotton and sugar plantations, yet their labor contributed directly to his fortunes. "A great deal, in fact their existence, depends on the crops," a credit reporter noted of Rice and Nichols in 1850, a year in which Texans exported 58,000 bales of cotton, most of it through the port of Galveston.[74]

Evidence of that interdependence appears in newspaper columns reporting cotton shipments in the area. Consider a few notices from just one year: 1852. On March 18, the steamship *General Hamer* arrived in Galveston carrying 331 bales of cotton from the Brazos River, including 177 consigned to Rice and Nichols. On May 13, the *Star State* arrived in Galveston bearing 628 bales, "the largest load ever brought from Houston." The *Star State* was a new steamer owned by a transportation company that Rice and several others had helped to capitalize, and in the next few weeks, the *Farmer*, another of the company's steamers, brought shipments of 235 bales, 231 bales, and 190 bales, all consigned to Rice and Nichols. Adding up only the 833 bales consigned to Rice's firm in this small sample yields a total of nearly 350,000 pounds of cotton, probably amounting at then-current prices to more than $30,000 worth of the crop. That is comparable to more than $1 million in 2022. And in addition to earning commissions on the cotton he himself sold, Rice had invested in the steamer companies that collected revenue by transporting other people's bales.[75]

Such shipments of cotton from Houston to Galveston completed a kind of regular circuit that began when steamboats traveled in the opposite direction, carrying supplies, goods, and enslaved people inland for sale to surrounding plantations. Texas planters in 1850 could count on producing, on average, a little more than one bale of cotton per person they enslaved—the larger the enslaved labor force on their plantations, the higher the average yields. Demand for more laborers therefore never flagged during the decade. On January 18, 1851, the *Farmer* arrived in Houston from Galveston with "90 negroes" on deck; three days later, it brought another twenty-six. Most of the enslaved people brought in this way from Galveston would have ended up in the fields, laboring from sunup to sundown. They produced the cotton bales that then made profits for commission merchants like Rice. And as with the cotton shipped on the *Farmer*, the steamboats in which Rice invested would have earned revenues from shipping "negroes," too.[76]

Rice and his partners sometimes handled slave-grown sugar on commission, as well. In 1853, for example, William J. Kyle and Benjamin F. Terry purchased the Oakland Plantation near present-day Sugar Land, so named because the region became a large producer of sugar with Black labor. Like other area planters, they relied on commission merchants such as Rice. As recorded in the 1855–56 ledger, Kyle and Terry consigned nearly $2,000 worth of molasses and sugar to Rice and Company for transportation and sale. And between 1858 and 1859, the Houston firm received another $3,000 worth of molasses and sugar from Kyle and Terry, who had become, by 1860, some of the largest slaveholders in the region, with 200 enslaved people under their control.[77]

These transactions were the sorts of business that Rice would later describe as his "extensive and laborious commercial pursuits." It is clear, both from his ledgers and from the Dun and Company reports, that the variety and scale of Rice's pursuits steadily enriched his firm over time. By 1856, the assets of Rice's company were "more than double their liabilities," and he had amassed considerable real estate and corporate stocks. By the end of the decade, he was "believed to be the richest man in the city," if not the state, and his firm had "property of every kind."[78]

As such reports indicate, Rice's portfolio, inventory, and clientele were broad and grew broader over the years. Toward the end of the 1850s boom, Rice and his partners seem to have devoted themselves more intensively to their mercantile business and real estate, perhaps to strengthen their ability to withstand fluctuations in the price of crops, which had sometimes imperiled Rice and Nichols. In 1858, a Galveston journalist encountered Rice on a Mississippi River steamboat as he was returning from a recent purchasing trip to New York, and reported that Rice's "stock this year will be found to comprise nearly every article in demand," including house furnishings, carriages, pianos, and many other fine finished goods.

But Rice's various partnerships also never detached themselves from the business of bringing cash crops produced by slaves to market. In 1856, under an image of a cotton bale marked with an "R" for Rice, he advertised for sale an experimental new machine called "Howe's Cotton Harvester," a portable, gin-like contraption that could clean cotton lint as it was picked through a "mechanical combination propelled by the hand." The machine, which was meant to be strapped to the shoulder of a picker "as the cotton sack usually is," was recommended for trial by "the cotton growing interest of the South." Three years later, Rice and Company were still advertising their services as "cotton factors."[79]

In sum, William Marsh Rice's business in Houston remained deeply tied to the plantation economy and the "cotton growing interest" throughout the 1850s. This was true even as the wealth he had amassed enabled his expansion into one of his most lucrative ventures: railroads. In 1856, Rice was one of the incorporators of the Houston Tap and Brazoria Railway Company, which was chartered to connect Houston's central business district to the Buffalo Bayou, Brazos, and Colorado Rail Railway, another line in which Rice was an incorporator. Yet even these enterprises were inseparable from the political economy of slavery in Texas; as with steamboats, their primary value was to help planters and merchants speed the flow of crops to market from plantations. "Railroads were linked with slavery," as one historian of Texas has put it, as a means of expanding cotton production in the state. And when the Tap company contracted with Kyle and Terry to construct the Tap, that project linked the company inextricably with "Negro Property," too. The two planters forced the people they enslaved to lay the railroad's tracks.[80]

The Edge Hill Plantation

Slavery touched nearly every aspect of William Marsh Rice's antebellum business. In addition to acquiring more "Negro Property" of his own over time, Rice earned interest on loans made to planters that were backed both by land and by enslaved people. He sold supplies to plantations; he sold the commodities produced there; and he sold finer goods to white Texans who were flush with new wealth from the 1850s boom. Far from moving away from the cotton economy with his investments in railroads and other companies, on the eve of the Civil War, Rice was working with other merchants to modernize and maintain it. In 1860, he helped to incorporate the Houston Compress Company, which aimed to industrialize and streamline the process of ginning, baling, and selling cotton.[81]

William Marsh Rice was hardly the only Houston merchant whose financial successes in Texas were entangled with chattel slavery. He was an exceptionally successful businessman, but not unique in his many connections to enslavement. Yet neither was Rice exceptionally disconnected from slavery, as his earliest biographers implied when they credited his wealth solely to his own "indefatigable" labors. In fact, by the end of the 1850s, William Marsh Rice's firm was also closely tied to a cotton plantation, operated with enslaved labor and controlled by his younger brother and business partner, Frederick A. Rice.

Sometimes known as Edge Hill Plantation and later described as "one of the largest cotton plantations on the Brazos River," this plantation has almost never been noted by William Marsh Rice's biographers or historians of the university. But its history deserves to be more fully told. Not only does Edge Hill illustrate the sorts of services Rice provided to many other plantations where enslaved people worked, but it also provides a window onto the antebellum activities of his brother Frederick A. Rice, who would later play his own roles in the formation of Rice University. In 1891, Frederick's signature would be the second name, just beneath his brother's, on the original charter of incorporation for the Rice Institute. It was Frederick who would rush to New York together with Captain James A. Baker to investigate William's suspicious death in 1900, ensuring that his estate would pass to the university. And by the special preference of their uncle, two of Frederick's sons—William Marsh Rice Jr. and Benjamin Botts Rice—would succeed their father after his death as long-time Rice Institute trustees.[82]

Frederick A. Rice had followed William south to Texas in 1850, joining the wave of new settlers to the state. He first established himself with a retail furniture business in Houston before becoming a full partner in his older brother's firm, Wm. M. Rice and Company, in 1853. Then, in 1854, Frederick married Charlotte Maria Baldwin, a wealthy widow whose first husband was a cotton planter named James N. Randon. In 1853, an inventory of the recently deceased Randon's estate valued his property at $41,515.90, which included a plantation in Fort Bend County on the Brazos River (appraised at $17,600) and thirty-four enslaved people (appraised at $15,850).[83]

Upon his death, Randon had numerous balances with area commission merchants, a typical situation for planters. His two largest debts were with William M. Rice and Company and another merchant, John Dickinson, who served as the first administrator of Randon's estate with Charlotte, Randon's widow. Charlotte and Dickinson sold some of Randon's land and cotton to pay off his debts, but after Charlotte's marriage to Frederick A. Rice, Dickinson and Charlotte resigned as administrators, and Frederick took over in the spring of 1855 as the sole manager of the Randon estate and plantation. Five years after coming to Texas, the younger Rice was a planter.[84]

Administering Randon's estate would be both an opportunity and a responsibility for Frederick. In the years to come, he was liable for preserving the value of the estate for Randon's heirs and regularly reporting to the county probate court on his management decisions, such as buying a new cotton gin stand or building new slave cabins on the property. In the Fort Bend County Tax Rolls of 1856, he also appeared, in his new role as estate administrator, as the enslaver of forty people.[85]

At the same time, taking over this valuable plantation profited Frederick and the firm he ran with his brother. Frederick Rice received permission from the probate court to grow cotton crops for the benefit of the Randon estate, and by the end of the decade, this practice had entwined the estate's affairs closely with Rice and Company. Probate records show that Frederick consigned cotton from Edge Hill to his and his brother's Houston firm. Rice and Company then sold the bales, collected a commission, and provided the estate with other provisions and services, linking both brothers' interests to the productivity of a large cotton plantation.[86]

One of the surviving ledgers kept by Rice and Company demonstrates the links. Entries for "The Estate of John Randon" between October 1858 and July 1859 show more than one hundred bales of cotton to the estate's credit, totaling more than forty-thousand pounds of crop picked by enslaved people under Frederick's control. The left side of the page records the estate's purchase of groceries, boots, axes, blankets, rope, and other merchandise from Rice and Company; other entries reveal that the company advanced cash to pay overseers for the plantation such as Thomas Phillips, as well as to rent additional enslaved labor during the picking season. The same transactions appear in Frederick A. Rice's report to the Fort Bend County Court, which listed them as expenses for the estate.[87]

Included among the enslaved people who made these transactions possible were men named George, Adam, and Steve; boys of uncertain age whose names were Butler, George, Toby, Charley, Simon, Henry, Hillary, and Bill; women of unknown ages named Milly, Mary, Harriet, Vicey, Malinda, and Jane; and girls of unknown ages such as Barbara; along with a dozen children whose names were also recorded.[88] Another line in the probate records noted the yearlong hire of "girl Grace" to the Randon estate for $145, while on the same day the amount of $145 for "negro hire" was credited to F. A. Rice's account in the ledger books of Rice and Company. Taken together, the entries could mean that one or both of the Rice brothers legally owned Grace, collecting a fee for her hiring to an estate that one of them managed.[89]

And yet, as with other enslaved people, such lines tell us painfully little about the life of women like Grace, who were reckoned in legal and financial records as assets or expenses, rather than as people with biographies worthy of narration. Frederick Rice's reports to the Fort Bend probate court also recorded deaths and births of enslaved people at Edge Hill, but only as additions to or subtractions from the estate's inventory. A typical notation read: "Since last report there has been born one negro female child. Negro man Adam aged about 70 years has died, and also four mules."[90]

In lumping the death of Adam together with "four mules," that notation sums up the grim calculus of chattel slavery in Texas, a system that profited white Texans at the expense of Black lives. But the probate records also contain occasional hints of how enslaved people lived and pressed against such indignities and their enslavers' control. In September 1859, for example, F. A. Rice reported a payment to a man named Greer for "taking up boy George." George had appeared six years before on the first inventory taken by the Randon estate, and in March and April 1860, two more entries appeared for "taking boy George."[91]

These and similar entries suggest that George had been repeatedly running away from the plantation in Fort Bend County, engaging in a form of everyday resistance to his enslavement similar to Merinda's flight from William Marsh Rice in 1856. In December 1860, Frederick Rice again paid a man named Fisher for "catching boy George." And in March 1861, another entry for "catching boy George" appeared, possibly a reference to the same man, or possibly a reference to a "George" who had just been hired out to the estate.[92]

Frederick Rice or his managers surely knew which person was meant. For historians, it is hard to know if the entries even refer to different men. As we have seen, the archives of slavery often work against scholars' efforts to see beyond financial abstractions to the individual lives of Black men, women, and children, who struggled against their confinement in space and on the page.

It would require a different kind of recordkeeping to distinguish one "George" from another. In 1870 the U.S. Census documented, for the first time, the full names of some of the people who had been enslaved ten years before. That census would better identify some of the Black people who worked for the Rice brothers' benefit at the Edge Hill Plantation. Yet this momentous change in their status on paper—from expenses in ledgers to citizens with surnames—had required the legal abolition of slavery after the bloodiest war in American history, epochal events that unsteadied, but did not topple, "money-making men" like the brothers Rice.

2 | RICE AND THE REBELLION

On June 12, 1863, in the middle of the U.S. Civil War (1861–65), a young Black man called Captain was on the move, traveling on the shallow waters of the Brazos River, when he was stopped by a white man and taken to a jail in Hempstead, Texas. The jailer determined that Captain was a fugitive from slavery and questioned him about his history. *Whom did he belong to?* the jailer wanted to know. Captain answered with the names of two men: William Marsh Rice and Frederick A. Rice.

The jailer quickly addressed a letter to the Rice brothers in Houston, scribbling his note on scrap paper that survived, seldom noticed, into the twenty-first century. "I have a negro boy who sais [*sic*] he belongs to both of you," he wrote. "He calls his name Captain." The jailer told the Rice and Company partners to come to Hempstead, prove that Captain was their property, and then take him away, "or he will be dealt with as the law directs in such cases." That meant, according to an 1861 law, that he would be forced into labor at the state penitentiary in Huntsville. The jailer surmised, or had been told by the fugitive himself, that Captain was seventeen or eighteen years old.[1]

It was likely not the first time that Captain had been taken up as a fugitive. Early in the war, Frederick Rice's reports about the Randon estate listed eight enslaved people "hired out" to work at Edge Hill, possibly by his and his brother's firm. Frederick gave the name of one of them as "Cap," and in May 1861, he reported expenses for "Catching Boy Capt." In October 1861, a similar note appeared again. If "Cap" or "Capt" referred to the same "Captain" jailed in 1863, he had been on the run before.[2]

In Texas, however, fugitives from slavery still had few places to go in 1863. From the earliest months of the war, freedom-seekers in other states had tested U.S. policy by running to military camps, pressuring Union officials to embrace emancipation. By June 1863, federal armies were dissolving slavery almost everywhere they marched in accordance with the Emancipation Proclamation, issued by Abraham Lincoln six months before Captain's capture. But military emancipation depended on the success of Union armies, and the Brazos River remained far from the front lines. Not until "Juneteenth"—June 19, 1865—did U.S. soldiers arrive in Galveston to begin enforcing emancipation across the Lone Star State.

William Marsh Rice was not in Houston when they came. At the very end of 1863, Rice had moved to Mexico, where he continued selling cotton and importing goods around a U.S. blockade of Confederate ports. His brother Frederick remained behind, managing their property and eventually closing up their Houston store. In a court document from the late 1890s, Rice recalled, "The war broke up my business." Much of Rice's wealth would nonetheless survive the fighting. And although the war did disrupt his business, not least by ending property rights in people, Rice could not blame the breakup entirely on others. There is good evidence that he supported the push for secession in Houston.[3]

That evidence flatly contradicts the story told for more than a century that Rice was a Unionist. A biographical sketch published in 1912 claimed that Rice's "sympathies were with the North" in the war and that his "opinions were known and respected" in Houston after his return from Mexico. Historian Andrew Forest Muir later agreed—though his early, unpublished work noted more cautiously that Rice's feelings about the Confederacy were "not entirely clear." Both cited unsourced anecdotes, posthumously told, about Rice's antebellum acquaintance with Sam Houston, who opposed secession. In her biography of Rice, Sylvia Stallings Morris argued that "it is only reasonable to suppose that he agreed with Sam Houston in seeing secession as a disaster" and found it "hard to imagine William Marsh Rice taking the opposing stand." These suppositions later hardened into accepted fact, embodied in the judgment reached by a key reference work on Rice: "Though he was a slaveowner . . . he identified with the Unionist cause."[4]

Both old and newly available sources reveal a more complex reality. At the outset of the rebellion, Rice favored the defiant steps that led to disunion, agreeing with others that only in this way could slavery and the wealth it supported be preserved. By the end of the fighting, like many wealthy white Texans, Rice may have been less supportive of the Confederacy than he was at the beginning, though that does not mean he identified with Unionists. Nor is there any evidence that Rice or his brother Frederick repudiated slavery before it was forcibly overthrown and legally abolished. With few exceptions, even the minority of white Texans who were vocal Unionists were still in favor of slavery—including Sam Houston, a slaveholder himself.

In short, William Marsh Rice's actions before, during, and after the War of the Rebellion did not mark him as exceptionally out of step with others of his class, as later descriptions of him as a Unionist implied. What the evidence shows instead is a larger truth that Captain surely knew well, and one with fearsome implications for the history that followed. At no point was slavery dying off or voluntarily discarded by white Texans like the Rices. It had to be defeated.

That defeat finally came almost two years to the day after Captain was jailed, with Juneteenth and the start of Reconstruction in the state. Only three years after that, in 1868, William Marsh Rice would write a long-forgotten will, analyzed here for the first time, that recorded his earliest intention to establish a school for "poor white children" in Texas. Written at the height of postwar struggles over voting, citizenship, education, and civil rights, the will demonstrates that the earliest seeds of the idea for what later became Rice University were planted not in the decade prior to its chartering in 1891, as historians have long believed, but in 1868, within the immediate aftermath of slavery, secession, and civil war.

"To Secure Our Institutions"

The documents Confederates left to posterity made clear that slavery was the cause of the Civil War. On February 1, 1861, some 177 county delegates gathered in Austin, Texas, where they overwhelmingly passed an ordinance of secession from the United States. The next day, they adopted a "declaration of the causes" explaining why Texas should secede and cast its lot with the Confederate States of America. The defense of slavery appeared at the top of the list.

Secessionists argued that Texans had joined the United States in the belief that "the servitude of the African to the white race" would continue to exist there "in all future time." Now, said the rebels, that institution was endangered by the election of Abraham Lincoln as president in November 1860. "We hold as undeniable truths," they continued, that the United States "were established exclusively by the white race, for themselves and their posterity; that the African race had no agency in their establishment; [and] that they were rightfully held and regarded as an inferior and dependent race." Freedom for Confederate Texans meant white supremacy and perpetual slavery for people of African descent.[5]

Secession brought to a culmination long-simmering tensions in the nation as a whole. In the 1840s and 1850s, fugitive slaves escaping into northern free states had galvanized a growing abolitionist movement. Closer to white Texans was a fear of enslaved people fleeing south to Mexico where slavery was illegal. By 1854, political struggles over fugitives and the status of slavery in federal territories had led to the founding of an antislavery, entirely northern party—the Republicans—and the new party's rapid success at the ballot box alarmed white southerners. After Abraham Lincoln, a Republican, won election to the White House in November 1860, a wave of secession swept the South.[6]

These crises divided the country and drew lines within some families, too. One of William Marsh Rice's nephews in Texas would join the Confederate Army as a private. Another nephew, William A. Rice, decided to leave his employment as a clerk for Rice and Company and return to Massachusetts in 1859; he later fought for the Union and came home with his arm in a sling. Many years afterward, William A. Rice recalled that his uncle William had "consented" to his nephew's decision to leave the firm and return to the North "when the War was threatening."[7] William Marsh Rice, meanwhile, chose to remain in Houston, where the possibility of war was rapidly sorting white Texans into four groups.[8]

One small minority had been hoping for secession for years, agitating forcefully for "Southern Rights." In Houston, their chief spokesman was E. H. Cushing, the editor and publisher of the Houston *Telegraph*. Born in Vermont and educated at Dartmouth College, Cushing had come to Texas around the same time as fellow New Englander Frederick A. Rice. Once in the South, Cushing quickly combined support for industry and railroads with full-throated support for slavery and cotton. Together with other newspaper editors itching for resistance, he devoted many column inches in 1860 to conspiracy theories that blamed a series of fires in Texas on an alleged alliance of abolitionists and enslaved rebels. Men like Cushing used the fires to raise alarms about what so-called "Black Republican" rule would mean. They were the first to push for secession when Lincoln won.[9]

On the other end of the political spectrum from aggressive secessionists was a small group of unconditional Unionists. Though not antislavery as a rule, this group firmly opposed secession, even after Lincoln's election. Their leader was Governor Sam Houston, whose election in 1859 had rebuffed extremists on the other side.[10]

In between these poles were two larger groups of white Texans. One defended the Union during the sectional crisis but embraced secession once Lincoln was elected. Another group defended the Union longer, but sided with the state once the Secession Convention's votes had been ratified. Both groups included merchants who worried that an abrupt breakup of the Union and any violence that followed would be bad for business.[11]

These various positions can make it difficult to determine precisely when a particular Texan who embraced secession (even one who had long worried about abolitionists and Republicans) definitively joined the secessionist camp. In 1860, for example, Frederick A. Rice publicly favored John C. Breckinridge for president, choosing the Democratic candidate who was most identified with an aggressive defense of "Southern Rights." Tellingly, Breckinridge was Cushing's choice as well. Yet although pro-secessionists all voted for Breckinridge, not all Breckinridge supporters were secessionists before the election.[12]

Is it possible, then, to know where William Marsh Rice himself stood on the question of secession, and when? No evidence from the time has been found to show that Rice stood with unconditional Unionists like Sam Houston. Whether he joined his brother in voting for Breckinridge is also unknown. But evidence does show that, over the course of the winter of 1860–61, and even before the secession convention in Austin, Rice was one of the leading Houstonians pressuring the governor to take the steps that diehard secessionists favored.[13]

Only days after Lincoln's victory, these disunionists began urging Sam Houston to convene the legislature to call a secession convention. The alternative, argued one correspondent to the Houston *Telegraph*, was submission to "Black Republican" rule and the "Africanization" of the South. Conversely, E. H.

Cushing predicted that Texas, once out of the Union, would be "the nucleus of slavery and the harbor of the wealth attached to slavery on this continent." He urged counties throughout the state to hold public meetings expressing the general will.[14]

William Marsh Rice attended the first such meeting to be held in Houston, on November 14, 1860, and was elected to a committee of twenty-one leading men (many of them known secessionists) charged with writing resolutions for adoption by the meeting. Their first resolution breathed defiance barely a week after Election Day. "Resolved," it said, "That the election of Abraham Lincoln to the Presidency by the Black Republican party of the Northern States, upon the principles of that party, is the denial of the right of the Southern States to equality in the Union, reducing them to the condition of provinces, and forces upon them the vital issue of emancipation of negro slavery, with all its evil consequences, or the withdrawal of the Southern States." The crisis demanded that the governor "convene the Legislature at the earliest practicable time" and that "all Federal officers" in Texas resign before Lincoln's inauguration.[15]

Not everyone on the Resolutions Committee signed their name to these statements, but according to E. H. Cushing, who was on the committee and served as secretary, William Marsh Rice did sign. As for the whole assembly, which was attended by "hundreds," it passed all of the resolutions "with but one dissenting voice." The mass meeting also appointed two temporary committees, one of which was charged with corresponding with similar groups in other counties. Among its members was Alfred S. Richardson, who would later be elected to the Confederate state legislature and, even later, would be named by Rice as a trustee in the 1891 charter of the Rice Institute.[16]

Historical context is key to understanding this meeting's demand that the governor convene the legislature. Outside of the context documented by historians of secession, the meeting may look only like a simple call for the legislature to gather and neutrally discuss the results of the election.[17] Within the fast-moving flow of events, however, such meetings were understood as an organized pressure campaign to move the state toward disunion. In an attempt to slow down the separatists' momentum, Governor Houston initially refused to call the legislature into special session. He proposed writing a letter to other southern governors to consult as executives, a step he took on November 28.

As historian William W. Freehling writes, "Houston counted on delay to calm the overly excited."[18]

But the men who had met in Harris County earlier in the month opposed any delay. On December 1, they convened again in Houston, and William Marsh Rice was again named to the committee charged with drafting a report and resolutions. While this group continued to hope that Governor Houston would relent and call the legislature (the only body authorized, they believed, to create a popular statewide convention), they stressed that there was no time to wait, not while "the day approaches for the inauguration of Black Republicanism." Steps were needed "to accelerate the movement."[19]

The December 1 resolutions in Harris County, drafted by Rice's committee and adopted unanimously, urged that "resistance to Black Republican misrule is necessary to secure our institutions, and to protect our peace and property," words that contemporaries would easily have understood as references to slavery and the calamities that would supposedly follow its abolition. The meeting called on local officials to prepare for a vote on January 8 that would elect delegates to a popular convention to push resistance forward. It also created a permanent executive committee to correspond with other counties organizing similar votes, while another committee was formed to raise funds for the executive group. Frederick A. Rice was on the fundraising group; Rice and Company donated funds.[20]

William Marsh Rice's involvement in these two meetings decisively refutes the long-held supposition that he was a Sam Houston loyalist to the end, but they do not necessarily show the same eagerness for disunion that men like Cushing had exhibited from the start. Rice could have signed onto the resolutions still believing that some form of resistance short of secession was possible. He may well have been among those white Texans who supported the governor in 1859 and came around to the idea of rebellion only after Lincoln's election, and then only gradually. Even E. H. Cushing acknowledged in a December 18 editorial that during the agitation immediately after Lincoln's election "there were many, especially among the commercial men, who deprecated the excitement," foreseeing the "pecuniary troubles" it might create for them.[21]

But by mid-December, Cushing wrote that even merchants who had held out hope for union "had come to the opinion that it was NOW, or NEVER, to settle this everlasting slavery agitation. . . . Submission now is [the] riveting of the chains upon us." According to the editor, some people in Houston were still claiming that disunionism was a movement of "reckless agitators who have nothing at stake." Cushing denied the claim by pointing to men like "Wm. M. Rice, W. J. Hutchins, W. S. Rogers . . . and twenty others of like standing." Rice was one of the merchants who was on his side.[22]

Further evidence of Rice's views appeared in the same newspaper issue. A few days before, Governor Houston had visited his namesake city to give a speech laying out his case for cautious deliberation and explaining his reasons for not convening the legislature. Houston was met, according to Cushing, with jeers from the crowd and a torchlight procession carrying banners that read "Cotton is King" and "We accept the Irrepressible Conflict."[23]

The organizers of the city's two previous mass meetings were also not impressed by Houston's speech. In an open letter "To the People of Harris County," seven men calling themselves the Harris County Committee criticized his tactics and declared the time for waiting over: "Now Abolitionism is in the ascendant, and the exercise of its power imminent. Then there was time for consultation and co-operation before the evil befell us. Now the time is short," they said. "Patriotism demands that all should actively participate in the election" of delegates to a popular convention, defying the governor's plodding course.[24]

William Marsh Rice was one of the seven who signed his name to that letter. The other signatories were all the members of the permanent committee established at the December 1 mass meeting except for one, suggesting that Rice had replaced the missing member.[25]

Contrary to earlier Rice biographers' claims, these sources make it not only possible, but necessary, "to imagine William Marsh Rice taking the opposing stand [against Sam Houston] and demanding to leave the Union."[26] Nor should that be surprising, given how intertwined his businesses and fortunes were with slavery. Secessionists believed, not entirely without reason, that the Lincoln administration would work to put the "peculiar institution" on a path to extinction. His election thus seemed to threaten the tremendous wealth of merchants and planters alike. By 1860, the nearly 4 million slaves in the United States were worth an estimated $3 billion to their legal owners, and that wealth was leveraged and relied on in countless ways.[27]

Confederate president Jefferson Davis saw the danger clearly in a speech made on April 29, 1861, upon the ratification of the Confederate Constitution, which explicitly protected slavery in its text. The "avowed object" of Lincoln's Republican Party, Davis said, would tend toward "rendering the property in slaves so insecure as to be comparatively worthless, and thereby annihilating in effect property worth thousands of millions of dollars." The ripple effects from such a destruction of property would extend, as well, to the investments, credit networks, and infrastructure that both undergirded slavery and assumed its indefinite operation.[28]

In the end, therefore, Confederates chose war over the risk of giving up slavery, white supremacy, and the unequally distributed wealth they had created. William Marsh Rice evidently supported their reasoning. The concerted efforts of disunionists forced Houston to resign as governor in March 1861, not long after Lone Star secessionists voted to join the Confederacy. Three weeks after the ordinance of secession was adopted, Texas voters affirmed it by a final statewide tally of 46,153 for secession and 14,747 against. In Harris County, the vote for secession was even more lopsided: 1,128 for to 163 against. Then, in April, with the firing on Fort Sumter in Charleston, South Carolina, civil war began.[29]

Slavery's Survival in Texas

The first weeks after Fort Sumter found white Houstonians unified and hopeful about the Confederacy. A meeting chaired by merchant B. A. Shepherd greeted Virginia's belated decision to secede with champagne toasts and "general jollification." Future Rice Institute charter trustees A. S. Richardson and Frederick A. Rice were elected officers in a local military company commanded by lawyer and judge Peter W. Gray. And city merchants, including Rice and Company, shortened business hours so that their clerks could perform military drills. "If there is a business man in Houston who does not most heartily support the government in all its measures," crowed E. H. Cushing, "we do not know who he is."[30]

Not all of the news over the next year was good for the rebels. "As Union troops made their way through Virginia and the Mississippi River Valley during 1861 and 1862," writes historian Andrew Torget, "reports streamed into Texas newspapers of enslaved African Americans escaping their masters," pushing U.S. policymakers to take ever more aggressive steps to weaken slavery in the South. By the middle of 1862, Lincoln told proslavery Unionists in border states that slavery could not long survive the "abrasions" of war. But Texas remained far from the battlefront, leaving enslaved people there with fewer opportunities for flight to military lines. Although not entirely insulated from war's abrasions, slavery in Texas survived and even grew.[31]

Wartime Houston prospered, too, enabling merchants like the Rices to continue business as usual—including the business of slavery. In December 1861, William Marsh Rice foreclosed on a mortgage on an enslaved teenager named Amanda, purchasing her at a trust auction for $1,050. In the summer of 1862, even as Lincoln began to speak more forcefully about emancipation, Rice and Company was selling luxury goods like pianos and extending credit to area planters. And in July 1862, Thomas Thatcher (a Wharton County planter who enslaved at least twenty-seven people) pledged three years of his cotton crop to William Marsh Rice for an advance of $6,000.[32]

That deal and others assumed that planters could continue to produce cotton and bring it to market during the war, pointing to a geographical advantage held by Texas over other rebel states. A Union naval blockade had quickly closed up southern ports. But since Texas shared a border with Mexico, planters and merchants there moved cotton by wagon trains to border crossings at Eagle Pass or Brownsville and on to Matamoros, Mexico, where thousands of bales were sold to eager foreign buyers and placed on ships waiting in international waters off the coast.[33]

For a few months at the end of 1862, U.S. forces did briefly capture Galveston, threatening Houston and throwing the city into a frenzy of military preparation. (The firm's records appear to show that Confederate quartermasters purchased $2,500 worth of material from Rice and Company that October for building defensive obstructions in the area, part of a much larger record of transactions between the firm and military purchasers.) But after a surprise New Year's Eve attack on Galveston, led by Major General John Bankhead Magruder, Confederates recaptured the island city as well as a gunboat, the USS *Harriet Lane*.[34]

These events caused a stir in Houston when prisoners taken from the *Harriet Lane* were found to include (in the words of Henry Perkins, then the district attorney for Harris County) "six negroes claiming to be free," bringing the effects of federal antislavery policies to Houston's doorstep. With the help of Judge James A. Baker Sr. (father of the future Rice Institute chairman), Perkins arranged to "hire out" the six Black prisoners to the state by forcing them to work in the state penitentiary in Huntsville. In a letter to the legislature, Perkins warned ominously that "we know not how soon we may have a Brigade of Negroes of like character" landing on Texas shores.[35]

Similar fears animated Texas governor Francis Lubbock's decision to call the legislature into special session in February 1863. As Lubbock later recalled, after the Emancipation Proclamation, "It became at once a matter of some concern to us to know what effect the proclamation would have upon the negroes, as it could not be kept concealed from them." In a message to the legislature, Lubbock warned that "Confederate laws have proved impotent to stay the progress of emancipation wherever the Lincoln soldiers have gone." So, at the governor's urging, the state legislature passed its own law defining harsh penalties for anyone, including prisoners of war, who incited slave insurrections or escapes.[36]

Worry about the war's corrosive effects on slavery may have influenced another matter considered in the same session: a petition to the legislature by Peter Allen, "a free man of color, aged about 49 years." Allen explained that he had worked in Houston as a barber for 17 years and had recently worked as a camp servant for an officer in the regiment formed by Sugar Land planter Benjamin F. Terry, who had been killed in battle in December 1861. On this basis, Allen petitioned for the right to stay in Texas, "the land of his nativity," as a free Black man, despite a longstanding law prohibiting free Black people from remaining in the state.[37]

Twenty-seven prominent white Houstonians—including William Marsh Rice—endorsed Peter Allen's petition, vouching paternalistically for the barber's "correct deportment" and reputation for "honest, sober, and industrious" living. Similar requests had very occasionally been granted before the war, and legislators who supported Allen made clear they viewed him as exceptional. Even so, the House of Representatives decided, by a vote of forty-eight to twenty-four, to deny Allen's request: He could only remain in Texas as a slave. In the perilous aftermath of Galveston and the *Harriet Lane*, the majority apparently feared to do anything that weakened slavery.[38]

In September 1863, a second attempt by federal troops to land on the coast and march inland was turned back by Confederates at the Battle of Sabine Pass. Slavery in Texas was never again seriously threatened by U.S. troops before Juneteenth. On the contrary, between 1862 and 1865, thousands of slaveholding Confederates from other states fled to the state's interior, forcing tens of thousands of enslaved people to move with them in an effort to keep them enslaved. Far from dissolving during the war, the Texas slave population swelled, flooding the state's markets with enslaved laborers for hire or sale.[39]

Prosperous white Houstonians capitalized on the surplus. Several area railroads, including the Houston and Texas Central, in which William Marsh Rice was now heavily invested, advertised a desire to hire enslaved people from owners. Meanwhile, the wave of new migrants set "Houston's slave market on a boom that continued to the war's end." One editorial in July 1863 noted that a recent sale of fifty people for an average of $2,600 per person "showed that negroes still bring all they are worth—if not a little more." In February of that same year, the Houston *Weekly Telegraph* listed skyrocketing prices for slaves as "evidence of the confidence of the people in the stability of property."[40]

The booming slave market also provided evidence of price inflation in Texas and waning confidence in a rapidly depreciating Confederate dollar. Nonetheless, the *Telegraph* was right: Purchases of enslaved people in wartime Texas demonstrated a widespread belief that slavery would survive the war, making property in people seem like a sound investment for Confederate Texans with capital.[41]

Creditors continued to accept enslaved people as security for wartime loans, as shown by two examples from the records of Rice and Company. In November 1862, the firm gave three notes totaling $4,000 to Thomas E. Bowdre and his wife at 10 percent interest, the last of which was to be repaid by October 1865. To secure the loan, Bowdre mortgaged nine enslaved people to Rice.[42] A few months later, in April 1863, Rice and Company extended a similar loan to Thomas W. Mitchell, a Fort Bend County planter who named ten enslaved people as security: Henry, Jack, Mary, Ann, Maria (and her one-year-old child), Patsy, Emily (and "her girl child"), and Phaby.[43]

Another document from around that time appears to show that in 1863, after the Emancipation Proclamation, Rice and Company engaged in purchases of numerous slaves as well. A small notebook, filled with Frederick A. Rice's handwriting, contains notations suggesting that he paid substantial sums to buy dozens of enslaved men, women, and children—either from several different sellers, or for several different buyers on commission, and probably drawing on the firm's account. Scattered throughout are names like Pleasant, "Ann and two children," Ellen, Abe, and Tom. The first two pages contain a tabulation of some thirty names, with their total price summed to $54,700.[44]

A separate, loose-leaf bill of sale from October 17, 1863, confirms that one person mentioned by name in the notebook, a thirty-five-year-old woman named Ann, "of black complexion," had been acquired by Thomas W. Mitchell in April 1863 and was then bought by William M. Rice and Company for $1,500. And in 1864, after several years of paying county taxes on forty-three people owned by the Randon estate and seven people he owned himself, F. A. Rice paid taxes on the forty-three Randon slaves in addition to forty enslaved people listed as his property alone, for a total of eighty-three people—a dramatic increase that probably reflects the purchases described in his notes.[45]

Like other Texas planters, Frederick intended to put this enlarged labor force to work growing cotton. In his administrator's report to the Fort Bend County Probate Court about the Randon estate in September 1863, Frederick formally asked, in the usual way, for permission to continue operating the Edge Hill Plantation for the estate. But he also added several details that had not appeared before.

First, F. A. Rice noted that he now had "27 hands his own property which could be worked with advantage" alongside the people belonging to the Randon estate. (This was likely another reference to people he had recently purchased, only some of whom would have been considered, in the reductive language used by slaveholders, full field "hands.") He proposed to cultivate two hundred more acres than he had the previous year, splitting the proceeds of any cotton between himself and the estate. And finally, Frederick indicated that he would send any bales made "to Brownsville or Matamoros."[46]

For that last step, he knew, Frederick Rice would have the expert help of his brother and partner. A letter written to Frederick by William from Matamoros on May 12, 1863, shows that the elder Rice was then on a visit to Mexico, scouting out opportunities for business. Though unsigned, the letter is one of the earliest available sources documenting William Marsh Rice's involvement in trade across the border. And it closed with a question that revealed how vital Texas plantations like Edge Hill, and the continued labor of enslaved people on them, would be in sustaining his business there.

"How much cotton have you started?" he asked.[47]

The Abrasions of War

While his May letter indicates that William Marsh Rice visited Mexico at least once in early 1863, it would be some months before he made a longer-term move across the border. By October 22, 1863, he was back home in Houston, where he addressed a letter to Frederick's wife, Charlotte, about the cotton crop. William told her to make sure that any bales that Frederick intended for sale weighed at least 550 pounds, because it was only possible to "get out a certain number of bales and the heavier they are the better." The advice showed the close eye Rice was keeping on operations at Edge Hill and the knowledge that he had already gleaned about the border trade in cotton—a business that had become, by then, a source of increasing conflict among white Texans.[48]

In theory, the ability to move cotton into Mexico could have solved urgent funding problems for the struggling Confederacy, primarily as a means by which the government could purchase military supplies and raise revenue. But from the beginning of the war, profits from the trade had proved difficult for officials to capture, eventually leading to clashes between civilians, state authorities, and the Confederate Army.[49]

One major problem was that rich, private speculators were able to outbid government purchasers by buying cotton with gold, driving up prices while contributing to the rapid depreciation of Confederate currency. When creditors responded by requesting gold for other transactions, the result was wider discontent. In June 1863, an article in a Houston newspaper complained that William Marsh Rice had recently refused to accept Confederate paper as payment for a loan; one year later, a local planter complained to Rice that it was not fair to make him repay a loan in specie, when the loan had been made in Confederate dollars. The growing demand for specie not only pinched debtors; it also hurt government buyers, who often had only cash or a promise of cash to offer cotton sellers.[50]

Over the course of 1862 and 1863, civilian and military officials in Texas experimented with various ways to combat inflation and profiteering. Raising taxes on cotton, stopping cotton at Brownsville, requiring special permits to export cotton—all of it was tried. But all of it only created what one general described as a "tangled snarl" of orders and counterorders by state, national, and military officials, each of whom had their own agents trying to buy up the state's limited supply of cotton.[51]

In the summer of 1863, the Confederate Army therefore took a more controversial step: impressing cotton—that is, confiscating it for a set price—to procure supplies in Mexico. But the new policy contained so many exemptions and loopholes that the gambit failed to meet the military's purchasing needs. And in the meantime, white Texans began to howl about impressment as a violation of individuals' and states' rights; one editor in La Grange said that anyone who submitted to the new rules "is already a slave and ready for the manacles." Even a revised military plan designed to be more palatable, in which planters would be required to sell only half of their bales to the army's "Cotton Bureau" in exchange for Confederate bonds, failed to quell the uproar.[52]

To further complicate matters along the border, a newly elected state government in Austin soon began resisting the Cotton Bureau's work. In December, Texas governor Pendleton Murrah announced a "State Plan" to buy up cotton with state bonds backed by land warrants, rather than depreciated cash. If planters sold half of their cotton to agents for the state of Texas on these terms, the state would not only protect their bales from military impressment, but would also cover the high costs of their transportation to Mexico. Murrah tapped William Marsh Rice's early partner, Ebenezer B. Nichols, to lead this "State Plan," which for months brought Texas state officials and their agents into open conflict with agents trying to buy cotton for the Confederacy.[53]

Despite their differences, all of these plans shared one thing in common: They took for granted that enslaved people could still be forced to produce the cotton being hauled south. Yet slavery, too, became a point of contention between military authorities and civilians in 1863. In March, the Confederate Congress passed a law empowering the army to impress private property for military use. Confederate major general Magruder interpreted that law to mean that he could force enslaved people to do work like digging trenches, driving teams, and building fortifications, in exchange for a small, set hiring fee to their owners. Even before the law, Magruder had been pressuring planters to hire out enslaved people to do the arduous work of erecting defenses along the Texas coast after the Battle of Galveston. But these requests soon intensified conflict between Magruder and planters, who were just as defensive of property rights in people as they were of cotton.[54]

In Fort Bend County, Frederick A. Rice was appointed in late 1862 as one of the agents working to round up enslaved laborers for Magruder's command and arrange for their transportation to labor camps. The Rice brothers also hired out: William Marsh Rice was paid by a Confederate officer for the services of an enslaved man named Charles as a messenger, while Frederick hired out people to an assistant quartermaster for work on a railroad to Galveston. Entries in a surviving Rice and Company ledger appear to show that two men enslaved by the firm, William and George, were hired out in 1863 at the going rate then being paid by the military: thirty dollars per month.[55]

From the beginning, Magruder found it difficult to secure all the labor he wanted through appeals to voluntarism. In January 1863, Houston editor E. H. Cushing noted with "regret" that "slave owners are not responding to the call of Gen. Magruder with that alacrity which the emergency of the case demands." Although one thousand enslaved men were already at work building fortifications in Galveston, Cushing warned that Magruder needed some two thousand more to put the coast's defenses "in a condition to fight off all the hosts of Lincolndom." B. A. Shepherd was heading a committee in Houston "to receive the negroes" for that purpose.[56]

When even these efforts failed to meet Magruder's demands, the general turned to the tactic already causing outrage over cotton: impressment. By July 1863, he had support from civilian and military leaders to take this more forceful step, though Magruder's superior officer, Lt. Gen. Edmund Kirby Smith, privately warned that enslaved property was "the last the owners are disposed to part with." Sure enough, when systematic impressment of slave labor began in August 1863, it proved no more popular than cotton impressment with propertied white Texans.[57]

Confederate propagandists like E. H. Cushing defended the military's increasing demands, insisting to his readers, "Gen. Smith is no tyrant. Gen. Magruder is no tyrant." But by the end of 1863, as one historian notes, Cushing's view was becoming a "minority opinion." The abrasions of war were unsettling the social order in Texas at last, though the friction there was caused less by Union armies than by internal unrest over perceptions of Confederate overreach.[58]

One planter who was in debt to Rice and Company could barely contain his mounting frustrations in a letter to the firm in January 1864. While noting that he would have liked to sell "50 or 100 bales at specie rates" to the firm as requested, he was "7 negro fellows and 8 of my plow-team out," presumably from impressment, making it too difficult to get his cotton out of the ground. And even if he could make bales, complained the planter, "what will the '*Cotton Bureau*' say? Will it allow me to sell without letting it have its first half?"[59]

Like other planters, Frederick A. Rice encountered the lengthening arm of the state when trying to move cotton. Some of his bales were redirected when they arrived at a Confederate government depot too late to count as payment of an in-kind tax on cotton for 1863. A different shipment of bales apparently sold to the military was sent back because it was poorly packed for transport to Mexico. On another occasion, his application to get a permit to export some bales was denied by a Cotton Bureau agent pending receipt of more information.[60]

On still other occasions, Frederick Rice himself represented the long arm of the state. After being exempted from conscription to the front lines in 1862 (the law allowed men who oversaw a plantation with more than twenty slaves, as he did, to stay home), Frederick served as an army officer on a series of military details in Houston, including for the Labor Bureau. And in early 1864, he became a purchasing agent for Texas under Murrah's "State Plan."[61]

As for William Marsh Rice, by the end of 1863, he had left home for Mexico again, and this time he would remain away from Houston for the rest of the war. "In August 1863," Rice later recalled, "my first wife died and in the December following I went to Mexico—Monteray [*sic*] and down to Matamoros and after a little delay on to Havana, remained there a month or two, then returned to Matamoros where I was in business until August 1865, at which time I returned to Houston." By late January 1864, Rice was well situated in Monterey, the first stop on that journey, when he wrote home that he hoped Frederick's family would have enough provisions to get by "if the Yankees come."[62]

Before leaving Houston, Rice had discussed in detail with his brother how to manage their affairs in his absence. He drew up a short will that left his entire estate to Frederick in the event of his death, as well as a list of treasury notes and state bonds in his possession. And on November 11, Frederick wrote William to remind his brother of some other instructions he needed to leave behind: "you had better leave a memorandum about the rents and negro hire."[63]

The last phrase, "negro hire," serves as another reminder of slavery's survival in Texas. In the midst of all the turmoil around impressment, William Marsh Rice still held slaves and still held promissory notes secured by slaves. Indeed, Frederick's letter raises a question that previous accounts of Rice's move to Mexico never asked: What happened to the people enslaved by William Marsh Rice when he left?

No source answers that question conclusively, but only a few realistic possibilities exist. The failure of Peter Allen's petition to remain in Texas as a free Black barber in early 1863 shows why manumission was unlikely. The jailing of Captain shows that escape was improbable. The booming slave market may have tempted Rice to sell. But another option was the one Frederick seemed to think his brother had in mind, at least for some of the laborers William Marsh Rice enslaved: he could hire them out to work—perhaps even to his brother for the use of the Randon estate—thus collecting fees from their labor even while he was away.

Of course, by the time Frederick wrote in November 1863, such arrangements were increasingly difficult to secure. The vise of impressment was closing in on various kinds of property: livestock, cotton, and enslaved people, too, as he well knew from his work in the Labor Bureau. So Frederick Rice also saw fit, in the same letter asking about "negro hire," to warn his brother about impressment. If he wanted to take his "white horse" with him to Mexico, Frederick advised, he should "send out and get him & keep him in Houston as they may press him. And," he hastened to add, "they may take 'Captain' too."[64]

That name—Captain—returns us to a jail in Hempstead in the middle of the year 1863. If Frederick referred to the same enslaved teenager who had just been captured there in June, then this November note indicates that the Rices or their agent had in fact gone to Hempstead and claimed Captain—only to now be faced with the possibility that he would be impressed. "You had better instruct Joe to release [Captain] with another horse," Frederick told his brother, "if he cannot save him without."[65]

But what did it mean to "release" Captain in a state that was still a stronghold of slavery on the far edge of the Confederacy? Where did Frederick mean for Captain to be sent? And what did it mean to "save him," an ambiguous phrase at a time when many Texans believed that Confederate officers were unjustly taking property and threatening the wealth they had stored up in Black people? Probably Frederick meant for Rice to hire Captain out somewhere he would be less likely to be taken by press gangs, but the letter does not explain Frederick's thinking fully. Captain's final fate remains unknown.

What is clear is that the war was producing increasingly intense disputes among white Texans over control of enslaved people. Secessionists in Texas had rebelled believing that "Black Republicans" threatened slavery. So when Confederate commanders encroached on slavery through impressment, some Texans resented the imposition on their power and property rights. And in the meantime, white Texans of all classes depended on slave labor to fuel a cotton trade across the border that no one fully controlled.

All of these internal disputes were made possible by slavery's continuation in Texas. Yet Captain's story also testifies to ongoing, everyday struggles between captors and captives in the midst of war. While white enslavers complained that Confederate policies like impressment riveted chains on them, Black Texans were straining against slavery itself. But a time would soon come, finally, when the system of chattel slavery as it had prevailed before and during the rebellion would be abolished. In Texas, Juneteenth was the beginning of the end.

Rice's Reconstruction Will

In June 1865, U.S. troops under the command of Maj. Gen. Gordon Granger arrived in Galveston to restore federal authority in the Lone Star State. On June 19—the day that Black Texans would soon begin to celebrate as a founding day for freedom—Granger issued General Order No. 3, affirming that all people enslaved in Texas were now free. This meant, he added, an "absolute equality" of rights between former enslavers and the formerly enslaved.[66]

Here was the vision of the state's future that secessionists had most feared, and many white Texans prepared to resist it with force. Violence marred the very morning after Juneteenth. At around 10 o'clock on June 20, train cars full of U.S. troops arrived in Houston from Galveston. Before the day was over, an unnamed "negro cook attached to one of the regiments was killed" on the streets of Houston in a dispute over access to sidewalks. The murder portended a terror campaign against Black Texans and their new allies that would soon engulf the state.[67]

E. H. Cushing, for the moment still in his editorial chair at the Houston *Telegraph*, would quickly become as virulent a critic of "Black Republican" rule after the war as he had been before it. By July 4, the *Telegraph* was urging "upon the Government the immediate and imperative necessity of adopting, temporarily at least, a compulsory system of labor for the blacks in this State." But on June 21, the paper made a more restrained report on the arrival of the new regime. The U.S. troops who arrived by train were likely "to remain for some time," Cushing said, before adding a notice about where some of them were staying. The "officers' quarters are at the residence of W. M. Rice, Esq."[68]

Granger's staff could occupy Rice's vacant home, which sat across from the courthouse, because he was still in Mexico at the time. Rice finally returned to Houston in August 1865, after a year and a half away. He remained only for a few days before rushing to the North to seek new lines of credit with which to stay in business. His stay, though, was just long enough for him to fill out an application in Houston to U.S. president Andrew Johnson for amnesty and pardon, which he did on August 23, 1865.[69]

President Johnson had recently required all Confederate citizens with more than $20,000 in property to petition for their civil rights to be restored, and Rice's wealth easily cleared that threshold. In his petition, Rice swore the required oath of allegiance to the United States and then wrote an appeal for amnesty that would quickly be approved. Rice listed "slaves" among the kinds of property he had possessed before the war, but he stressed that he had never taken up arms or office for the rebels. He had been guided above all, he claimed, by the duties of business. Passing over the secession winter in silence, and stretching the truth by claiming he had never run the Union blockade, Rice's narrative moved quickly to the end of 1863, when he had "left for Mexico to avoid the oppressive tyranny of the Confederate Government."[70]

That reference to "tyranny" is one of the few expressions of Rice's feelings about the Confederacy since the war had begun, but his audience must be considered: He wanted his amnesty application to succeed. The statement also may have been meant as a comment on the Confederacy at the time of his departure for Mexico in December 1863, when impressment was angering many Texans. If so, Rice found a way to express his frustration with Confederate policy in a comment that could only have helped his amnesty case. His petition likely simplified a more complex story of growing disaffection from the government that secession had created—the story, in other words, of many other Texans in his class.[71]

What is certain is that, while he was abroad, Rice had brokered deals that directed huge quantities of cotton to foreign buyers, sometimes for his own benefit and sometimes to help various parties. Correspondence with his one-time partner, Ebenezer B. Nichols, suggests he may even have handled some cotton for the state of Texas in support of Governor Murrah's "State Plan." In one of his first letters home from Monterey, Rice wrote, "I am off to Matamoros to attend to Nichols matters." And as late as 1867, E. B. Nichols was still sorting through his account books from the war and writing to Rice about settling up what he called their "Matamoros matters." One series of letters between the men concerned an apparent dispute about what had happened to a shipment of sixty-eight bales of cotton from Col. T. C. Armstrong, a purchasing agent for the state of Texas, though exactly what had transpired is unclear.[72]

Clearer was the fact that going to Mexico had helped Rice to remain a wealthy man. By November 1865, Rice had already secured large loans in Cincinnati and New York City. By March 1866, credit reports about him described his "considerable means and real estate at least $125,000," and a follow-up report in July concluded with this short description of Rice: "Wealthy. Claims versus him perfectly good." As several historians have noted, by going to Mexico, "William Marsh Rice had managed to be where the money was waiting."[73]

Not long after the war, following the money would prompt Rice to leave Texas again, this time for the North. The rapid postwar expansion of railroads like the Houston and Texas Central was confirming the status of Wall Street in Manhattan as the nerve center of national finance, where private investors speculated in railroad securities and reaped the benefit of legislation favorable to corporatization. In June 1867, Rice married Julia Elizabeth Baldwin, the sister of Frederick's wife, Charlotte, and soon thereafter the couple moved from Houston to New Jersey, eventually settling in New York City, where he kept an office and worked as a director and financial agent of the Houston and Texas Central. But Rice retained numerous interests in Texas, kept close tabs on the state, and returned often. On July 4, 1868, for example, William Marsh Rice was back in Texas visiting Frederick's family when he drew up a new last will and testament and had it witnessed in Houston.[74]

This postwar will, found deep in the Rice University archives and unmentioned in any previous histories, began by naming Frederick A. Rice as his executor. It directed large bequests to various relatives, demonstrating that Rice had more than regained his prewar worth. But then the will concluded with a remarkable coda: Rice wished that "from the balance of my estate the sum of three hundred thousand dollars ($300,000) be set apart to endow an institution for the education of the poor white children of Harris County." It was the earliest known sign that Rice was thinking of founding a school in Texas to serve as his legacy after death.[75]

To oversee the new institution he envisioned, Rice named his brother, Frederick, as president of its board of trustees for life, with the power to veto all other trustees. William left it to Frederick to compose that board after he died, but he nominated several men drawn from his and his brother's social networks in 1868. They included Peter W. Gray, Alfred S. Richardson, Benjamin A. Botts, George R. Ennis (son of Rice's early partner Cornelius Ennis), George Goldthwaite, and John Shearn.

Some of these men knew each other as fellow business partners and lawyers; in 1865, Gray and Botts's brother had founded the firm that later became Baker Botts, one of Houston's most influential legal firms. William Marsh Rice was an early client. At least four of the trustees had served as vestrymen of Houston's Episcopal Christ Church, and Peter Gray and William Marsh Rice had once served, along with Cornelius Ennis, as trustees of the Houston Academy, a coeducational private school that closed during the war.

Most of the men listed in Rice's 1868 will were also closely associated through their recent wartime service. Peter Gray and B. A. Botts had served with Rice on the committees that pressured Governor Houston during the secession winter. Richardson, Botts, Frederick Rice, and Goldthwaite had all been officers in an 1861 military company formed in Houston under the command of Gray—who represented the city of Houston at the secession convention, was later elected to the Confederate Congress, and finished the war as a Confederate treasury agent. Finally, the will was witnessed with signatures by Botts and the arch-secessionist newspaper editor E. H. Cushing.[76]

Though it would later be revoked by Rice's other testaments, his 1868 will is thus a significant source for understanding his Civil War years. The will locates the origins of Rice's decision to endow a school in the era of Reconstruction, at least fourteen years before the events usually cited as progenitors for the charter of the Rice Institute. It demonstrates the importance of Frederick A. Rice to the story and identifies an earlier circle of men who may have played a role in inspiring the 1891 charter. It shows that Rice's earliest intention was to plant the school in Texas. And it shows that Rice wished to exclude Black students from the beginning. The institute he envisioned in 1868 was for "white children" alone.

The will also offers a rare glimpse of Rice's affiliations and thinking at a time of intense political conflict over the place of Black Texans in postwar society. On the one hand, by 1868 the war had permanently uprooted slavery as a system of property and credit relationships. For years after the fighting, William Marsh Rice could not collect many of the debts still owed him by Texas planters, some of whom wrote him blaming their inability to pay on the loss of their slaves.[77] Whereas Rice had once rented out the labor of people he enslaved, he now rented some of his real estate holdings to Black tenants and wrote small checks, presumably for wages, to Black men like "Ben," the name of a person who had once been listed as "belonging" to him.[78] Labor relations were rapidly changing in the countryside, too, as Frederick A. Rice noted in his report about the Randon estate in 1866. "The slaves of the estate have all been emancipated by action of the United States Government by their military success in the war," he told the Fort Bend County Probate Court, through an attorney. "In consequence laborers had to be hired and paid wages for most of the year 1865," and the "value of the Estate has been greatly impaired."[79]

But what would the new system of free labor look like? Who would determine the terms of work and the kinds of wages freedpeople received? And what other rights did freedom entail? For most formerly enslaved people, working for a wage signaled the dramatic changes wrought by the war. Yet Granger's Juneteenth order had also advised freedpeople to remain at work where they were, and over the next year, planters used various means of coercion, violence, and threat to ensure that they did. In response, Black Texans after slavery would fight collectively to secure a fuller set of rights, protect their families, get land of their own, and negotiate the terms of labor.

For a few years during Reconstruction, the federal government served as an ally in that fight, albeit an imperfect one, through the Bureau of Refugees, Freedmen, and Abandoned Lands, better known as the Freedmen's Bureau. As they arrived in Texas after Juneteenth, U.S. agents and military officers began to oversee labor contracts in the cotton districts and sometimes intervened in labor disputes. One Freedmen's Bureau ledger shows that, in January or February 1867, Frederick A. Rice entered into a two-year contract with a Black foreman named George Wheat and thirty-one other freedpeople working at Edge Hill. Among them were many persons whose first names, including "George," had appeared in the lists of people owned by Frederick and the Randon estate before emancipation. Now they were identified as members of families, sharing surnames such as Randon, Wheat, and Blue.[80]

The Freedmen's Bureau also created new opportunities for Black Texans and their children to pursue formal education, after years of being denied it by law and custom. By the end of 1865, Black children and adults were flocking into schools created and staffed by the Freedmen's Bureau. Black families supported these schools through tuition paid from their own meager wages and savings, and school openings proliferated over the next few years. On Chenango, the Brazoria County plantation where Rice's firm had advanced the money for a sugar mill in the 1840s, a teacher sent by the Freedmen's Bureau in the summer of 1866 briefly turned the sugar house into a schoolroom.[81] But such schools struggled to overcome the challenges of teacher attrition, high tuition, and—most of all—hostility from white locals. In February 1867, a building being used by a Black church as a school in Houston was burned to the ground in an apparent act of arson. Other acts of terror across the state made clear that Black Texans would face massive resistance in their quest for the "absolute equality" mentioned in Granger's order.[82]

Indeed, only one year after Juneteenth, President Andrew Johnson's lenient approach to Reconstruction had enabled the election of a conservative state government in Texas and the adoption of a new state constitution crafted exclusively by white men. The 1866 constitution provided for a segregated, unequally funded system of public schools. (White schools would be funded by the sale of public lands, while separate Black schools would be funded by a special tax levied only on Black Texans.) Yet the all-white legislature elected under this constitution did little to advance education. Instead, it passed a series of "Black Codes" that regulated labor in the interests of white planters, criminalized refusal to work as vagrancy, mandated segregation on railroads, prohibited transfers of public land to Black people, and barred Black Texans from voting, holding political office, serving on juries, or testifying against whites in court.[83]

Alarmed by the signs that former Confederates were trying to recreate slavery in all but name, the U.S. Congress finally wrested control of Reconstruction away from President Johnson. With the Reconstruction Acts of March 1867, Congress placed the rebel states under military rule until they adopted new state constitutions and ratified the Fourteenth Amendment. Southern voters who could prove their loyalty would cast ballots to determine whether to hold state conventions to draft these new constitutions. Crucially, too, Congress required that Black men be allowed to vote in these elections, as well as to vote for and serve as delegates to the conventions.[84]

Throughout the summer of 1867, tens of thousands of Black Texans braved threats of violence and retribution by registering to vote for the first time. Among them was George Wheat, who signed his legal mark to the voting rolls in Fort Bend County on August 8, only a few months after he had signed a labor contract with Frederick A. Rice. The mobilization of new Black voters by Republican groups known as Loyal Leagues also helped to inform and empower many freedpeople to assert their rights in ongoing conflicts with employers. On January 6, 1868, for example, a man named Anderson Hall appeared before a Freedmen's Bureau agent to protest officially that F. A. Rice had never paid him any wages for the past two years of work.[85]

The outcome of Hall's protest is not recorded. The fierce reaction of white Texans to the Reconstruction Acts is. In a letter sent to William Marsh Rice in September 1867, white planter W. A. Delespine condemned Black voter registration and denounced Congress's policies as "practically committing the destiny of ten states to ignorant Negroes." Murders and outrages against Black Texans spiked in 1867 and 1868, led by terrorist groups like the Ku Klux Klan working in concert with state Democrats. And in January 1868, a large assembly of white Democrats assembled in Houston at a "Conservative State Convention" to adopt plans for resistance to Congress. The meeting passed resolutions urging conservatives to vote against a state constitutional convention, but also, failing that, to vote for delegates who would produce a "constitution without negro suffrage." An address issued by the meeting argued that Black voting rights would lead to "Africanization and a war of races." Better, it said, to continue under military rule than to accept "the greater evil of negro supremacy."[86]

The coauthor of that address was one of the men Rice would nominate only a few months later in his will as a trustee for his school—former Confederate congressman Peter W. Gray. Rice himself was not in Houston at the time of the conservative convention; after his second marriage, in June 1867, he and his wife traveled to the Northeast. But one of the Rices' first return visits was in 1868 to see Frederick and Charlotte, which explains why he was in Texas for the drafting of his July 4, 1868, will.[87]

By then, Gray and his fellow white conservatives had failed to prevent the calling of a new constitutional convention. In a statewide referendum held in February, more than thirty-six thousand newly registered Black voters cast ballots in favor of drafting a new constitution, dwarfing the turnout of opponents. Black delegates were also elected to serve in the constitutional convention, which began meeting in Austin on June 1, 1868, one month before Rice drew up his will. The state seemed on the cusp of a new moment of biracial democracy.

For delegates to the convention in Austin, even interracial schooling was on the table. As white and Black delegates gathered that June to work on a new constitution, they quickly took up a number of progressive policy ideas, including a report from E. M. Wheelock, a northern abolitionist who had overseen bureau schools in Texas. Wheelock proposed a compulsory system of free public schools for all of the state's children, equally funded from the treasury and "open to all upon equal terms." Whether individual schools would be racially "separate or mixed," he would leave it to the new legislature to decide—thus theoretically leaving open the possibility of integrated schooling, too. Wheelock's main point was, "Universal suffrage necessitates universal education," and universal manhood suffrage was what the delegates in Austin intended. The convention endorsed the removal of racial restrictions on the right to vote, a policy later required by the Fifteenth Amendment to the U.S. Constitution.[88]

It was amid this immediate political context that William Marsh Rice took pen in hand that same summer to pledge a significant sum—$300,000—to the creation of a private school for "poor white children" in Harris County. His Reconstruction will showed that on one point, at least, Rice agreed with the likes of Wheelock: Education was vital to the future of Texas. But while the delegates in Austin worked on a system of common schools funded by all for all, Rice instead envisioned a private institution from which Black students would be excluded.

More egalitarian alternatives were not unthinkable in the heady days of 1868, even if they were violently opposed by most white southerners. Earlier that year, Louisiana's biracial state Reconstruction convention had produced a new constitution that mandated integrated public schools, "without distinction of race, color, or previous condition." And in Reconstruction South Carolina, African Americans were appointed as trustees of the state's university system in 1868. These policies built on a long history of advocacy for equal schools by free Black activists in the North, as well as antebellum precedents at interracial abolitionist colleges like Oberlin in Ohio and Berea in Kentucky. While few examples of integrated public schools actually materialized in the postwar South, the provision for them in states like Louisiana and South Carolina suggested the revolutionary possibilities suddenly opened up by Reconstruction.[89]

But to white reactionaries, the prospect of interracial schooling only proved the need to resist Black suffrage. "Any attempt to force mixed schools would result in much evil," thundered the Houston *Telegraph* in December 1868, though it was of the opinion that "the sensible blacks" preferred separate schools and would not press the issue in Texas. Another writer warned against complacency, however, pointing to Louisiana and South Carolina as warnings: "It is an undeniable fact that the negroes of the South have persistently and clamorously contended for every real or imaginary right."[90]

Opponents of mixed common schools further argued that poor white parents would refuse to send their students into integrated classrooms but also could not afford private school tuition. Presaging later arguments that affirmative steps to educate Black students would result in unfairness to whites, conservative editorialists complained that northern philanthropists cared more about "negro equality" than about white southerners: "while freedmen's schools are dotted all over the South and Yankee school-mistresses are everywhere—

and some of them most laudably—engaged in teaching negroes, not one school has it yet entered into Northern minds to establish for the poor white children of the South." In 1866, after noting that a freedmen's school was to be built in Brenham, one Texas editor railed against the neglect of white families: "We would suggest to such communities, that some building that the colored children have no use for, might, perhaps, be obtained for a school for the orphans of Confederate soldiers and poor white children generally, which is needed in every county in the South." Perhaps it was even to address this common complaint that a free school for "poor white children" had entered into the minds of William Marsh Rice and his circle.[91]

Whatever the case, the wider debate about education makes clear what was at stake in the summer of 1868, as the newly remarried Rice visited with his old friends and tended to his business in Texas. In the end, the state constitutional convention of 1868–69 adopted Wheelock's forward-looking proposal for public education virtually to the letter. Rice, on the other hand, together with a trusted group of white men and former rebels, decided to draw up a well-funded plan for the free, private education of white children alone.

Rethinking the Founder

The school that Rice sketched in 1868 never came to pass. After settling in New Jersey, Rice drafted a new will in 1882. It would have endowed a school there instead for "poor, male white children of American birth," with preference shown to orphans from Harris County, Texas, or Somerset County, New Jersey. His plan evolved again with the chartering of the Rice Institute in 1891. Yet these later visions were clearly descended from his original idea. Two of the surviving trustees named in the 1868 will, Frederick A. Rice and Alfred S. Richardson, were named trustees in the Rice Institute charter. And as in 1868, so in 1882 and 1891, Rice chose racial exclusion.[92]

History did not stand still in the intervening years. White Democrats regained control of Texas in 1874 and soon rewrote the state constitution, undoing Republican reforms and mandating segregated public schools. After Reconstruction effectively ended in 1876, lynching, white terrorism, convict leasing, and voter intimidation deepened Black Texans' political and economic disempowerment in the following decades. By the mid-1880s, the U.S. Supreme Court was interpreting the Fourteenth Amendment in ways that did more to protect the rights of corporations than to prevent racial discrimination. And in the meantime, former Confederates worked hard—through popular histories, textbooks, and rituals—to portray their rebellion as a principled stand for states' rights, not slavery: a "War Between the States" in which they had fought nobly and been defeated by the North's numbers and industrial might, rather than by the sorts of internal divisions that had wracked Confederate Texas.

Known as the myth of the "Lost Cause," this effort to reshape the memory of the war began before Reconstruction had even ended. At an 1870 meeting in Houston to establish the Texas Historical Society, Ashbel Smith (a slaveholder who later became first president of the University of Texas Regents, and who had served with Rice on a disunion committee in the secession winter) revealed that he still had a Confederate flag and wished to be wrapped in it for burial when he died. Botts, Gray, and Goldthwaite—all nominated as trustees in Rice's 1868 will—were officers in the new state historical society, which professed to be nonpartisan but pledged cooperation with the Southern Historical Society, a seedbed of the "Lost Cause." One reporter heard Gray tell the founding meeting of the Texas group that "he had nothing to take back, had been right all the time," while another speaker, ex-Confederate John H. Reagan, declared that "the negroes of the South were in a better condition in every respect before their freedom." The proslavery lie that enslaved people were happy and well-treated by benevolent masters would remain a touchstone for generations of Confederate apologists, as well as a cornerstone for Jim Crow.[93]

Rice's 1868 will reveals that his first idea to endow a school for white children was forged within this postbellum crucible. Yet because the will apparently was never made public, those origins were forgotten, unknown, or suppressed by 1891. Observers at that time were thus more likely to trace the roots of the Rice Institute to William Marsh Rice's Yankee birth and later years in the North, rather than to his time in Civil War Texas. When the charter for the Institute was first published in 1891 in the Texas press, an early headline introduced him as "Mr. W. M. Rice of New York," and the story that followed mentioned only the Cooper Union, founded before the war in New York, as his inspiration. To others, the Rice Institute seemed closer in time and spirit to schools endowed by titans of industry such as Vanderbilt, Stanford, or Carnegie, than it was to the Civil War. In early speeches about the Institute's history, Edgar Odell Lovett stressed Rice's origins as "a native son of Massachusetts" and an heir to the educational ideals of the Pilgrims. The idea for the Institute, he said, was "born in the early nineties . . . a period prolific in new undertakings in American education."[94]

But at least one Houstonian later told a different origin story for the Institute, one that connected it more directly to Rice's activities during the war. To this day, the papers of historian Andrew Forest Muir contain a penciled account, written by a close associate of Texas lumberman John Henry Kirby (born in 1860), of a story that Kirby had told him sometime in the early twentieth century.

Kirby, who worked closely with two of William Marsh Rice's nephews in the lumber industry, claimed to have heard that Rice ended up in possession of a large amount of cotton at the end of the "War Between the States." According to Kirby, the cotton was owned either by Texas or by the Confederate government and had been collected as part of a levy on cotton. But with the war over, or so the story went, Rice could not find any official authorized to take the cotton off his hands, so he sold it and kept the proceeds: "He always felt, however, that it belonged to the people of this section of the country and it was his desire to return it to them. And so it was that he finally decided to endow a school of higher education for the benefit of the progeny of them who had actually paid the [cotton] tax"—in other words, for the benefit of the children of white Confederate Texans.[95]

Spoken sometime before Kirby's 1940 death, but not written down until after that, this account never appeared in Muir's publications or in Sylvia Stallings Morris's biography. Understandably, earlier researchers likely chalked the story up to hearsay. The details of Kirby's memory have not been corroborated. Nonetheless, the discovery of Rice's 1868 will, composed only a year after he was still settling up "Matamoros matters," shows that Kirby was not wrong to root the Institute's origins in the immediate postwar era. Nor was he wrong to connect Rice to the handling of cotton during the Rebellion. Muir, working under the inaccurate assumption that Rice was a Unionist, may have set aside Kirby's story on those grounds alone. Rice's political sympathies and wartime activities do not by themselves confirm Kirby's story, but they do make the story more difficult to dismiss out of hand.

Captain James A. Baker, who knew Rice better than Kirby, framed the older man's sense of indebtedness to Texas more generally, though his own story about the origins of the Rice Institute bears some resemblances to Kirby's. According to a speech he first delivered in 1929, Baker recalled Rice telling him that, after 1883, as he traveled to Texas and "would come into contact with his old friends of the '30s, '40s and the '50s," he "realized that all he had in the past, and would get in the future, was built from the foundation of his fortune, which started right here in Houston, and he determined then that the boys and girls of Texas should have the benefit of his fortune." Baker did not mention, and perhaps did not even know about, the 1868 will. But he also made no claim that Rice had ever been a Unionist, stating only that he had continued in cotton and the merchant business "until the course of the war between the states."[96]

In any case, what is known and still unknown about Rice University's founder must be reconsidered. The record shows clearly that William Marsh Rice's involvement in slavery was not small or somehow softened by his New England origins or mercantile pursuits. It was significant and consistent across his years in Texas. When slavery and the anti-Black racism it both engendered and required faced an apparent threat in the form of Abraham Lincoln's Republican Party, he abetted the movement in Houston to accelerate secession. Then, working in concert with his brother and business partner, he continued to profit from the labor of enslaved people and traffic in cotton during the war, a conflict that further splintered the political allegiances of white Texans but did not erode their commitment to slavery or white supremacy.

In the early years of Reconstruction, Rice also remained close to conservatives who sought to shore up white supremacy in the face of new Black political mobilization. His racial restriction of the Rice Institute's benefits was therefore not a sudden decision made in and shaped only by the context of 1891, but a continuation of older choices and commitments. Nor did Rice ever become estranged from the elite southern men he named in his 1868 will. In the 1870s, he served as director of a Houston bank and of a Houston insurance company alongside Botts, Gray, and Cushing. In 1879, Botts, Goldthwaite, and Richardson headed a list of Houston friends who threw an honorary dinner for Rice upon one of his return visits to the city. And in 1895, another of Rice's visits to Texas coincided with a national reunion of Confederate veterans in Houston, one of the largest such assemblies to date.[97]

That May, thousands of ex-Confederates crowded into Houston's hotels, auditoriums, and streets. They heard reports about the importance of vindicating the Lost Cause in classrooms and textbooks, as well as updates on plans for erecting Confederate monuments. They witnessed a battle reenactment by the veterans. But the highlight for many attendees was the appearance of Jefferson Davis's daughter, Winnie Davis, at several social gatherings hosted by local white elites.

One such gathering was held by "Mr. and Mrs. William Marsh Rice," who opened their apartment in Houston to Davis and an entourage of Confederate luminaries. At another reception, Davis was supposedly approached by an "old negro" who greeted her with smiles and tears—a performance that confirmed, for Confederate apologists, cherished white myths about faithful slaves and the righteousness of their cause. Finally, as part of a floral street parade conceived and planned by Rice's wife, one report noted that "Mrs. William M. Rice . . . very properly headed the procession with Miss Davis," in a carriage decked out with magnolias.[98]

These events at the 1895 Confederate reunion said much about Julia Elizabeth Baldwin Rice's own image of herself as a southerner and socialite. But they are no less revealing of her husband's self-image and the world in which the Rice Institute had been chartered only four years before—a world that Rice and his peers had helped to build. In their social world, whatever internal divisions had once riled Confederate Texans were now subsumed in nostalgia and the New South; the violence and wealth of antebellum slavery were covered by a gauzy veil of moonlight and magnolias; and there were no tears shed for the end of Reconstruction, a period most white southerners—and many northerners as well—denounced as a misguided experiment.

Yet, in the very same city, there was another world whose foundations were simultaneously being laid. It was built by the Black Texans whom William Marsh Rice's vision for his institute had always excluded. Reconstruction and the Rebellion had represented something different to people like "Captain" or George Wheat. In contrast to the Texas that Rice or his peers imagined, the collective dreams of Black Texans would be shaped by memories of Juneteenth, with its promise of freedom and equality for all. And in the decades to come, these conflicting ideas would continue to define the founding and earliest development of the university, as the various stipulations in Rice's final will began to take shape on the streets of Houston.

II

THE FIRST FOUNDING

3 | THE LOUISIANA STREET PROPERTY

After 1865, thousands of formerly enslaved people in Texas began to migrate from plantations into towns and freedom colonies, pursuing work, education, and new futures for their children. As ex-slave Felix Haywood later recalled, after Juneteenth, "colored folks started on the move. They seemed to want to get closer to freedom, so they'd know what it was—like it was a place or a city." Many came to Houston, settling on its southwestern edge in a place called Freedmen's Town.[1]

One who came was a woman named Sallie Wicks. In 1870, Wicks appeared in the U.S. Census as a forty-five-year-old resident of Harris County. Born in Virginia, she lived with her sixteen-year-old daughter Bettie, who had likely been born enslaved in Louisiana. The distance between their places of birth—Virginia, Louisiana—evokes the scale of a domestic slave trade that had relocated close to one million Black people from the upper to the lower South before the war. But exactly how Sallie and Bettie got to Texas is unknown. What is known is that, in 1873, after several years of laboring in freedom, Wicks had saved enough money to purchase some land near Freedmen's Town, in Houston's Fourth Ward.[2]

Wicks paid at least $125 for the modest hundred-by-fifty-foot lot, making her home there with Bettie. When she died in 1891, Wicks passed the property on to her daughter. For both women, though, the lot was worth more than its monetary value alone. Close by was the original location of the Gregory Institute, the first public school in Houston open to multiple grades of Black students. And equally important was the symbolic power of land. As Haywood remembered, freedom felt like finding a place. Bettie—who became Bettie Leonard after her marriage in 1876—would stay on her mother's lot for more than fifty years.[3]

To keep the land for that long was no easy feat. In the fifty years after Reconstruction, white Houstonians worked to realize their own dreams for the city, and the designs of white developers and planners led to the neglect and depreciation of many early Black neighborhoods. In other cases, white Houstonians coveted Black land and sought to get it. Bettie Leonard learned this firsthand when in 1892, the year after her mother died, a powerful new neighbor acquired property yards away from her front door, and later began trying to acquire hers too: the William M. Rice Institute for the Advancement of Literature, Science, and Art.

Few Houstonians may realize it today, but Rice University's history as a place began there, in the Fourth Ward. The trustees of the Rice Institute did not originally intend to build a campus at the university's current location on Main Street. Instead, as Leonard soon learned, they first planned to site the campus on a smaller tract closer to downtown, at Leeland Avenue and Louisiana Street. William Marsh Rice had acquired this approximately six-and-a-half-acre tract (sometimes called the Swain or Ennis Tract, but referred to here as the Louisiana Street Property) as payment for a debt in 1877. He then deeded the tract to the trustees of his newly chartered institute in 1892, with instructions that it be used for its future grounds after his death. That plan would not come to pass in the end. Still, the Rice trustees kept most of the Louisiana Street Property for nearly four decades, acquiring more property nearby before they sold it all away in 1929.[4]

Before that, the trustees of the Rice Institute also made concerted efforts to grow its footprint in the Fourth Ward. That included buying up lots where other Black property owners had settled around Wicks, Leonard, and the site of the Gregory Institute. The first business manager of the Rice Institute would later testify that he became "well acquainted with the negro woman, Bettie Leonard," from having "numerous talks" with her about buying her land for Rice. But Leonard always refused to sell.[5]

On the contrary, in 1909, Bettie Leonard and two Black neighbors filed a lawsuit against the Rice Institute in defense of their property rights. The suit remained unresolved in 1912, when the Institute began its first academic year with an elaborate opening ceremony on its Main Street campus, several miles away. In later years, Rice's trustees began renting the vacant parts of the Louisiana Street Property out to traveling circuses; they permitted a controversial Ku

Klux Klan event to take place there, too. Yet through it all, Leonard held on to her land. When the Rice Institute commissioned a survey map of its downtown site in 1923, the blueprint showed a five-sided shape labeled "Wm M. Rice Institute Property," bordered on the right by Louisiana Street. But just beneath it, to the left, was a smaller rectangle—easy to miss at first glance, yet crying out for explanation once seen. The caption on the rectangle read: "Negro Lot." It was the lot that belonged—still—to Leonard, daughter of Sallie Wicks.[6]

The first founding of Rice University as a segregated institution had multiple origin points, from Rice's 1868 will to the 1891 charter to the 1912 opening. But much can be learned about the founding if we start here, with the questions raised by a little-known map from 1923. What did Leonard's "Negro Lot" look like from the perspective of the Institute? And what did the Institute look like from the perspective of Leonard's neighborhood, which by the time of Rice's charter had already served for a quarter-century as a vital center of Houston's African American community? What happened, in other words, when the founders of a whites-only university began to plant their visions for the future in a place where Black futures and freedom had already taken root?

The answers shed light not only on the origins of Rice University, but also onto a larger story that historians have only begun to tell: the story of how segregated universities shaped modern, segregated American cities, and the steps that Black families and communities took to stand their ground.[7]

The Gregory Institute's Neighbors

Today, what used to be Rice's Louisiana Street Property sits squarely in the downtown of the nation's energy metropolis, surrounded by skyscrapers and a nearby expressway. Less than a mile south of present-day City Hall, and two blocks south of Antioch Missionary Baptist Church, the property is the current home of Chevron and the former headquarters of Enron. In the immediate aftermath of Reconstruction, however, when William Marsh Rice first acquired the property, it still sat on the outskirts of Houston's business district in what was, for African Americans, a historically significant corner of the city's Fourth Ward.

At the time, Fourth Ward residents were not exclusively African American. Nor was the Fourth Ward the only part of the city where "freedmen" settled. But in the late 1860s, "Freedmen's Town" quickly took on material and symbolic significance as home to important institutions built by Black Houstonians after slavery: mutual aid societies, churches, businesses, and schools. Pioneering Black leaders lived, worked, or worshiped here, including Sandy Parker, a founding minister of Antioch Missionary Baptist Church; John Henry (or "Jack") Yates, longtime pastor of Antioch; and Richard Allen, a deacon at the church and one of the first Black men elected to the Texas legislature during Reconstruction.

By 1870, the Fourth Ward was also home to the Gregory Institute, the product of a partnership between the city's Black community and the Freedmen's Bureau. Since the start of Reconstruction, Black Houstonians had rented out space in their own houses and churches to the Freedmen's Bureau for classrooms.[8] Demand for schooling soon outstripped available space. So in 1868, a group of Black trustees led by Allen, Parker, and Elias Dibble (minister of Trinity Methodist Episcopal Church) raised $330 from donations made by Allen himself and around two dozen white benefactors. The Black men then used those funds to buy a one-acre lot for a school called the Gregory Institute, about two hundred feet from the acreage that later became the Rice Institute's property.[9]

The next year, the Freedmen's Bureau paid nearly $7,000 to erect a two-story, furnished brick building on the lot, capable of seating 230 students. In January 1870, a "large concourse of citizens, white and colored," met for the Gregory Institute's dedication and heard addresses from a Freedmen's Bureau official as well as Parker and Dibble. Members of Antioch and Trinity would raise more funds two years later to purchase ten acres in the Third Ward, dedicating this larger tract for annual community celebrations of Juneteenth. But in 1870, before Emancipation Park existed, a large congregation celebrated the fifth anniversary of Juneteenth on the Gregory Institute's acre.[10]

On that Juneteenth, according to one city newspaper, the streets were filled with Black Texans from Houston and "the surrounding country" who had assembled for the "freeman's demonstration." The day began with a parade up Main Street from downtown, complete "with drum and colors and a Marshal" leading the procession to the Fourth Ward. There the assembly heard two addresses and a public reading of the Emancipation Proclamation. Then they danced and played baseball in the open field by the Gregory's new building, into which hundreds of students would crowd for lessons over the next twenty years. Two months later, in August 1870, the state legislature passed a law incorporating the Gregory Institute of Harris County and naming Allen, Dibble, Parker, and two other men as its first trustees.[11]

These events showed what Juneteenth had made possible and deepened the identity of Freedmen's Town as a center of Black institutional life. At the same time, the history of the Gregory Institute underscored the disparities in resources and power that still divided Black from white communities in the wake of slavery. The $7,000 spent on the school's building represented a significant investment. Yet it was much less than the $300,000 that William Marsh Rice could earmark for a school for "poor white children" in his will of 1868, the same year the Gregory trustees began raising money to buy their one-acre lot. Some white Houstonians contributed money to the purchase of that lot (including B. A. Shepherd and, from the list of possible trustees in Rice's 1868 will, Benjamin A. Botts and John Shearn). But many more were hostile to such efforts and agreed with the reactionary view expressed by one Houston newspaper in January 1870: "the negro is but of small value except as a slave."[12]

Indeed, another, more valuable piece of land had initially been identified as an ideal site for the schoolhouse, but planners were unable to raise enough to meet the $3,000 asking price. Some white donors promised money only "conditionally provided the house was put in such a place and built according to their ideas or plans." Then, after the eventual new site was selected, Freedmen's Bureau agents discovered that the owner of the tract, Melissa Ammerman, was unwilling "to deed the land to a board of trustees for a colored school." Bowing to her wishes, a deed was first made out conveying the acre to the trustees as individuals, and then another was drawn up investing the property in the trustees as a school board. The whole saga led the bureau's local agent to revise his initial optimism about white locals' support for the Institute. "After subscribing money for school purposes," he wrote, "nine tenths of them refused to pay and some of them have used their influence to prevent a school house being put up here by the government for the education of the colored people."[13]

In truth, freedpeople had to contend with the prejudices of allies as well. In 1869, Richard Allen—a skilled carpenter himself—protested when the Freedmen's Bureau awarded the lucrative contract to build the Gregory Institute to a white firm, without consulting the Black trustees and with insufficient notice of the call for bids. One bureau official reacted by saying he wished Allen could be removed from the group, while another grew "wrathy" in a meeting with the Black trustees, complaining later of the board's "big head."[14]

The dispute nonetheless demonstrated the agency of Black Houstonians in the struggle for equal rights and respect. After the confrontation over the construction contract, the Freedmen's Bureau disbursed funds directly to Allen to raise a fence around the Gregory Institute, maintain the building, and pay laborers. And in December 1870, the government deeded the building to Allen and his fellow trustees, with the condition that "pupils shall never be excluded therefrom, or from the benefits arising from the rental or sale thereof, on account of race or previous condition of servitude." The Black trustees' title to the land had mattered.[15]

No wonder, then, that Black Houstonians in the Fourth Ward prioritized getting land. In 1875, Antioch Missionary Baptist Church broke ground for a new brick sanctuary on the lot where the church now stands. It was designed by Richard Allen.[16] Yates, Dibble, and other Black leaders also worked to assist freedpeople in purchasing homesteads of their own in the neighborhood. In 1866, Dibble's church acquired a city block bordered by Travis, Bell, Clay, and Milam Street, just east of the future Gregory Institute site. The Black Methodist congregation placed its sanctuary on one-half of the lot and then subdivided the other half for congregants' homes.[17]

Other Black families built a cluster of homes right beside the Gregory Institute. The first to arrive was Robert Shaw. Born in 1840 in Virginia, Shaw paid $200 for ten thousand square feet on the southern border of the Swain Tract in 1871, residing there until his death in 1917.[18] Shaw's homestead was steps away from the Gregory Institute to his south, while to his north, it adjoined the property that William Marsh Rice would acquire in 1877. A "bird's eye" map of Houston in 1873 showed that city streets had yet to reach the Gregory Institute, but the neat brick school building was shown near a house, encircled by trees, that may well have depicted Robert Shaw's home.[19]

More Black families joined Shaw after 1872, when white developer W. J. Fredericks bought a tract running from the north line of the Gregory Institute acre to the south line of the Swain Tract and divided it into nine lots, all fronted by a narrow path that became known as Smith Alley. Fredericks sold lots 4, 5, and 6 to Black buyers in 1873. Lot 5 went to Sallie Wicks.[20]

Three years later, Wicks's daughter Bettie married Samuel J. Leonard, who served as a trustee of the Colored Emancipation Park Association in 1881, and took his last name.[21] Four years after that, Henry C. Hardy, a Jamaican-born teacher who served as the first Black principal of the Gregory Institute, married Laura Hardy and then moved with his new family onto Lot 3 of the Fredericks Addition.[22] That same year, another Black woman, whose wedding had been officiated by Jack Yates in 1878, acquired Lot 7.[23]

By then, all nine of Fredericks's lots had been occupied by Black households, while across the alley, a large lot between Shaw's property and the Gregory Institute's acre had also been purchased, but not occupied, by Robert Fairchild, another Emancipation Park trustee. Fairchild's 1868 wedding to Amanda Fairchild was officiated by Elias Dibble. His daughter was one of several schoolteachers in the family; she taught at the Gregory Institute. One of his sons would later leave Texas to attend the Tuskegee Institute, while another son's name would later grace the first building erected on the campus of what became Texas Southern University.[24]

These Gregory Institute neighbors endured various trials, public and private, over the next few decades. Many worked in low-paying jobs such as domestic service or driving drays. In 1900, Shaw's land would be seized by the city for back taxes and sold to the highest bidder, a white doctor who immediately mortgaged it back to Shaw; two years later, Shaw regained the title to half of his original lot, but only by selling the other half to a third party who assumed his new debt.[25] Laura Hardy and Bettie Leonard would both divorce their husbands as the century closed, leaving the two women in sole legal possession of Lot 3 (Hardy) and Lot 5 (Leonard). Sallie Wicks died in 1891.[26]

Still, the small settlement along Smith Alley was a clear illustration of what Black Houstonians had managed to build since slavery's defeat. During and after Reconstruction, Black and white politicians occasionally used the Gregory Institute next door for county Republican Party conventions. While living by and teaching at the Gregory Institute, Henry C. Hardy founded a benevolent society for Black Texans, the Ancient Order of Pilgrims, and started a business selling pianos. His wife, Laura, briefly taught music. Charles N. Love, the publisher of the Black newspaper the *Texas Freeman*, would later say that whatever he achieved was "due primarily to what I was taught and learned from two Negro men, namely, Rev. Jack Yates in Sunday School and Professor H. C. Hardy in the public school."[27]

In 1892, however, a new educational institution took charge of the six-odd acres lying between the Gregory Institute and Antioch Missionary Baptist Church, bringing a different vision to their corner of the Fourth Ward. The newcomer was the Rice Institute for the Advancement of Literature, Science, and Art.

The Rice Institute's Neighbors

Despite all that the builders of Freedmen's Town had achieved by 1892, the Rice Institute arrived in the Fourth Ward at a time of worsening conditions for Black Texans as a whole. Statewide, de facto segregation had hardened into laws like the one passed in 1891 requiring railroad companies to provide separate cars for "white" and "colored" passengers. An 1893 law mandated the racial segregation of public schools. Lynch mobs were terrorizing Black communities across the South, and by the first years of the twentieth century, Black men had been deprived of the vote throughout the former Confederacy, including Texas. With the full approval of the U.S. Supreme Court, Jim Crow states were confining African Americans to a lower sort of "citizenship" not worthy of the name.

In some ways, the fate of the Gregory Institute gave the measure of the decline. From its opening in 1870, the school had stood as a beacon of one of Reconstruction's highest ideals: equal education, irrespective of race. State lawmakers elected under the 1869 Constitution, a group that included Richard Allen, had carried the fight for that ideal into the Texas House of Representatives. Allen sponsored a public free-schools bill in 1870 that, like the new constitution and the Gregory Institute charter, contained no mention of racial distinction in schools. As one Freedmen's Bureau official reported that year, Black lawmakers "justly regard[ed] a 'separate system' as a violation of their Constitutional rights, both National and State."[28]

Unfortunately for their cause, Black representatives were outnumbered by white reactionaries who opposed Reconstruction. The state Senate rejected the first nominee to serve as public school superintendent "partly because he was understood to be in favor of [racially] mixed schools," according to a Freedmen's Bureau report. An 1871 law repealed Allen's 1870 bill and restored a separate funding model for Black schools. And in 1876, as federal support for Reconstruction cratered, the state's conservatives succeeded in adopting a new constitution providing for "separate schools . . . for the white and colored children."[29]

That same year, the Houston School Board assumed control of the Gregory Institute as one of the district's "colored" public schools. It was the beginning of a long-lived "separate system" that the first generation of Black legislators in Texas had fought to forestall.[30] With little public and private support, the Gregory Institute building quickly fell into disrepair. In 1893, all classes taught there were relocated to Houston's already overcrowded "colored high school" several blocks north. And within two years, the original Gregory Institute building had been demolished, making way for an extension of Jefferson Avenue by the city over the lot. A potent physical reminder of Reconstruction's early promise was gone, though many of its Smith Alley neighbors—including Bettie Leonard—remained.[31]

As for the Rice Institute, its origins can be traced at least to 1868, when William Marsh Rice signed the postwar will that envisioned a school for the "poor white children of Harris County." In the years since, while living in New Jersey and New York, Rice had continued to ruminate on that idea and to investigate institutions like Girard College in Philadelphia and Cooper Union in New York. In an updated 1882 will, Rice created an endowment for a "William M. Rice Orphans Institute," now intending it to be built in New Jersey. But around 1887, Rice was approached by Cesar Lombardi while on a visit to Houston. Lombardi was president of the city's school board (a role in which he also oversaw the Gregory Institute's final years), and he told Rice that the city urgently needed another municipal high school.[32]

Rice finally settled on endowing a version of his original idea for an educational institution in Harris County, though it would not be a public high school or an orphanage. In 1891, he instead endowed the Rice Institute, chartered that same year for the benefit of the "white inhabitants" of Houston and Texas. In the years since the Civil War, Rice's wealth had increased dramatically through his investments in real estate, railroads, lumber, and associated enterprises. After making an initial gift of $200,000 to the Institute, he pledged to give more after his death. Then, in 1892, Rice and his wife, Elizabeth Baldwin Rice, signed a deed conveying his property on Louisiana Street to the Institute's board of trustees, comprising Rice himself, his brother Frederick, Lombardi, Emanuel Raphael, Alfred S. Richardson, James E. McAshan, and the board's chairman and Rice's lawyer, Captain James A. Baker. The board, in various configurations and with new members filling seats as they became vacant, would oversee the university down to the present day.[33]

Although Rice did not wish construction to begin until after his death, he and the board made clear their intention to use these acres in the Fourth Ward for the Institute grounds, which they hoped would include a polytechnic school, art collections, a library, and other features. In fact, the trustees' first official action concerned the Louisiana Street Property. The ink on the deed was barely dry when they learned of a proposal to the city to open a street through the tract. The board met quickly to draft a petition to the City Council, asking the city to dedicate the grounds in perpetuity to the Rice Institute and protect it from encroachment by streets.[34]

The city granted that petition, persuaded by the trustees that the grounds would serve as a site for free education and also function as a public park, "under proper regulations." A fence with padlocked gates soon encircled the property, and the board erected a house for a white caretaker to protect the lot and "keep out trespassers." Over the next few years, the Institute would plant hundreds of trees on the site, some selected and placed by William Marsh Rice himself. According to charter trustee Emanuel Raphael, Rice's wife, Elizabeth Baldwin Rice, also visited the site on occasion and took a lively interest in it on their visits to Houston: "She and Mr. Rice and myself drove out to the grounds, and Mrs. Rice suggested where the principal buildings were to be placed; and wanted the whole plat to be parked out in landscape gardening."[35]

As the fences went up and the trees went in, what did the property's Black neighbors think about these changes happening in their backyard? No direct evidence addresses the question. But two of the Black residents of Smith Alley—Bettie Leonard and Laura Hardy—did get an especially close look at the wealthy couple behind it all. In one sign perhaps of how small a city Houston still was, Leonard and Hardy both worked for about a week in the Rices' hotel apartments in 1896, when Elizabeth Rice was incapacitated by a stroke on a visit to Houston. Both women would be listed in the 1900 census as sick nurses, and as William Marsh Rice himself later recalled, his wife was attended by "two colored nurses," though he did not mention Leonard and Hardy by name.[36]

Indeed, there might never have been a record identifying Leonard and Hardy as nurses for the Rices if Elizabeth had not drawn up a new last will and testament during that time. In the surprising will, Rice's wife gave away large amounts of property that she claimed to own jointly with her husband. She denied having ever consented to the deeds conveying real estate to the Rice Institute. Then, not long after signing the will, Elizabeth Rice died.[37]

In the disputes that followed over the legitimacy of Mrs. Rice's last will, Leonard and Hardy were called to testify in court about her soundness of mind while they had cared for her. Both Black women told the court that Mrs. Rice had been able to converse and make decisions, though Leonard called her "irrational" at times. Their testimony thus became a small part of the evidence a probate judge heard before he approved the contested will, triggering a cascade of lawsuits that would not be settled even by the time of William Marsh Rice's own death in New York in 1900.[38]

As generations of Rice University students and visitors would later learn from campus tours, Rice's death led to another tangle of lawsuits when it was discovered that his butler and an attorney had conspired to murder the widower and steal his fortune, threatening the Rice Institute's future. Ultimately, James A. Baker, Rice's lawyer, defeated these efforts in court, saved the Rice endowment from Elizabeth Rice's executors, and confirmed the Institute's title to the Louisiana Street Property.[39]

In the meantime, the trustees did little to move their plans for an institute forward. But the tract they had designated for the grounds did occasionally crop up in the years-long morass of litigation. In 1899, for example, trustee Emanuel Raphael was asked in a deposition to describe the Institute's property in the Fourth Ward. Tellingly, given what came later, the questioning drew out his thoughts on the area's racial composition.

> Q. What is the value of the Louisiana Street property in Houston, Texas, that Mr. Rice conveyed to the Institute? A. I suppose that would be worth somewheres along $15,000.00 or $20,000.00.

Q. What sort of a neighborhood is there around it? A. Not very good.
Q. Isn't it most all colored population? A. On two sides it is colored but one side is white people.

Raphael's description of the by-then predominantly Black neighborhood as "not very good" may hint at the worry of an early board member about the Fourth Ward as a site for the Institute.[40]

At that moment, though, Institute trustees had bigger concerns: the lawsuits over the Rice estate that threatened the endowment itself. Not until about 1905, when those suits had been mostly resolved, did board members begin to refocus on plans to develop the Rice Institute. More change was coming for those first Gregory Institute neighbors who still lived beside the Rice grounds, including Laura Hardy and Bettie Leonard.[41]

The Neighbors versus Rice

After Rice's murder and the conclusion of all related lawsuits, the full extent of the wealth he had bequeathed to the Institute became clear. By 1905, the trustees held more than $4.6 million in assets and real estate in Texas, including some especially rich lumber lands in Louisiana. The prospects of Houston had also been boosted by the nearby discovery of oil at Spindletop in East Texas and by the flattening of Galveston in the great hurricane of 1900. As the ambitions of the trustees for the Institute grew in turn, they began to explore ways to secure a larger campus site, ranging from choosing a different location to expanding the Louisiana Street Property, which was barely larger than the current historic quadrangle on the Rice University campus.

Ideas about race and space would never be far from these discussions, as Raphael's 1899 deposition suggests. One possibility considered by the board was locating the Institute on a fifty-acre former golf course it acquired after Rice's death. But the presence of Black residents in that area struck one advisor to the board, future Houston mayor J. J. Pastoriza, as a problem. Pastoriza had been approached by Baker to offer feedback on the Institute's prospects, and in October 1905, Pastoriza penned a letter to Baker with his thoughts. He argued that the former golf course was "an ideal place for the Rice Institute," more appropriately sized than the Louisiana Street Property. There was only one defect in the bigger site, said Pastoriza: "the unsightly approach to it. I find a great many small houses occupied by negroes, on both sides of the street leading to the grounds."

Pastoriza advised Baker that this "could be remedied by purchasing the property and demolishing the houses." The trustees could lend funds to a third party to purchase the surrounding land, concealing the Institute's identity as buyer to keep prices low. Then, after razing the Black families' houses, they could make a profit by selling the lots to "individuals who desire to be near the college, and who would agree to erect first class houses thereon." Alternatively, the trustees could turn the empty space into "a beautiful park."[42]

Baker's reactions to Pastoriza's letter are unknown, but its proposal for how to deal with "negroes" around the old golf grounds was similar to what the Institute trustees had already begun to do around the Louisiana Street Property, which at that time they were still envisioning as one possible campus site. In December 1904, the board hired a surveyor to plot the grounds and the tracts next to it, "so that the Board may, if they see fit, make purchases of the adjoining property." And the next year, an agent named Henry M. Curtin began buying lots from Black landowners on behalf of the Institute, concealing from sellers that Rice was actually the interested party.[43]

In March 1905, for example, the Fairchilds sold Curtin nearly 19,000 square feet next to Shaw's for $1,800. Around the same time, Curtin bought lots 2, 6, 7, 8, and 9 in the Fredericks Addition from their owners, paying between $500 and $700 each for the lots closest to the Institute's property. He also acquired a triangular piece of ground on the north side of Jefferson Avenue, left over from the Gregory Institute's acre.[44]

Curtin transferred all of these properties to the Rice Institute, keeping most of the transactions off the public record at first. In 1907, he reported at a board meeting "as to what property is purchasable in the neighborhood of the Institute Grounds" and was told to keep buying. Two years later, the Rice Institute bought Lot 4 in the Fredericks Addition, too.[45]

The flurry of purchases left only a few of the original Gregory Institute neighbors on their homesteads—Bettie Leonard, Laura Hardy, and Robert Shaw. They had watched as their neighbors, one by one, were bought out by

Curtin, who finally recorded all the transfers to Rice with the county in 1908. But then, in 1909, Shaw, Leonard, and Hardy filed a lawsuit in Harris County District Court against Rice and Curtin, drawing a line in the sand.[46]

The suit's immediate cause concerned access to Smith Alley, the narrow path that had always served as a border to the Fredericks Addition. After purchasing the triangle on Jefferson from the Gregory Institute acre, the Rice Institute tried to erect a fence that ran along the north side of the triangle and enclosed a tiny part of Fredericks Lot 1. Leonard, Hardy, and Shaw sued in the Eleventh District Court for an injunction, because that fence would have walled off Smith Alley completely—leaving the remaining residents no access to the street from their own homes. The Institute's intention seemed clear: to force the neighbors out.

Shaw and Leonard told the court they were too poor to pay any court fees. (Leonard signed her autograph in a shaky hand, while Shaw made an "X" on court documents for his legal mark.) Nonetheless, they were determined to fight, and subpoenas were issued to several of their former neighbors to testify. The case was still pending two years later, in 1911, when a lawyer for the Rice Institute reported at a board meeting on the suit "by Leonard, Hardy, and Shaw vs. the Institute to prevent the Institute from closing off egress from their homes."[47]

By then, under the leadership of their newly hired president, Edgar Odell Lovett from Princeton University, who also joined the board, the Rice Institute trustees had decided to build the much larger current campus on a nearly three-hundred-acre tract on Main Street, abandoning their original designs in the Fourth Ward. (Lovett had visited Louisiana Street while interviewing for the job but decided the site was "too small and too close in" to the city.) The Institute's lawyers thus recommended that the board purchase the lots owned by Leonard, Hardy, and Shaw to settle the suit.[48]

The neighbors were not interested in selling, however. Matters came to a head again in January 1912, when the Institute completed its fence anyway, blocking off the Black residents' access to and from Smith Alley. The neighbors responded, with the help of a white lawyer, by filing a new petition to the court.

The lawsuit underscored the plaintiffs' awareness of their civil rights to own property and to sue, rights made all the more vital by the erosion of Black southerners' political and social rights under Jim Crow. As historian Dylan Penningroth has argued, even white southerners who were staunch segregationists had a vested interest in the idea that Black persons could legally hold title to property, not least because this meant white developers could market real estate to them. White lawyers also recognized a circumscribed set of Black civil rights when they represented Black clients like the Smith Alley neighbors in court, hoping to win a fee. Black litigants did not sue white defendants often or face them on a level playing field; in the suit with Bettie Leonard and her neighbors, the Rice Institute board was represented by the city's most experienced, well-connected, and deep-pocketed lawyers. Nonetheless, by taking legal action, the Smith Alley neighbors tested the power they had to obstruct the Institute's plans—and to lay their own claims before the court.[49]

Their amended pleading gave a detailed history of the property that predated the Rice Institute, conjuring up the area's Reconstruction past. Smith Alley had long been "the only way they have to go to and from their respective homes," explained the plaintiffs, who pointed out references to the alley in original deed records. During the twenty-five years when "the Gregory Institute premises" had been in use as a school ground, "the public and the plaintiffs' ancestors and their grantors constantly passed [it] going to and from" their homes. Black children, they noted, had used the alley on their way to the old school. Now, the Rice Institute had "unlawfully fenced the Southern end" of Smith Alley, blocking Leonard, Hardy, and Shaw from entry and exit. They had a "right to said alley" based on its dedication for that purpose in the past, and "by the right of necessity" to access their property.[50]

The main injustice alleged by these Black plaintiffs against Rice, in other words, was not their exclusion from a university that did not yet even exist. Rather, the Rice Institute was trying to eject them from a place that had long been theirs. And they intended to stay.

The Circus Grounds

The suit over Smith Alley was still ongoing in October 1912 when the Rice Institute held a celebrated opening ceremony for its first academic year, with invited guests from around the world. The overlapping of those events in 1912—one well-known, one long forgotten—reveals that the Rice Institute's history of relations with Black Houstonians began even before its first students entered the Sallyport, and long before the first Black students and faculty did.[51]

Rice's history at the Louisiana Street Property continued even after the Institute opened on Main. For several years, beginning in 1910, the trustees decided to rent the Louisiana Street Property to traveling circuses like Ringling Brothers and Barnum and Bailey. As Rice students attended their first classes in September 1912, the famous Buffalo Bill and Pawnee Wild West show was playing on the original Institute grounds.[52]

That October, the trustees also received the first of several proposals for leasing the Louisiana Street land. The board liked one early pitch from the Chamber of Commerce for a playground and park for (white) children, though it also advised the chamber about "a suit now pending" against the Institute by "colored inhabitants" of adjoining lots, "by which said negroes are trying to force the Institute to keep open a street known as Smith Alley." If Rice were to lose its case to Leonard, Hardy, and Shaw, the Institute recommended that the Chamber of Commerce build a "solid picket fence" on the southern border of the tract. The "dead end" to Smith Alley would ensure that its Black residents could not access the proposed (but never completed) park.[53]

The alternative to leasing the Louisiana Street Property was to sell. In 1914, the City of Houston purchased a significant section of the Rice tract and used it to erect the Taylor School, an impressively modern new building for students—white, exclusively—through the seventh grade. The Rice board continued to entertain proposals from lessees for the remainder of the tract; for many years, the trustees gave the YMCA permission to operate athletic fields and tennis courts beside the Taylor School, without paying rent. But the board's emerging preference was to sell the remnant of the Louisiana Street Property and its adjoining lots.[54]

Standing in their way were the Black neighbors on Smith Alley. In February 1917, after the YMCA had inquired about growing its footprint, business manager A. B. Cohn sent Chairman James A. Baker a map and memo, detailing approximately "14 lots on Jefferson Street" that the Institute had bought through Curtin. Cohn was forced to say the area comprised "about 14 lots" because that number included "3 lots owned by negroes which were not purchased by the

Institute." Until the Institute possessed titles to all contiguous lots, specifically those occupied by Leonard, Hardy, and Shaw, it would be difficult to find a buyer for the tract as a whole.[55]

In the meantime, temporary leases continued. The Ringling Brothers returned in 1915. An industrial fair was held on the Louisiana Street property in 1920. And then, in 1923, James A. Baker received an inquiry about using the Louisiana Street tract from a far more controversial party: Houston's Ku Klux Klan.

The twentieth-century Ku Klux Klan had made its first public appearance in Houston only a few years before. Klansman from the local chapter (Sam Houston No. 1) marched in robes at a Confederate veterans' parade in 1920, not long after national Klan organizers had come to town with fear-mongering stories about a "secret military society" that had supposedly been formed by armed "negroes" in Houston. Casting themselves as defenders of white supremacy, moral virtue, and native-born American Protestants, Houston Klansmen held large initiation meetings with flaming crosses in the city's suburbs, and in 1921 the local Klan committed a string of violent crimes with both white and Black victims. The local wave of terrorism included the abduction and castration of a Black dentist, J. Lafayette Cockrell, for allegedly associating with a white woman.[56]

The organization's reputation for vigilantism explains why some city leaders began sounding alarms in the fall of 1922, when the Texas Klan entered publicly into electoral politics. Local judge Murray B. Jones, who was married to Captain James A. Baker's daughter Alice, became the Klan's nominee for mayor of Houston in 1922. Jones lost, but the Klan's candidate for U.S. senator from Texas won. Meanwhile, a number of other white elites in the city began organizing to defeat Klansmen at the polls, denouncing the Invisible Empire's anti-Catholicism, lawlessness, and secrecy.[57]

Some members of the Rice Institute community, such as Lindsey Blayney, professor of German, joined those who denounced the Klan's resurgence. But at least one leading anti-Klan voice in Houston, oilman Joseph Cullinan, suspected the secret order had infiltrated the Rice Institute, too. In November 1922, Cullinan replied to a solicitation from Rice's Student Loan Fund Committee saying that he would not donate because he had been "advised" that a "substantial" number of Rice Institute students were members of the Klan.[58]

Cullinan had understandable reasons for suspicion. At least two members of the twenty-four-person Student Loan Fund Committee were widely reputed to be Klansmen: Judge Chester H. Bryan and store owner W. C. Munn. Billie Mayfield, publisher of the Houston Klan newspaper, *Colonel Mayfield's Weekly*, was well-known as a booster of Rice football with ties to the Institute. Most troubling to Cullinan was this: When young Rice alumnus and family friend James L. Autry died at age twenty-four in 1922, his funeral was visited by a "little band of klansmen, hooded and robed," according to newspaper reports, and on his casket they laid a "flowered fiery cross bearing the initial 'R' [which] represented the grief of the Rice Institute chapter of the Knights of the Ku Klux Klan." That same year, the school yearbook would publish a now infamous photograph of the "Ku Klux Klan of Rice Institute."[59]

These events were still in the recent past when, on November 3, 1923, James A. Baker received a letter from the Sam Houston Klan No. 1. It was openly signed by H. H. Collins, the chapter's leader, and printed on official letterhead with Klan iconography. Collins wanted Baker, as chairman of the Rice Institute, to let the Klan use the Louisiana Street grounds (primarily the part then being used by the YMCA) to hold a circus raising funds for "charitable purposes." The Klansman pledged that "no objectionable features" would be allowed at the Klan's "charity circus" (he likened it to a popular minstrel show held at the City Auditorium the year before) and predicted that the Klan's event would draw a crowd of seventeen thousand over nine days.[60]

By that time other chapters of the so-called "second" Klan had hosted such events in other parts of the country, including carnivals complete with picnics and Ferris wheels. But as Cullinan's letter the year before shows, the Klan's request to Baker came at a moment of increasing contestation over the secret order in Houston. Undaunted by its defeats in the city elections of 1922, the Klan had responded in 1923 with a public relations campaign, portraying itself as a philanthropic organization.[61]

The plan to hold a "charity circus" was part of this charm offensive; the proceeds would be used to purchase Thanksgiving dinners for poor white families. The Klan launched similar campaigns in other places. In north Texas, local Klansmen even offered a donation to the president of Abilene Christian College. Still, the Klan was controversial enough that YMCA officials wrote to

Baker on the circus matter. While the YMCA general secretary was "perfectly willing" to let the Klan use the field his organization was leasing for free from Rice, he evidently wanted the consent, tacit or otherwise, of Baker and the board of trustees.[62]

Given that wider context, it is unsurprising that the Rice trustees did not respond to the Klan with an unequivocal "yes." More notable is that they did not say "no." After a series of off-the-record conversations among the trustees, Rice business manager A. B. Cohn jotted their decision, in pencil, on a note filed away with Collins's letter. On November 19, 1923, trustee Benjamin B. Rice, nephew of the founder, telephoned Murray Jones (a local judge, Baker's son-in-law, and the Klan's nominee for mayor in 1922). Rice informed Jones that the Institute "would not act. If YMCA gave permit, Inst. would do nothing."[63]

And so it came to pass: a "K.K.K. charity circus" held over nine consecutive days on the Rice Institute's downtown property, with games, vaudeville shows, and a nightly automobile giveaway. Organizers encouraged Klan groups from surrounding areas to visit, hoping for a show of regional strength, and on the first night, the press reported a "capacity crowd" numbering in the thousands. The throngs gathered within shouting distance of Antioch Missionary Baptist Church to the north and Smith Alley to the south—but a far cry from the early days of Reconstruction, when Black school children had crossed these grounds on their way to the Gregory Institute.[64]

Much had changed in fifty years. And yet, even as the Klan circus took place, Bettie Leonard (once a sick nurse to Elizabeth Baldwin Rice, later a plaintiff in the 1909 suit against the Rice Institute) was still living nearby, on the same property her mother had bought after emancipation. By then Robert Shaw had already died at nearly eighty years old in January 1917, after which the Rice Institute acquired his property. His death may have convinced Laura Hardy to finally sell her property to Rice, too, obtaining a higher price ($4,000) than earlier sellers by holding out until 1917. Four years later, with Shaw and Hardy gone, the injunction suit that they and Leonard had filed against Rice was finally dismissed by the district court "for want of prosecution." Meanwhile, according to the 1920 census, Leonard had reunited with her ex-husband Samuel J. Leonard, who was shown living with her again on Smith Alley. Only the Leonards now remained from among the first Gregory Institute neighbors.[65]

Despite pressure from the Rice Institute to leave, and in the face of dramatic changes around her, Bettie Leonard had held on to the land bought by her formerly enslaved mother in 1873. In 1925, however, Bettie Leonard died. She was buried near her mother, Sallie Wicks, in Olivewood, an African American cemetery near a bank of White Oak Bayou northwest of downtown. And the very next month, Cohn appeared at a meeting of the Rice Institute trustees to inform them of the news. Lot 5 in the Fredericks Addition was, finally, available to buy.[66]

Houston in Black and White

By the time of Bettie Leonard's death, sixty years after Juneteenth, the city of Houston had ballooned from a population of under 9,000 to nearly 300,000, making it the largest city in Texas. It had also become increasingly segregated by race, through a process that was the work of many hands, public and private, visible and invisible. Laws about who could attend which schools or ride in which railroad cars, for example, interacted with decisions by groups like the Rice Institute board about how to value property, where to put fences, and what parties to support with favorable leases or loans. As the holder of significant real estate in the city, Rice University was a major protagonist in the history of segregation's rise, even before it opened its doors in 1912 and even beyond its Main Street campus.

The story of the Louisiana Street Property is one example of the role Rice's first founders played in the development of the segregated city, though it is not the only one. Many of the men who managed the Institute's interests (including Rice architect William Ward Watkin and trustees such as James A. Baker and A. S. Cleveland) were real estate developers, investors, and planners who helped to build elite subdivisions like Courtlandt Place (1906), Shadyside (1920), Southampton (1923), Broadacres (1923), West University Place (1924), and Southampton Extension (1925). Lots in these leafy enclaves near the Institute were sold exclusively to white buyers, thus achieving by design what the Rice trustees had gradually and with some difficulty pursued by purchase in the Fourth Ward: a white residential zone around the school's main site.[67]

Key men in the early history of the Rice Institute also supported abortive attempts to provide Houston with a zoned city plan. Inspired by early twentieth-century urban reform movements on both sides of the Atlantic, in 1912 the Houston Park Commission (appointed by Houston mayor H. Baldwin Rice, the nephew of William Marsh Rice) engaged architect Arthur C. Comey to sketch out a master plan for the city. Mayor Rice then commissioned a study of European cities by Frank Putnam, who praised Germany's modern urbanism and recommended that Houston establish a planning commission. A later mayor took up that suggestion in 1922, appointing early Rice Institute professor Lindsey Blayney to lead a planning commission. Another Rice professor, John Willis Slaughter, served as the group's secretary.[68]

Little came of these early moves until later in the 1920s, when Will C. Hogg, the son of a Texas governor and founder of Houston's most exclusive neighborhood, River Oaks, threw his wealth and clout behind a new city plan proposal, complete with zoning ordinances, municipal utility improvements, and a street grid. A close associate of Baker, and a friend of the Institute who had helped start its Student Loan Fund, Hogg led a city planning commission that was established in 1927. He also created a group called the Forum of Civics, whose mission was to promote the commission's plan.[69]

Baker and Lovett belonged to the forum in their roles as chairman and president of the Rice Institute. Early campus architects John F. Staub and William Ward Watkin, as well as early Rice professors Stockton Axson and Lewis B. Ryon Jr., also wrote for or served as associate editors for *Civics for Houston*, a pro-planning magazine backed by Hogg. And Hogg's new city planning commission hired Ryon, the first civil engineering professor at Rice, to serve as its engineer. Professor Ryon, who had also been elected the first mayor of West University Place in 1924, worked for two years with the Kansas City architecture firm Hare and Hare to publish an influential report in 1929, replete with maps, data, and graphs about the city.[70]

These city planners understood themselves as part of an international movement for progressive urban reform: They believed in modern sanitation, traffic control, public health, and parks. As in other American cities, however, they also believed cities should be spatially organized by race. All of the above efforts included the gathering of information about where and how Black Houstonians lived, as well as suggestions about where they should—and should not—be allowed to live in the future.[71]

In 1913, for example, Comey's early plan included a map showing areas where "colored" residents were then concentrated (one was Freedmen's Town), noting that this information would be "vital in the determination of school, playground, and park locations." City engineers produced an even more detailed map of "Negro Distribution" in Houston in 1924. Ryon, the Rice engineering professor, worked to update this information for Hogg's commission later in the 1920s, while the consultant S. Herbert Hare corresponded directly with Hogg about the potential impacts of their city plan on the racial layout of the city.[72]

Hare noted that "the city plan will tend to drive the colored population out of some of the localities now occupied by them," so they would need somewhere to go. Despite recent rulings against racial zoning by the U.S. Supreme Court, Hogg believed that his commission's report should identify a few districts for Black citizens that white buyers would voluntarily avoid and "beyond which the colored population will not undertake to encroach." He told Hare that he would enlist Professor Ryon "to mark out with me some boundary lines describing these districts."[73]

Two years earlier, an associate had noted to Hogg that a racial zoning law would likely violate the Constitution; Hogg replied that he knew this, "but [that] does not keep us from planning [the] ideal layout." In another letter, Ryon advised the city secretary that, because courts now routinely struck down any provision for racial segregation by public ordinance, a plan like Hogg's would be the only legal way to segregate: "racial segregation is practical only where effected by mutual agreement of all the property owners within a given territory that they will not sell or rent to the opposite race."[74]

When the Hogg commission finally published its report in 1929, it sought to mark out those territories by first identifying three existing "negro colonies" in the Third, Fourth, and Fifth wards. It also noted a few "other smaller negro sections, some of which should be eliminated in the development of the city and others enlarged," especially in areas close to wealthy white neighborhoods like River Oaks whose residents wanted their "negro servants" to live nearby. The report then included two shaded maps, one showing the present "race distribution" and the other showing "proposed race restriction areas." The first map still showed Black residents around the Rice Institute's Louisiana Street Property, where Sallie Wicks and others had purchased homes during Reconstruction. The second map did not.[75]

As for Bettie Leonard's lot, after her death the Rice Institute purchased it from her only heir, a son named Clifton. For $3,000, the trustees had finally completed their control of the whole, contiguous tract on the Jefferson side of its original Fourth Ward property.[76] Then, in 1927, the Institute reached an agreement to sell it all to the Houston Independent School District, which wanted to use the enlarged Louisiana Street Property for the first of two new junior colleges it planned to build—one for whites, and one for "colored" students. The final sale was completed in 1929 for $236,250, not long before the stock market crashed.[77]

In the end, school officials chose other locations for both the white junior college (which later evolved into the University of Houston) and the Houston College for Negroes (which eventually became Texas Southern University). Classes for the latter were housed initially in the Third Ward's Yates Colored High School, built in 1926 and named after Jack Yates, the important Fourth Ward pioneer. But the 1929 sale highlighted how dramatically the Louisiana Street Property and its surroundings had been transformed over the previous six decades—from the home of the Gregory Institute and a key site of Reconstruction's promise of racial equality, to the site of a "charity circus" held by the Ku Klux Klan, to the real estate of a rigidly segregated school district. The transformation told in miniature the larger story of Jim Crow's rise in Houston, which by 1930 was divided in numerous ways by race.[78]

Just how divided became clear in the 1930s, when the federal Home Owners' Loan Corporation (HOLC), part of the New Deal response to the Great Depression, produced maps that graded urban areas across the nation for their perceived risks to mortgage lenders. By then, Hogg's city planning campaign had fizzled. Nonetheless, the HOLC's City Survey largely adopted the assumptions and local data that had gone into recent maps like the ones made by Ryon and Hare, and it drew on new "social scientific" theories about property valuation and race that were being promulgated in academic circles. In city after city, African American neighborhoods were graded as "hazardous" and shaded on the maps as red, a process known as "redlining" that raised barriers to Black home ownership and exacerbated the racial wealth gap between Black and white Americans.[79]

Houston was no exception. In the Bayou City, the HOLC would ultimately shade all of the Louisiana Street Property and Freedmen's Town to its north and west as "red," thereby warning lenders away from investment in that area and others where Black Houstonians were clustered. By contrast, white neighborhoods like those surrounding the Rice Institute campus on Main Street were rated "Best" and shaded in green. The maps would make it more difficult for later Black Houstonians to acquire even the modest real estate that some Black landholders after emancipation had been able to acquire and pass down to children. Simultaneously, white perceptions of rental property in Black neighborhoods as overcrowded and run-down would go hand in hand with white fears of such spaces as literally "hazardous" and crime-ridden, leading to over-policing.[80]

In short, forty years after Raphael worried about the Fourth Ward being a "not very good" neighborhood and Pastoriza advised Baker about how to ensure that the Rice Institute would have no "unsightly" Black neighbors, the federal government's discriminatory maps cemented such private prejudices into social policy. The story of the Louisiana Street Property is only one episode in the much larger saga of racial segregation in Houston. But in it we can see evidence that the Rice Institute did not float above the many events and decisions that built a Jim Crow city. Its leaders were instead intimately involved in the creation of a segregated urban future.

At the same time, the history of the Fourth Ward points to another truth. After slavery, Black Houstonians had persevered in the face of mounting challenges to their rights. They built institutions like the Gregory Institute and nurtured citizens like Bettie Leonard who could not be easily moved. And in the years to come, numerous people who were born, raised, and rooted within Black communities like theirs would play key roles in moving Houston and Rice University in a different direction, closer to freedom.

4 | BEING BLACK AT THE RICE INSTITUTE

On November 29, 1923, as the Ku Klux Klan's "charity circus" entered its final days on the Rice Institute's downtown property, the student-run newspaper, the *Rice Thresher,* was full of anticipation for that week's homecoming football game. The paper teemed with greetings to alumni, historical reminiscence, and tributes to school spirit. Yet it also contained another tribute, of sorts, to a Black woman whose work on campus dated to its earliest days. An article on the third page profiled Jenny Pettit, who parked her horse-drawn cart at the Institute's gates every Monday and Thursday to take up laundry for students: "The boys say she is always on time with the washing and it is always good work." Pettit had been coming to campus since 1912, said the *Thresher,* and "most of the football men know her."[1]

Even better known on campus by 1923 was Jack Shelton, another Black Houstonian who had been at the Institute almost from the beginning. Shelton worked as a trainer for Rice sports teams and as a caretaker for the athletic fields, and he would appear in every volume of the yearbook from 1916 to 1929, plus a few more volumes after that. To the Institute's white students, faculty, alumni, and administrators, Shelton seemed to be, according to one *Campanile,* "almost as permanent as the Institute itself."[2]

Black Houstonians were indeed present at Rice from the creation, performing work that was vital to the institution's success. Though long overlooked in histories of the university, both Pettit and Shelton were trailblazers in the history of Black Rice. Even in the era of racial segregation, the white students who profiled Pettit and Shelton seemed to recognize these early Black figures for their roles in, and claims on, the history of William Marsh Rice's university.

These profiles more clearly belonged, however, to another long history: a record of demeaning stereotypes and racism meant to justify the legal and economic subjugation of Black Americans. Quotations from both Shelton and Pettit were rendered in racist dialect by writers at Rice. References to Shelton in campus publications often paired or replaced his name with "Nigger." And the *Thresher* applied the same racist epithet to Pettit in its profile of "Aunt Jenny," which also described her as "corpulent" and an "old Negro mammy."[3]

Even when recognizing Pettit and Shelton, in other words, white observers at the Rice Institute repeatedly and willfully misrecognized both. In their distorted pictures of Black workers on campus, long-standing service even became evidence of an unquestioning love for the university, the kind of loyalty befitting a faithful "mammy." "Ah, Ah wants yuh to tell all the fellers 'at I'se allus a backer o' Rice Institute," Pettit supposedly said in her homecoming interview. Likewise, although the *Campanile* noted of "Dr. Jack Shelton" that any athletic season would be a failure "were our beloved nigger to leave us," students were confident that Shelton never would. "He takes our abuses," the yearbook said, "and returns them with smiles and willingness."[4]

Or so the *Campanile* imagined. In reality, the images of Shelton created by white observers show how common assumptions of white supremacy were in the culture of the Rice Institute. These assumptions drew both on Lost Cause myths about "faithful slaves" and on well-established tropes from American popular culture. The name that came to define legal segregation—Jim Crow—was derived from a character and song associated with blackface minstrel shows before the Civil War, suggesting how long cultural and political forms of power had worked together to maintain white rule. In the segregated "New South," the expectation that Black figures like Shelton should smile in the face of abuses was part of a rigid system of racial caste that early twentieth-century white Americans both inherited and modernized.

This racial order was vigorously challenged by Black Americans at the time. Jim Crow racism was routinely exposed and attacked by "New Negro" writers, artists, and civil rights activists at the turn of the century, from Harlem to Houston. But in southern states like Texas, Black voters had been systematically disenfranchised by the beginning of World War I, and the constant threat of spectacular anti-Black violence constrained social change. A different perspective on Shelton's smiles is suggested by a famous 1895 verse from African American poet Paul Laurence Dunbar, who better understood the experiences of Black men and women in the era described by some historians as the "nadir" of American race relations: "We wear the mask that grins and lies. . . . With torn and bleeding hearts we smile."[5]

How, then, should we interpret Jack Shelton's smiles or Jenny Pettit's comments? What did the culture of the Rice Institute expect them to conceal? What did they decide to mask, and what did they choose to reveal? In short, what was it like, and what did it take, to be Black at Rice? The first to confront those questions at the university, though they would not be the last, were the Black pioneers who came to the Institute not for classes, but to work.

"A Beautiful Type of the Old South"

Tracing the history of Black workers in Rice's earliest years is not an easy task, not because African Americans were absent, but because institutional records seldom took careful note of their presence. Photographs show Black men in early campus construction crews but do not identify them. Similarly, a letter from 1918 by campus architect William Ward Watkin speaks of a "darkey" who drove a wagon for groundskeeper Tony Martino and was "jointly employed" by the Institute. Martino commended the driver to Watkin as "very careful" and "capable," but the architect did not name him. In some cases, the refusal to name was itself a way of marking race. The early records of the Institute's faculty club, where members were served by Black attendants, contain references to the "help," "the servants," "the Cook," and even a "Cook's helper" who was injured in a kitchen gas explosion, but no names. Blueprints for the on-campus club later noted the segregated bathrooms Black employees were required to use.[6]

The Rice Institute hired Black Houstonians off campus, too. When the city complained of trash accumulating on the Louisiana Street circus grounds in 1912, the Rice business manager told the property's white caretaker to have the debris cleared: "We think there are some negroes in your neighborhood who do hauling of this kind." On other occasions, the Institute tried to find "a cheap negro" to pull down an old building and depended on an "old colored couple" to look after the old golf-course grounds owned by the Institute in 1910.[7]

Houston's segregated labor market in the early 1900s confined most Black workers to low-wage jobs like these, offering few chances for upward mobility. In areas such as construction, groundskeeping, transportation, and more, white employers valued the "cheap," anonymous labor often provided by Black men. Meanwhile, hotels, boardinghouses, and wealthier white families relied heavily on Black women who worked as housekeepers, cooks, laundresses, and nurses, occupations that were also low-paying, if sometimes less anonymous.

Domestic work brought some Black Houstonians into especially close contact with white employers, including key figures in Rice's history. In 1928, the Houston *Post* reported on the death of a ninety-year-old Black woman named Mary King who was a "negro mammy of the Old South and servant in the James A. Baker family for 30 years." Baker, who served as Rice's chairman from its chartering in 1891 until his death in 1941, told the *Post* that "'Aunt Mary' was a beautiful type of the Old South, a faithful mammy, a devoted friend and a Christian spirit. As such she will be remembered by those who knew her best."[8]

Baker certainly knew Mary King better than Watkin knew Martino's unnamed driver. However, as with the *Thresher* profile of "Aunt Jenny" a few years before, Baker's brief eulogy to "Aunt Mary" primarily illustrates the racialized lenses through which white employers saw Black women. While Baker undoubtedly saw the article about King as a kind of recognition, Black Houstonians could not have failed to notice all that he failed to see. Mary King was a worker in the Baker household, but "Aunt Mary" was a "type," as Baker put it, a palimpsest onto which white southerners inscribed their own images of what it meant to be "negro," both in the "Old South" and in their new era of racial segregation.[9]

Indeed, Baker's description of "Aunt Mary" epitomized the culture of race relations in which he and other elite Houstonians had been reared since Reconstruction. In 1874, as a teenager, Baker had enrolled at Texas Military Institute in Austin, where he (along with two of Frederick A. Rice's sons) studied under Confederate veteran and influential pedagogue John Garland James. Not long before he assumed the presidency of Texas A&M University in 1879, James compiled a *Southern Student's Hand-Book of Selections for Reading and Oratory*, and it offers a revealing glimpse into the curriculum that TMI cadets like Baker were taught.[10]

Garland James's primer combined heroic Lost Cause portraits of Confederate chivalry with vehement denunciations of Reconstruction. It praised the White Leagues that had "redeemed" the South from "negro rule." Yet it also contained maudlin depictions of loyal slaves, singling out for praise "the old negro nurse, with her head in a white handkerchief and her consequential gait." The anthology taught students that the "African race" was an inferior civilization for whom slavery had been a blessing, and who now depended on the enlightened but firm rule of white men. "We are under the very highest obligations of a brave manhood to do justice to the negro," advised one excerpt in the *Hand-Book*, though "justice" did not mean "negro" equality. "He is not our equal. He is in our power, and cowardice takes no meaner shape than when power oppresses weakness." Still, the reading continued, "in the name of civilization, in the name of our fathers," white men should never sacrifice "the rights and liberties of the white race in crazy wranglings over the rights and liberties of the black race."[11]

Such passages tutored students in an ideology of white supremacy and paternalism that suffused elite organizations in the Jim Crow South, from segregated churches to civic clubs and fraternal organizations like the Houston Light Guard. In 1879, Baker acquired his lifelong title of "Captain Baker" when he was elected captain of the Light Guard, a militia founded in 1873 by former Confederates and initially led by Edwin Fairfax Gray, the brother of Peter W. Gray. In 1875, members of the Light Guard threw a reception for Jefferson Davis upon his visit to Houston, where the former Confederate president appeared on a platform with older guardsmen Benjamin A. Botts and Frederick A. Rice. William Marsh Rice owned fundraising bonds issued by the Light Guard. And two of Frederick's sons served alongside Baker as guardsmen, traveling with the group to march in parades and drill exhibitions like one at the 1895 Confederate veterans' reunion in Houston. In these and other settings, young men like Baker learned to apply the lessons about white manhood they had learned from rebel officers like James.[12]

In its early years, the guard was more than ceremonial; the militia was called out by public officials in the 1870s and early 1880s to break up strikes by Black workers and to restore order in moments of racial unrest, including on occasion by restraining white rioters. But in later years, as younger men stepped into leadership positions, the Light Guard lived on primarily as a military dress company for elite Houstonians who adhered to the Lost Cause even if they had not been old enough to fight for it themselves. Some members of this generation preached the virtue of sectional reconciliation and the need for improved (but still segregated) conditions for Black southerners. Simultaneously, though, they kept the faith that calls for racial equality were "crazy wranglings," and they heaped praise on Black southerners who seemed to accept their place. Beginning around the time of Baker's captaincy, for instance, the guard was often joined at its events by a drummer, John Sessums Jr., who was born enslaved and served for fifty years as a token Black member of the Houston Light Guard's drill team. After he died in 1928, veterans of the guard paid to erect a tombstone at Sessums's grave. It memorialized him as "faithful unto death."[13]

As with "Aunt Mary," so with Sessums: Nostalgic stories about loyal Black subordinates absolved white southerners of injustice in the past while justifying Jim Crow's hierarchies in the present. Nor were these ideas confined to the South. In 1923, five years before Baker eulogized Mary King as a "faithful mammy," Confederate heritage organizations proposed a monument to "mammys" on the national mall in Washington, DC. Though that was never built, Lost Cause apologists were more successful in their push to have their views represented in textbooks, school curricula, and local monuments nationwide. And all the while, despite the opposition of groups such as the National Association for the Advancement of Colored People (NAACP), founded in 1909, new media technologies were mass-producing cartoonish images of Black life and disseminating them around the nation and the world.[14]

As a result, by the time students matriculated at the early Rice Institute, most had been reared in a mass culture premised on white supremacy. White students could draw on a range of sources for what they presumed to be knowledge about race, from interactions with Black domestic workers to contemporary advertisements for Aunt Jemima pancake mix; and from Tin Pan Alley sheet music to movies in which white actors wore blackface, like *Birth of a Nation* (1915) or Al Jolson's *The Jazz Singer* (1927). Many students would have seen touring vaudeville troupes like the Old Reliable Virginia Minstrels, the "World's Best Colored Show," which rented Rice Institute land near the Louisiana Street property when it brought its large musical act to Houston in 1924.[15] And once they arrived at the Institute, Rice students continued to consume popular music containing stereotyped images of Black life. In 1917 and 1918, sophomores organized boating trips to the San Jacinto Battlefield for freshmen, who danced on board to common minstrel show tunes: "'Turkey in the Straw,' 'Nigger Blues,' and all the other latest hits."[16]

Hovering over all of these events was the gray ghost of the Lost Cause, which stalked the campus in formal as well as informal settings. At the first commencement, in 1916, graduating seniors performed a historical tableaux featuring "a host of grey clad veterans marching toward the Spirit of the Confederacy as symbolized by a girl who was draped in the Confederate flag." Four years later, on October 8, 1920, classes were canceled at Rice because of a major national reunion of Confederate veterans in Houston. President Lovett (whose father-in-law had been a prominent Confederate Army officer) issued an announcement requesting trustees, faculty members, and members of their families to assemble in the Sallyport to receive a delegation of "the soldiers and their friends" for a campus visit; students were also asked to assemble that afternoon in the quadrangle for a cheer session in honor of the veterans, who were to be served tea on campus. And in 1927, the Institute hosted a guest lecture in the physics amphitheater by noted historian Ulrich B. Phillips, whose 1918 book *American Negro Slavery* gave scholarly legitimacy to racist myths about the institution. White audiences who heard versions of Phillips's lectures delivered that year in Houston, Austin, and Galveston returned home with the lesson, as one listener reported, that "the relationship between master and slave was fine" and the latter was not "badly" treated.[17]

The same nostalgic ideas about the Old South shaped numerous student dances at the Institute in this period, which were frequently staged as racial fantasias. At one dance in 1920, for example, students and faculty chaperones were entertained by "negro comedians" (white performers in blackface), while at another, in 1929, the River Oaks ballroom was changed "as if by magic into an old-fashioned southern plantation." As Rice guests arrived, "they were presented with Owl shaped programs by typical plantation-type darkies" standing before a likeness of a southern manse, while across the room stood a cabin representing the "servants' quarters." "Herein was seated an old-fashioned and very stout black mammy, bandana and all."[18]

Early twentieth-century mass culture encouraged amateurs not just to consume, but to perform and reproduce the images of Blackness they saw and heard in popular media. Recent studies have emphasized the central role that segregated colleges played in this process of social reproduction, and Rice was no exception. Many cartoons and jokes in early student publications mimicked the caricatured "darkies" and "mammies" seen in other humor magazines, advertisements, and minstrel shows. At one writing-club meeting in 1921, a female student read "a poem, 'Little Sambo,' in negro dialect, which was pleasing"; at another, a male student "read a story about the southern country negro which showed a delightful familiarity with the subject."[19]

Other students went beyond mimicry of Black voices and wore blackface, too. In 1921, the College Women's Club performed a "jazzy" show with stock characters from minstrels, performing songs like "Pickaninny Kid" in "negro dialect" and "negro makeups." It was only one of multiple blackface shows by Rice women in that decade, which concluded with a male student performing as a "pickaninny" at an annual spring festival in 1930. Similarly, when the Dramatic Club staged *The Dreamy Kid*, a one-act play by the New York playwright Eugene O'Neill with exclusively Black characters, student actors put on blackface and diligently rehearsed their dialects. Afterwards, the *Thresher* had special praise for the actress who played the "Mammy."[20]

With lampoons like these, students at the Institute clearly chose to follow the wider trends that made "mammy" characters and blackface pervasive in American culture, even if they sometimes tested local convention. In 1933, when the Dramatic Club announced plans for a production of *Uncle Tom's Cabin*, based on the antebellum antislavery novel, a local chapter of the United Daughters of the Confederacy publicly opposed it. The student club bowed to the protest by agreeing to stage a different play, a melodrama about the postwar South titled *Rose of the Southland*. But the replacement hardly challenged the genre's customary racial tropes. When "Miss Billie Knight as Mammy Evelina, appeared on the scene with her face blackened and received applause," she practically stole the show.[21]

In its review of that production, the *Thresher* commented that a "jovial negro mammy, filled with the superstitions of a Eugene O'Neill dark boy, is good for several laughs in any play," especially when her costume was stuffed with pillows to enlarge "various conspicuous portions of her anatomy." If there was anything on which white audiences of all sections and political sympathies could agree, the *Thresher* seemed to say, it was laughing at a comically large "mammy." Truly, by 1933, nothing could have been more common in American theaters.[22]

Still, what did it mean when racist entertainments were performed on a campus where Black people like Jenny Pettit and Jack Shelton labored, to audiences who sometimes went home to houses where Black women like Mary King worked, and at a school that excluded Black students from admission? In that context, even popular culture took on local meanings, and what students thought of as humor reinforced the Institute's identity as a white southern university. To take one illustration from a later period, consider a 1950 cartoon from the student-run *Rice Institute Magazine.* The caricature depicts several partially nude Black women, drawn to fit the artist's idea of savage African cannibals (a common motif in early twentieth-century white visual culture). While ogling the women, a white male student has collided with a tree and sits in a daze. His white companion then leans over and says, "Use your head, Joe; They couldn't be Rice girls."[23]

The same punchline seemed to be the point of a gag repeated in two earlier volumes of the *Campanile.* In 1926, the yearbook's humor section contained a series of photographs purporting to depict Rice buildings and classes. In place of the Administration Building (later Lovett Hall), for example, the photo showed its satirical opposite, a rickety wooden structure. Then, over the caption, "The Co-Ed Gym Class," editors printed its supposed opposite: a photograph of three African American girls playing in a field. A similar *Campanile* photograph from 1931 captured a different group of Black children, presumably somewhere in Houston. Next to it, an article and caption implied that these were the latest in a group of new football players who had been admitted to the Institute despite poor academic records, winking to the reader who knew the truth: These couldn't be Rice boys.[24]

White students who gathered for the Pre-Law Society's annual banquet in 1928 made explicit what usually went unsaid in these attempts at humor. As a prompt for the evening's dinner debate, a letter was read announcing that the Rice administration would soon "consider accepting negro applications." A chaotic debate ensued, with the majority taking the side of one student who said, "I'll be damned if I'll go to school with a negro," though a handful made the case that integration would be "a normal thing to do in this free land of

Equality." Chaos erupted again when the program committee revealed that the letter was a fake. Afterwards, the *Thresher* reported that the debate had been heated enough to verge on violence, and noted that the Black wait staff had taken special note of the argument: "The negro waiters became excited; they began to gather around supposedly taking off the dishes, but vitally interested in the hectic oratorical struggle."[25]

The mention of the waiters is another reminder that Black Houstonians were at Rice from the beginning, though their experiences remain difficult to glimpse through the scrims of racist stereotypes and Lost Cause myth that were also there from the start. In its report on the Pre-Law banquet, for example, the *Thresher* described the waiters' "enormous white teeth," "thick lips," and "low brows," projecting onto them the exaggerated features pervasive in blackface minstrelsy. Earlier that same year, the *Thresher* called attention to another group of Black servers who had worked at the Junior Prom, which was held off campus at a venue once again decorated as a "Southern Colonial Garden." Sets for that dance depicted the Sewanee River and an "old-fashioned cotton-field with the 'colored folks' picking cotton." Rice boys stood on the sidelines like "afternoon callers waiting for the young ladies to take one last look in the mirror and to have 'mammy' smooth down their ruffles for the last time." For dinner, guests enjoyed a "typical Southern fried chicken course in the dining room; the negro waiters," noted the *Thresher*, "fit in well with the general scheme."[26]

In sum, at the banquet, as at the prom, white observers saw the unnamed waiters as crude racial types of the Old South, casting them to "fit in well" with their own imaginations of what it meant to be Black. Nor do most adult leaders of the Institute appear to have challenged such images, whose outlines had long been taught to them in their own, usually segregated circles. Speaking to freshmen in his matriculation address in 1935, President Edgar Odell Lovett encouraged new Rice students worried about how they might perform in their classes by quoting a recent quip from a Cambridge don in England. The don knew a mathematics student who seemed "idle, stupid" at first, but the pupil soon found success by applying himself to the material: "He began to work like a nigger and in one year's work got a good place."[27]

In Lovett's casual use of a racial slur, combined with the joke's backhanded recognition of the hard labor of Black people, the story drew the same stark, racial lines as examples of student humor in the period. A "darkey" might work hard, but he could not study mathematics at a place like Rice. And all the while, Black waiters, Black laundresses, and Black groundskeepers in Houston continued about their work.

Being Jack Shelton

If being Black at the early Rice Institute meant having to do two jobs at once, the work at hand *and* the work of navigating through and around white images of Black life, no single figure illustrates that predicament better than Jack Shelton.

Born in the 1880s near Goliad, Texas, to parents who had been slaves, Shelton grew up in Beeville, a predominantly white rural community in South Texas. There, as in Houston, the African American community had mobilized after the Civil War to build vital institutions, including churches and a school. An 1897 issue of the Beeville *Bee* reported on Jack Shelton winning a cakewalk put on by "the elite colored society of the city," though it is unclear whether the lucky dancer was the Shelton who later worked for Rice or his father, also named Jack.[28]

Bee County in the 1890s was also a place of rising interethnic tensions during a national economic downturn. As growing numbers of Mexican Americans began migrating to Beeville from the South and West, they competed with Black laborers for scarce jobs in an economy dominated by Anglo-Texans. In 1894, competition over wage rates, encouraged by white employers who wanted the cheapest possible labor, led to a spate of violence, reportedly involving an attack by local African Americans on Mexican American workers. The younger Shelton remained in Beeville in 1900, now married with a son of his own. But conditions in the county, combined with a separation from his wife in 1902, may help explain why he soon joined a great migration of rural Black Texans to Houston.[29]

By 1908, Shelton had found new work as a porter and masseur at a bathhouse in Houston operated by Dr. Edwin D. Lunn, a physician and practitioner of chiropractic techniques. Then, in 1914, a new job opportunity appeared when Phillip H. Arbuckle, the Rice Institute's first coach, brought his football team to Lunn's sanitarium for treatment after a particularly bruising loss to the Aggies of Texas A&M University.[30] Shelton later remembered Arbuckle being so impressed by his work as a masseur that the coach began bringing Shelton to campus every day to rub sore muscles. The football team beat the Aggies two years straight after that trip to Lunn's, and in November 1916, Shelton appeared in a photograph with the winning squad on the front page of the *Thresher*, a towel draped over his shoulder. The caption described him only as "Jack," the "rubber."[31]

Other portraits would appear regularly in Rice publications over the next two decades. Yearbooks from this era include photographs of Shelton delivering water or administering first aid during games. Others picture him standing with his signature towel in group portraits of the football, track, and basketball teams. Two of those pictures included hoops star H. Malcolm Lovett, son of Edgar Odell Lovett. In the 1920 basketball team photo, the younger Lovett, who would serve as a member and chairman of the Rice Board of Trustees in the 1960s when the university began to desegregate, sits cross-legged in the first of three rows. Shelton stands, arms crossed behind him, in the third.[32]

In addition to publishing photos of Shelton, student publications in these years claimed to respect and appreciate his skill as a trainer. In 1921, the *Thresher* regretted to hear that Shelton might be quitting Rice, describing "Jack" as "one of the best negro trainers in the country." The paper breathed a sigh of relief when, only three weeks later, Shelton was back on the job: "His difficulties were settled satisfactorily to all parties involved." That same year, after a new field house was constructed on campus, the *Campanile* reported that "Dr. Jack has his little room for treating charley-horses, sprains, bruises and cuts, and other minor injuries."[33]

Less than a decade after it began, Shelton's job at the Institute thus seemed secure, and his duties eventually expanded to include care of the athletic fields. In 1923, the *Campanile* published a photograph of the "Doctor" in the section normally reserved for coaches, noting that "his interest in the university he works for and the men he works with should place him there." According to the previous yearbook's editors, he was "a fixture as permanent in the minds of football men and other athletes as Rice Field itself—'Dr. Jack' Shelton, suh, right heah!"[34]

In reality, of course, Shelton was not a permanent fixture at Rice. He had a history before the Institute and a life beyond it, too. Houston's annually published city directories first contained an entry for Shelton in 1907. Five years later, the directory showed Shelton rooming briefly at 1107 Andrews Street, and the next year he had moved to 1312 Frederick, just north of the Rice Institute's Louisiana Street property.[35]

Both addresses placed Shelton's home life in the heart of the Fourth Ward, indicating that Shelton, like many African American migrants to the city, put down new roots in the established Black community around Freedmen's Town. In February 1917, he was remarried at a wedding officiated by Rev. F. L. Lights, the successor to Jack Yates as minister of Antioch Missionary Baptist Church. In 1919, a column on Antioch in the Houston *Informer*, the city's leading Black newspaper, acknowledged Jack Shelton for his help in planning a congregational trip to the beach.[36]

Shelton's residence on streets like Andrews and Frederick (and, later, Howe) also put him in the neighborhood of Booker T. Washington High School, Union Hospital (the city's first Black hospital), the Carnegie Colored Library, and an academy for Black students on San Felipe Street. All four institutions owed their existence to a small but rising Black professional class whose aspirations were documented in *The Red Book of Houston: A Compendium of Social, Professional, Religious, Educational and Industrial Interests of Houston's Colored Population*, published by the city's Black elites in 1915. Echoing Booker T. Washington's gospel of uplift and strategic accommodation to the Jim Crow social order, the authors of the *Red Book* highlighted the many community achievements that made the Fourth Ward so attractive to newcomers.[37]

The Rice Institute attracted Shelton for different reasons: His job at least brought reliable, if modest, pay. Even so, whenever he traveled from the streets of the Fourth Ward to the Rice athletic fields, Shelton had to navigate through and around the numerous color lines that limited his rights. If he rode out to the Institute on the street car, for example, Shelton would have been required to make his way to the rear seats reserved for "colored" passengers. Stepping off the trolley and entering his workplace, where he might be called simply by his first name—or worse—Shelton knew he would be expected to answer "sir" or "ma'am." Leaving campus again at the end of a long day, Shelton went home through a city where most parks, schools, hospitals, and public spaces were barred to him. Black citizens, who could enlist in the military's segregated units, could not even vote in party primaries by 1923. And they were routinely harassed by Houston's civilians and police.[38]

The harsh reality in which Shelton lived was never clearer than in the late summer of 1917, when a case of police brutality in his neighborhood sparked one of the worst episodes of racial violence in the city's history. It began when a group of Black soldiers in the U.S. Army's Twenty-Fourth Infantry, then stationed at a World War I training camp just outside of town, learned that a Black woman in the Fourth Ward had been harassed and physically assaulted by a white policeman. The same policeman had then pistol-whipped Black soldiers who tried to intervene.[39]

Members of the Twenty-Fourth Infantry, most of whom hailed from the North, had experienced racial discrimination themselves since arriving in the Jim Crow city for guard duty at Camp Logan. But they had been warmly welcomed by members of Shelton's church and other Black Houstonians in the Fourth Ward. So on the evening of August 23, when word spread about the outrage committed by police against the Black woman, Sara Travers, and the Black men who had come to her defense, a group of Black soldiers began to march from Camp Logan (where Memorial Park sits today) toward the heart of Freedmen's Town.[40]

Two hours of bloody clashes between the armed soldiers and white locals followed, and when the smoke cleared, 15 white Houstonians and 2 Black soldiers lay dead. Several others injured that night later succumbed to their wounds. After hastily assembled court-martials found 110 Black soldiers guilty of mutiny, in the largest murder trial in American history, 19 Black soldiers were summarily executed by hanging, while scores of others were sent to federal prison.[41]

The aftershocks from these events were felt in Houston and the nation for years. African American soldiers had served proudly in the Southwest as "Buffalo Soldiers" and in the Spanish-American War; many had been hoping that service in the Great War might advance the cause of democracy at home as well as abroad. Yet for activists like W. E. B. Du Bois, the Harvard-educated Black intellectual and cofounder of the NAACP, Camp Logan was a reminder that even uniforms offered no sure protection for Black citizens. According to Du Bois, the hangings exemplified "the deep resentment mixed with the pale ghost of fear which Negro soldiers call up in the breasts of the white South," as well as the uneven application of justice under Jim Crow. After all, an anti-Black pogrom earlier that same year had killed "125 Negroes" in East Saint Louis. Yet in that city, only "20 white men were imprisoned, none for more than 15 years, and 10 colored men with them," a stark contrast to the iron fist that fell on the 19 Black soldiers hung and the "51 imprisoned for life for killing 17 whites in Houston." An NAACP investigation concluded that "The primary cause of the Houston riot was the habitual brutality of the white police officers of Houston in their treatment of colored people."[42]

Locally, the violence of 1917 only intensified white policing of Black neighborhoods like Shelton's. It also sparked increasingly public debates among Houston's African Americans about how to meet the crisis. The NAACP's investigator reported that many were leaving for the North. "Having a home is all right," one told her, "but not when you never know when you leave it in the morning if you will really be able to get back to it that night." Some in the Fourth Ward still favored the philosophy of Booker T. Washington; through education, business, and accommodation to the racial protocols of the Jim Crow South, they hoped to staunch the worst violences of white supremacy while carving out space for Black economic development well within the confines of racial segregation. But members of a younger generation were increasingly dissatisfied with Washington's approach. They founded Houston's first local chapter of the NAACP in 1918, blasted the Klan and police brutality throughout the 1920s, and advocated pardons for the Black soldiers of the Twenty-Fourth who were unjustly tried en masse for the so-called Camp Logan mutiny—a campaign that finally bore fruit more than a century later, when the soldiers' convictions were overturned by the U.S. Army in November 2023. Clifton F. Richardson, a graduate of Bishop College in Marshall who moved to Houston in 1909 and founded the Houston *Informer* in 1919, became the leading local spokesman for this increasingly confrontational movement for civil rights.[43]

It is only possible to guess where Jack Shelton himself stood on the spectrum of postwar opinion, but he was clearly among those who decided to remain in Houston, settling down for good in a house he eventually owned in the

Fourth Ward. In 1918, when Shelton moved into this residence on Sherman (later Valentine) Street, he made his new home near the very blocks where Black soldiers had marched from Camp Logan the year before. Perhaps he contemplated their defiance of Jim Crow—and what it had cost them—when he registered for the draft in 1918, listing his occupation as an "athletic attendant" at the Rice Institute.[44]

Meanwhile, at Shelton's workplace, a student who read nothing but the *Thresher* would never have known that a cataclysm had shaken the Fourth Ward that the trainer knew so well. The Rice Institute spent the World War I years preparing young Owls to become officers, organizing male students into companies of cadets, and imposing new wartime rules on campus over the protests of students. All of these topics garnered extensive coverage by the *Thresher.* But not the violence of 1917 in Houston. No mention of the Camp Logan mutiny has been found in any contemporary publications or records at Rice, even though it unfolded only a few miles away and came very near the Louisiana Street property still owned by the Rice Institute.[45]

On the contrary, in the weeks after the bloodshed, the football team carried on with preparations for its first match of the year: an October 6, 1917, exhibition game against white soldiers of the First Illinois Hospital Corps, then stationed at Camp Logan. When time came for the football team's annual group photo, after its best season to date, Shelton draped his towel over his shoulder as usual. He smiled for the camera. And in a nod to the military mood on campus, the *Campanile* editors identified him in the caption, just this once, as "Jack (Red Cross Man)."[46]

"The Rigidity of Castes"

In retrospect, Shelton's experience at Rice highlights some of the flexibility—as well as the absurd paradox—of the Jim Crow South. Even as white Houstonians opened their newspapers to fearmongering stories about mutinous Black soldiers, many still had regular interactions across the color line. "Talk of segregation! Southern homes are swarming with colored servants," exclaimed Professor Albert Guérard, a Frenchman who taught at Rice from 1913 to 1924 before leaving Houston. In a 1948 memoir about his decade at Rice, which had "confirmed" his views about the injustice of Jim Crow, Guérard noted that his white neighbors would have balked if a "Negro preacher" built a house next door, even though "there are servants' quarters in every back yard." And no one batted an eye if a Black nurse sat "with the white folks in a streetcar, if she is escorting a white child." For Guérard, such contradictions proved that the point of segregation was never the avoidance of all "physical propinquity" or contacts between white and Black southerners. Rather, the point was white people's power to dictate the terms of those contacts and thus preserve "the rigidity of castes."[47]

At Rice, that power was reflected in the ease with which white students could turn from hailing Shelton as an icon to mocking the older man with impunity. During this period, student hazing rituals featured elections for freshman class officers in which sophomores would convince new students, known colloquially at the time as "slimes," to vote for imaginary candidates such as Hermann Park (the name of the park across the street from campus) and Sally Port (the nickname for the iconic archway under the Administration Building). And on more than one occasion, "Jack Shelton" was elected class president by the unsuspecting freshmen. The mock elections made the trainer the butt of a cruel joke: An African American could be a "Red Cross Man," but he could not be a slime.[48]

In 1926, the editors of the *Campanile* made a series of even more malicious jokes at Shelton's expense. One cartoon in the humor section infantilized the trainer with a racist caricature of a young boy eating watermelon, his eyes wide and his lips enlarged. The drawing was captioned, "The pickanninnyhood of Dr. Jack Shelton." Another page in the same volume, by contrast, hypersexualized the adult Shelton by describing him as "famous as a Don Juan," while a spoof on a third page jokingly named him as a member of the administration for "The Vice Institoot." Alluding to San Felipe, a Fourth Ward street where the city had located its red light district at the time, the *Campanile* described Shelton as the "H. P. (Hot Papa), (San Felipe); Professor of the plain and fancy massage; familiarly known as Nigger Jack, the boy with a 'high brown' [woman] in every college town in the South."[49]

As with their depictions of mammies at Rice plays and dances, students may have regarded such crude jokes as a perverse kind of homage or harmless fun to which they were entitled. Either way, Shelton knew that he could neither reciprocate nor resist such jokes without real danger. For Black Houstonians, stereotypes about the sexual prowess of a Black man or the sexual availability of Black women could easily become matters of life or death. After all, newspapers frequently carried stories of Black men killed by vigilantes for looking the wrong way at white women or for other perceived violations of the racial order. In 1928, after Robert Powell allegedly shot a white police officer in the Fourth Ward, the Black man was abducted from Jefferson Davis Hospital by a lynch mob and hung from a bridge over the bayou, and all on the eve of the Democratic National Convention held later the same month in Houston. The lynching was another paroxysm of racial violence that sparked national media attention and an investigation by the NAACP—but apparently no comment in any Rice Institute publication or record.[50]

Even seven years later, a white newcomer to Houston was startled when he asked two female Rice Institute students if their sociology professor ever spoke in class about "the Negro problem." The students could make no reply. Not long after, their interrogator confronted the professor, John Willis Slaughter, at a dinner meeting arranged by future Rice trustee Harry Wiess. But when asked why he, a professor of civics and philanthropy, did not talk about race relations in class, Slaughter dismissed the concern. "Problem" sounded too much like conflict, and Houston's white leaders preferred not to give any impression of that in the city.[51]

This studied silence was not the result of total ignorance at Rice about the conditions of Black life after World War I, either in Texas or elsewhere. In 1925, an alumnus who was then attending graduate school in Chicago wrote back to the *Thresher* about the racial integration he saw in the North and challenged his alma mater to become more democratic. Black Texans occasionally appeared on campus in other than laboring roles, as when students from Prairie View State College came to Rice Field in 1925 to watch a football game between the Owls and the Aggies from segregated seats. And prominent members of the Institute's faculty were well aware of the concerns of local civil rights activists through their participation in a segregated network of social service organizations. Yet such contacts did not appreciably weaken what Professor Guérard would later call "the rigidity of castes" in Houston—or at Rice.[52]

In early July 1927, for example, engineering professor L. B. Ryon had proposed to Will Hogg that their urban planning commission (discussed in chapter 3) conduct a new door-to-door survey of the city's "racial distribution." Ryon drew up a questionnaire to administer to Black households and suggested that Rice students could be hired to do the "fieldwork" over the summer. But at a meeting later that year, attended by Hogg and Ryon and called together by Houston's Inter-racial Commission (a group with two boards, one white and one Black), Black leaders voiced concern about the survey. They worried, not without reason, that it would be used in the service of segregation.

Ryon was appointed to "collaborate with the colored committee" and devise the best plan for the survey. According to a report by C. F. Richardson in the *Informer*, the Rice engineer reassured the committee enough that some volunteered to collect the data themselves. Mutual suspicion remained, however. Richardson promised that the *Informer* would "reserve the right to survey the surveyors," and the next year, only two months before Powell's lynching, Black leaders requested a budget for paying their own fieldworkers to conduct a survey. But when Hogg asked Ryon to assess whether it was worth the cost, the professor demurred. While Ryon believed the data collected would be useful from a "social services" point of view and thought the budget was reasonable, it was not crucial to Hogg's city plan: "Doubt whether it could successfully be used for segregation."[53]

Knowing that Hogg's vision of "voluntary segregation" depended on cooperation from Black community leaders, the Forum of Civics (whose executive committee was now chaired by Rice Institute English professor Stockton Axson) did make a modest effort to mitigate tensions in the weeks after Powell's lynching. The August 1928 issue of *Civics for Houston* was focused on "Houston's Colored Citizens." It pointed readers to books on the subject at the Houston Public Library, including Du Bois's *Souls of Black Folk*. And it printed a lengthy cover article by Richardson, who delivered a fiery report about the "shameful, shocking, and startling conditions under which thousands of colored Houstonians are forced to live," even as he also said that it was "next to impossible to give a free and full account in such an article as this."[54]

The incongruity of the article's appearance in *Civics for Houston* (which Richardson described in the *Informer* as a "white monthly magazine") was suggested by its very first page. Richardson opened by noting that Houston's Black professional class included "graduates and post-graduates from some of the leading colleges and universities of the country, including Harvard, Yale, Columbia, Pomona, Illinois, Chicago, Northwestern, Howard, Meharry, Pennsylvania, Fisk, Bishop, Wiley, Prairie View and other institutions of learning." But, for an illustration placed beside that passage, the white editors selected a photograph of a Black woman identified only as "Sunshine Mary at the Old Folk's Home." She was dressed in domestic garb that many white viewers would have connected to their stereotypes of Black women.[55]

Ultimately, the special issue laid bare the conflict between a paternalistic approach to race relations, favored by even the most sympathetic white elites in Houston, and the refusal of Richardson and other "New Negro" activists to abide by old protocols of racial deference—or what one historian has called "the Jim Crow routine." Some white elites in Houston were willing to go as far as Booker T. Washington's vision of white and Black southerners remaining "as separate as the fingers" in "all things purely social," even as they joined in efforts at "mutual progress." Edgar Odell Lovett had even exchanged cordial letters about the Rice Institute's opening with Washington, founder of the Tuskegee Institute, and his close Houston ally, Emmett J. Scott. But Richardson's model of a new kind of assertive activism was less palatable to local whites.[56]

One particularly revealing clash took place in 1929 between Richardson and Slaughter, the Rice Institute professor who later said he preferred not to teach about "the Negro problem." Slaughter belonged to many philanthropic boards in the city throughout the 1920s, including the advisory board of the Houston Negro Hospital, established in 1926 with funding from oilman Joseph S. Cullinan. That gift was praised by Richardson in his *Civics for Houston* article. Yet the governance of the hospital had been a source of controversy from the beginning. It had a Black advisory board (on which Richardson served) whose decisions had to be approved by the white board (on which Professor Slaughter sat).[57]

In 1929, after the latest in a series of disagreements between the two hospital boards, the Black members all resigned in protest. Richardson published a stream of hard-hitting editorials blaming the white board's condescending rule for the break-up. But in reply, Slaughter's allies fired back in the *Gargoyle*, another elite white magazine. The *Gargoyle* praised the white professor for his "unselfish" service, cast doubt on the ability of Black Houstonians to run a hospital themselves, and blamed Richardson most of all: "It is such as he that makes impossible any widespread faith that his race is ready for self-help, much less self-determination."[58]

The whole episode exemplified the fraught relationship between Black civil rights activists and white philanthropists in the years after the first World War. W. E. B. Du Bois himself memorably described such tensions in the same 1920 essay that had denounced the treatment of the Camp Logan mutineers. "My friend," he began, "who is pale and positive, said to me yesterday, as the tired sun was nodding: 'You are too sensitive.'" Du Bois then responded by detailing the heavy weight of moving through a segregated world under the constant gaze of whites, foes and friends alike: "I hurry home through crowds. They mutter or get angry. I go to a mass-meeting. They stare. I go to a church. 'We don't admit niggers!' Or perhaps I leave the beaten track. I seek new work. 'Our employees would not work with you; our customers would object.' I ask to help in social uplift. 'Why—er—we will write you.' I enter the free field of science. Every laboratory door is closed and no endowments are available."

Du Bois conceded to his skeptical white friend that not all of these things happened every day: "Not all each day,—surely not. But now and then—now seldom, now, sudden; now after a week, now in a chain of awful minutes; not everywhere, but anywhere—in Boston, in Atlanta. That's the hell of it." Jim Crow forced Black citizens to spend their lives "looking for insults or for hiding places from them." And at any moment, into the midst of this "mental turmoil," there might break the news of another brutal atrocity against Black citizens: Wilmington in 1898, Waco in 1916, Chicago, Elaine, and Longview in 1919, Tulsa in 1921, or (to cite the example Du Bois himself gave) Houston in 1917.[59]

If such was the lived experience of racial caste for even the most highly educated and well-connected men, such as Du Bois or Richardson, it was likewise so for Black men like Jack Shelton. At times, perhaps, Shelton's long-standing position and fame at Rice Institute may have seemed to provide him some protection from the worst indignities of being Black in a Jim Crow city. Yet Rice, as we have seen, was no hiding place from insults. And although Shelton may not have left behind his own list of those insults, it is easy to surmise the likely contents of such a list.

It might have included hearing jokes like the one the *Thresher* saw fit to publish in 1923, about a Black man hanging from a tree. Surely it would have included the countless times he was referred to with a racist epithet, or sarcastically as "Doc." And perhaps Shelton might also have listed the time, either in 1921 or 1922, when a group of more than twenty robed figures assembled for a well-known yearbook picture of the "Ku Klux Klan of the Rice Institute." Hooded in the official regalia of a resurgent national Klan, the Klansmen posed with their backs against the Rice Field House, right outside one of the main places on campus where Shelton regularly came to do his job.[60]

It is possible that even the Rice "Koo Klucks," as the *Thresher* once called them, saw no contradiction between their activities and expressions of affection for Jack Shelton, known to successive classes of Rice students as "physician, surgeon, rubber, trainer, tailor, Lord High Keeper of the Track, Baseball diamond, and Gridiron." Perhaps, like other white Houstonians, they made special allowances for a trusted, exceptional "negro" who they believed would not (like Richardson) transgress Jim Crow's racial codes. Or did they even consider how the photo might have affected him at all?[61]

The *Thresher* once claimed that Shelton "takes all the gaff from the boys in good spirit and makes a friend of every athlete he trains." Students loved to see "his dusky smile about the athletic fields." It is possible that he did appear to take it all, or most of it, in good spirits. It's also possible, and more probable, that he took very little of it this way. So we should at least wonder, as Paul Laurence Dunbar did, about what Shelton may have concealed behind his seemingly effortless smile, and whether he wore it all the way back to his home—in Freedmen's Town.[62]

"This Little Recognition"

The available evidence suggests that Jack Shelton brought care and skill to the work he did for more than two decades at the Rice Institute. In 1925, the *Campanile* boasted of his "reputation of never having a man that has been taped by him receive a sprained ankle in a football game." In the early 1930s, as Shelton's work shifted away from his early role as a trainer and toward exclusive work as a groundskeeper, he gained a reputation for excellence there, too. The condition of Rice's football and track fields was often praised in the sports columns of Houston papers.[63]

The historical record also shows that many Rice students developed what they viewed as friendly relationships with Shelton, whom they revered for his knowledge of Rice football and his witticisms about the sport. One such quip was printed in a 1931 issue of the Houston *Post-Dispatch.* In response to a question about why Rice could not defeat the squad from Southern Methodist University, Shelton reportedly said, "It ain't no use to try to beat dem church schools in football, 'cause if de Lawd ain't on dere side, whose side can he be on?"[64]

Jack Shelton died of a heart attack in 1937, around the age of fifty. Obituaries were published in the *Thresher* and in both of Houston's major newspapers, which noted that Shelton's "black hands have rubbed out many a muscular kink at Rice in the last quarter of a century" and described him as "faithful," "loyal," and "wise." A large crowd of current and former Rice athletes reportedly attended his funeral. They heard the presiding Black minister remark that Shelton "must have been a good citizen—and a Christian—because so many persons gathered to pay him their last respects."[65]

Clearly, for many who graduated from Rice in those early years, what they thought of when they remembered their time at the Institute was as likely to be "Jack" as it was to be the founder or the school song. In 1928, a Rice sophomore and future student body president wrote a profile of Shelton in the Houston *Post-Dispatch,* which also published his photograph. "Jack has hundreds of friends among the Rice alumni and students," claimed the *Post-Dispatch.* "He has served loyally, and we are glad to give him this little recognition."[66]

The writers for the *Post-Dispatch* may have been more accurate than they knew, for as we have seen, even when giving Shelton a "little recognition," white contemporaries only partially recognized the man. Profiles of Shelton—described by one issue of the *Thresher* as a "genial old darkey" with "kinky hair"—were warped by the pervasive myths, dialect, and epithets that sought to rationalize Jim Crow. The reports of his funeral mirrored the eulogies published almost a decade before to John Sessums Jr., the "faithful" drummer for the Houston Light Guard. But in a biting commentary on the encomia paid to Sessums by whites at that funeral, the Houston *Informer* could not help but notice (in satirical dialect) that the "w'ite jintmen, dident hav mutch ter say bout John sept'n in gards ter his loyalty an 'voshun ter his w'ite folks." As for Sessums, the *Informer* claimed that he was an enigma to many Black Houstonians, hinting at the mistrust that elite white patronage may have cost him—and perhaps Shelton, too—with some in the Black community.[67]

Most profiles of Shelton also showed little understanding of the life that Shelton led beyond the boundaries of Rice Field. A 1933 article in the Houston *Chronicle* at least noted some of his personal history in Bee County, but it concluded that Shelton had found the real meaning of his life at the Institute: "Plans for the future? Ambitions? Jack has few of either," said the writer, except to stay at Rice. The eulogy to Shelton in the *Thresher* claimed that he "had little thought for material gain for, as is common with his people, he possessed little of intrinsic worth."[68]

Such lines flattened Shelton into a stereotype that eventually became as common on southern college campuses as the "faithful mammy" was in the nation as a whole, that of the Black trainer and mascot who lived for nothing else but devotion to white student-athletes. By the time of his death, descriptions of Shelton by white writers mirrored those of Black men who were identified in similar ways with other southern football programs, such as "Blind Jim" Ivy at the University of Mississippi, Bolling Fitzgerald at Vanderbilt University, Garrett Turner at Southern Methodist University, Henry "Doc" Reeves at the University of Texas at Austin, Merrill Collins at the University of Alabama, and Washington "Wash" Randall at Louisiana State University (LSU). Viewed in that context, Rice's treatment of Jack Shelton clearly belonged to a wider set of practices by which white colleges in the South—the institutions where the region's future leaders went to learn and practice the privileges of race—collectively reinforced white supremacy in the nation as a whole.[69]

In fact, after Randall's death, LSU students flocked to his funeral, too, and remembered him in the student newspaper with lines that could just as easily have appeared, verbatim, in the *Thresher* about Shelton. According to the *Reveille,* Randall "seemed to be as much a fixture here as the team itself, attending every game and practice session, caring for the field, lining it off for games, rubbing kinks out of sore muscles, sponging off the hot faces of athletes as they came off the field." He was, according to a white-run Louisiana newspaper, "the most loyal Tiger of them all."[70]

Loyalty, subservience, a comical aloofness to everything except college athletics: These were also the themes of a final reminiscence of Shelton published in 1950 by Paul Hochuli, a Rice alumnus, former football player, and sports columnist for the Houston *Press*. Writing thirteen years after Shelton's death, Hochuli's 1950 article recounted again the story of the rubber's discovery by Coach Arbuckle, recalled his encyclopedic knowledge of Owls football, and described him as an indispensable man at the Institute. After graduation, Hochuli had personally visited Shelton on his sickbed at "his home on Valentine Street" and invited Shelton to attend the funeral of Hochuli's father, a Rice booster. Hochuli remembered being among those former students who attended Shelton's funeral and found themselves "crying without shame." He was "proud to call [Shelton] friend."[71]

And yet, as a student twenty-five years earlier, Hochuli (Class of 1927) had been at the Rice Institute, and even on the staff of student publications like the *Campanile* and the *Rice Owl*, in the very years when Shelton had been the target of some of the most malicious caricatures ever aimed at him by students. Evidence of the "gaff" that Shelton long endured survived even in Hochuli's eulogy, which said that Shelton was once nominated as Rice football's most valuable man at the team's annual banquet: "It was a gag, of course . . . but it wasn't far wrong at that." "To those of us on the team," Hochuli continued, "Jack was 'the cullud gentleman' at times, but mostly 'Nigger Jack,' called that in the same spirit of deep friendship that allows one man to cast aspersions on another."[72]

By then, Shelton was no longer alive to counter Hochuli's particular way of recalling those aspersions. Even if he had been alive, he might not have felt free to disagree. Then too, by 1950 Hochuli's own memory of his student days could have been refracted through complex feelings about Shelton's illness and death and the growing momentum of civil rights activism in the United States after the Second World War. Hochuli's nostalgic recollections of Shelton—much like Captain Baker's earlier eulogy to Mary King as a "devoted friend" and "mammy" of the Old South—may have reassured him that the racial disparities of the New South had not been, and still were not, necessarily experienced by Black "friends" as injustice.[73]

Whatever the case, Hochuli's 1950 sketch of Shelton shows how, long after graduation, white students carried with them the supposed truths about race that they believed they had learned at Rice. Early Owls adapted and reinforced anti-Black stereotypes that were drawn from Lost Cause myths and popular culture in their social lives, publications, performances, and dances. And for some of them, those images fused with the moments they would cherish most about their college days, leaving indelible marks in their yearbooks and their memories.

Partly for that reason, disentangling the institution from the webs of racial caste, when that process began in later years, would ultimately take much more than only a change to the Institute's legal charter, and even more than the presence of more Black men and women on campus in more and different roles. The early Rice Institute had not only kept Black students and faculty out, it had produced and reproduced cultural ideas and practices designed to hold African Americans down. Becoming a desegregating university would thus require later Rice students and leaders to attend more carefully to what Black men and women themselves had to say about their experiences—and to reckon more honestly and fully with the history and consequences of racism on campus and beyond.

5 | REHEARSALS FOR DESEGREGATION

Readers who picked up the Wednesday issue of the *Rice Thresher* on February 12, 1949, saw a picture rarely seen before in the paper's history: the photograph of a Black man on the front page. Centered, above the fold, and just below the masthead was a portrait of Dr. Henry Allen Bullock, head of the Department of Sociology at Prairie View A&M College in nearby Waller County. He had recently come to deliver a speech on the Rice Institute campus.[1]

The subject of Dr. Bullock's lecture was "The Role of the Negro in the South." Invited to Rice by the Forum, a speaker series organized by students and faculty, Bullock told his audience of about ninety people that Black southerners were struggling for "the American creed," the principle that each individual had dignity and rights. That ideal, he said, could be "seen in the Declaration of Independence, in Wilson's Fourteen Points, in the Four Freedoms of Franklin Roosevelt," and it would ultimately prevail. After a historical survey of the Black freedom struggle narrated like a "great drama," with a cast of heroes and villains crossing the stage, Bullock predicted that "the unnatural lines of segregation are soon going to drop 'with a thud.'"[2]

Though African Americans had fought Jim Crow from the beginning, many critical battles in that long struggle came to a head during World War II and its aftermath, the period in which Bullock and his Rice audience then found themselves. Mass Black protests, civil disobedience, and urban rebellion crystallized in the wartime period, heightening civil rights discourse and expectations to unprecedented levels. Relatedly, significant gains in Black political power distinguished the period, owing to court battles begun in Houston to end whites-only primary voting and a Depression-era shift that brought Black voters and influence into a politically dominant Democratic Party. Fueled by wartime gestures meant to stave off disruptions to critical defense industries,

Black labor activists and their allies saw ways forward for the creation of fairer workplaces. Conditions seemed ripe for the lifting of more Black workers into more secure working-class and middle-class positions, as well as into the kinds of political influence that could follow.[3]

For the moment, then, Bullock's bold prediction was also a reasoned and sober one. As the nation emerged from the World War and entered into the Cold War, some white liberals in the United States were turning a more critical eye on the contradictions between American creed and practice. Even at private southern universities such as Duke, Emory, Vanderbilt, and Tulane, white students, faculty, and alumni were beginning to lobby for a loosening of racial restrictions. Racial bars to admission would fall at Washington University in St. Louis by 1952. And at Rice, Bullock's speech came amid a weeks-long campaign by student editors at the *Thresher* to encourage debate about Rice's policy of racial exclusion.

Nothing drew more attention to the injustice of segregated universities in particular than the appearance of scholars like Bullock on their campuses. Black men and women had long occupied campus jobs like Jack Shelton's, even at whites-only schools. But after the war, a rapidly growing Black professional class made up of college graduates and postgraduates "started to come to campus for other reasons," such as to hear a lecture or (as in the case of Bullock, who received his bachelor's degree from Virginia Union University and his doctorate from the University of Michigan) to deliver the lecture. Contacts between white and Black faculty members in professional scholarly settings were also increasing. And if such things were allowed, that begged the question: What else should segregated universities permit?[4]

Postwar civil rights activists were not waiting passively for an answer. By 1949, lawyers for the NAACP had launched successful or promising lawsuits that tested the rights of Black applicants to enter graduate programs at flagship public schools in the South. One landmark suit, *Sweatt v. Painter*, had ties to Houston and would reach the U.S. Supreme Court the year after Bullock spoke at Rice. Four years after that, the Supreme Court's decision in *Brown v. Board of Education* (1954) overturned the precedents supporting segregation in public schools, setting the stage for the later court-ordered integration of state universities in the South.[5]

At Rice, however, and not only at Rice, the "unnatural lines of segregation" did not come down all at once with a thud. There would be no sudden collapse of segregation in 1954, no Black students at Rice for another decade, no tenured Black professors for long after that, and no Black chair of a department (such as Bullock was at Prairie View A&M) for even longer still. Bullock was not only the first Black professor that readers of the *Thresher* had ever seen on its front page, but the last for many issues to come. Bullock's moment at Rice in 1949 is therefore worth lingering over for more than a moment, both for what it reveals about the agency of Black Texans themselves in the earliest efforts to challenge segregation at Rice, and for what it suggests about how long the struggle would be. Tentative rehearsals for desegregation in the decades before the fall of racial bans foretold some of the difficulties that the first generations of Black students at Rice would confront when, in the late 1960s, they eventually arrived.

A New "Negro University"

As historian Melissa Kean has shown, the story of how the South's elite private universities desegregated is "a story about how a group of very powerful people . . . came to do something that many of them did not want to do: admit black students." Facing pressure from northern foundations, the federal government, some faculty and students, and, above all, a civil rights movement led by Black southerners themselves, most white trustees and presidents sought to maintain racial bars at their colleges for as long as they could, taking advantage of their legal status as private organizations to maintain the status quo—both on campus and beyond it. In 1940, for example, when the Houston School Board approached the Rice Institute about using its stadium as a venue for all of its public high-school commencement ceremonies that year, the "School Board was told that Charter restrictions of the Rice Institute prohibited the use of the School's stadium by Colored People." The city would have to find a different venue in which to honor the graduates of the "Colored High Schools."[6]

In many ways, the Rice Institute of the 1940s was even better positioned to resist change than peers like Vanderbilt, Duke, Emory, and Tulane. Small, independently wealthy, and with a limited number of graduate programs focused on engineering and science, Rice also lacked a seminary, law school, or medical school. At other universities in the South, the faculties and students of these kinds of professional schools often had more pressures from within their disciplines to question Jim Crow, as well as more interactions with Black colleagues in their cities.[7]

To be sure, white students, faculty, and staff at Rice never lived in complete racial isolation. Student groups in the 1930s and 1940s hired Black entertainers for social events, as when a young Milt Larkin (later a Houston jazz legend) brought his big band to River Oaks for Rice's annual Archi-Arts Ball in 1937. And Rice Owls sometimes traveled downtown to shows by Black performers like Cab Calloway or the operatic singer Marian Anderson, occasionally returning to campus with new reflections about race relations. But Black entertainers performing for white audiences did not necessarily challenge segregation's norms or displace stereotypical racial shows. At a dance in 1943, a "Negro entertainer" performed an "Old Plantation style" minstrel show in blackface just off campus at the Autry House, Rice's student center at the time.[8]

More revealing of the emerging cracks in Jim Crow's edifice that Bullock identified were examples of interracial competition in athletics. Even before the war, student athletes at Rice competed against, and sometimes with, Black athletes from other schools. In 1932, Rice tennis players put on exhibition matches at Prairie View A&M College, and in 1938, two Rice student-athletes and one Rice coach accompanied an intercollegiate track-and-field team on a tour through Europe on the eve of world war. They traveled with several Black student-athletes, including sprinter Mozelle Ellerbee, an NCAA national champion from the Tuskegee Institute. A photograph of the integrated team appeared in Rice's campus magazine at the time.[9]

Back home, religious clubs at the Rice Institute participated in citywide forums on interracial understanding and invited Black ministers to speak just off-campus at the Autry House, then the student center. In 1943, for example, Dr. L. S. White, a Black minister at the BeBee Tabernacle, addressed the Methodist Student Union on "Race Tension in Houston." According to a detailed *Thresher* summary, White "spoke plainly" to the students on segregation, calling out the indifference of white Houstonians to attacks on Black girls by white men, their use of racist slurs, the humiliation of segregated buses, the denial of voting rights, the displacement of Black communities by white real estate developers in the Fourth Ward, and "the way in which the race of a Negro criminal is played up in the newspapers," while the "race of a white offender is never mentioned." "We know you because you don't care what we think of you and don't try to conceal your thoughts from us," White told the students. "But you don't know us because we Negroes have to hide our feelings or place ourselves at a great disadvantage."[10]

White's 1943 speech gave Rice students a particularly clear view of the concerns of Houston's Black community, which in 1950 would comprise more than one-fifth of the city's booming population. Houston was also home to one of the NAACP's largest and most active southern chapters, led by the indomitable activist Lulu B. White, a graduate of Prairie View. In the early 1940s, Houston's chapter worked with Thurgood Marshall and national NAACP attorneys to defeat Texas's white-primary laws, winning a victory before the U.S. Supreme Court in 1944. The next year, as NAACP lawyers began planning a suit to challenge the exclusion of Black students from the prestigious law school at the University of Texas in Austin, Lulu White recruited Heman Marion Sweatt, a graduate of Houston's Yates High School and Wiley College in Marshall, to serve as a plaintiff.[11]

In February 1946, Heman Sweatt's application to UT's whites-only law school began a long legal battle, as well as a statewide debate about segregated education that spilled onto campus at Rice too. UT officials conceded that the Houstonian was fully qualified to enter the law school, except for his race. But they had no intention of letting him in. Instead, Texas appropriated funds to turn a Black junior college in Houston into the new Texas State University for Negroes (TSUN). The state then hastily created a miniature law school for TSUN that would temporarily operate in an Austin basement before moving to Houston, arguing that this would give Sweatt a "separate but equal" option for his legal education. In early 1947, three UT faculty members were given joint appointments to teach courses in the pop-up program. One of the three was Rice alumnus and future Rice professor and board member Chalmers M. "Hank" Hudspeth, then a twenty-seven-year-old assistant professor of law at Texas.[12]

Rice students learned of the new Houston school's creation in the *Thresher*, which gave its March 6, 1947, editorial an arresting headline: "Negro University." As the editorial noted, some conservatives who spoke in favor of the newly minted TSUN argued openly that it was needed to avoid federally enforced integration across the state. From this fact, observed the *Thresher* wryly, "the impression might be gained that the state intends merely to pay token homage to its moral obligations." The Rice editorialist hoped otherwise, in one of the earliest positions ever taken by the *Thresher* on a civil rights issue. "Let us hope that Texas is at last going to live within the realm of moral justice instead of just going outside of Federal jurisdiction."[13]

The *Thresher* did not go so far as to endorse integration. It hoped, rather, that the new "Negro University" might "provide this minority group with first class tools needed to produce its own leaders." But Sweatt refused to take the state's bait. Although some Black leaders welcomed the creation of a minority-serving state university in Houston and lobbied to secure more resources for it, no one immediately enrolled in its makeshift law school. As Hudspeth told the Associated Press in Austin on March 13, he and the other professors assigned to the basement courses were still waiting for students: "We have had no registrations and no inquiries since Monday." That was because Sweatt's legal team was determined to challenge the idea of "separate but equal" education itself. Sweatt filed a lawsuit against UT president Theophilus Painter for denying him admission, setting his case, *Sweatt v. Painter*, on a path to the U.S. Supreme Court.[14]

Despite the famous case's connections to Houston, Rice Institute officials apparently made no public comments about *Sweatt v. Painter*, even after Hudspeth left Austin to become a faculty member at Rice in the fall of 1947. An initial draft of plans for the inauguration of William V. Houston, Rice's recently hired second president, did include the idea of inviting Theophilus Painter to speak at the ceremony on the subject of "Education in Texas." In January 1947, Houston privately expressed concerns about that idea to the chairman of the Rice board, Harry C. Hanszen, referring obliquely to the fact that Painter might be seen, especially by "those from out of the state," as too "tied up with the recent political difficulties at the University of Texas." President Houston confessed he was "anxious . . . to avoid becoming involved" in those "difficulties," which he never explicitly named, and after discussing the subject with his predecessor, Edgar Odell Lovett, he wondered if it might be best to request a lecture from the president of a private school outside Texas. In the end, Painter did attend Houston's inauguration, but he did not speak.[15]

President Houston's caution about Painter may have indicated a desire to distance Rice from Texas's hardliners on segregation, if for no other reason than to protect the Institute's national reputation. Even so, Houston also kept his distance from the other side in the state's rapidly brewing fight over segregated higher education. In his first years at Rice, he declined several invitations to attend presidential inaugurations at Black universities in the region, including Sweatt's alma mater, Wiley College. In 1948, the newly appointed president of TSUN invited the Rice leader to participate in a panel there on "Possibilities of Inter-College Cooperation on Common Problems." President Houston apparently sent no reply.[16]

Some Rice students, on the other hand, did show an early interest in cooperation with the newest university in town. Rice undergraduates could already look back on some history of interaction with students at TSUN when it was still only the smaller Houston College for Negroes. In 1937, members of the YWCA at the two schools had collaborated to plan a conference for campus "Y" groups from across the region, including delegates from Prairie View and from Tillotson College in Austin. But ten years later, as Sweatt's case began to wend its way through the courts, the initiative for a new and more politically charged series of interracial contacts among students in Houston would arguably begin hundreds of miles away, at a conference for student leaders in Madison, Wisconsin.[17]

The Education of Brady Tyson

In September 1947, delegates from college student-government organizations around the country gathered in Madison to found the National Student Association (NSA). Among the delegates was a Rice history major from San Antonio named Brady Tyson. Tyson returned to Houston in the fall of 1947 energized by the group's constitutional convention, but also with "a great deal of worry and thought." The Madison delegates had fiercely debated a resolution condemning segregated schools, and Tyson was uncertain about where he stood on the issue.[18]

Tyson reported his concerns in an October column in the *Thresher*, where he was then an assistant editor. "I believe that segregation is morally wrong," Tyson began, "but that it is deeply rooted in the prejudices of the people of Texas, and I consider the people of Texas the salt of the earth in spite of this." Despite his felt responsibility to work for change, Tyson concluded that, until "the people of Texas" were ready (by which he clearly meant white Texans), he was bound to abide by Jim Crow laws and customs. He voted against the NSA resolution. Still, Tyson was troubled by his vote. "In a time when the segregated school system of Texas is under attack," he wrote, alluding to Sweatt's case against UT, "it would be well for us to re-examine our own views." Tyson invited students to send in their own reactions to his vote for publication in a new *Thresher* column: "Readers Write."[19]

Tyson heard quickly from two students who told the *Thresher* they supported change. "Since, so far as I am aware, there are no facilities for graduate study in the sciences open to Negroes in Texas, why should not Negroes be admitted here," asked Ward Whaling. June Davis agreed, citing her familiarity with Vassar College, "where Negroes were admitted and treated exactly as whites, including Negro girls and white girls rooming together." A third student, Clarke Foster, wrote that he was raised to believe in the Bill of Rights, but "I have trouble reconciling what I learned in school to what I read in the papers," including "the refusal of the Texas University to admit a negro to its law school."[20]

In early November, Brady Tyson received a new commission from the Student Council. Along with Jimmy Meyers, he was "delegated to meet representatives from the Texas State College [*sic*] for Negroes to discuss the organization of the NSA." By December, when Tyson and Meyers were named as delegates to an NSA meeting at Southern Methodist University in Dallas, the Rice students were preparing to "present a plan whereby a regional survey of comparative Negro and white educational opportunities in Texas and Oklahoma will be made." At SMU, officials gave special permission for an "inter-racial meeting" on their campus, and Rice delegates attended sessions alongside students from TSUN. Tyson served on a committee about educational opportunity gaps.[21]

Tyson was not the only Rice student becoming increasingly curious about the disparities between Black and white schools in the Jim Crow South. In November 1947, *RI: Rice Institute Magazine*, edited by senior Fance Frank, opened its first issue of the year with two essays on the question, "Should Negroes Be Admitted to Rice?" Frank answered, "Yes," presenting statistics to show that "education for the majority of children in the state is a farce and a disgrace. And the negro children get the least share." Surveying expenditures on Texas public schools, she found that 65 percent of Black children were taught in classrooms that only received $200 to $1,000 a year, while only 8 percent of white children were in that low-spending bracket. Attributing the plight of Black Texans to poor educational opportunity, Frank concluded that a "logical place to begin correcting the situation is at Rice and other colleges."[22]

The magazine also published an opposing column by Rice student Bob King, who left no doubt where he stood: "I believe in segregation." Basing his arguments on false pseudoscientific myths about "racial ties and heredity," King defended the continuation of separate schools for Black students, and he asked why Rice students would want to invite the "social dilemma" of integration. Raising the specter of interracial mixing to defend the status quo, King asked, "are you girls willing to dance with tall good-looking colored boys?"[23]

King's essay was an ugly example of racial prejudice, but it was followed two months later by a remarkable sign of the ferment on campus that year. King later remembered that, in January 1948, Brady Tyson invited him and Fance Frank to go with him downtown to talk with an African American businessman, the "president of the Watch Tower Life Insurance Co." "The purpose of the trip," King recalled, "was to influence me." The businessman, Tyson, and Frank all tried to persuade King that segregation was wrong and even contended that there was "no reason why negroes and whites should not date each other if they so wished." King conceded that the executive was "a very fine man," but he still left the meeting unconvinced. Racial integration, he said, would be "disrespectful to our Maker."[24]

The downtown trip may have failed to convert King, but it did offer a tantalizing glimpse of new contacts between Rice students and Houston's activist Black community. The Watchtower Life Insurance Company, headquartered in the Third Ward, had been founded by Thornton McNair Fairchild, son of the early Emancipation Park trustee whose family owned land by the Gregory Institute decades before. By 1947, the company was led by Charles A. Shaw, a Howard University graduate and Army veteran who arrived in Houston in 1932.

Formerly an official in the Atlanta NAACP and the National Negro Business League, Shaw was now prominent in Houston as a civil rights activist, businessman, philanthropist, and frequent public speaker. In 1943, for example, Shaw spoke on a panel alongside Dr. H. A. Bullock from Prairie View (the professor who later spoke at Rice) about "The Negro in Post-War America." Though unnamed by King, Shaw had to be the man that he was taken to see.[25]

Tyson had good reason to bring his classmates to Shaw, a man skilled at speaking on race relations in a variety of settings. In February 1949, as part of a series of events hosted by the NAACP for Negro History Week, Shaw would speak on a panel about "Negro education" alongside Heman Sweatt. That same month he appeared on a Brotherhood Week panel about civil rights with Rice's own Hank Hudspeth. How Tyson learned of the insurance executive is unknown—perhaps from newspapers or a public event, perhaps through his conversations about the NSA with Black students at the new state university in the Third Ward, or perhaps even through a professor like Hudspeth. Whatever the case, the contact better informed the Rice student about the active Black community that stood behind Sweatt's challenge to segregation.[26]

In the 1948–49 school year, Tyson (now a senior) resolved to keep a spotlight on the color line, both in his role as a member of the Forum committee and as the new editor-in-chief of the *Thresher,* which he turned into a twice-weekly paper. Tyson's staff covered that fall's U.S. presidential election with special attention to the candidates' views on civil rights. On October 2, 1948, days after the Texas Supreme Court denied Heman Sweatt's appeal in his case against UT, Tyson ran an editorial blasting state leaders as out of step with the times. Then, later that month, Tyson's reporters began a multi-issue series comparing educational institutions in Houston. The series included stories on St. Thomas University, St. John's School, the University of Houston, and, on November 20, a full-page report on the history and prospects of TSUN, "a new school with deep roots."[27]

The writer of the report, Abraham Nad, noted that the hastily created state school had started with temporary structures and only one permanent building, named after Thornton M. Fairchild. But more construction was coming, and the halls were already "filled with conversation" between classes, suggesting Nad had visited the new university's campus for his report. He concluded with admiration for the nearly three thousand Black students across town, many of them military veterans, who were "trying to make the most of opportunities that are just now beginning to open up to them."[28]

Tyson's *Thresher* saved its most explosive article that semester for December: an interview by student reporter George McCelvey with Heman Sweatt himself, conducted inside Sweatt's home in Houston. "Mr. Sweatt contends there is no equality in a system of segregated education," McCelvey wrote. Soft-spoken and affable, Sweatt gave updates about his impending case before the U.S. Supreme Court and shared details about Black southerners who had been admitted to graduate schools in other states. He told the *Thresher* there was a moral issue involved in his exclusion from Texas's law school and concluded, much like H. A. Bullock would in his speech at Rice a few weeks later, that the struggle to end segregation was "purely in line with our democratic ideals."[29]

McCelvey's conversation with Sweatt laid a fuse that was lit two weeks later, when the *Thresher* published an outraged letter from Coy W. Mills, the principal of Houston's Jefferson Davis High School. As a Rice alumnus from the Class of 1925 and the current parent of a Rice student, Mills demanded to know the purpose of the interview with Sweatt and echoed Bob King's fears with a final, inflammatory question: "What will be your attitude if Sweatt or another Negro is admitted to Rice and tries to date the Co-eds, perhaps your best girl friend or sister?"[30]

In reply, assistant editor Robert McIlhenny published a statement in boldface that avoided Mills's final question but took what looked to be a straightforward position on the question of whether African Americans should be admitted to the university: "Any student admitted to either the graduate or undergraduate school here should not expect and should not receive special privileges, restrictions, or attention because of nationality, race[,] creed, or political belief. Similarly, all students who apply for admission to the Institute should be judged equally and solely upon scholastic qualification and capabilities."[31]

Three days later, the Houston *Post* carried a story with the headline, "Rice Editor Seeks Admission of Negroes." It included an announcement about Bullock's upcoming speech to the Forum. And it quoted Tyson claiming that the *Thresher*'s editorial calling for an end to racial restrictions in Rice admissions represented the view of "about everybody I know on the campus."[32]

Over the next month, a number of students loudly objected to Tyson's assessment of campus opinion. Tyson and Mills exchanged another round of sparring letters, sparking more coverage in the Houston press. The *Thresher* also published letters supporting its position, including from writers who reported on their positive interactions with Black servicemen in the armed forces during the war.[33]

Two of the most revealing letters Tyson received were ones that he did not publish. The first came from Lulu B. White, executive secretary of the Houston NAACP, who wrote "to commend" the student editor. The other came on Watchtower Life Insurance Company letterhead from Charles A. Shaw, who remembered Tyson well. "It has not been my privilege to see you for several months," Shaw wrote, "and on several occasions I have thought of you and of the pleasant contacts it was my privilege to have with you and your friends." He hoped that "during the New Year our contacts may be more frequent." The letters from White and Shaw are intriguing signs of the roles that Black Houstonians themselves had played in the education of Brady Tyson and like-minded students at Rice, an education that would continue with Bullock's lecture on campus a few weeks later.[34]

A more discouraging lesson came, though, on February 14, when Rice president William V. Houston wrote a letter to the *Thresher* that summarily dismissed the debate over integrating Rice by pointing to its 1891 charter, just as the Institute had done before he arrived when refusing the use of its stadium for Black high-school graduations in 1940. "The Rice Institute was founded and chartered specifically for white students," President Houston now told the *Thresher*. "The question of the admission of negroes is therefore not one for administrative consideration, and the discussion in this connection is entirely academic."[35]

The blunt response made clear the official attitude at the Rice Institute in 1949. Publicly, administrators and trustees claimed forcefully that the charter was an insuperable obstacle to change. Whatever they said privately remained off the record. But several months after Houston's letter to the editor, Brady Tyson would receive one final lesson about the institution's resistance to change, delivered in the very last moments of his education at Rice. In the spring of 1949, as Tyson was waiting in line to pick up his class ring, an unnamed administrator approached him with a withering message. "You have done more damage to Rice," the official told the graduate, "than any student in history." Forty years later, Tyson could still remember the stinging rebuke.[36]

The "Counter-Stimulation"

Official discouragement did not end Rice students' desire to learn more about the civil rights movement swirling around them in postwar Houston. In April 1949, Heman Sweatt was invited to address a Rice group at the First Unitarian Church near campus. The next year, Methodist students invited R. O'Hara Lanier, first president of the Texas State University for Negroes, to speak. He was followed by a Rice lecture from TSUN art professor and muralist John T. Biggers. Rice faculty occasionally visited Prairie View A&M, too, or vice versa. Contacts with students at local Black universities also continued, most notably in the Texas Intercollegiate Student Association (TISA), which voted to admit TSUN in 1951.[37]

President Houston's administration, meanwhile, remained fully committed to a segregated university while avoiding conflicts on the matter with those who could imagine a different way. On the one hand, unlike at some peer institutions, administrators and trustees at Rice did not go out of their way to bar contacts between faculty or students and African Americans. In 1953, TISA hosted its fifth annual convention on the Rice Institute campus, with at least one Black delegate in attendance. President Houston issued a statement welcoming the TISA delegates, and a musical show featuring dancers from Rice, Baylor, and Texas Southern University (TSU, the newly renamed TSUN) was held on the TSU campus in conjunction with the meeting. On the other hand, whenever students at Rice or elsewhere pressed on the issue of integration, they hit the same wall. Again and again, writes Melissa Kean, "Rice simply removed itself from the debate with an appeal to its charter language."[38]

Across town, Black students writing for the TSU *Herald* highlighted the problem with that approach in an editorial published in 1949, the week after President Houston's letter to Brady Tyson: "The students at Rice, and more specifically The Thresher, have not attempted to attack the legality of the situation, rather the morality," noted the *Herald*, "and that, to our way of thinking, is the way in which the lasting desirable effect will come." The TSU students also noted that eight Black students had recently enrolled in the School of Social Work at Washington University in St. Louis, "not because of the charter, but in spite of the charter."[39]

At the same time, the *Herald*'s careful parsing of student opinion at Rice ("students at Rice, and more specifically The Thresher") suggested an awareness that "executive sentiment" was not the only obstacle to change at the Institute. Social events in the period showed the persistence of racial stereotypes that had deep roots. On January 19, 1949, in the middle of the controversy at the *Thresher*, the paper published on its front page a photograph of two female students dancing in blackface for an annual melodrama hosted by the Elizabeth Baldwin Literary Society. And after Tyson was quoted saying in 1948 that the majority of students he knew supported integration, another student (Coy Mills's son) fired back in the Houston *Post* that "Mr. Tyson certainly must know very few people on the campus."[40]

Indeed, the authors of a brief history of the Class of 1949, shared at that year's senior banquet, hinted that Tyson's "caustic regime" at the *Thresher* had inspired a notable backlash: "the negro situation became acute, and the liberal student body received a counter-stimulation." In the larger context of American society, too, the postwar civil rights movement increasingly faced a fierce movement of "counter-stimulation" from diehard segregationists. Though Sweatt ultimately succeeded in winning his case before the Supreme Court in 1950, the court's decision in *Brown v. Board of Education* four years later met with massive resistance from white southerners.[41]

The depth of racism at Rice may be gauged partly by a *Thresher* survey of 522 students and faculty in 1957. Significantly, the poll showed that 171 respondents now favored Rice's immediate integration, with another 150 open to its "eventual" integration. But 197 still "opposed integration at any time." That fall, barely a week after a showdown over integration at Central High School in Little Rock, Arkansas, students at the Rice-Stanford football game hung a large Confederate flag from the student section at Rice Stadium, brandishing what had by then become a ubiquitous symbol of resistance to integration across the South. And the next month, at a Forum debate on segregation, a student arguing against integration again cited the dangers invoked by King and Mills almost a decade before: "social mixing and miscegenation." A home video of a pep rally at Rice from sometime in the 1950s captured a female student jumping up on the shoulders of two male students just outside Fondren Library, a small Confederate battle flag clenched between her teeth.[42]

Clearly, a decision to enroll Black students in 1949 or 1957 would not have immediately made the Institute a welcoming place for all. Even Rice students who supported integration still had only a partial grasp of the issues that would face Black students if and when official policy did finally change. In one comment to the Houston *Chronicle,* for example, Brady Tyson expressed doubt that there were many Black students in Texas who would be "qualified" for admission to Rice's graduate school, even if the racial bar were dropped.[43]

Birdelle Ransom, a thirty-four-year-old mother of three who lived in the Third Ward and was studying at the Texas State University for Negroes, seized on Tyson's wrongheaded comment in a typed letter to Tyson the next day. "You should get to know us better," Ransom said, adding: "I have friends of colour who have degrees from Michigan State, The University of Chicago, The University of Colorado, Cornell, Purdue, and others too numerous to mention. My neighbor, Jimmie Law, is studying at Yale. Being a senior within the hallowed walls of Rice, you ought to know that geography is no criterion of intellect. I'm just a sophomore and I know that."[44]

Still, it would take many "within the hallowed walls of Rice" much longer to learn what Ransom already knew. In future years, Black students at Rice would often confront questions from others, sometimes spoken and sometimes unspoken, about their ability to meet the school's high academic standards.

Indeed, well before the admission of the first Black students, the question of "qualification" had a way of popping up in campus discussions about integration, even when the well-meaning intended to tamp the question down. In 1953, when TISA delegates meeting on Rice's campus elected TSU student Lloyd Riley as the group's parliamentarian, the *Thresher* took pains to say, "There is no doubt that he is qualified for the job. . . . His election serves as a symbol of recognition of ability regardless of other factors, and should not be taken as a lean-over-backwards policy to the Negro race."[45]

Such comments suggest that, even when the ideas of dogmatic segregationists could be overcome, those working for desegregation at Rice would face additional trials. These included the pernicious but long-lived myth that Black students must somehow be less qualified than others to enter Rice. Also harmful was the belief that no one should do anything perceived as "leaning over backwards" to support Black students once they arrived. When Rice eventually began in the 1960s to remedy its long history of racial exclusion, these and other obstacles to full inclusion would still loom large. And in the years to come, variations on Ransom's 1948 admonishment of Brady Tyson—"You should get to know us better"—would become a recurring refrain for the Black students, faculty, and staff who struggled to make Rice a place of belonging for all.

III

THE SECOND FOUNDING

6 | CHARTER TRIALS

A new era in the history of Rice University—a second founding of the institution—began in 1963 when Raymond Lewis Johnson, who graduated that year with highest honors from the University of Texas at Austin, decided to pursue a doctoral degree in mathematics from Rice.

Johnson's illustrious academic career began in the small town of Alice, Texas, where he started elementary school by skipping ahead to the third grade. Though he attended segregated schools throughout childhood, Johnson entered Alice's newly integrated high school just after the Supreme Court's landmark 1954 decision in *Brown v. Board of Education*. An influential math teacher there encouraged Johnson to apply to college at the University of Texas at Austin (UT), where he enrolled as a National Merit Scholar in 1960.

In Austin, Johnson entered what he later recalled as a "strange world" precariously suspended "between integration and segregation." Though admissions had been integrated for almost a decade, Texas was not yet "a desegregated university." Black students lived in separate dormitories on a still segregated campus, and a powerful mathematics professor, Robert Lee Moore, was known as a diehard white supremacist. But Johnson found a more supportive mentor in Dr. Howard B. Curtis, who had also taught Johnson's high-school math teacher. Curtis received his mathematics PhD from Rice in 1958. As an alumnus, he knew that in 1963 the Rice University board had at last declared its intention to remove racial barriers to admission. Johnson applied to Rice's Department of Mathematics for graduate study, received a favorable reply from the department, and headed to Houston that summer expecting to begin his degree.[1]

In Houston, though, Johnson found another strange world also stuck between segregation and integration. As the fall 1963 semester approached, Johnson learned that Rice University was embroiled in a lawsuit over the school's racially discriminatory 1891 charter. Two alumni had intervened in the suit that summer in a brazen attempt to prevent Rice's integration. Johnson was informed that, until these legal issues were resolved, he would not be allowed to enroll formally as a graduate student. Instead, he would have to be employed in the math department as a research assistant.

For Johnson, the news came as a surprise and a disappointment. Since his enrollment at UT, a mass movement for civil rights had won some significant gains, though not without struggle. Beginning in 1960, sit-ins led by college students had challenged segregation at lunch counters, restaurants, and other public spaces. In 1961, President John F. Kennedy had issued Executive Order 10925 banning racial discrimination in federal employment, and the following year, the Kennedy administration backed James Meredith's application to integrate the University of Mississippi in the face of violence from local white supremacists and intransigent state leaders. Efforts by Black students to integrate other public universities in the Jim Crow South had helped to push an initially reluctant Kennedy administration toward more affirmative support of civil rights.

On June 11, 1963, just nine days before a group of alumni filed their lawsuit to slow or stop efforts to integrate Rice University, a television address by Kennedy had connected civil rights and the desegregation of higher education to the nation's Cold War struggle against communism abroad. Commenting on the registration of the first Black students at the University of Alabama that same day, which had required the president to dispatch the National Guard to its campus, Kennedy described the continuation of racial injustice one hundred years after the Emancipation Proclamation as a "moral crisis" facing the whole nation. "Today," Kennedy noted, "a Negro is attending a state-supported institution [of education] in every one of our 50 states, but the pace is very slow." With the March on Washington later that summer, thousands of civil rights activists ratcheted up the pressure on Kennedy's administration and the nation to pick up the pace.[2]

Based on the momentum of the national civil rights movement and Johnson's positive relationship with Dr. Curtis, who was spending a sabbatical year at Rice, the gifted young mathematician had been hopeful that Rice would offer him something more than the grudging acceptance he and other Black students experienced in Austin. But the sudden change in his status for the fall of 1963 was his first indication that Rice might not be so different from UT after all. "Jim Crow may have seen its twilight," Johnson later said of those days, "but there were plenty of people who wanted to keep the sun up just a little while longer."[3]

Johnson would not finally be admitted to Rice as a doctoral student until 1964. The first Black undergraduates matriculated at Rice one year after that. By then, those steps had already been taken not only at formerly segregated public schools across the South like the University of Alabama, the University of Mississippi, the University of South Carolina, and the University of Houston, but also at Vanderbilt University, Tulane University, and every other private southern university that Rice's senior administrators considered to be a model or peer. Moreover, Johnson's enrollment at Rice was greeted with the opposite of fanfare or celebration. It was not even reported in the Houston press until months after it occurred.[4]

What was it like, then, to become one of the first Black students at one of the last universities to integrate? Why did it take so long for the sun to begin setting on Jim Crow at Rice? What trials did Black students such as Johnson face in that protracted, twilit process? And in the years that followed Rice's first steps toward desegregation, what, if any, would be the longer-term consequences of the university's peculiar and halting start?

Maintaining the Bar

Back in the late 1950s, as Raymond Johnson began attending an integrated high school in Alice, Texas, federal prohibitions against racial discrimination in hiring and contracts were placing new pressure on the Rice Institute's racial policies. Simultaneously, the Supreme Court's decision in *Brown v. Board of Education* was inspiring new resistance to integration by many white southerners, including in Texas.

At Rice, President William V. Houston and the board showed little desire for proactive change and continued to rely on the Institute's charter language as a rationale for the status quo. As Melissa Kean notes, many leaders of elite private southern universities claimed to believe that integration, if and when it came, needed to be managed carefully by the region's "intelligent white men." In practice, private southern universities, including Rice, "followed rather than led." In 1958, for example, at the instruction of board member H. Malcolm Lovett, a secretary at Rice wrote to Girard College in Pennsylvania to ask about a "suit that was filed against your college with reference to accepting negroes." Girard had managed to fight off a challenge to its own racially restrictive charter, and Lovett wanted to know "on what basis you were successful in maintaining your school 'For White Male Orphans.'"[5]

A shift came when Houston stepped down as president in 1960, and a new president arrived at Rice at a time of rapid change, beginning with the change of the institution's name from the Rice Institute to Rice University. President Kenneth S. Pitzer, a noted chemist with a national reputation, was recruited to Rice from the University of California at Berkeley, and he later recalled agreeing to helm the newly christened university only on the understanding that Rice would soon abandon a racial bar in admissions that he considered "ridiculous."[6]

Pitzer's insistence on that point was motivated partly by pragmatism. He knew attracting a top-flight faculty to Houston would require integration. Nondiscrimination clauses in research grants from national foundations and the federal government were also a growing concern; in fact, the transfer of Pitzer's own federal research grants to Rice forced the board, in October 1961, to openly discuss the possibility of ending racial restrictions for the first time. Funding considerations weighed especially heavily on the board, which was simultaneously in the process of trying to bring the National Aeronautics and Space Administration (NASA) to Houston.

Pitzer urged "active attention to a solution" and left his earliest meetings with the board convinced it was just a matter of time and logistics before integration began. He must have been encouraged, too, by a poll run by students in December 1961. Three-quarters of the student body participated in the vote, which showed support for "desegregation" by a roughly two-to-one majority among students and by an eight-to-one majority among faculty.[7]

Yet there were also indications that the road ahead would not be smooth. A few weeks before the 1961 referendum, history professor Louis A. Galambos published an opinion column in the *Thresher* lamenting apathy on campus and the dearth of serious discussion among students about segregation at Rice. But even his modest proposal—that professors bring up the subject more often with their students—was denounced as "an inflamatory [*sic*] crusade" by his senior colleague Andre Bourgeois, a distinguished professor of French. In a retort to Galambos published in the *Thresher*, Bourgeois raised the familiar specter of racial mixing often cited by segregationists in the past. Students, he suggested, should be polled on the question of whether they would be willing "to eat your meals with colored students" or "to sleep with colored students in your rooms," and he added that students and professors "who do not like the way things are on this campus should have the good taste of going back to where they came from." A senior undergraduate likewise criticized Galambos's claim that the integration question was a "fundamental issue" for everyone at Rice: "I have no Negro friends or relatives that want to get into Rice," said the student, "why should I care?"[8]

Although the results of the student-and-faculty poll that December suggest that such views were increasingly in the minority on campus, they also give some sense of the ideas motivating the 36 percent of the students polled who still firmly opposed "desegregation." What students meant by that term also varied widely. An editorial by the *Thresher* told students the poll was about "desegregation," not "integration," before referring to a recent student protest of segregated dormitories and campus facilities at the University of Texas. The *Thresher* hoped that a vote for "desegregation" by Rice students would send a signal of support to the students campaigning for social integration in Austin. Even so, other students may have understood the subject of the poll as something far more limited than full inclusion. "We don't want to recruit Negro students," the Student Association president told the *Thresher* in explanation of the resolution put to students for a vote, "but we don't want to bar Negro students—we just don't want to make any judgements based solely on race."[9]

Even apart from the poll results, it is clear that campus opinion at the end of 1961 remained heterogeneous. On the one hand, a small minority of students and faculty had actively joined or openly supported civil rights protests in Houston, including downtown sit-ins led by Texas Southern University students in 1960. Two Black student leaders in the local sit-in movement, Curtis Graves and Otis King, even visited the Rice campus in April 1960 to participate in a student forum. On the other hand, opposition to the sit-ins and to integration at Rice also survived on campus, along with many of the cultural practices that had long made the Rice campus inhospitable for Black people.[10]

On November 8, 1961, for example, President Pitzer received a letter from a student officer at Hanszen College, an all-men's residential hall, inviting him to attend a recently inaugurated tradition: the second annual "Hanszen Minstrel," to be held in Hamman Hall at that weekend's homecoming events. Pitzer declined the invitation to the show, which featured a large chorus of Hanszen students in blackface singing tunes like "Dixie" and "Pick a Bale of Cotton." But a photograph in the 1962 *Campanile* captured what the president missed. It showed a group of students on stage, their faces blackened with thick paint, over the caption "Hanszen proceeds with deliberate speed"—a mocking allusion to the famous integration order in the Supreme Court's second *Brown v. Board* ruling from 1955.[11]

Another indication of the roadblocks ahead appeared a few months later in February 1962, when the Rice Alumni Association hosted an invitation-only lecture on physics by former president William V. Houston in Hamman Hall, the same space where Hanszen students had recently performed in blackface. When several honor students from Texas Southern University showed up to attend the lecture, to which students from other area schools had been invited, the Alumni Association refused to admit the Black students into the event.[12]

Incidents like these suggest why Pitzer was anxious to change Rice's policies; more such episodes, he knew, would further embarrass the university. In light of the sit-in movement locally and high-profile civil rights cases nationally, Pitzer and other administrators also knew that more direct challenges to segregation at Rice certainly would come. Indeed, just weeks before Black students showed up at former President Houston's lecture only to be turned away, a Kenyan-born senior at Texas Southern named James N. Hinga had written to ask for an application for graduate study in mathematics at Rice.

Hinga was mailed an application as requested, but because his letter mentioned being an "African student," he was advised by the registrar, M. V. McEnany, that "the charter of Rice University places some restrictions of a racial nature on our student body." McEnany added that "a legal review of the interpretation of these provisions is currently underway, but its outcome cannot be anticipated at this time." A little more than a year before another young Black mathematician would turn his sights on Rice, it was clear that the bar to Black students remained firmly in place.[13]

"Exasperating Timidity"

In February 1962, McEnany was correct in telling James Hinga that "a legal review" of the charter was then underway. The previous September, board chairman George R. Brown had asked the university's lawyers to prepare an opinion on the legal validity of the racial restriction in Rice's founding documents. Then, in October 1961, board member Newton Rayzor made a motion, approved by the trustees, that instructed the university's attorneys to explore all the "ways and means" available to adopt "broader policies of admission" and make recommendations accordingly.[14]

Since then, the trustees had moved very slowly. Not until February 1963, a full seventeen months after Rayzor's motion, did the board file its famous lawsuit seeking permission from the Texas state attorney general to change the Rice Charter by lifting racial bars to admission and charging tuition. Though it had been contemplated for months, the suit was also the first public statement the board had ever made announcing an intention to alter its racial policy. In contrast to segregationist leaders at state-run schools in places like Mississippi and Alabama, Rice's trustees eschewed any dramatic public performance of blocking the schoolhouse door. But as Kean notes, with the exception of Brown and Rayzor, "there was no real appetite for desegregation among the Rice trustees, no eagerness to step forward and make what they believed would be an unpopular change." English professor Alan Grob, who was hired in 1961, would later recall that in a moment calling for boldness, Rice leaders had shown an "exasperating timidity."[15]

In retrospect, the board's reluctance to move quickly can be seen even in the fateful decision to file a lawsuit that not everyone believed was legally necessary. From the beginning, Pitzer had suggested to the trustees that the charter's seventh article already gave them power to determine criteria for admissions. And they had done so already in ways that departed from other provisions in the indenture containing William Marsh Rice's founding gift.[16]

After all, the indenture had named as its beneficiaries the "white inhabitants of the City of Houston, and state of Texas." Yet the Rice Institute had admitted non-Texans from its very earliest years, including students of Latin American and Asian descent, a point also made by Galambos in his letter to the *Thresher*. Given this, Pitzer later recalled asking, "Why sue the Attorney General over this question? Why not just admit Negroes next year?"[17]

The idea of proceeding without a suit had a powerful opponent, however, in board member H. Malcolm Lovett, the son of Rice's first president. Lovett's opinions carried considerable weight. As an alumnus whose school career dated back to the days when Jack Shelton was still wrapping ankles for student-athletes like himself, Lovett also showed a greater willingness than Brown, Rayzor, or Pitzer to defer to the racial sensibilities of white locals and alumni who viewed Rice as an elite regional school. Lovett was a lawyer with Baker and Botts, the firm that represented Rice, and so his views on legal strategy were usually considered decisive by the rest of the board.[18]

In September 1961, it was Lovett who relayed to Brown the opinion of his firm. Because Rice was a private institution, he argued, the racial restriction in the charter was legally "valid." Citing (among other precedents) a decision by the Supreme Court in the case of Girard College, the private institution in Philadelphia whose founding documents restricted admission to "poor white male orphans," Lovett and his colleagues concluded that the Fourteenth Amendment did not protect individuals from discrimination by a private school. They therefore recommended that the board file a lawsuit in district court, naming the state attorney general as defendant, "seeking authority" to disregard the charter restriction before acting. The lawyers added—with prescience, as it turned out—that in such a case, "Persons who were for or against the proposal might intervene as friends of the court."[19]

The board took a year to weigh and explore that idea before endorsing the lawsuit plan in September 1962. In December, a federal judge in a different case ruled that Tulane University's own racially restrictive founding documents were no longer legally enforceable. Yet Lovett counseled the board to stay with its original strategy. That winter, a frustrated Pitzer drafted a letter to Lovett, who served as liaison between the board and the law firm, urging that the suit be immediately filed. "It is not my purpose to re-open the question whether court approval should be sought but rather to urge promptness in following the chosen path," Pitzer wrote, adding, "Even a day of unnecessary delay should be avoided." Nonetheless, the suit to change the Rice charter was not filed until February 21, 1963, one month after the first Black students at Tulane had registered for classes.[20]

The board's determination to pursue the matter in court (instead of acting as it had in earlier decisions to disregard geographical restrictions in the charter) had the effect of elongating the timetable of integration. It had other consequences, too. For the duration of the suit, trustees and administrators remained highly alert to anything on campus that pressed issues related to desegregation or racial justice—attention that they perceived as damaging to the suit in the court of public opinion.

For example, on the same day the charter-change lawsuit was filed, student Mike Jaffe of the Rice Forum wrote the Rev. Dr. Martin Luther King Jr. to ask him to postpone a planned visit to the Rice campus, reportedly after being told by university officials that King's visit could interfere with the litigation. Later that year, lawyer and future congresswoman Barbara Jordan was invited to a residential college to address the Young Democrats, but she was brought onto campus unannounced. King never came.[21]

Of all the people affected by the board's chosen path, none would be more directly impacted than Raymond Johnson, who was completing his final semester at the University of Texas when the charter suit was filed and announced. Johnson's advisor at Texas, Dr. Howard B. Curtis, a Rice PhD alumnus, encouraged him to go to Rice for graduate study in mathematics that fall. The Mathematics Department at Rice, led by Chairman Jim Douglas, was impressed by Johnson's academic record and accepted his application. Johnson arrived in Houston that summer for a pre-matriculation "boot camp" for graduate students and moved into temporary housing at Baker College, where he was assigned a white roommate who became a lifelong friend.[22]

At least some people at Rice had foreseen developments like these in the summer after the charter lawsuit was filed. In a January meeting of deans, college heads, and department chairs on charter changes and "racial matters," the academic leaders were told by Pitzer that "if racial restrictions [were] removed, then [they would be] removed completely." Although the "expectation is small numbers & mostly graduate students living off campus in near future," the president told the group that "some undergrad & residents can be expected."[23]

An article in the *Rice Thresher* on February 27 likewise noted that, although undergraduate students were not expected in the fall, graduate admissions were conducted through a different, advisor-led process, and "it is possible that a department which had not filled its quota by September could accept a Negro student." A Rice spokesman also told the *Thresher* that the removal of racial restrictions, when it came, would apply to "'all areas,' including residence and athletics."[24]

Malcolm Lovett and the university's lawyers were not happy, nevertheless, when they learned that Johnson had arrived on campus before a ruling had been issued in the charter suit. Lovett, in particular, became convinced that Douglas and Curtis had overreached their authority by soliciting an application from Johnson and then admitting him. At some point between February and June, a solution was found that was apparently acceptable to the Mathematics Department. While awaiting the court's ruling, Johnson would be employed as a research assistant and paid through a government grant, instead of enrolled as a student. He would also, meanwhile, have the ability to audit courses. After a board meeting on June 26, 1963, Newton Rayzor spoke with George R. Brown and Lovett about the proposed plan, which Brown readily supported. But according to Rayzor, Lovett "differed with him very sharply."[25]

Just how sharply Lovett disapproved of Johnson's arrival became clear in a confidential letter composed by Rayzor to Pitzer the next day. "A rather serious little episode has developed over the colored gentleman on the campus by the name of Johnson," Rayzor wrote. Lovett was troubled by his perception that Douglas and Curtis had conspired to bring Johnson to campus prematurely as a student. He and the lawyers handling the case claimed that this could create a "bad impression" among alumni, the community, and the attorney general's office that the board had "not waited for the results of the law suit but have taken it upon ourselves arbitrarily to obliterate the color line."

Rayzor, himself an accomplished attorney, felt that this concern about damage to the lawsuit was making a "mountain out of a mole-hill," but he also shared another complaint from Lovett about Johnson that Rayzor found more difficult to dismiss. "Another thing which is very troublesome—and I think this point is very embarrassing to us all—is that this man has been given the run of the facilities on the University campus," including a room at Baker, a locker, and "permission to use the swimming pool and eating facilities." According to Rayzor, Malcolm Lovett had "almost become obcessed [*sic*] with the imaginary seriousness of the situation," and had even "gone so far as to say that, as a Trustee, he will not vote to give this man a degree if, at a later date, he enrolls as a student."

Though he deplored Lovett's reaction as "badly overdone," Rayzor agreed that, if word got out of Johnson's presence on campus that summer, it was likely to stir up a "hornet's nest." He wondered if Johnson could be persuaded "voluntarily to forego use of the University's facilities." Perhaps, he suggested, Pitzer could ask Douglas to tell Johnson that his use of campus facilities touched on a "very sensitive" issue that "could do great harm to the University . . . and, in addition, it could also bring great harm to Johnson himself by creating a prejudice which he could not live down at Rice, or perhaps at any other University in this part of the country."[26]

At least some of the reaction to Johnson's presence on campus may have been informed by another development that occurred almost simultaneously with his arrival. On June 20, one week before Rayzor wrote to Pitzer on the subject, a group of discontented Rice alumni, led by John B. Coffee (Class of 1934) and Val T. Billups (Class of 1919), had filed their own suit in intervention, claiming that, as beneficiaries of William Marsh Rice's original indenture, they and like-minded former students had a right to contest the board's action before the court. Although the earliest brief prepared for the board by Baker and Botts in 1961 seemed to foresee the possibility of such a thing happening, by the summer of 1963, the intervention was causing major consternation at Rice and beyond, especially since the attorney general had signaled in April that he did not oppose the charter change. Because of Coffee's and Billups's action, a judgment in the case would be even further delayed.[27]

Now despairing of the quick end to segregation that he had anticipated when he took the presidency, by the fall of 1963 Kenneth Pitzer was ready for the trustees to reopen the question of whether it even needed court approval in the first place. In a memo to the board in October, he reiterated that "it seems to me that the Board may take the position that the Charter as written does not prohibit the admission of Negroes any more than it prohibits the admission of out-of-state students" who had attended Rice from the beginning. He put the point more forcefully in an additional memo on January 29, 1964, noting the "very great damage" that would be done if the court sided with Coffee and Billups. "I urge the Board to be courageous and to act now on its own authority."[28]

Yet the board and the university's lawyers did not deviate from their chosen path. On the contrary, they agreed to a motion from Coffee and Billups to try the case before a jury—a highly unusual, legally unnecessary, and potentially perilous concession in a case like theirs. Not long after Pitzer's memo urging the board to act on its own, the case came to trial before a jury that included two Black jurors and five college graduates. Fortunately, after hearing voluminous testimony showing that Rice could not be a great university without the proposed changes, the judge and jury both sided with Rice's trustees, but Coffee and Billups promptly appealed the decision, and they eventually attempted to take their case all the way to the Texas Supreme Court. The litigation would not be entirely resolved in Rice's favor until 1967.[29]

Cautions and Crusades

When Raymond Johnson began his career at Rice in 1963, he was not yet fully aware of all that was happening in the courts and behind the scenes. "What I knew and what was actually going on" at Rice were two different things, he later recalled.

Johnson was especially unaware of the hand-wringing over his presence on campus among some members of the board in June 1963. In fact, Johnson remembered that Rice seemed more welcoming at first than Texas had been. Unlike Heman Sweatt at UT, he did not have to file a lawsuit to break the color line at Rice, and he was assigned a white roommate at Baker College when he arrived. When the summer program for new graduate students ended, Johnson and two of his fellow students, both of them white, rented an apartment on the other side of Hermann Park from campus.

At some point before the fall semester, Johnson was told by Jim Douglas, chair of the Mathematics Department, that he could not yet matriculate as a student due to the suit. While attending courses without being officially enrolled in them, he would be hired as a research assistant for Douglas, tasked with translating advanced mathematics articles from Russian into English. But even after learning of the alumni intervenors, Johnson was confident that Rice would win its suit, and he found the Mathematics Department congenial. He and other students often walked to lunch at Sammy's and enjoyed intramural sports after work. Johnson later remembered where he was on November 22, 1963, when he learned that President John F. Kennedy had been shot: playing touch football with students at Rice.

Aside from sports and Sammy's, Johnson recalled limited contact with other parts of campus outside of mathematics. From the beginning, he found more community off campus in Houston's African American neighborhoods. He enjoyed eating and listening to jazz music on Dowling Street, found a barber in the Third Ward, and made friends with students at Texas Southern University, where he attended a party on his first day in Houston. Years later, that event at TSU was clearer in Johnson's memory than his first visit to the campus at Rice.[30]

Still, Johnson confronted challenges not faced by other Rice students as he began his graduate work under the long shadow of Jim Crow. One challenge was finding suitable housing off campus. Although the Supreme Court's decision in *Shelley v. Kraemer* (1948) had ruled that racially restrictive deeds and residential covenants were unconstitutional, exclusive white neighborhoods around campus, such as Southampton, had long found creative new ways to keep Black residents out. One method favored by the Southampton Civic Club was to forbid the subdivision of properties into rental units. In 1948, the president of the Southampton Civic Club had explained to Rice officials why they could not allow off-campus Rice students to rent there: "the only legal means we now have of preventing the renting of servants quarters and garage apartments, duplexes and apartment houses to members of the Negro race is to prevent the renting thereof to every race and to every class." In later years the club lobbied the university to remove Southampton from lists of rental properties provided to Rice students; in 1956, the university had complied.[31]

That history helps explain why, seven years later, Raymond Johnson and his two white roommates from Rice initially found an apartment south of campus, about a thirty-minute walk away and closer to the Black community in the Third Ward. Yet Johnson soon learned that, even there, his presence disturbed some white neighbors. Apparently, Johnson's light complexion had led his landlord to mistake him for a Puerto Rican or South Asian renter, which made him eligible to rent in the eyes of the apartment manager. But after neighbors complained to the landlord about visits to the apartment by Howard Jefferson, one of Johnson's Black friends from UT, he and his roommates were asked to leave the complex. His Rice colleagues decamped for a new place north of campus, while Jefferson and Johnson moved into a new apartment together on South MacGregor, still south of campus. Without an automobile, Johnson walked to campus every morning to arrive by eight o'clock and then walked home at the end of the day. "If I lived closer to campus," he noted wryly at the time, "I could get more studying accomplished."[32]

Johnson also joined a growing student movement for civil rights in Houston. He later recalled being invited by fellow math student and roommate Jeff Lewis to join an interracial group of students from Rice and TSU who were visiting restaurants to test their willingness to serve Black diners. On one of these outings, he met a sociology major from TSU named Claudette Smith, and the two became a couple, deepening Johnson's connection to the Third Ward campus. In the spring of 1964, he was part of an audience of fifteen hundred people who heard Martin Luther King Jr. speak on the Civil Rights Bill at a TSU auditorium.[33]

Meanwhile, back at Rice, the board's suit against the state attorney general had finally come to trial in February 1964. A resounding verdict in Rice's favor came quickly as March began. And despite an expected appeal by Coffee and Billups, a university lawyer announced publicly that the trustees could now, if they chose, move forward with admitting Black students and charging tuition.[34]

Behind the scenes, though, caution remained the watchword for university leaders. In April, Pitzer jotted down some notes either for or at a meeting with board chairman George R. Brown, Malcolm Lovett, and treasurer Leo Shamblin to discuss next steps for the university. The third item on the president's list was "Negro admission," and below the agenda he made some notes about an unnamed "Graduate student" that must have referred to Johnson. The student was "from Texas, live[s] off campus, High academic quality," and was "not a crusader."[35]

The last point was of particular importance to those leaders who had long expressed concern about racial controversies that might interfere with the suit. In November 1963, the formation of ACCORD, a student advocacy group focused on civil rights, had attracted attention at the highest levels of the administration; at least some of its plans were actively discouraged by officials "because of the existence of the suit." And in May 1964, the student leader of the Rice Forum reported that several speakers who had been expected to appear on campus that semester, including Roy Wilkins, the executive secretary of the NAACP, had not appeared after all "because of problems in finding open dates, and due to complications involving the 'suit.'"[36]

The week after Pitzer discussed Johnson's status with Brown and Lovett, similar "complications" arose when the president learned that students at Jones College, a women's residential hall, had extended a special invitation to Geraldine Williams, a senior at Texas Southern University. Williams, who had been crowned "Miss TSU," was to be the first ever Black honoree at Rice's Rondolet, an annual spring pageant and formal dance.[37]

Malcolm Lovett, however, objected to the idea. Although Coffee and Billups had not yet filed an appeal of the court's March 1964 decision in the charter case, they were expected to do so. And as he had the previous summer when he learned that Johnson was on campus, Lovett believed the invitation to Williams might somehow endanger the litigation. Pitzer called Lovett directly to ask "if it was serious enough that the obviously embarrassing step of withdrawing the invitation ought to be taken." Apparently, in the trustee's view, it was.[38]

The board agreed, according to a statement on the Rondolet issue later released by Pitzer: "The Trustees considered, at my request, possible changes in those campus customs and practices which might be requested by students and faculty in anticipation of the final legal authorization for the complete removal of racial restrictions." They decided that "so long as the present trial court decision was subject to appeal or in other litigation, no changes of this character should be made without the explicit approval of the Trustee representing the Board in legal matters"—in other words, without the agreement of Lovett. In the end, a tearful Jones College president, Ann Lassiter, made the phone call disinviting Williams, who consoled Lassiter by saying that such experiences were not surprising for her.[39]

In retrospect, Rice policy about which events rose to the level of administrative concern about the suit proved highly selective, and tended to apply more often to events that favored desegregation than the other way around.

As Hanszen College officers prepared their budget for 1963 to 1964, at least one noted that the college's blackface minstrel show, started in 1960, might not be allowed to go on, in which case the show's budget (categorized under "cultural activities") would be absorbed into a more "enlightened social committee budget."[40]

Yet in November 1963, the show did in fact go on, with its usual combination of blackface minstrelsy, scatological jokes, and thinly veiled contempt for civil rights struggles. Billed cheekily as "the absolute last of the Hanszen Minstrels," the 1963 show was described in the *Campanile* as sticking to its usual "vein" of humor: one "flowing with dark blood." Accompanying photographs of the performance showed one student in blackface with a graduation cap. Another student, his face and arms both blackened with paint, wore a Jack Yates High School T-shirt. The highlight of the show, according to the yearbook, came when a third student portraying a character called "Supernigger" emerged from an outhouse on stage. That same year, the 1922 yearbook photograph of the Rice Ku Klux Klan was republished in the advertisement section of the *Campanile*.[41]

With or without knowledge of such events, Raymond Johnson later remembered feeling some concern in his first year that he might not be able to stay at Rice after all. He applied to the National Science Foundation for a graduate-student fellowship that could be taken elsewhere, just in case, and in the summer of 1964 he also took a job translating Russian articles for the Humble Oil Company. Then, at the beginning of June, Pitzer evidently began to make inquiries with the Mathematics Department about converting Johnson's status from a research assistant to a student.[42]

The department replied enthusiastically that Johnson had "done very well" and "should be registered as a student," though it seemed at first that he would need to fill out a new application, since the one he filled out "a year and a half ago" could not be found. The application eventually turned up, prompting Pitzer to write a memo reminding someone to "send word to Mr. Johnson that we now have his old appl. for graduate study" and it was complete. Pitzer was confident that the board would grant permission to Johnson to enroll by the end of June.[43]

Even that step would not come without speed bumps. University lawyer Tom Davis saw no objection to enrolling Johnson, Pitzer noted, "indeed he favors it." Yet Lovett remained cautious. On June 16, he sent to Pitzer and Brown a draft of a letter that he thought should be sent to Johnson before admitting him. "Dear Sir," it began, "You have applied for admission to Rice University in September 1964. As you know we could not have admitted you as a student prior to the favorable judgment rendered in Cause No. 612,668, styled WILLIAM MARSH RICE UNIVERSITY, ET AL, VS. WAGGONER CARR, ATTORNEY GENERAL OF THE STATE OF TEXAS, IN THE 28TH JUDICIAL DISTRICT COURT OF HARRIS COUNTY, TEXAS. An appeal from this judgment has been perfected by the Opposing Intervenors."

The proposed letter continued by informing Johnson that, if the opposing intervenors succeeded, Rice University would have to return to its position immediately before the first judgment was rendered. In that case, Lovett's letter told Johnson, "you would have to withdraw as a student and Rice University could not give you credit for work done and satisfactorily completed." Any credits, diplomas, or degrees earned in the meantime would be "withdrawn, cancelled and of no effect."

This remarkable draft, which would undergo significant revision before it reached Johnson's eyes, underscores just how wedded Lovett remained to the very legal theory that, by some reasonable interpretations, the District Court had set aside that spring: the idea that the 1891 charter had always restrained the board from acting on its own to admit Black students. The trustees' leading legal advisor seemed to believe that an appellate court could still stop Rice from admitting Black students or force it to expel one already admitted.

Or perhaps Lovett simply remained as disturbed as Rayzor had found him to be the previous summer over what he regarded as Johnson's premature arrival on campus. Now, in a cover memo to Pitzer explaining his thinking but never mentioning Johnson by name, Lovett wrote, "If an applicant wishes to enter under the conditions outlined in the proposed form of letter, I still question the advisability of permitting him to do so." It was possible, Lovett predicted, that the case could continue for another "two years or more," and it would be "a most unfortunate situation" if a student took classes during this time that later had to be wiped from his record: "I doubt whether we would be justified in any way in permitting the youthful enthusiasm of an applicant to result in a delay of one or two years toward completion of work incident to an advanced degree."

He recommended that the university not give any course credit or degrees to Johnson until all litigation had ended.

In the letter that Pitzer was obliged to send Johnson after this exchange, the president did not go as far as Lovett suggested. He toned down the trustee's draft in several ways, adding in its second line, "We find you to be qualified academically," and concluding: "we sincerely hope that the adverse contingencies will not materialize." In place of Lovett's impersonal "Dear Sir," Pitzer addressed "Mr. Johnson" by name. Still, Lovett's basic message—that an outcome in favor of the intervenors would force Johnson to withdraw, and that Johnson would in that event have to "relieve and release Rice University from all liability of any kind"—remained in Pitzer's letter, which ended with a place for Johnson to sign, indicating his acceptance of admission only under these terms and conditions.

Pitzer sent the letter to Johnson on August 18, 1964. The remainder of the month passed without a reply. Then, on September 7, 1964, Raymond L. Johnson reviewed the letter, took up a pen, and signed his name on the provided line, returning it for the university's files.[44]

"Special Circumstances"

That fall, Johnson applied himself to his studies in the place on campus where he had always felt most at home: the Department of Mathematics. He later described graduate school as a kind of "cocoon," a fitting image for the collegial environment that nurtured his development as a scholar and, to some extent, insulated him from many events on campus. Working during normal business hours on most weekdays, Johnson rarely attended Rice activities, though he did recall making it to see the Rice basketball team in December 1966 when the Owls hosted the Bengals of Idaho State, led by star African American shooting guard Ron Boone. Johnson cheered for the Bengals.[45]

Rooting for Boone was the kind of stand that would come to exemplify Johnson's style: understated, yet clear-eyed about the moral wrong of racism and his own responsibility as a Black scholar to combat it. Even his attendance at the Rice–Idaho State basketball game may have been more pointed than it appears at first glance; earlier that season, some white students in the Rice cheering section had shouted slurs and phrases like "White Power" at athletes of color on the visiting Trinity University squad. From his own experience at UT-Austin, Johnson knew what life was like for Black undergraduates at a historically and predominantly white institution. And even in his few years at Rice, Johnson showed early signs of becoming the award-winning mentor for Black students that he would later be as a professor of mathematics at the University of Maryland.[46]

Throughout the 1964–65 academic year, Johnson officially remained the only Black student at Rice. Far from admitting Black undergraduates that fall, Rice leaders continued to preach caution while the Coffee-Billups appeal awaited a hearing. On October 1, 1964, the *Thresher* reported that residents of Jones College had been asked by officials to "limit Negro guests until [the] conclusion of [the] Trustees' suit." While President Pitzer said the request to Jones students was only advisory, the administration "suggested that they sort of 'go slow' on this" for the time being.[47]

Pitzer clarified a few days later that "the University is now following a completely non-discriminatory policy" and only "recommended that all members of the Rice community consider carefully any actions or statements" that might interfere with the successful conclusion of the suit. Still, in the wake of the administration's similar decision about Rondolet in the spring, some students and faculty were becoming more dissatisfied by the day with the pace of change at Rice.[48]

After students at Hanszen College reprised their blackface minstrel show a fifth time at homecoming in 1964, for example, critics wrote the *Thresher* to denounce the obvious "contempt" that the performers had once again shown for Black Americans. Student Derald Glidden, then president of ACCORD, laid the blame for the show's survival at the feet of the administration and board, which for almost two years, "out of fear of unfavorably prejudicing the suit, created a spurious dichotomy between integration on the intellectual level and integration on the social level."[49]

An editorial in the *Thresher* on March 4, 1965, brought an even more biting indictment. While noting (for the first time in the *Thresher*) that a Black graduate student was now studying at Rice, the editorial argued that leaders had done nothing to prepare for or recruit Black students and had used the "incomplete state of the charter suit" to justify delay. Pointing to the Rondolet episode, to Pitzer's advice to "go slow" from the year before, and to a more recent report that officials had tried to tamp down publicity for an upcoming campus lecture by Roy Wilkins of the NAACP, the *Thresher* wondered when, or whether, the institution would align itself, not with mere expedience, but with "racial justice."[50]

About three weeks after the publication of that editorial, Raymond Johnson (with the help of his soon-to-be-wife Claudette Smith as typist) took time away from his studies to compose a personal letter to President Pitzer that asked many of the same questions, albeit in the measured and diplomatic way that had helped him navigate a world in which Jim Crow was not yet dead. Referring to the "incidents of the past few weeks" (including the reports about Wilkins) and the events of the previous year (including the withdrawal of Geraldine Williams's invitation to Rondolet), Johnson told Pitzer that he was perplexed.

Just over a month before, Johnson explained, he had been called by the Development Office at Rice and told that "the suit had reached the stage at which the University felt it would be possible as well as desirable to allow the press to interview me." (That February, the Houston *Post* had published the first story in a city paper about Johnson's admission at Rice, and the Black-owned newspaper the *Forward Times* would publish its own profile of Johnson in April.) But if "the extreme caution exercised on all matters concerning integration" was no longer necessary in his case, Johnson wondered, why had it been necessary in the case of publicity for Wilkins's speech? Would students who had been previously told to exercise caution, like those at Jones College, be informed as he had been that the situation had changed, if it had?

Of even greater concern to Johnson was "the administration's plans with respect to Negro undergraduates." Though he did not mention it to Pitzer then, Johnson's own experience had taught him the value of active recruitment of Black students to once-segregated schools. Had it not been for the recommendation of his teacher in Alice, he would not have considered UT-Austin; had it not been for the urging of Howard B. Curtis, he would not have considered Rice. "I do not feel that in general a University should recruit students," Johnson said, perhaps for the sake of argument. But, he added, "special circumstances seem to call for it in this case."

Those "special circumstances" included the fact that "Rice has been segregated for its entire life span." It was no wonder that "Negro counselors and teachers have little or no basis on which to recommend Rice to the students." The charter trial's dual purpose meant that, anytime it was mentioned in the press, the new tuition policy came up too, which Johnson predicted would be a concern for Black students. Moreover, the university's constant reminders to the public and the campus that the suit was still in progress would tend to discourage Black applicants, and here Johnson may well have thought about the foreboding letter he had been required to sign the summer before. "It seems to me that there is a need for information or explanation and for clarification of Rice's position. Has the administration taken any such steps or planned any such activity?"[51]

Pitzer took a few days before sending Johnson a reply. While disputing some of what the student had heard, especially about financial aid and the Wilkins visit, the president welcomed suggestions from Johnson about how to reach prospective Black students. The exchange was a promising start, but in a few years Pitzer would leave Rice to become the president of Stanford. In 1967, Johnson's advisor Jim Douglas would leave for the University of Chicago. Johnson followed him there before returning to receive his PhD at Rice, which awarded him its first degree to a Black graduate in 1969. That same year he began his long career at the University of Maryland.

Meanwhile, many of the questions Johnson had asked about Rice's plans for the future remained open as the 1960s came to an end. In the usual understated style that had led some at Rice to underestimate him as "not a crusader," Johnson's letter to Pitzer had grasped precisely the issues now facing Rice. The charter trial was effectively over, even if some in the university were slow to embrace that reality. But Rice was not yet a desegregated university. The hard work of becoming one—the work of the second founding—was in fact just beginning.

7 | A TOKEN START

In the spring of 1970, for the first time in its history, the Rice *Campanile* offered every graduating senior one whole page of the yearbook, a blank slate on which students could publish whatever they chose. The senior pages would differ greatly in style, length, and tone. But for Linda Faye Williams, who would graduate that May as the first Black woman with a Rice University degree, the blank page raised a serious question: How did she want her four years on campus—and by extension the beginnings of integration at Rice—to be memorialized?[1]

Linda Faye Williams had come to Rice in 1966, hoping to become an English teacher. Since then, a transformative sociology course with assistant professor Chandler Davidson, taken in the spring of her junior year, had redirected those plans. After graduation Williams would embark on a distinguished academic career in political science, earning a doctorate from the University of Chicago, faculty positions at Cornell and Howard, a research fellowship at Harvard, tenure at the University of Maryland, and national visibility as a political commentator on television. In her award-winning 2003 book, *The Constraint of Race,* she would later acknowledge Davidson as one of the "mentors, assistants, and just plain encouragers" who supported her "scholarly journey."[2]

In 1970, however, as Williams looked back on her time at Rice, constraints, as well as encouragement, came readily to mind. In 1965, the year before she arrived, the university had enrolled its first two Black undergraduates: Charles Edward Freeman III and Jacqueline McCauley. It would graduate neither. When Williams walked the stage to take her diploma in 1970, receiving a standing ovation from the crowd, Rice still had fewer than forty Black undergraduates, comprising less than 2 percent of students. Not a single member of the faculty was Black. No wonder, then, that when Williams thought about what to put in the yearbook to reflect the realities of Black life at a slowly desegregating university, she settled on a stark, sobering image: a photograph of a single coin on an empty white page.[3]

"I chose a picture of a bus token," Williams explained in an interview in 1988. "That seemed to bother a lot of the progressive faculty, but that was how I felt."[4]

Williams's selection of a "token" for her senior page was more than an expression of personal feelings alone. It addressed a wider debate in 1970, both at Rice and around the nation, about what it would take to realize the promise of integration. Many Americans believed the promise had been realized already with the passage of federal civil rights legislation and court decisions. But in the 1960s civil rights activists were challenging the idea that racial justice had been achieved by the end of legal segregation alone. In 1963, Malcolm X had critiqued integration by pointing out that, nearly ten years after *Brown v. Board of Education* in 1954, fewer than a tenth of the nation's Black students were in integrated schools: "That isn't integration, that's tokenism!" Martin Luther King Jr. used the same term that year to describe the slow integration of restaurants and hotels in the South, noting that the "sedative of tokenism" could not cure the "cancer of segregation." The words "tokenism" and "token" served many other activists, too, as ways to criticize the slow pace of change at institutions with long histories of exclusion, and to talk about the consequences for those who became the first to enter predominantly white spaces.[5]

Though it may well have troubled some who viewed themselves as her allies and who saw her graduation as proof of how far the university had come, Williams's senior page thus reveals another side to the story of integration at Rice: a story about the burdens shouldered by its earliest Black undergraduates. After Williams's death in 2006 at the age of fifty-seven, following a long battle with chronic illness, Davidson remembered her years on campus as "extremely stressful" for her, and she herself had spoken about the isolation she felt.[6]

To be sure, the university had already undergone some changes between the admission of McCauley and Freeman and the moment of William's graduation. As early as January 1969, English professor Alan Grob, a vocal advocate for integration, was even confident that Rice had turned a corner, telling the *Thresher*, "The University has now broken its racial barriers not in a token legal sense, but in the spirit of a desire to fully integrate." One year later, however,

Williams submitted her picture of a token to the *Campanile*. The image suggested, without a word, that the university's desire to integrate was still open to question, and that the varied experiences of the first Black students at Rice had yet to be fully understood.[7]

Students who came to Rice in the late 1960s arrived at one of the most eventful and polarizing eras in the history of the nation—and the university. Nationally, political violence, the 1960s counterculture, the rise of Black Power, and generational conflict over the Vietnam War sparked unprecedented protests at colleges and universities, as the struggle over civil rights evolved into a movement of movements. Locally, protests over the selection of a new university president in February 1969 sharply divided the Rice campus and made national news, while at the very same moment, disagreements over desegregation also divided students, faculty, administrators, and trustees. "One of the things I recollect about the period," Davidson later said, "is that so many things began happening at about the same time. Movements were spawned and transformed at a very rapid pace."[8]

Attending a four-year college during all of this upheaval proved impossible for some students, life-altering for others, and consequential even for some who did not receive a degree. Black students, no less than others, fell into all of those categories, but they also faced unique challenges on a long-segregated campus that was, in many ways, not transforming rapidly enough. If, for many Americans and some at Rice, the late 1960s proved the need for further change, for others it taught the opposite lesson: Rapid change was unwise, even dangerous. While the turbulence of these years sometimes spurred the efforts of those who tried to accelerate desegregation at Rice, more often the swirl of events hampered and interrupted the kinds of social transformations that many desired from integration. And so, by the end of the decade, what Linda Faye Williams had concluded (and hoped, through her senior page, that posterity would not forget) was that Rice's earliest efforts to integrate were not spirited or concerted, but sluggish and conflicted. It was a token start.

"Alone at Rice"

Linda Faye Williams came to Rice in 1966 from tiny Lovelady, Texas, a town one hundred miles north of Houston where she and three younger siblings were raised by their parents, Washington Columbus ("W. C.") Williams and Wilma Juanita Jackson Williams. Both parents were accomplished teachers with undergraduate degrees from Black institutions of higher learning in the state: Paul Quinn College in Waco and Huston-Tillotson College in Austin. Her father, a high-school principal, also held a master's degree in education from Prairie View A&M, and as Linda's high-school graduation approached, he first encouraged her, too, to consider Prairie View.[9]

The Williamses had a hard-won knowledge of the obstacles their daughter would face as she entered adulthood. W. C. Williams once composed a reflection on the life of Martin Luther King Jr. (shared with Chandler Davidson by her sister after Linda's death) that began with an illustration of racial prejudice. "Suppose you were given the task of swimming from one side of a pool to the other," he wrote. "Let's assume you know how to swim and under normal circumstances, it would present no problem to you." Now, Williams continued, imagine diving eagerly into the water and preparing to cross the pool, only to be suddenly stopped, when "someone comes by and tells you that you had not understood; you had to swim the pool wearing a special pack that contained a hundred pounds of lead weights." W. C. and Wilma Williams may have had those weights in mind as they advised their eldest daughter on her choice of college.[10]

Linda Williams, a National Achievement Scholar and the president of her senior class, nonetheless had her sights set on Rice University. She described Rice in her application as the place most "suited to my interests and abilities where I can best develop my potentialities." And in the fall of 1966, she dove in, enrolling at Rice with the hope of becoming a teacher, like her parents.[11]

Williams's experience of Rice would be encumbered by race from her earliest hours on campus. On move-in day, she was assigned a white roommate whose mother "went through a great deal of hysteria" about the pairing, said Williams, who recalled "standing there and thinking, 'Oh, no.'" Williams remembered that time as the "loneliest" of her life, and that sentiment was echoed by another early Black student, Charles Edward Freeman III, when he reflected on his own campus experience. Freeman's time at the university was very different from Williams's but very like it in this: "I was alone at Rice," he said.[12]

Williams's matriculation in 1966, along with that of Theodore M. Henderson from Galveston at the same time, briefly brought the number of Black undergraduates at the university to four, out of a total population of about two thousand. Jacqueline McCauley (a National Merit Scholar from Kashmere Gardens High School in Houston) and Charles Freeman (a valedictorian and National Merit finalist from Lincoln High School in Port Arthur) had matriculated in 1965.[13] Midway through McCauley's sophomore year, however, she withdrew from Rice. Freeman left at the same time, enrolling at Texas Southern University after three semesters of being placed on academic probation at Rice. Gloria Darlene Oliver from Waco joined Rice the next fall as the lone Black freshman in the entering Class of 1967, but she, too, did not remain for long. Though the university did not list race on any official student forms, a faculty member in the summer of 1968 estimated the number of Black students as "about two."[14]

These paltry numbers were no accident. They were the products of deliberate policy choices and institutional priorities at the time. President Kenneth Pitzer had assured the Houston *Chronicle* in March 1964 that Rice "will make no effort to recruit members of any race into the student body. We are not conducting a crusade. We are simply removing restrictions." As Rice's admissions director later explained to another journalist, officials had moved "carefully" with integration, offering admission in the first year to only three out of no more than "half a dozen black applicants."[15] Recruitment of Black students was virtually nonexistent or, when it occurred, too little and late to persuade recruits with other attractive offers.[16]

In addition, Rice officials had publicly emphasized that the university's admissions criteria would remain otherwise unchanged. In a speech about the charter trial in November 1963, trustee H. Malcolm Lovett assured alumni that "we will maintain the high standards we have always had." According to the *Thresher,* Lovett declined to say how many Black students would be admitted, "since this would depend on 'how the ball bounces,' that is, on how many meet the entrance requirements." Pitzer reiterated the point the following semester: "Our first principle will be that Negro students should meet the same qualifications as every other candidate for admission." "We are removing restrictions," the president stressed, "rather than doing special things for Negroes."[17]

Lovett and Pitzer may have intended their statements, at least in part, to place the qualifications of Black students who did enroll at Rice beyond doubt; McCauley remembered the president kindly welcoming her to campus with a personal meeting. Yet the repeated invocations of "high standards" also posed a false dilemma between excellence and equity that would trouble discussions of race on campus for decades. By insisting that Black students could come and succeed only if they met Rice's exacting standards, officials also implied that nothing about Rice itself would be to blame for poor outcomes in admissions or academic performance.[18]

Accordingly, when three of the first four Black undergraduates immediately found themselves on academic probation after one semester, and two of the four were gone after three semesters, university officials initially showed little curiosity or concern about the reasons. A short memo listing Rice's Black students in early 1967 only reported each student's most recent grades, without the course titles, instructors, or additional comment. Under "Charlie Freeman," the entry read: "Probation 3 times (busted)." From the university's perspective, it seemed, Rice's high standards simply had not been met.[19]

Those Black students who did remain at Rice later remembered how these prevailing attitudes affected them. "After the first two black students didn't graduate," Linda Faye Williams felt increased pressure to succeed. "I really felt that I was an experiment, and everybody would blame other blacks if I didn't do well," she recalled in 1988, adding, "That was a pressure I did not like."[20]

Henderson likewise remembered hearing stories about Freeman and McCauley when he arrived. He recalled the campus as mostly friendly and supportive. Still, he resolved to be "sure I was on my p's and q's," and before long, other students had taken to calling Henderson "The Bishop" for his habit of cloistering himself in his room or the library to study, alone, deep into the night.[21]

The pressures felt by Black students in the late 1960s were not unique to Rice, of course. But at Rice, the challenges faced by Black students were compounded by the university's smallness, as well as its lateness and slowness with desegregation. At the University of Texas at Austin, for example, Black students still comprised less than 1 percent of the student population in 1971, fifteen years after the first Black undergraduates had enrolled. In Austin, though, the first Black student cohorts were larger than those at Rice, which facilitated the early formation of African American social clubs and Greek life. More than one hundred Black students enrolled at UT in 1956, and by the early 1960s, Black students there had already joined together to lead protests against segregation in Austin theaters, restaurants, and housing. Although leaders at UT were slower to integrate dormitories than classrooms, some Black students in Austin had found support in residential communities just off campus like the Almetris Co-Op, where renowned housemother Almetris Duren provided many of the first Black women at UT with what one described as "an oasis in a sea of white." It was from supportive environments like these that Black students launched the sit-ins and lawsuits that pushed UT to begin integrating its residence halls in 1964.[22]

In Houston, Rice's first Black undergraduates arrived in 1965 without having to protest for equal on-campus housing—but also without the Black student community and support that co-ops, clubs, fraternities, and sororities provided some of their counterparts in Austin. They were also newcomers to a residential plan at Rice that was itself relatively new: the college system. In 1957, the university elected to convert its four residential halls into "colleges" modeled on similar living and learning communities at Oxford or Yale. The four colleges designated exclusively for men and housing about 220 students each—Baker College, Will Rice College, Hanszen College, and Wiess College—were joined by one new college on the other side of campus for women: Jones College. A period of expansion, beginning in the mid-1960s, brought three more colleges to campus: Lovett and Sid Richardson for men, and Brown College, adjacent to Jones, for women.[23]

More than simply dormitories and dining halls, the colleges were promoted by the university as environments for "complete living," each with its own student government, a sizable budget managed by students, and a full calendar of social events and extracurricular activities, including "college courses" students could apply to teach. A faculty head of the college, then known as the college "master," resided with his family in a house on campus, alongside other resident faculty fellows, creating what one promotional video in 1962 called "an atmosphere ideal for the development of the student." Despite the adjustments the system required to student life and government, which had previously been organized more around graduating class than residence hall, by 1966 the colleges had quickly become central to student identity and traditions, including intramural competitions such as Beer Bike, which began in 1957.[24]

For Black students, however, the college system created unique challenges. Already small in total numbers, Black students were further isolated by their separation into colleges. Upon matriculation in 1965, Jacqueline McCauley moved in at the all-women Jones College, on the opposite side of campus from Wiess College, where Charles Freeman was placed. She was joined at Jones by Linda Faye Williams the next year, while Ted Henderson was assigned to Will Rice College. These and other early Black students navigated living and social spaces in which, as in their classrooms, they were virtually alone. And after nearly a decade of developing traditions in the absence of Black students, the residential colleges had done only a little to change in preparation for their arrival.

Recall, for example, that at Hanszen College, students had put on a popular blackface minstrel at homecoming for five straight years, beginning in 1960. At the first such show, a quartet of faculty members performed in blackface, too; the quartet included college master William H. Masterson, a historian who later found himself at the center of campus protests over his appointment as president. As the annual date for the show approached in 1965, students in charge of the tradition planned to produce what the college newsletter called a "slightly modified" version, designed as a melodrama. Advertised as the First Annual Hanszen College Non-Minstrel and held as usual in Hamman Hall, the show was to retain "'humor' characteristic of and appropriate to the occasion" and again featured a large chorus of seated students, this time without makeup. In another respect, though, the tradition remained unchanged for Homecoming 1965, the first for Freeman and McCauley on campus. One main actor in the melodrama still performed in thickly applied blackface paint.[25]

At times, interactions within the colleges confronted Black students at Rice with expressions of ignorance and hate that had seldom, if ever, intruded on their domestic spheres before. Century-old symbols of the Lost Cause and white supremacy were not unusual on campus. As Williams would recall, "I had friends—and they really were my friends—who couldn't understand why I hated them having a Confederate flag hanging in their room." In January 1966, George Lincoln Rockwell of the American Nazi Party also spoke on campus at the invitation of Wiess College, where Charles Freeman then lived. According to the *Thresher*, it was his "first invitational appearance at any Southern university." And in February 1967, at the start of what was Ted Henderson's second semester on campus, his college cosponsored and hosted a speech in the commons, replete with vicious slurs, by J. B. Stoner, a notorious white supremacist who was later convicted of having bombed a Black church in Alabama. The speech ended only when a group of Texas Southern University students entered the room in silent protest.[26]

At other times, the residential colleges offered more positive experiences to their first four Black students, all of whom seized opportunities to participate in student life. McCauley starred in theater productions; Williams and Henderson joined their college choirs. Freeman, a state-champion tuba player in high school, played in the band, tried ROTC, and (during his freshman year) took part in a Beer Bike practice at Wiess. Henderson recalled Freeman's roommate reaching out to welcome him to campus, a gesture he appreciated even many years later. The same roommate whose mother had humiliated Williams on move-in day later said that she had requested a Black roommate. She and Williams eventually worked together for a time as tutors to Black school children at Harper Elementary School, in a student-run effort supported by the federal Volunteers in Service to America, or VISTA, program.[27]

Some colleges made space, too, for events that organizers may have believed would hold interest for (or at least demonstrate sympathy with) Black students. In February 1966, only a few months after Hanszen's first "Non-Minstrel," the college sponsored a talk by white journalist John Howard Griffin, author of the 1961 book *Black Like Me.* Griffin spoke to students about his by-then well-known experiences traveling through the segregated South disguised as a dark-skinned Black man; his remarks denouncing racial prejudice received a standing ovation from the crowd.[28]

That spring, and again in the fall, James Forman, a leader in the Student Non-Violent Coordinating Committee (SNCC), spoke at two Rice colleges on the group's new orientation toward the philosophy of Black Power. His October 1966 talk at Wiess College received a chillier reception than Griffin's from white students, who objected to what the *Campanile* called Black Power's "shock treatment." But there was standing room only in the commons a few months later, when Wiess hosted a talk by heavyweight champion Muhammad Ali and presented him with an honorary Wiess necktie.[29]

That same winter, several white students at Jones College also planned and held a daylong university symposium on Houston's "minority problems." (The initial brainstorming discussions occurred at Jones during the same week Williams moved in.) Billed as Rice's first "teach-in," it took place in December 1966 and featured TSU alumnus Curtis Graves (newly elected as the first Black state representative in Texas since Reconstruction) and TSU student Millard Lowe (a local SNCC coordinator). TSU professor Earl W. Rand, who a few months later would speak at Gloria Oliver's high-school graduation in Waco, spoke at the teach-in, too.[30]

By themselves, though, events like the "teach-in," framed in ways that focused on minority groups' "problems," could only do so much to alleviate feelings of isolation for the still vanishingly small number of Black students at Rice, especially since that number would be halved—from four to two—by January 1967. The teach-in proved to be one of the last Rice events attended as a student by McCauley, who withdrew before final exams to focus her time on social activism with her husband, a VISTA volunteer. Around the same time, after being academically suspended by Rice, Freeman left for TSU, gravitating towards an activist group there led by teach-in speaker Millard Lowe.[31]

As a result, before Linda Faye Williams and Ted Henderson had even completed one year of classes, they suddenly found themselves left alone, like McCauley and Freeman before them, as the only two Black undergraduates at William Marsh Rice University. Integration had started once, it seemed, only to start over again.

"Rice Is a Segregated Institution"

While the virtual absence of other Black students on campus was impossible for Black students not to notice from the start, by the spring of 1967 others at Rice were beginning to ask why integration was moving at an inchworm's pace. The question would swell in volume over the next two years, until scarcely a week passed without some reminder, either in the university's public or private records, of an ongoing debate over "minority student admissions." Yet those conversations revealed little consensus among white observers about the nature of the problem facing Rice, the best solutions to the problem, or even whether there was a real problem at all. And even those who agreed that there was a problem disagreed, more basically, about why it needed to be solved.

In May 1967, for example, the outgoing president of the Student Association criticized the "token admission of Negro students" at Rice, making an argument in favor of diversity that the Supreme Court would accept eleven years later as a rationale for affirmative action: "The average WASP [White Anglo-Saxon Protestant] at Rice needs exposure to a diversity of cultural, social, and economic groups."[32]

But in October 1967, after Oliver arrived as the only Black student in that fall's entering class, English professor Alan Grob took to the pages of the *Thresher* to criticize the university's slow pace of integration on other grounds, basing his arguments less on the promise of what diversity would do for white students than on the necessity of redressing Rice's "long history of legal exclusion." The professor then floated several proposals for "how to achieve a truly integrated community here at Rice." "By this I do not mean the token Negro student at Jones or at Will Rice," Grob wrote, referring impersonally (but obviously, to readers at the time) to Williams and Henderson. The professor wanted to see a Rice in which "a substantial number of Negroes significantly participates in every facet of University life."[33]

In response to such concerns, Rice's director of admissions, James B. Giles, denied that the administration had tried "to keep integration here down to token levels." He expressed openness to some of Grob's proposals, especially the idea of faculty visiting "Negro high schools" and recruiting "leading students" to apply and enroll, while disagreeing with other ideas, such as the preferential admission of some Black students with below-average test scores. "The ultimate test of any candidate for admission," Giles told the *Thresher,* "is whether he can do the work."[34]

Such exchanges could not have done much to assuage sophomore Linda Williams's suspicion that she was viewed by some at Rice as an "experiment," but they did point to the growing concern of others that Rice was not doing enough to integrate. Those voices only grew louder after the assassination of Martin Luther King Jr. and the urban uprisings that followed it in April 1968, which prompted several professors to write President Pitzer directly, urging more aggressive action on desegregation. A "spontaneously generated" faculty group led by Grob formed that spring, with Pitzer's blessing, to analyze admissions procedures, consider federal grants that might help bring minority students to Rice, and develop more tutoring and counseling resources on campus.[35]

The work of responding to such proposals would fall mostly to different administrators, however, when Pitzer left later that year to become president of Stanford University. Beginning in August 1968, a new Campus Executive Committee (CEC) took on the president's duties until a successor could be named. The CEC was chaired by engineering dean William E. Gordon, and as time would tell, Gordon had been given a taller order than he knew.[36]

Pitzer's abrupt departure left Rice with interim leadership at one of the most tumultuous moments in the history of American higher education. The Vietnam War, urban unrest, and a panoply of social movements were roiling American politics and society, due in part to student activism at universities. Students, faculty, and administrators also clashed over issues specific to college life, such as speakers' bans, ROTC, defense research, parietal rules, and the very purpose of a university, making protest commonplace on campuses in the late 1960s. Black student groups alone would organize nearly two hundred demonstrations across the United States in 1968 and 1969, many of them calling for more Black students, more attention to Black history and culture in university curricula, and the hiring of more Black faculty.[37]

Rice would see protests, too, on a much smaller scale and with ambiguous results. To many Americans, the student turmoil of 1968 and 1969 capped a decade that seemed to threaten "the unraveling of America," and college administrators everywhere struggled to understand and regulate the national groundswell of protest. Their worst fears about such activism came to pass at Columbia University in April 1968, when students occupied five buildings and temporarily shut down university operations; bloody clashes between students and police officers made headlines around the world, and Columbia's president would resign in August 1968, just days before more violence erupted at protests outside the Democratic National Convention in Chicago.[38]

Headlines from Columbia were still fresh in May 1968, when Dr. William H. Masterson—then president of the University of Chattanooga, but formerly a Rice student, history professor, and dean, as well as master of Hanszen College from 1957 to 1966—addressed the Class of 1968 as Rice's commencement speaker. In his speech, "The Troubled Search," Masterson argued that universities had a crucial role to play in solving social problems, but only if they focused on their main purpose: intellectual inquiry. Echoing the views of many higher education leaders at the time, Masterson worried that recent demonstrations by students risked "a subversion of intellect by emotion," which was "more perilous than the ghetto, more insidious than racial prejudice, more complex than [the] technology of war." Emotional protest, Masterson implied, was a cure worse than the disease.[39]

The historian believed that Rice, at least, had stayed above the fray—little knowing that within the year he would be at the center of the university's own campus crisis. When Rice trustees announced in February 1969 that their choice to succeed Pitzer as president was none other than Masterson (an unpopular figure among those faculty and students who remembered his time as a strict professor and dean), surprise, then outrage, and then mass protests consumed the campus over a long, tense weekend. Masterson would resign the post less than a week after accepting it.[40]

Throughout the 1968–69 academic year (the third for Linda Faye Williams and Ted Henderson on campus), all these events inevitably shaped the ways administrators and trustees at Rice viewed new demands from students and faculty, including about integration. Although the immediate cause for what came to be known as the "Masterson crisis" in February 1969 was the board's failure to consult sufficiently with a student and faculty advisory committee on the presidential search, it also brought to a climax months of growing disagreements among university leaders, faculty, and students on many other issues that often became tangled up together. One of the most contentious of these debates concerned what the university should do, or not do, about "minority student admissions."

The debate was joined in earnest in September 1968, as ten or eleven new Black freshmen joined the university, comprising its largest entering class of Black students yet. That month, minority admissions came up at the very first fall meeting of Rice's student government body, the Student Association (SA), which opened with a question about how "events this summer have affected everyone in our age group." In the ensuing discussion, senators identified a few major questions for the SA to tackle as priorities for the year. The first question was whether students would have a voice in the selection of the university's new president: "If so, how?" The second was: "Can the admission policies which have so limited the number of minority students on this campus be effectively improved?"[41]

The next week, the SA hosted an open forum on "Integration and the Rice Admissions Policy" that drew seventy-five students and faculty members, including Alan Grob, who recommended to the Faculty Council, a faculty governance body, that his small group of concerned professors from the previous spring should be appointed as a formal committee and empowered to make recruitment trips to area schools during that year's admissions season. The council agreed in early November, naming Grob the chair of an Ad Hoc Committee on Problems of Recruitment of Students from Minority Groups.[42]

In the meantime, an independent group of eleven white students, styling themselves the Student Committee on University Research (SCOUR), a division of the Student Action Committee, had begun meeting to discuss and study the same issue. And in November, just before Thanksgiving, SCOUR published and widely distributed a thirty-one-page report entitled *Who Enters Rice?* The report laid out a detailed "proposal to the community at large on underprivileged and minority group admissions," and it had been prepared, according to the authors, in consultation with unnamed Black students.[43]

The SCOUR report first gave a bracing review of the current situation at Rice. "A Black enrollment of substantially less than one percent of the overall enrollment is not even significant enough to be a 'token,'" the students concluded. "Rice is a segregated institution." Much like Fance Franck in the *Rice Institute Magazine* twenty years before, SCOUR surveyed recent studies on racial disparities in the nation's schools. And much like Raymond Johnson's letter to Pitzer in 1965, it argued that active recruitment of Black students would be necessary given Rice's long history of exclusion. "With this history," the students said, "it is not enough to say, come if you can get in but we won't encourage you in any way."[44]

Impressively written and researched, *Who Enters Rice?* received official endorsements from several residential colleges, the SA, prominent faculty members, and the *Thresher.* Parts of it overlapped with arguments that professors like Grob had been making for months. SCOUR agreed, for example, on the need to recruit at area high schools, except that the students wanted students to make the trips. While its focus was on Black students, the report called for the admission of more Mexican American and low-income students as well, and it even proposed some far-sighted reforms (such as assigning counseling staff to the residential colleges, offering pre-matriculation summer programs, and hosting recruitment dinners on campus) that the university later adopted, in some cases decades later.

Yet the report also touched on political live wires that were particularly polarizing in 1968. Unlike Grob's committee, for example, but like activists at some other universities that year, SCOUR proposed that a certain percentage of new admissions each year should be reserved for Black students. Other students quickly took to the *Thresher* to describe that idea as "racism" or reverse discrimination. For key leaders at the university, the SCOUR report suffered, too, from its seeming association with the ideals and tactics of the Students for a Democratic Society (SDS), the New Left group whose leaders had spurred the unrest at Columbia.[45]

SCOUR was, after all, a subcommittee of the Student Action Committee (SAC), which aimed at "the restructuring of the University and society so that at each level, all those affected share control in policy-making." That rhetoric unmistakably echoed the ideas advocated by the SDS, whose national leaders embraced the counterculture, opposed the Vietnam War, and called for revolution. The Student Action Committee was established at an SA meeting on October 8, and on October 10, the university's executive committee added a new item to its own meeting agenda: "SAC."[46]

Rice did not have an SDS chapter—yet—but SAC certainly looked like one. The committee inaugurated its efforts at Rice in October 1968 with a "Life Week against the Death Culture," featuring a performance by a Black theater group from Texas Southern University, guerilla street theater in the quadrangle, and a lecture by a recently fired UT philosophy professor who had served as a faculty sponsor of the SDS in Austin. Capping it off was a weeklong protest against the Vietnam War held at the statue of William Marsh Rice in the center of campus.[47]

"Life Week" also brought another controversial speaker back to campus: Charles Edward Freeman III. After his academic suspension from Rice in early 1967, Freeman had enrolled briefly at TSU, becoming a vocal leader in a Black Power group called Friends of SNCC. (The 1967 *Campanile* would call him "our own TSU-SNCC leader Charlie.") In May 1967, Houston police responded to weeks of student protests on the Third Ward campus by firing a fusillade of bullets into a men's dormitory. After one officer was struck and killed by another officer's stray shot, the police forcefully ejected all students from the dorm and arrested five hundred African American students. And in the chaotic aftermath, five protest leaders were charged with murder for allegedly inciting a riot. Freeman was one of the five.[48]

The former Rice student maintained that he was a scapegoat for a death he did not cause. He secured legal representation from the NAACP for a trial that would take place at the end of October 1968. And in the weeks before the trial, he appeared on the Rice campus to speak at least two times—once at Brown College, and once at Baker College, with the TSU theater group that performed for Life Week. In a front-page story, the *Thresher* excerpted some of the poetry he wrote and read at the event, remarking of Freeman, "He sees things severely, sometimes radically, always sharply."[49]

The next week, Freeman was on the front page of the *Thresher* again. The October 31 issue opened with an article reporting on the formation of a new faculty-student committee elected to advise Rice's board of governors and trustees on the selection of a president. Immediately below that story, under the fold, was a lengthy story about Freeman's trial in Victoria, Texas, which a group of Rice students had driven south to attend. Outside the courtroom, they spoke with Freeman, who thanked them all for coming but waved off one of the students who tried to hand him a copy of Chinese communist leader Chairman Mao's *Little Red Book*, a totem of leftist politics at the time. "Oh no man," Freeman told the student, "they'd give me 20 more years if they even saw me looking at this."[50]

October 1968—the month that began with the formation of an SDS-like group on campus—thus ended with a small group of Rice students rallying around Freeman at his trial on charges of rioting and murder. The SCOUR report, when it emerged the next month as a SAC publication, would inevitably be viewed in that context by university officials. At first glance, it may have seemed that the disruptive radicalism that had upended universities elsewhere was coming to Rice.

In truth, the events organized by SAC never attracted as much turnout or interest as organizers desired; the reach of the New Left at Rice was clearly shorter than it was at places like Columbia. And even the awkward interactions between Freeman and those few Rice students concerned about his plight suggested a solidarity often mixed with misapprehension, betraying an undercurrent of racial division that also had emerged in student movements elsewhere. A *Thresher* editorial deemed the speech by the fired UT professor "the most worthwhile" event of Life Week, but it panned the Black student group from

TSU, which "found it hard to communicate with its audience in any but the most primitive and halting way." Though the reviewer did not wholly blame the Black students ("The 300-year-old chasm separating the blacks from most of the audience is a pretty broad one to be bridged in a single evening"), he concluded that the TSU group's performance "did not entirely succeed."[51]

Another student recalled—in May 1969—that her attempts to interest classmates in the SCOUR report had met with both apathy and resistance that year. She remembered that even students who identified as "liberal" objected to some of the report's specific proposals. And she also met many "people who reacted with—asking me, for instance, why I felt that diversifying the university was good, basically why that was good, and who were just against the entire idea of bringing Black students, for any number of reasons, either because it would cheapen the Rice degree, was one thing I heard, that it's not Rice's responsibility to educate Blacks." Proponents of radical change at Rice were not in the majority.[52]

Still, to university administrators unnerved by events on other campuses, even small signs of unraveling could cause concern. In November 1968, at San Francisco State College, members of that school's Black Student Union (joined by white students who called themselves the Third World Liberation Front) launched a student strike after months of agitation for admissions reforms and a Black studies program. Violent confrontations between students and police followed. At a convocation at Rice that December, the CEC's Dean Gordon referred indirectly to such events when he issued a warning to students about campus protest. "Irresponsible actions on the part of unkempt students at certain other universities have cooled Congressional interest in support of higher education, resulting in tighter budgets," Gordon said. "The same factors which hurt universities in general, hurt Rice, and therefore hurt you."[53]

Just a week after that convocation, nonetheless, a group of demonstrators announced plans to return to the William Marsh Rice statue for another rally—this time to protest what they perceived as Gordon's slowness to act on the SCOUR report. Among the planned speakers were the SA president, that year's homecoming queen, and, finally, John Birotte—a Lovett College freshman from Houston's Third Ward, a National Achievement Scholar, and, said the *Thresher*, "one of Rice's 17 black undergraduates."[54]

What Birotte had to say was apparently not recorded. Nor was the size of his audience, suggesting that the rally was small. Even so, behind the scenes, the growing incidence of student protest was beginning to stimulate concern among the university's interim leaders, who were also dealing, in the very same weeks, with another sensitive matter. On November 26, just as copies of *Who Enters Rice?* began to appear across campus, and after he had been freed by a hung jury in the trial at Victoria, Charles Freeman had applied for readmission to the university. Then, in December, around the same time as the SCOUR rally in the academic quad, the faculty committee in charge of student readmissions had voted unanimously, in a closed meeting, to approve Freeman's request.[55]

Gordon's Campus Executive Committee received the news about Freeman on December 17 with alarm, but there was little that could be done about the situation over the winter break. Freeman was left to wait for news of his fate back in Port Arthur with his parents, who wrote to the university three times that year, pleading for a clear and timely decision so they could advise their son.[56]

The CEC did not return to the issue until a meeting on January 6, 1969, the first of several at which the Freeman case would be "discussed at length." The committee worried about the possible "political" effects of overruling the faculty's decision in favor of Freeman, who was still under disciplinary suspension at TSU due to his indictment. Some members predicted that "there will be a small group of activist students who can seize upon this issue as a question of faculty rights as well as one of racial discrimination," clearly thinking of SAC and SCOUR.

But Rice's interim leadership was evidently more worried about Freeman's potential return. The CEC asked Gordon to speak with the faculty committee that had approved his readmission, and the dean reported back about the conversation on January 9. He had induced the faculty to reverse their decision and return later to Freeman's case.[57]

So Many Things, at about the Same Time

Throughout the fall 1968 semester and into the winter break, the course of events had pulled separable threads of discussion about desegregation and student power tighter and tighter into what was beginning to seem, to some on campus, like a single knot. And in the meantime, the ad hoc faculty committee led by Alan Grob had also begun its work. In fact, at the same January 9 meeting at which Gordon told the CEC about the reversal of the Freeman decision, the committee also discussed the activities of Grob's group.

With coordination provided by Grob, some twenty faculty members had spent the winter visiting high schools and learning more about African American and Mexican American students who might be interested in Rice. Administrators had also met with Grob and others to discuss steps the university might take to recruit minority students, including through a National Science Foundation grant won by Rice to support science and engineering training for high-school students. The results of these activities were encouraging, suggesting the gains that could be made by concerted effort along these lines. By February 1969, nearly one hundred Black students had submitted applications, almost five times more than had ever been received in one year before.[58]

On January 21, 1969, Grob told an audience of students at Hanszen College that he was newly optimistic about Rice. The university was increasingly committed, he believed, not only to "equal opportunity," but more broadly to "social justice." In retrospect, though, that conclusion was premature, as even reports of the Grob committee's successes were not greeted with universal enthusiasm by campus leaders. At its January 9 meeting, the CEC discussed a question from the university's director of development, who wondered whether Grob's committee would cause "a difficult public relations problem."[59]

Gordon addressed this concern by noting that Grob's group was not a policymaking body. Nevertheless, those worried about public relations may not have been pleased to learn that, when Grob later spoke at Hanszen about his efforts, he referred approvingly to SCOUR and reportedly named two prominent Black activists as examples of the kinds of students Rice should pursue. "We don't want to take in merely white students with black skins," Grob was quoted in the *Thresher* as saying. "We don't want to exclude entirely the Malcolm X's, the Elridge [*sic*] Cleavers, men of intellect and potential" whose conventional academic records might appear to be weak. With national news headlines reporting on a gun battle between two Black Power groups on the campus of UCLA only days before, such statements were not likely to assuage Rice administrators concerned about student radicalism.[60]

Meanwhile, student protests about the reception of *Who Enters Rice?* had resumed in the new year. On January 7, SCOUR wrote a statement decrying what they considered the tepid institutional response to their report and revising an earlier demand: Rice should "set aside 50 places in the in-coming class for Black admissions and 25 places for Latin American admissions." Two days later, on the same day that the CEC had discussed Freeman and Grob, Gordon then spoke about "Minority Admissions at Rice" to a large group of students and faculty at Will Rice College. The evening meeting would be covered, the next week, by two front-page articles and an editorial in the *Thresher*.[61]

At the Will Rice meeting, Gordon pledged that the university would do more to recruit Black students, while cautioning that change took time. He said he had forwarded the SCOUR report to the Grob committee for review (he sent it on January 3). But according to the *Thresher*, the students in attendance "remained entirely silent, including the few 'minority group' students there." And conspicuously absent from Gordon's talk were the students who had spearheaded the new SCOUR statement. They met separately that night at Lovett College to screen a film on the "Columbia student rebellion last spring." A few days later, they met to form a Rice chapter of the SDS.[62]

Gordon's speech also failed to impress the editor of the *Thresher*, who saw—in the growing distance between administrators, faculty, and students over the SCOUR report—the "shadows of apocalypse." "The administration here does not have a reputation for inaccessibility, facelessness, and intransigence," the editor said, "unlike those holding the reins at institutions like Columbia . . . and it is not faced with a host of directly conflicting demands clamoring for immediate solution, as is that at San Francisco State." The *Thresher* also noted (thankfully? regretfully?) that Rice was "troubled by no militant black student minority." All of this made it unlikely that Rice would "follow the same paths and make the same errors as these schools. . . . But it's hard sometimes to avoid the feeling that the chances are becoming greater all the time."[63]

With hindsight, such fears of apocalypse might seem overwrought, but the editorial's concern about the disconnects between students and campus leaders did eerily prefigure the events of the next month's better-known Masterson crisis. The editorial was not wrong to note a conflict "between the Rice administration and certain vocal segments of the student body" in that year's ongoing "debate on minority admissions." And finally, the *Thresher* was not alone in thinking about this discussion in the context of unrest on other campuses. That larger "political" context was explicitly on the minds of the CEC as it weighed Freeman's case, and other sources suggest that it was also on the minds of prominent Rice alumni and trustees that winter.[64]

In fact, on January 14, 1969, a few days after Gordon spoke at Will Rice College, H. Malcolm Lovett himself weighed in on the debate about SCOUR, in a lengthy and revealing letter addressed to two other trustees and copied to Gordon and McEnany. Lovett, now serving as chairman of the board, was about to enter some of the most challenging weeks of his tenure, which would include hospitalization for major back surgery after an injury suffered that winter. The trustees, then deliberating about their search for a new president, were only weeks away from voting on and announcing their controversial choice of Masterson. After that announcement, they would face massive faculty and student uproar over the process behind that selection, and especially over the breakdowns in communication between the board, faculty, and students. But all of that was still in the future on January 14. And for Lovett, the matter of minority student admissions and the manner in which some students had raised it were urgent enough to deserve a response.[65]

The chairman's letter began with a critical review of *Who Enters Rice?* and the January postscript released by its authors. Lovett had read the report and allowed that it was well, even "forcefully," written. He wondered if someone else was doing the writing for the students. Either way, Lovett concluded, "I don't believe their assertions have any validity as far as Rice is concerned, or that they should be encouraged to think that their views are going to be adopted by the Board."

Having thus dispatched SCOUR's specific proposals, Lovett went on to rebut the report's major arguments. A basic premise for SCOUR was that Rice's long history with segregation necessitated further action on the university's part to encourage Black students and increase their numbers. Lovett's view, by comparison, was relatively unburdened by that past. "Rice was established, as you know, as an institution for the white inhabitants by direction of the Founder," he wrote. "This was in keeping with applicable mores at the time, which may not have been right, but they certainly were accepted."

Lovett conceded that times had changed, to exactly this extent: Now that the trustees had changed the charter, Rice "will be glad to admit any young man or woman who meets its entrance requirements," regardless of race or creed. Yet Lovett did not see the need for measures far beyond that. Instead, he thought it imperative to maintain that the university had, except for the amendment of the charter, otherwise stayed the same. "When it was an institution for white people, as Scour would say, it established a policy of relatively rigid selectivity in order to promote and realize its goal of academic excellence." And when the trustees "made it possible for Rice to admit students without regard to race," the chairman continued, they agreed that "there would be no change in the admission policy of selection on the basis of excellent academic achievement."

This core principle of excellence, Lovett believed, was the one now being threatened by student agitators whose ultimate motives he questioned. "In more recent years," he wrote, "as groups have come forward trying to draw the universities into an activist role in supporting their particular philosophies or recognizing their sense of guilt, pressure builds up to lower standards." Not unlike many leaders at desegregating universities elsewhere at the time and later, Lovett clearly worried that the SCOUR proposals urging the university to take more affirmative steps to recruit and admit minority students would require it to compromise on "academic excellence."

The chairman even feared that this lowering of standards had already occurred with the entering Class of 1968. "I understand that last year at the behest of someone and without knowledge of the Board, a very few, possibly three, students of below standard achievement were admitted on an experimental basis," Lovett said. "These experimental projects have a way of maturing into a full fledged program and I don't believe that such a program would have the support of the Board." The chairman concluded by reminding the letter's recipients that no major changes to admissions could be made without approval by the trustees. He advised James U. Teague (the trustee who chaired the board's Faculty, Student, and Alumni Committee) to "keep abreast" of SCOUR's activities.[66]

Barely a month before the crisis over Masterson would hit the campus like an earthquake, a fault line was thus beginning to emerge, even if some administrators still believed that matters were well in hand. On January 29, 1969, two weeks after receiving a copy of Lovett's letter, the dean of undergraduate affairs, Michael V. McEnany, dictated a typed reply to the board chairman. His aim was to reassure Lovett that the threat posed by SCOUR was, for now, minimal. McEnany told the chairman, based on conversations with students involved, that the student committee had actually splintered over the proposal to set aside racial quotas for that year's entering class. Those favoring such a step had left the SAC to form the new chapter of SDS, McEnany believed, and he informed Lovett that the new SDS chapter was small. "We have here a possible source of real trouble on the campus," said the dean. "But, in my view, no immediate danger." McEnany hoped that administrators could stay in touch with students, work with them, and "perhaps even ultimately get their assistance in some of our projects."[67]

Even so, the CEC was not taking any chances when it came to "the problem of student militancy," which had dominated the group's agenda at a meeting held the day before McEnany wrote. The CEC had talked about student activism for "about an hour and a half" and drew up contingency plans in the event of "Attempts to Disrupt Campus Affairs." One of the items before them for discussion was an antiwar leaflet created by students from SDS. Another was a recent *Wall Street Journal* article, circulated by Rice's treasurer, on "Black Student Revolt," which touched on events at San Francisco State and carried an ominous headline: "Colleges' Bid to Enroll 'Disadvantaged' Brings Problems and Protests."[68]

By the end of the meeting, the CEC had resolved to publish a statement declaring that disruptions to campus activities would not be tolerated. Student culprits would be expelled, nonstudents treated as trespassers. And at a meeting held on February 6 (eight days before the trustees would finalize their choice for president), a draft of the statement on disruptions was presented to Teague's board subcommittee, which approved "the steps which were being taken in this direction."[69]

At the same meeting, Gordon also invited McEnany and admissions director Giles to speak to the trustees about the university's admissions policies. Doubtless with the recent letter from Lovett in mind, Teague read into the minutes the clause of the Rice charter giving the board full "discretion" over "the requirements for admission" (the very clause that Pitzer had once cited in trying to persuade trustees not to wait on the charter trial to begin admitting Black students). McEnany "assured the committee that the policy on admissions had not changed" and "emphasized that the standards of admission would apply to all races and not a select few."[70]

In sum, as February 1969 began, the debates over student activism and minority student admissions that had grown louder over the previous year had clearly become entangled and top of mind for university leaders. McEnany, at least, remained hopeful that Rice could move forward without trouble. On Monday, February 17, the dean wrote to Alan Grob that Gordon wished to appoint two or three undergraduates to the ad hoc committee on minority admissions, which would signal the important role that could be played by students within normal channels. The Student Association nominated six names for the group, among them John Birotte, Linda Faye Williams, and two students from SCOUR. McEnany suggested appointing three, leaving Birotte off the list—but Grob replied that he wanted all six, and the professor scheduled a meeting with the expanded committee to be held at the end of that week, on Saturday, February 22.[71]

What Grob could not have known was that, by Saturday, the campus would be roiled by a rapid and unprecedented sequence of events. On Thursday, February 20, the *Thresher* bristled with argumentative columns and letters about the ROTC on campus; the postponement of an appearance at Rice by Columbia student activist and SDS leader Mark Rudd (he was sick); student reactions to the new proposals on penalties for campus disruptions; and notices of two upcoming events promoted by members of the Rice SDS. The first was a meeting on the plight of Lee Otis Johnson, a TSU student who had recently been arrested. The second was a meeting to discuss the idea of a Black Studies Department at Rice.[72]

But then, on Friday, February 21, an unforeseen event suddenly interrupted all these discussions. News leaked out that the trustees had selected William H. Masterson as Rice's next president without consulting with the faculty and student committee formed the previous fall, igniting a weekend full of the largest demonstrations the university had ever seen. The shocking news broke as severe storms swept across Houston, swamping campus streets. By the end of Friday, hundreds of students had braved the weather to attend an SA meeting and discuss a resolution protesting the trustees' move. Trustees Herb Allen and James Teague announced the board's decision at a meeting of all faculty held that same afternoon, describing Masterson as a timely leader who would appeal to the local community and keep a "firm hand on the tiller in these troubled times." But the faculty, presented at that meeting with a petition started by Grob and several other professors, passed its own resolutions "vigorously" protesting the procedure by which Masterson had been selected.[73]

In the furious hours that followed, a teach-in was planned at the Rice gym for the next day (Saturday), to be held at the same time that the board was planning a press conference to introduce Masterson at the faculty club. The teach-in would be followed by a silent protest march to the front of Lovett Hall, which would pass by the press conference in Cohen House while it was still in progress, and end in the grassy area outside the Sallyport known as the Founder's Court.

As Davidson later put it, however, in those years many things were happening, all at the same time. That Saturday morning, at nine o'clock, Grob's Ad Hoc Committee on Minority Admissions went on with its already scheduled meeting, the first to be attended by the committee's six new student members, including Linda Faye Williams and John Birotte.[74] The committee spent the first half-hour talking about the Masterson news before turning to admissions business (hurriedly, one member recalled, so that they could make it to the teach-in). In the end, those who attended the Grob meeting arrived late to the gym, too late to catch most of a series of speeches but not too late to join the march, which soon swelled to more than one thousand faculty and students as it proceeded down the inner loop toward Lovett Hall.[75]

Also joining the march—in another sign of how many things were happening, all at once—was a prospective Black student from Galveston, whose parents had arranged for him to meet that day with history professor and new Hanszen College master Ira D. Gruber. Gruber, an active participant in that winter's recruiting activities with Grob, told the high-school student that he wanted to attend the march and invited him to come along as they talked along the way. "You've come on a very wild day," the professor informed the teenager, as they fell in with the marchers.[76]

"Wild" was just the impression the marchers were hoping to avoid. Seeking to preempt any criticisms based on "unkempt" appearances, most of the men came to the march clad in coats and ties; the women wore skirts. Many pinned a simple, suggestive protest sign to their clothes, bearing the words, in capital letters, "It Can't Happen Here." Assembled just outside the Sallyport, they waited for the press conference in the nearby faculty club to conclude. Then, in a dramatic moment that would be splashed across the next day's Houston newspapers, Masterson approached the crowd to speak.

The newly announced president made some brief remarks through a bullhorn and took only six questions—one from a professor, the other five from students, and all of them captured on a recording by student-run KOWL radio. Unrecorded, and only possible to imagine, is what Gruber's guest from Galveston must have been thinking as the protest unfolded, or what he inferred from the sixth and final question being asked by none other than John Birotte, the Black freshman who had spoken out about SCOUR at the William Marsh Rice statue in December.

Birotte had just come that morning from his first meeting with Grob's committee. That same day, in a special edition of the *Thresher,* he would sign his name (along with twenty-six others) to a statement criticizing the board's action and connecting it to a larger series of recent events, including the "handling of the Charles Freeman admissions case, [and] the handling of the SCOUR report." Now, as Birotte stepped to the microphone in Founder's Court, he seized his chance to address Rice's new president directly.[77]

"I'd like to ask you point blank," Birotte began, in a loud, clear voice,

> whether or not you consider the forming of a community mind, the first community mind that's ever been at Rice University, virtually since the beginning of its history, something which you can refute by going ahead and just accepting what the board of trustees has said. . . . Do you still believe that you can form a workable rapport with the students and the faculty of this university and do you feel that if you do accept this appointment as president . . . that Rice University will ever be any university worth what it has been in the past . . . under your reign as president?[78]

Birotte's concluding line was greeted by raucous applause from the crowd. Masterson declined to say what he would do next and took no further questions. A long series of additional meetings took place that night and into Sunday, before a student-and-faculty poll was taken on Monday to confirm the widespread opposition to his selection. On Tuesday, Masterson resigned.

In hindsight, and from one point of view, Birotte's statement had been only a small part of those historic events. Yet from another point of view, it also had a larger significance. With just a few words, the first-year student from the Third Ward had boldly staked out his position on a vital and historically significant community issue, in the middle of a year in which "minority student admissions" had been a virtually unceasing topic of conversation and controversy, and in full view of hundreds of Rice professors and fellow students. Birotte had identified himself with the broader "community mind" on display outside the Sallyport. And he had also laid claim, notwithstanding his own very recent arrival and the recent arrival of Black students in general, to the long history of the university and its traditions of excellence, challenging its new leader to be worthy of what Rice had been, at its best, in the past. Finally, Birotte had given voice to what many protesters later said that they felt that weekend: something new and transformative at Rice. To many standing outside Lovett Hall that afternoon, and perhaps to Birotte, and perhaps even to the visiting Black recruit from Galveston (who joined Gruber at Hanszen for lunch afterwards, along with a Black female student whom they had encountered during the march), the university appeared more open and inclusive and fearless of high emprise than it had ever been.[79]

But hard realities were yet to come, for not everyone saw the events of that day in the same light. A sizable segment of the student body was not there at Lovett Hall and did not approve of those who were. One senior who supported Masterson wrote to the *Thresher* that he felt the president would do a good job, especially as "student unrest becomes more troublesome at Rice." Afterwards, in the hearing of at least one person, H. Malcolm Lovett was to describe the peaceful protest that Saturday as nothing less than a "riot." And in the succeeding weeks and months, even those who had been central movers in the protests began to wonder what exactly, aside from one man's resignation, the events of that weekend had truly achieved.[80]

After all, on all of the major issues that had roiled the campus before February 21, including "minority student admissions," the Rice community remained as divided as it had ever been, and now there was one important difference. Henceforth campus debates and conversations would continue on ground shaped by aftershocks from the Masterson affair.

Persistent Fights

In the spring of 1969, as protests over Masterson engulfed the Rice campus, Linda Faye Williams was taking "Political Sociology" with Professor Chandler Davidson, the course that, she later said, played a key role in redirecting her career plans toward political science. The class required a research paper, but Williams was initially unsure of which direction to take, so she went to visit the professor in his office hours. There, Davidson suggested to Williams that she write a paper on a seemingly simple question. What would happen to Texas politics if Black, Latino, and poor white voters turned out to vote at the same rate as affluent whites?[81]

In between her other classes and activities, Williams disappeared into the library to read and research the issue, draft and rewrite, then research and read some more. When she was finished, her tightly argued paper had run to fifty typescript pages, and she had concluded that the question was not as simple as it seemed. At first, Williams had hypothesized that even a higher turnout of minority voters in Texas would still be defeated by white voters acting as a bloc. By the end, after closer investigation of the evidence, she instead found that poor white voters, as a class, shared economic interests and voting preferences in common with nonwhites. Their alliance had the potential to transform politics in the state.

There was a caveat, though, to Williams's conclusion. Since the passage of major civil rights and voting rights legislation, it had become tempting for even white liberals in Texas to begin thinking that racism was now a thing of the past. But nonwhite voters knew that inclusion at the polls alone would not "melt the obstacles standing in the way of minority groups like snow in the summer sun." No movement appealing to Black and Latino voters would succeed if it missed the continuing salience of racism in American life, and that was precisely what many white liberals in Texas tended to miss. Williams predicted, therefore, that minority group interests would still have the best chance for political success only when they happened to converge with the interests and values of white elites.

Williams was already beginning to hone a set of scholarly questions that would occupy her throughout most of her subsequent academic career—questions about race, class, politics, and what her seminar paper called "a persistent fight for full citizenship." She was also already formulating answers marked by ambivalence and complexity. In her junior-year paper, closely mentored by Davidson, she had arrived at a somewhat guarded forecast for the future of racial liberalism through a careful study of Texas state politics up to 1968. And yet, looking back, a careful study of what happened at Rice in her junior year could well have yielded similar findings, on a smaller scale.

On the one hand, the Masterson crisis had brought together a remarkably broad coalition of groups to protest his appointment—faculty members from various places on the political spectrum; students who belonged to the SDS, the Young Democrats, and the Young Republicans; students both from the white majority and from among the small number of Black undergraduates at Rice. Yet that broad coalition had relied on a unique convergence of interests—namely, opposition to the process used to select Masterson, mingled with dislike for the man himself. By contrast, issues pertaining directly to minority student admissions had failed that year to rally consensus across political lines. Birotte's question to Masterson in February was recorded and applauded; his comments on SCOUR in December apparently were not.[82]

Such contrasts became even clearer later that spring in the final resolution of Charles Freeman's readmissions case. After a faculty committee returned to Freeman's case in April 1969 and voted (again) to readmit him, acting president Frank Vandiver (who was appointed by the board after Masterson stepped down) vetoed the committee's decision. Vandiver announced to the press that, given Freeman's failing academic record at Rice and TSU, "Any other decision would have compromised the academic integrity of Rice."[83]

Emboldened, perhaps, by their success in defeating Masterson's appointment, some students and faculty started a petition campaign and gathered at the statue of William Marsh Rice to oppose Vandiver's veto of the faculty committee's decision. They framed the issue, as the CEC had predicted in January that some would, largely as one of faculty rights, but they also hinted that racial discrimination was at work. Freeman, too, returned to campus to speak about his own case, dressed for his speech (as the anti-Masterson forces had been) in a dress shirt and tie.[84]

But unlike in February, when some 1,200 students and faculty had marched against Masterson, a meeting called to support Freeman attracted fewer than 350 supporters. While many across campus had found, in the Masterson crisis, a shared rallying point, or what Birotte had called a "community mind," the case for Freeman underscored the sharp limits of their consensus. And when student members of the SDS insisted that Freeman's case was connected to another decision made by Vandiver that April—the acting president's refusal to permit the SDS to host a regional conference on campus—efforts on Freeman's behalf quickly began to fracture, losing their focus and moral clarity.[85]

At the rally in the quad, for example, ostensibly held to support one of Rice's first Black students in his quest to resume his college education, SDS leaders sported black armbands and small Confederate flags (a jab at Vandiver's scholarship on the South in the Civil War), ate watermelon, and attached a list of demands to a melon left at the president's office, using symbols charged with histories of racism to advance concerns about the powers of faculty committees and student free speech. One of the white student leaders at the rally, a classmate of Linda Williams in Davidson's course that spring, told the press that the choice to use the watermelons was fitting, "because Vandiver treats us like a bunch of niggers." Pictures of watermelons also appeared in the 1969 yearbook, along with a summation of the differences between the Masterson and Freeman cases: "While the Masterson protest gained support from widespread personal feelings against Masterson, the Charlie Freeman protest had little support because not enough people cared about Charlie."[86]

A few years later, Freeman (by then working as an insurance agent after completing an undergraduate degree at Lamar University in Beaumont) told a reporter from the Houston *Chronicle,* as he looked back on that moment, that he felt the SDS "were more interested in promoting themselves than in helping me." In the aftermath of the Masterson crisis and widening protests over Vietnam, he had become "a convenient issue" for student radicals. By the same token, however, as a growing national conservative movement won major political victories in the coming years, the Freeman case and the SDS became convenient talking points for those who opposed the changes taking place at American universities, especially the behavior of activist faculty and students. Indeed, letters praising Vandiver's decisions that spring poured into the president's office from community members, alumni, faculty, and students, one of whom wrote that she was glad "Rice standards are high" and "the admission of Charlie Freeman would be a step in the lowering of these standards." That fall, when letters appealing for alumni support in a $33,000,000 fund drive went out, the responses also showed general support for Vandiver's actions, including from one alumnus who felt he had not gone far enough: "You also *need*—to get rid of the hippies & foreigners so as to permit Texas white students to attend Rice in accordance with *the will of the Founder.*"[87]

While few on campus may have shared that sentiment exactly, the ease with which Vandiver defused the Freeman crisis by appealing to "academic integrity" was telling. And more evidence of the narrowness of campus consensus came that May, as participants in the Masterson crisis began to sit down for interviews with a university-funded oral history project to document their reflections on what had happened. In January, Grob had been sure the university was beginning to embrace social justice as a core value. Only a few months later, speaking to an interviewer after the Masterson crisis and the Freeman case, Grob was less sure. The professor now predicted that there would be, at Rice, a larger "retreat from national goals, a growing conservatism about student affairs, minority groups, a resistance to change."[88]

Others at Rice saw the February crisis as the product of personal vendettas against Masterson, held by craven or overly idealistic faculty who had manipulated the students and did not know the first thing about being a university president. That was the perspective of at least one member of Gordon's CEC, who contributed an oral history to the archives in 1969. Never mentioning Grob by name, dean of humanities Virgil Topazio (a Masterson supporter) gave minority student recruitment as just one example of the wishful thinking to which some faculty, in his view, were prone. "Why can't we have a hundred black students?" he claimed that some professors and students were asking. "Go out and get a hundred black students—recruit them from the boon docks. As soon as you come across someone who's black, bring him in."[89]

What such idealists failed to consider, according to Topazio, were the practicalities. "Just look at the financial picture now, aside from the standards of the school or anything else." It took money to "go scouring the country to find these students, which we did, incidentally, and we have infinitely more black students this year." And then it would cost even more money to "subsidize" their education. "This is not exactly a pittance. I mean, somebody has to make a decision. We have so much money to play with, and how much of this can we afford for this, and so on."[90]

Such comments exposed the cleavages that remained at Rice on the question of what to do about "minority student admissions." That March, just before Vandiver's appointment, the CEC formally expressed concern about rumors that the university was applying "different admissions criteria" to the Black applicants who had been recruited by Grob's committee, prompting a detailed review by the registrar of the class ranks, test scores (including IQ scores when available), and evaluations of all African American students considered since 1965, with comparison to a small sample of white students. The review concluded "that the policy on admissions had not been changed; that it had been and still was, the objective to select the best qualified students," and that "the standards of admission would apply to all races and not a select few." Nonetheless, the questions about standards and the qualifications of minority students, which had been raised earlier that year by Lovett and Teague as well, would persist.[91]

So would questions about the university's investment in minority student recruitment. In a report to the Faculty Council that February, Grob estimated that, to continue its recruiting efforts in the 1969–70 school year and implement its other recommendations, his committee would need at least $20,000. A few trustees that spring, led by Teague, agreed to help raise money from local corporations for individual scholarships for minority students. But they balked at the idea of adding that need to the general fund drive, which would have flagged it as more of a budgetary and strategic priority. And when acting president Vandiver later broached a request by Grob for more recruitment funds, the "Board hit the ceiling."[92]

As for Linda Faye Williams, how much she knew about any of this as a new member of Grob's committee may never be known. By the time she joined the group, much of its work for the year was already concluded. The application deadline had passed, and on February 24, 1969, the day before Masterson resigned as president, Grob presented his committee's formal report to a regular meeting of the Faculty Council. According to the meeting's minutes, the committee recommended a possible reduction in freshman course loads, an expanded system of tutoring, and the hiring of "at least one Negro on the staff who could serve as a counseling friend for the disadvantaged Black students." Grob focused above all on what the committee justifiably regarded as its most significant work, the recruitment trips by faculty members over the winter break. That fall, a total of eighteen Black students would enroll at Rice, more than all of the Black students who had enrolled in the first four years of integration at the university combined.[93]

In view of those gains, which were thanks in large part to the Grob committee's efforts, it is not difficult to imagine why (as she later recalled) Williams's decision to place a bus token on her senior page the following spring seemed to "bother a lot of the progressive faculty." And yet, in view of the complex history that had led up to those gains, it is also crystal clear why Williams still felt there was so much more to do.[94]

After all, some of the students who entered in the fall of 1969 would arrive under circumstances similar to those Williams had experienced as a matriculant in 1966. One first-year student would become the first (and, for all of the 1969–70 school year, the only) Black student at Brown College. At least one college still asked new residents if they would be "willing to room with a person of another race." In January 1970, a regular columnist for the *Thresher* asserted in print that "the mean intelligence quotient of the Negroid race is . . . lower than Caucasians and Orientals of equivalent socio-economic circumstances." Around the same time, arrangements were made to hire a Black counselor as recommended by Grob's committee, but he was given a job description that did not explicitly include support for Black students. And there was still not a single member of the faculty who was Black.[95]

There were, however, Black students, with more on the way. And if Williams's senior page served as a reminder of the burdens still being shouldered by some who entered Rice, it served, too, as a harbinger of how Black students would challenge convention, bring new distinction to the university, and push the institution to higher, more inclusive, ideals. Seen in the light of what was to come, the token symbolized not only integration's conflicted beginnings, but also the beginnings of Black student protest at Rice. With her sights now set on the University of Chicago, as the winner of a coveted Woodrow Wilson Fellowship for graduate study, Linda Faye Williams did not remain on campus long enough to see the fruits of that protest firsthand. But by the time Williams's two sisters followed her to Rice from Lovelady, Texas, enrolling at the university in the fall of 1973, there would be, waiting for them, something truly new in the university's history: a Black Students Union to join.[96]

8 | BLACK STUDENT UNIONS

On Saturday, February 12, 1972, as basketball fans streamed towards the Rice Gymnasium for a televised home game against the Texas Longhorns, a small group of Black students gathered just outside the gym, holding protest signs. The students had stayed up the night before to hand-letter the posters, one of which asked, rhetorically, "All for Rice, Rice for All?" Another read: "INTEGRATION with SEGREGATION brings about DEMONSTRATION." And to any spectators who noticed the group as they rushed towards their seats, the implication of all the signs, taken together, was clear: Rice remained, in important respects, far from desegregated.

Few passersby that day would have recognized all of the protesters by name, but many would have known the one identified as a spokesman: Rodrigo D. Barnes. An all-conference linebacker on the football team, Barnes had joined Rice in 1968 as one of the first four Black student-athletes at the university, and the local sports reporters on campus that day certainly knew him. The next morning, articles about the protest appeared in the Sunday editions of Houston's two newspapers, alongside reports of the Owls' loss to the Longhorns. The *Thresher* published a photograph of the protest on its own front page a few days later, just beneath a story about Rice's plans to build a thirty-eight-thousand-square-foot addition to the gymnasium.[1]

The *Thresher* did not publish a story about the protest, however. Only the city papers tried to describe the students' aims. And perhaps because Barnes was involved, or perhaps because the article was published in their sports sections, or perhaps because Southwest Conference football was something close to a civil religion in Texas in those days, the initial articles focused primarily on only one of the students' posters: the one highlighting the absence of a Black coach at Rice. Barnes was asked to speak on that point. Both the athletics director and newly hired head football coach Al Conover were asked for comment, too. Yet as Barnes made clear in his comments to the press, the hiring of a Black coach was only one of the protesters' concerns that spring. The university still had only fifty-nine Black students, graduate and undergraduate. There were still no Black officials in admissions or administration. And most concerning of all to students was the number of Black faculty members then teaching at Rice. That number was zero.[2]

True, the *Thresher* had reported in January that one Black professor, identified elsewhere as Dr. Marion Oliver, would be joining the Mathematical Sciences Department in September. (One of the signs outside the gym in February appeared to comment on the news: "One WHOLE BLACK Professor. Give Us Another Token, PLEASE.") A Black woman was reportedly under consideration for a new faculty position as well.[3]

In the end, though, only one of those two prospects came: Myrtle Francis, who held two degrees from Texas Southern University and started in the fall as an instructor in the Health and Physical Education Department, likely making her the first Black woman to teach, briefly, at Rice. The university would soon approach Professor Thomas Freeman from TSU about teaching religion part-time at Rice, but that appointment would not be offered or accepted until after the students' picket. As early as 1969, an official with the federal government's Office of Civil Rights had noted the absence of even one Black professor at Rice and told acting president Frank Vandiver that it was "perhaps the last major university in the Southwest to be without such a faculty member." Three years later, the fact remained.[4]

With these realities in view, the protesters who assembled outside the Rice gym in February 1972 knew that the university needed change, change that required united student action. On April 10, the Student Association approved a constitution for the Black Students Union (BSU) of Rice University, making it an official student organization for the first time. And in the weeks after its formation, members of the BSU began working together on another collective goal: a new campus building, to be called the "Black Student Union Center," that they hoped could serve as a headquarters for the BSU and make more space for Black life on campus.[5]

That spring, now more than fifty years past, a majority of the Black students at Rice would sign a petition calling on the university to build such a center. The petition, which survives today in the Woodson Research Center, was signed by Curtis Davis and Derrick Lewis and Don Fredieu "Esq."; by Leroy L. Sterling Jr., Gerald Lyons, and Stennis Lenoir. It was signed by Kenneth Walker and Kenneth Prevot and Gary Fry; by Goldie Domingue, Brenda James, Regina Tippens, Mike Tyler, Alpha Morgan, and Althea Jones. The petition was signed by Rodrigo Barnes and Jan Faye West. And there were other names, too, as well as other actions taken that year by the BSU, including the organization of an Easter Egg hunt for community children and the university's first-ever memorial event to honor Martin Luther King Jr.[6]

In short, the first members of the Black Students Union were clear and convinced about the kinds of steps that Rice still needed to take to continue its desegregation. The question was: How would the university respond?

"Situations Which Must Be Corrected"

By 1972, Black students at many universities had formed organizations similar to Rice's BSU, and in many places their formation had coincided with and created pressure for the establishment of departments, centers, and programs in Black studies, Africana studies, or African and African American studies. In the years after the rise of the Black Power movement and the King assassination, hundreds of such initiatives began across the country, including at schools that Rice was beginning to see as aspirational peers.

The advent of Black studies and related disciplines was never uncontested, nor was the formation of Black student groups. On many campuses, Black studies arose from student, faculty, and community movements that aimed at the radical reorganization of universities in the service of social justice. On other campuses, administrators, faculty, and funding agencies viewed Africana or African American studies programs in more utilitarian terms, hoping their creation would help diversify student and faculty ranks while blunting student radicalism. In either case, such programs championed the proposition that Black life, history, and culture in the Americas deserved, needed, and rewarded scholarly study in any modern university.[7]

Even after universities created Black studies or Afro-American studies programs, fierce debates continued over their curriculum, governance, hiring, and funding. Still, on many other campuses, these debates were well underway by 1972. In February 1969, for example, while Rice University was consumed with the Masterson crisis, student activists at the University of Houston were engaged in protests that resulted in the creation of an African American Studies Program at UH that year. A Center for African and African American Studies would not launch at Rice University until 2019.[8]

The protest outside the basketball game in February 1972 makes clear, nonetheless, that the history of Black organizing and Black study at Rice dates back to the dynamic years in which Black student movements were taking shape across the city and the country. The aims of the BSU at Rice reflected many of that broader movement's concerns, particularly in their calls for Black faculty, more support for Black student life, more courses and programs on Black history and culture, and spaces on campus for all of the above.

The origins of Rice's BSU can be traced at least to March 1971, a year before the protest at the basketball game, when John Birotte announced in the *Thresher* that Black students had recently met in the Will Rice College commons to found an "organization of Afro-American members" of the colleges. As cochairman of the new group, Birotte explained to the *Thresher* that it was the culmination of "many pressures" felt by students over the first few years of integration. He singled out the "separation and breakdown" of Black students' community through their dispersal in the residential colleges, which functioned too much like "another type of fraternity." But this, Birotte said, was only one of the "situations which must be corrected one way or another" if Rice was to become "the rational university community it claims to be."[9]

The next fall, an editorial in the *Thresher* by Professor Chandler Davidson offered more information about the range of Black students' concerns, highlighting in particular the absence of a single Black or Mexican American professor or administrator at Rice. "Black students I have discussed the matter with at Rice and on other campuses stress the importance of this fact," Davidson said, adding that more and better-funded recruitment efforts were needed to convince prospective Black students "that they will be welcome."[10]

Two weeks later, Richard Tapia, assistant professor of mathematical sciences, wrote the *Thresher* to agree with Davidson. Though he clarified that Rice did now have, in Tapia, at least one Mexican American member of the faculty, he shared Davidson's dismay about "the very sad situation at Rice, namely the lack of minority students and minority faculty." Since his hire in 1970, Tapia had found the attitude of most faculty and administrators on campus to be that "blacks and browns lower the standards; minorities have nothing to offer. It is this latter attitude," he added, "that I find the most difficult to understand since I have never experienced it on any other campus." The next year Tapia would assist Mexican American students (who were also underrepresented at Rice, due to a long history of prejudice and discrimination directed at their own communities both at the university and beyond it) in founding the Rice Association of Mexican-American Students (RAMAS).[11]

New student organizations like the BSU and RAMAS, along with faculty like Davidson and Tapia, posed a series of critical questions to the newest president of Rice University, Norman Hackerman, who came from the University of Texas to take the top post at Rice in the fall of 1970. At the time, federal officials charged with enforcing new equal employment opportunity regulations were asking questions, too. At a Faculty Council meeting early in his tenure, Hackerman noted that representatives from the Department of Health, Education, and Welfare (HEW) had repeatedly criticized Rice's record of "passive rather than active" recruiting of Black faculty applicants and had warned that federal grant funding could be in jeopardy. He "urged" departments to become more active.[12]

Yet when it came to increasing the numbers of minority students and faculty numbers at Rice, Hackerman did not express the same degree of urgency as faculty colleagues like Tapia and Davidson. In an interview granted with the alumni newsletter just before he arrived, for example, Hackerman was asked, "Do you favor any particular increase in the minorities at Rice?" The new president replied with what was, by then, a common line at Rice: "I think those in minority groups who can take the courses and the program that Rice offers, certainly ought to be encouraged to come." But when presented in December 1970 with a request to fund the Grob committee's minority-student recruitment trips, Hackerman agreed to give the group only $1,000 from the president's discretionary funds, far less than the committee needed to maintain and expand its travel, and said that the funding would be reviewed in one year.[13]

Hackerman showed a similar caution in response to a memorandum from a newly formed Affirmative Action Committee (created largely in response to prodding from HEW officials), which recommended that the university set aside $40,000 or $50,000 to be used by departments in the recruitment of minority faculty candidates. In a marginal note next to that proposed amount, Hackerman wrote, with an eye on Rice's then-straitened finances, "From what!" But whereas the budget presented itself to Hackerman in this instance as a constraint, to some others the budget itself reflected Rice's skewed values. "Somewhere along the line priorities must be changed," Davidson told the *Thresher* in January 1972, "when the university spends only $1,000 for minority recruitment but it spends $76,000 on recruiting for the football team."[14]

A similar argument was made to Hackerman around the same time by one of the star members of that team, Rodrigo Barnes, who certainly had no problem with funds for football but believed that Black students needed more financial support. A dedicated squash player, Hackerman made time for a regular game at the racquetball courts on campus, and Barnes later recalled approaching the president at the gym and engaging him in "several personal discussions" about the concerns of Black students. "Our discussions frequently centered on money—or the lack of it—for student support," remembered Barnes, who also said the president suggested that Black students organize themselves to improve conditions at the university.[15]

"Dr. Hackerman is faced with a number of problems," Barnes would tell the Houston *Post* in April 1972, not long after the student protest outside the UT basketball game: "'He's trying to get his budget together. I respect him as president and as a man. But as chairman of the Black Student Union at Rice University,' [Barnes] added, 'I have a job to do, too.'"[16]

The Education of Rodrigo Barnes

Rodrigo De Triana Barnes had arrived at Rice in the fall of 1968, bringing with him a long and hard education in the depth, breadth, and endurance of anti-Black racism in Texas. The highly touted recruit had grown up poor in all-Black public housing projects in Waco and spent parts of his early childhood raised by his grandmother in an old "plantation shack" outside Calvert with no running water or electricity. As a boy, while collecting firewood, Barnes once came upon the corpse of a Black lynching victim hanging from a tree; on another occasion, while out with his grandmother, he witnessed a white sheriff walk into a local beer joint and shoot the unarmed Black proprietor in the head, right in front of a large Friday evening crowd.[17]

In a memoir published in 2021, Barnes would later recount these and other experiences of growing up in the shadow of Jim Crow, but he also recalled the strong guidance he received from his middle-school band director and high-school football coach (both graduates of Prairie View A&M University) at his all-Black school, George Washington Carver in Waco. Opened in 1956 by a district intent on avoiding school desegregation, Carver High had nonetheless become a source of pride and considerable achievement for members of Waco's Black community. By his senior year, Barnes's performance on the gridiron was drawing the attention of recruiters from predominantly white universities both inside and outside the state, so many that it was difficult to sift the offers. "The main problem I had in doing that," Barnes remembered, "was that I didn't know any adults—teachers and coaches included—who'd gone to any of these other colleges." No one could tell him what to expect.[18]

Though Barnes lacked "a trailblazer to show me a clear path," he would become that trailblazer for others at Rice University. During his senior year of high school, Barnes and Mike Tyler (a fellow Black student-athlete from Waco) were hospitably welcomed for a recruiting visit in Houston by upperclassmen Tommy Alexander and Bucky Allshouse. After one look at the scenic, tree-lined entry onto the Rice campus and the towering height of the Sallyport, he recalled, "I was instantly hooked."[19]

Even before he arrived at Rice that fall, Barnes soon began to learn about the power and benefits of the Rice alumni network, a group from which Black communities had so long been excluded. In the summer after graduating high school, he received a job offer from Mrs. Baird's Bread, a Texas bakery owned and run by a family with several generations of Rice graduates and football patrons. After matriculating at Rice, he would also encounter many white students who welcomed him to campus just as Alexander and Allshouse had, including some who engaged him in late-night conversations in their colleges about music, culture, and life. Some (surprisingly to Barnes, given his experiences with white people in Waco) were willing to lend him their cars.[20]

And yet, like the few Black students who had arrived before them, Barnes's few Black classmates encountered racism on campus, too. During his first week,

Barnes later recalled, a white student in his own college approached him and bluntly asked, "Hey, nigger. Where you from?" Taken aback, Barnes tried to explain why the slur landed like a slap, but the student said that where he was from, that was what all Black people were called. Stahlé Vincent, a fellow Black scholar-athlete who matriculated that year, recalled attending a freshman-week dance at which two Jones College residents made clear they would not dance with "people like you." Later that same week, while Vincent walked in the quad, two female students circled him and said, "I thought you people had tails." Vincent, like Barnes, wondered, "What have I gotten myself into?"[21]

Piercing as these experiences were on their own, they were sharpened by the many other challenges that came with moving from all-Black schools and communities to a virtually all-white space. White students had developed college traditions—like planting stink bombs in a dorm cooling system, or pelting freshmen with water balloons, or raising funds through "slave auctions" in which students "sold" dates or services to other students—that may well have been intended as harmless pranks, but were not always easy to see as such in the murky twilight of segregation.[22] Even the music white students played at their parties was unfamiliar to Barnes, as was the experience of hitting and being hit by *white* teammates and opponents in a football practice or game. Though Barnes opened himself to new experiences, it was not easy to adjust. "It was a complete culture shock," Vincent added later. "The feeling of isolation was intense."[23]

As difficult as they found it to relate to some of their new peers, both Barnes and Vincent found it more difficult to deal with campus adults. "Students had no real power over you," Barnes later observed, "so what they thought and said was relatively innocuous compared to how faculty or staff could treat you." Some professors were known for being sympathetic and welcoming. But when an advisor did not show up to scheduled meetings, or an instructor ignored Black students when calling roll, or a coach kept Black players out of the positions they came to play, or a "reputed liberal" professor refused to lend a Black female student a book she needed for a paper, but then gladly loaned the requested book to a white classmate instead—all of it gave Black students the clear impression that some faculty and staff did not think they belonged at Rice. One of Barnes's professors publicized his poor grades to the whole class and read racist passages from American literature aloud in a supposedly comical dialect that demeaned Black people. On another occasion, an assistant football coach pulled him aside to advise him not to flirt with white girls.[24]

These experiences added significantly to the challenges faced by Black students when, like a great number of freshmen at Rice, they struggled in first-year courses. At the time, Barnes recalled, "Rice didn't provide much at all in the way of services to any student, white as well as minority, but it was minorities and international students who suffered the most from the lack of a support infrastructure." For example, all students faced the common challenge of overcoming the fear of asking for help when needed. Yet for Black students, the question of whom they could trust was fraught: Some professors—and *which* was not always clear—"really did not want African American students to succeed."[25]

Black students did find mentors on campus, particularly among the nonacademic staff in custodial, secretarial, and dining services, where African Americans were more numerous and often forged close relationships with students. As in earlier decades going back to the Rice Institute's origins, Black staff members faced their own challenges in the struggle for equal respect and equitable treatment at Rice. One white professor surmised before leaving the university in 1968 that "among the Houston Negro community [Rice] has the reputation of being a white Mecca, a white Holy-of-Holies." Yet Black staff members in the early years of integration also clearly took pride in and cared for the first generations of Black undergraduates at Rice. Jan F. West, who matriculated in 1969, later recalled those who "nurtured us—the ladies in the kitchen" and people like Mrs. Alberta Nobles, a Brown College housekeeper who made sure she got to class on time. West's comments were echoed by another student, Karen Kossie-Chernyshev, who said of her later undergraduate experience at Rice, "Some of my fondest memories are the conversations I had in the early 80s with cooks."[26]

Even so, Barnes's early experiences often left him feeling that there was "nobody to go to, and nowhere to get help." He wondered if he had been "naive" in coming to Rice and struggled with self-doubt.[27] With time, though, Barnes came to see that the problems he and other Black students encountered had a history that long predated their arrival in the late 1960s. "Rice had been established to educate Caucasian Houstonians," as Barnes wrote in his memoir, "and the culture of the university had emerged from the prevailing white culture, so white students already had a hand up over minority and international students in learning the Rice ropes."[28]

Despite—or because of—that long history, Barnes recalled, "the university wasn't providing leadership in supporting students who were struggling with issues of race, culture, and socialization, not to mention academics." The question that he could not immediately answer at the time was *why*, along with the question of *how* things could be changed.

The answer to the first question became clearer to him over time. As for the other question, one answer was suggested to Barnes in only his second semester at Rice, when several days of protest led to William H. Masterson's resignation as president. "I didn't know anything about Masterson," Barnes remembered, but "the fallout from his appointment taught me the power of demonstration" on campus. Three springs later, at the Rice-UT basketball game in February 1972, Barnes and his fellow Black students decided they would test the power of demonstration again.[29]

"A University Can Do Things If It Wants To"

The student picketers in February 1972 had several aims, including (as Barnes later wrote) "to appeal to the university to hire a black coach and African American administrators who could provide guidance as well as justice." Barnes hoped that his presence, as perhaps the most famous Black Owl at the time, would raise the profile of the BSU. And although the protest did not make national news like the one that led to Masterson's departure, the picketing did seem to garner some immediate results.[30]

One apparent result was the almost immediate hiring of McCoy McLemore (an alumnus of Jack Yates High School and a former professional basketball player with the Houston Rockets) as the university's first Black assistant coach. "Before that demonstration," Barnes told the Houston *Post* in April 1972, "they said they didn't have any more funds to hire a coach of any kind. But they wound up getting them somewhere, which goes to show you that a university can do things if it wants to."[31]

As if in further illustration of that fact, that April the chair of Rice's Department of Religious Studies approached Thomas Freeman, the legendary Texas Southern University professor and nationally renowned coach of the TSU debate team, to ask about his interest in a guest lecturer position at Rice. Before Freeman could even interview with the dean or fill out an application, he was called and congratulated by the president of TSU, who said that he and Hackerman had spoken personally and agreed that Freeman's appointment at Rice would be good for both schools. He started that fall in a part-time teaching position that would be renewed each year for the next two decades.[32]

Two other hires made after the basketball game protest also suggested that students' direct action was continuing to reverberate. First, Samuel A. Forney, a graduate of Fisk University, was hired that year as the first Black admissions counselor at Rice, part of a broader reorganization that involved shifting official university recruitment efforts away from the ad hoc faculty committee led by Grob and into the Admissions Office. Second, the Office of Information Services, a forerunner of Public Affairs, hired Arthur Pfister, a twenty-two-year-old Black poet who had studied at Tuskegee and now taught at TSU, to be a freelance feature writer for Rice News. In March 1972, Pfister wrote five remarkably unfiltered and culturally sensitive profiles of Black student leaders at Rice (Barnes, Goldie Domingue, Leroy Sterling, Brenda James, and Mike Tyler) for official release through the university's press service.[33]

Clearly, the early members of Rice's BSU had succeeded in getting the attention of university officials. No wonder that Brenda James told Pfister that she was "very much in favor of the recent demonstration at a Rice basketball game in which Black students at Rice made a few situations known to the Rice community that they thought should have been brought to the attention of faculty, staff, and alumni alike." Still, Black students were also under no illusion that one protest had solved every problem at Rice. James also told Pfister, speaking of the protest, "We need more."[34]

Even after the spate of quick actions that spring, many of the substantive issues raised by the students' protest (and by the protests of Black students at many other universities at the time) remained standing concerns. Of the several new Black professional staff and faculty who began working at Rice in 1972, only Freeman would remain for a significant length of time. Moreover, in a pattern that would be oft repeated, the small number of Black faculty and professional staff at the university took on additional work that often went beyond their job descriptions. McLemore helped coach football as well as his own sport (basketball), and in the fall of 1972, he assisted the admissions office with the recruitment of minority students, too.[35]

Black psychologist Dr. Robert Bell was given a similarly broad set of responsibilities when he was hired by Rice the following year. Bell, who received his PhD from UT-Austin and his undergraduate degree at TSU, had previously worked as a consultant for psychiatric services at Rice from 1970 to 1972 before leaving for a job at Vassar College. In 1973, he returned to Rice as director of student advising, though that title failed to convey all of the formal and informal roles that Bell would assume in his years at Rice. In addition to leading academic advising efforts, he served as a consultant in Rice's psychiatric services and its tutorial program; as a sponsor for the BSU and unofficial counselor to Black students; as an appointed member of the Affirmative Action Committee; and as a teaching faculty member in the Department of Psychology, where he began as a professor but was later redefined as an adjunct. That varied workload was due in part to the fact that even after Bell's return to Rice, it was still possible to count Rice's Black faculty members, full time or part time, on one hand. As Bell noted to the Houston *Post* in September 1973, he was one of only three.[36]

Meanwhile, the basketball protest had not fully addressed some of the students' key concerns, such as the need for funds to support Black students, as well as for university leadership on what Barnes called issues of "race, culture, and socialization." At the time, for example, Rice offered only one course about African Americans, a permission-required seminar first taught by southern historian Sanford Higginbotham in 1969 as "Readings in the History of the Negro American." The course was retitled in 1970 as "Readings in the History of the Black American," but even it would disappear from the catalog between 1974 and 1978.[37]

The distribution of Rice's small number of Black undergraduates across the residential colleges also still made it difficult for minority students to connect with each other, as Birotte had noted in 1971. Brenda James, who told Arthur Pfister she had attended a predominantly Black Fort Worth high school "where the ratio of Black students to white *student* was 1600 to 1," encountered a very different situation at Rice, where she was one of about five dozen Black students in a total population of around three thousand. "There are so few of us that we hardly see each other," James said, "and thus hardly have any interrelationships to improve on."[38]

The desire to build more of a community for Black students was one of the reasons why, in the weeks after their protest, BSU members also began to press the university to designate a building on campus as the Black Student Union Center. "We would like to have somewhere to study the black culture," Barnes said. "A building where we could have a library, a meeting room and game room." James believed that such a center could serve as a "catalyst" for other improvements on campus. Mike Tyler told Pfister that it would provide Black students with "a place of our own" while also "improving the school for everyone." And Jan Forney, a freshman psychology major from Waco, predicted to a reporter from the Houston *Post* in April that a BSU building would help Rice attract more Black students, "because these are the things black recruits notice when they come to look at the campus. They always wonder where there's a place we can go."[39]

Student leaders had even identified, in March 1972, an unoccupied building that they believed could work in the short term as a center: a modernistic structure, designed by William Ward Watkin and once used by the campus's Naval ROTC program, that was slated to be demolished. With the support of the chairman of the Department of Architecture, the BSU suggested that students could turn the redesign and renovation of the building into a hands-on, experiential learning project.[40]

The new BSU Center, as the students imagined it, would serve several purposes. The building would provide space for social activities planned by Black students and featuring Black culture. It would house an office for BSU leaders and a faculty sponsor. The building could also, the students hoped, serve some of the functions performed at other universities by academic departments. It would hold a library, like many of the residential colleges did, but stocked with books and art about Black culture and history. It would have space for special courses (similar to Rice's unique student-taught "college courses") on the Black experience, thereby supplementing a formal curriculum at Rice that largely neglected the subject. And it could host lectures, presentations, and concerts for the whole campus, sponsored by the BSU.[41]

Rice administrators, however, were not easy to persuade on these points. On April 12, dean of students F. A. Wierum met for about an hour and a half with Curtis Davis, an architecture student from Florida who had just become the new chairman of the BSU. Wierum told Davis (in the dean's own words) "that I did not think his arguments justified the University setting aside a facility" for Black students. In a handwritten memo after the meeting, Wierum put down his suspicion that what Black students really wanted was "a combination of non-residential college and black studies department." To Wierum, such proposals smacked of "separatism," and they would grant the BSU "a power status not enjoyed by any other student group except the colleges." The dean of students told Davis that the Naval ROTC building was going to be demolished and could not serve as a center for Black students; Davis, according to Wierum, "would not accept the answer, but wanted to discuss it and try to convince me of their real need."[42]

Wierum was far from alone in his skepticism, which reflected widespread suspicions among white higher education leaders at the time about race-conscious policies generally and Black studies in particular. In a 1968 speech that was published in 1970 in the *Sallyport*, Rice's dean of humanities, Virgil Topazio, even ventured to say that "rash demands" at some universities "for the establishment of Afro-American studies taught by black professors under black administrators in completely autonomous black departments" represented an "attempt to shelter" student "misfits" and campus activists, who were not prepared "for the rigors of an intellectual life."[43]

Such attitudes illustrated some of the political headwinds that Davis and the BSU students still faced in their quest for a center, while also underlining why a Black cultural space seemed so important to students. On the day after his meeting with Wierum, Curtis Davis published a letter in the *Thresher* laying out the case for a BSU Center, calling on students to sign a petition in its favor, and—without naming the dean—responding to some of the objections he had heard Wierum express. The goal of the BSU, Davis explained, was not to create a "separatist feeling on campus." Rather, "the overall cultural and educational aspects of the center would be to the benefit of the university as a whole," especially through the events the BSU would host there.[44]

The kinds of events Black students had in mind became clear a few days later, when the BSU held the campus's first-ever memorial event honoring Martin Luther King Jr. On April 15, 1972, BSU students hosted a Black art exhibit in the Rice Memorial Center (RMC); a lecture by a Southern Christian Leadership Conference speaker on King's life and legacy; a panel with local Black Houston leaders in the Grand Ballroom of the RMC; and an evening dance and concert (also in the RMC) by a six-piece band and vocal group from Baton Rouge, Louisiana, called Black Blood.[45]

BSU students envisioned more events like these being hosted in their proposed building. So on May 9, 1972, before leaving campus for the summer, Davis wrote directly to President Hackerman to "once again emphasize the need for a Black Student Union Center at Rice" and to ask how much the university would be willing to invest in remodeling the NROTC building. About a month later, dean of undergraduate affairs M. V. McEnany was tasked with telling Davis that the proposal could not be approved; the NROTC building had to be torn down. "I know this will be a disappointment to you," McEnany wrote Davis, "but no other conclusion was possible under the circumstances. I hope that your group will continue to work for the interest of the black students on campus and will let me help you toward realization of your objectives in any way that I can."[46]

Davis may have been disappointed, but he and other members of the BSU were no less determined. After returning to campus in the fall, they managed to identify an alternate location for their proposed center. It was a small, steel shed, tucked behind the bleachers of the track stadium, that had been once used as a studio by the Fine Arts Department. The old building was now set aside for use primarily by the Athletics Department, but by the start of October 1972, BSU students had secured permission to redesign, furnish, and use the space as their own. Their continued lobbying of the president's office also bore some fruit that autumn, when Hackerman approved the use of $2,000 from the President's Discretionary Fund for remodeling the metal shed.

So it was that in 1973, despite the resistance students had encountered from multiple officials since first proposing the center, a new caption appeared on the official campus map published each year in the *General Announcements*. The shed behind the bleachers was marked as number "40" on the map. And it was labeled in the legend as the "Black Student Union Building."[47]

"A Tin Shack Located in the Middle of a Swamp"

The creation of the Black Student Union Building and its designation as such on Rice's official campus map demonstrated just how much the BSU had managed to achieve in its first year as a formal organization. It was not, however, a panacea. One problem was location. The Naval ROTC building had been right on Rice Boulevard near a heavily used part of campus, just behind the Mechanical Engineering Lab. The shed behind the stadium sat on what was then the far outskirts of campus, in an unlit, unpaved area prone to flooding from Harris Gully. It stood adjacent to a ramshackle wooden house that served as the campus recycling center, which was regularly surrounded by heaps of aluminum cans and scrap metal. And it was accessible by car only via one shell road that could only be reached from Stockton Drive.

Conveniently located, the Black Student Union Building was not. Nor was the unfurnished and unfinished metal shed (which lacked a bathroom and had been used most recently by the Art Department for projects that were especially "noisy, odorous, and messy") in any way prepared for occupancy by a student group. A significant amount of remodeling work—which students estimated would cost $13,000—needed to be done. Yet only $2,000 had been allotted for the work from the President's Discretionary Fund—an amount roughly equivalent to the budget just for replacing the furniture in one residential college lounge.[48]

Throughout the 1972–73 school year, BSU members worked hard to make up the gap in their budget, while also taking on some of the remodeling work themselves. They organized a homecoming raffle that netted around $250 in proceeds, held a spaghetti dinner that raised around $100, and even collected glass Coke bottles to recover $7 in returned bottle deposits. At the start of October 1972, BSU officers also approached the Student Association (SA) to seek funds. In response, senators agreed that BSU students could keep the profits the SA earned from the use of Xerox machines in the library—provided that Black students accepted the job of servicing the copiers and keeping them supplied with paper.[49]

Nevertheless, by the end of the spring semester, the BSU was still well short of the money needed to make its building usable. The Xerox concession had earned only about $500, half of the amount projected when the deal was made. BSU officers were informed by the Building and Grounds Department that they had quickly run through all but $29.32 of the $2,000 from the president's office on lumber, interior lighting, and hourly labor costs for university electricians and carpenters, who for that amount had only managed to take out an old wall and cabinets, install new framing, and put in overhead light fixtures.

Meanwhile, flooring, wall panels, exterior lighting, landscaping, a bathroom, and lounge and office furniture had yet to be purchased or installed in the shed, which also lacked air conditioning of any kind. Even with its fundraisers, BSU members had barely been able to cover expenses for the year's activities, which included hosting an on-campus production about Martin Luther King Jr. performed by the Black History Club of Galveston's Ball High School; making a pamphlet used by the Admissions Office in recruiting Black students; buying a used stereo for their space; and renting equipment they had used to paint the BSU Building themselves.[50]

Such was the situation inherited by new BSU chairperson Gloria Guilford, who became, in March 1973, the first woman to lead the organization. In the month after her election, therefore, Guilford's first priority was to write directly to President Hackerman with an itemized list of charges by Buildings and Grounds for the BSU center. Guilford asked Hackerman for an additional $583.66 to at least finish flooring and paneling before the new school year. He approved $490.[51]

Simultaneously, Guilford wrote to the president of the SA to request $1,385 for the coming year. About half of that amount, she said, would cover a "Get Acquainted Party," a charity dance to buy toys for local children, and two movie screenings in the coming year; the other half would go towards furniture for the building. The discouraging reply was that it was against SA policy to grant funds to student organizations, and even the Xerox concession might not be available to the BSU again: "Next fall the Student Association will decide whether it will service the machines itself or contract with a student group to do that job."[52]

A few months later, in September 1973, the SA did decide that it would award the Xerox concession to a student group again. But conflict arose when KTRU Rice Radio, which already received two dollars each year from each student in a blanket tax, submitted its own bid for the right to operate the machines, vying with the BSU for the extra money. At a contentious SA meeting about the issue, discussion eventually turned "to a search for other sources of funds, especially for the Black Student Union."[53]

One college president suggested that the BSU's representatives should approach each residential college instead to ask for donations, on the grounds that "since there are such small proportions of blacks in each College, the average black at the University gains more from the BSU than from his or her particular College." On this proposal, if the colleges devoted some of their budgets to the BSU, the SA could then award the Xerox concession to KTRU and both groups would be funded.[54]

But the proposal sparked what the *Thresher* called a "major controversy" over the next week. Only two of the eight colleges agreed to give $100 each to the BSU, and even those that donated sharply rebuked the SA for trying to "pass the buck." The dilemma was resolved only when KTRU's student manager withdrew the radio station's bid, leaving the BSU to maintain the Xerox machines again, but not before an SA vice president proposed an amendment requiring that any BSU events funded by the concession had to be open to *all* students. Guilford objected to the implication, noting that "BSU policy is that all events are open to everyone," and the amendment was dropped.[55]

Though the debate over the renewal of the Xerox concession had ended (for the moment) in the BSU's favor, it also underscored the precarity of the group's funding, as well as the difficulty Black students still had in convincing others that their organization was not separatist but performed a vital service to the university. In the months that followed, Guilford sent letters to off-campus groups, including the Dow Chemical Company, asking for financial support. (Dow's reply: "that they are sympathetic toward the appeal but that they contribute directly to Rice University for all students.") Uncertain of whether the BSU would be able to fund a speaker itself as it had long hoped to do, she wrote the university's Committee on Public Lectures to suggest a list of prominent Black speakers for consideration. (She was informed the suggestions came too late.) And she wrote to the Admissions Office, arguing that more of its own budget should be put into recruiting Black students.[56]

Finally, in April 1974, BSU leaders met with the college presidents and masters to put forward a new funding proposal: that each Black student should have the option to direct $15 of the $20 in student fees that they paid to their residential college to the BSU instead. The BSU's need remained great; as Guilford pointed out, they had not yet been able to finish their building, much less build up the library of "Black History volumes" originally envisioned for the center. And the idea of an optional student fee was not entirely without precedent; another student organization, the public interest research group TexPIRG, funded itself by receiving a two-dollar fee collected by Rice from every undergraduate each semester, unless the student opted out.[57]

The masters and presidents decided instead to revive an earlier approach, first suggested during the controversy over KTRU and the Xerox concession. The presidents would seek to persuade each college to make a "one-time-only allocation" to the BSU for the coming year, covering its short-term budget until some more permanent solution could be found. Five of the eight colleges agreed, even though (as then dean of undergraduate affairs Katherine Tsanoff Brown later noted) an "arrangement by which the B.S.U. goes begging to the Colleges for a yearly or sporadic handout also seems improper and makes their advance planning difficult." When students returned to campus that fall, Dean Brown composed a memo to Hackerman with what she felt would be a better proposal. "On the grounds that the Black Students Union as an organized group can perform certain useful functions for the University," Brown asked Hackerman directly, "would you consider the University's supplying some support to the activities of the organization on an annual basis?"[58]

Brown's letter to the president went on to detail the work that the BSU was performing already. When it came to assisting new Black students with "social adjustment" to Rice, which had a direct bearing "on their chances of academic success," Brown was sure that the BSU "can do this more effectively than any other person or group on campus." The BSU planned to bring "black speakers, musicians, artists, etc. and other activities in support of black culture which would have interest and value for the whole Rice community." (Brown did not mention, but could have, that the BSU's proposed budget for 1975 included plans to support campus programming for Black History Week for the first time.) Finally, said the dean, the BSU was already helping Rice with the "recruitment of qualified black applicants."[59]

Several BSU leaders had indeed been working for the Admissions Office. In addition to putting together a brochure used by recruiters to attract Black students, since 1973 the BSU had organized and funded a welcome mixer for new Black students during freshman orientation week. And even those faculty members most committed to minority student recruitment had noticed that nothing was more effective than testimonies from students themselves. In a public exchange with Hackerman on admissions policies at the faculty club in 1973, Richard Tapia had told the president, "We have students here who are willing to help recruit. I think that would be a very wise thing to do."[60]

Even so, when Brown's memo outlining the arguments in favor of annual BSU funding received its first hearing at a presidential staff meeting on September 9, 1974, "Initial reaction of the staff was negative." Fred Wierum agreed with Brown that the university should support Black student recruitment and mentoring, but he was not convinced by her point about the promotion of Black culture; that was "not truly an area the University should support through BSU." In a note scrawled in pencil on the margin of Brown's memo, Hackerman recorded his own objection to her plan: "can't agree to supp. 1 stud. org. & not others."[61]

In the end, Brown's efforts resulted only in another ad hoc solution. Hackerman agreed to put $2,000 from his discretionary monies into a fund that would now be split between three organizations: the Black Students Union, the Rice Association of Mexican American Students, and the Chinese Student Association. The funds, whose disbursement would be controlled by the SA, would not be available after the 1975–76 school year, as a spur to students to find another long-term solution.[62]

The minority student organizations fund was not nothing, but it fell far short of permanent funding for the BSU. During the fall of 1975, with support from Brown and other student life administrators, all three of the supported student groups sought to make their funding more secure. First they lobbied within the SA for an annual fee of one dollar paid by all students to support "Minority Cultural Affairs." But this proposal, framed even by proponents as a "tax" and by opponents as undue "affirmative action," was resoundingly defeated in a student referendum that November. A revised proposal, which would have allowed each student to direct up to five dollars of their fees from the Rice Program Council (RPC) to a selected student organization instead, was quickly defeated too.[63]

In sum, by the bicentennial year of the United States and the eleventh year of Black undergraduate admissions at Rice University, and despite the Black

Students Union having steadily grown in size (to 85 members by 1975) and in services rendered to the university, and although Rice still had no office or academic unit devoted specifically to the study or promotion of African American history, art, and culture—the BSU still possessed no stable source of funding. A one-time grant from the president of $2,000 had been reduced first to a one-time share of $2,000 and now to nothing guaranteed at all. And in the meantime, the process of seeking funding—every year, over several years—had begun to take a toll on the confidence of student leaders in the university's commitment to Black students at Rice.

In the fall of 1974, for example, as Brown prepared her proposal to Hackerman for BSU funds, she first directed a member of her staff to contact Gloria Guilford for an account of how the group had spent the original $2,000 allotted by Hackerman. In a handwritten reply, Guilford, who had already provided such an itemization more than a year earlier, vented her frustration over having to make the BSU's case once again and marveled at how much "heartache" and explanation it had taken just to secure insufficient funds "to simply *renovate* a tin shack located in the middle of a swamp."

Guilford invited Brown and Hackerman themselves to visit the "tin shack," which was still unfinished, as the only way she could think to convince administrators of the BSU's continued need for funds. "Please excuse my bitterness," the senior's letter concluded, "but at this point I cannot understand why everyone seems to find it so hard to understand why car washes, raffles, and dues *are not enough* to meet the needs of a portion of the student body not wholly affected by actions on the part of the RPC and colleges."[64]

Finally, a few months later, in an even more pointed commentary on the extent of unmet need at Rice, Guilford would petition for permission to take all her courses in the spring of 1975 (her last semester as a Rice student) at Texas Southern University instead. Guilford's petition expressed a desire "to have the experience of attending a predominantly black university" before she graduated. Her request was received by Rice's faculty Committee on Examinations and Standing, whose members "were in sympathy with her proposal." At the committee's December 5, 1974, meeting, "it was moved and seconded that it *be approved*."[65]

The motion unanimously passed, and the committee moved on. But when time came for Gloria Guilford to submit a senior page to the 1975 *Campanile*, just as Linda Faye Williams had done five years before, she wrote and typed a mini-essay that filled every available part of the four-by-five-inch space. "It is my opinion that it is the university's responsibility to see that . . . minority students are made to feel as integral a part of the university as are other students," she wrote. Noting the presence of only "two Blacks on the faculty" and detailing some of the "overt" and "covert racism" that persisted at Rice, Guilford also cited her experiences with the BSU as evidence that too many on campus "simply shake their heads and/or wring their hands refusing either to believe, accept, or acknowledge that such problems exist." It was an analysis that other Black students in the 1970s and later would validate, and it concluded, for Guilford, with a challenge to the university: "I wish Rice would approach the social-psychological problems of minorities and racism with the same fervor that it approaches the problems of engineering, science, and technology."[66]

All for Rice, Rice for All?

Two years after Gloria Guilford spent her final Rice semester across town at TSU, the Black Student Union Building disappeared from the Rice campus map. The outline of the structure was still there on a new version of the map in the 1977 *General Announcements*. The "tin shack" itself still stood in 2023, now repurposed as a storage shed surrounded by tall weeds and used by groundskeeping crews. But its association with the BSU was, apparently, already at an end five years after it had first been proposed.[67]

Few appeared to mourn the ending at the time; after all, the BSU Building had never become what Black students thought it should be. In the meantime they had found other spaces in which to meet and make community, imbuing the campus landscape with a complex and expanding geography of Black life at Rice. There was a BSU office on the second floor of the RMC, and a college commons where a group of Black women met once a week for dinner. In 1977, in collaboration with the RPC, the BSU even recruited Bubbha Thomas and the Lightmen, a nationally renowned African American jazz band from Houston, to perform in the campus pub for Black History Week. On a surviving recording of the two-hour concert made for KTRU radio, it is still possible to hear the audience's stirring, collective response to the music from Thomas and the band.[68]

Still, while the end of the Black Student Union Building did not stop the BSU from continuing its founding mission ("to help establish a total understanding of the Black subculture and to enhance the social and intellectual participation of the Black students in the University and the community"), it is difficult not to see the building's disappearance from campus maps as a case of ground lost, especially amid the gathering signs, both locally and nationally, that concerted efforts to desegregate American higher education were also losing ground.[69]

In 1974, for example, Rice provost Frank Vandiver opined in a speech at Texas Tech University that "affirmative action" had already gone too far, producing in many cases "unqualified job holders" at universities and leading to "compromised standards." Coming as they did from the highest ranking academic officer at Rice, the comments suggested to longtime advocates of minority hiring that Rice still remained unserious about diversifying its ranks. "In a community which is nearly 50 percent Black and Mexican-American, Rice has two Black and one Mexican-American faculty members," Richard Tapia told the *Thresher* in response to Vandiver's comments. "Isn't Dr. Vandiver confusing Equal Opportunity and Affirmative Action with tokenism?" Robert Bell was likewise "appalled" by the speech, signing his own letter to the *Thresher* with a mordant flourish: "Robert Bell, Professor of Psychology (one of three faculty members who may be unqualified jobholders forced on the university by affirmative action)."[70]

From the beginnings of the BSU, students had also decried Rice's poor record with hiring Black faculty. They continued to speak out on the problem. In April 1977, a group of eight graduating seniors wrote the *Thresher* to highlight an "aspect of the University that has bothered us here as Black students." Namely, "no real effort is being made to locate Black scholars" for the faculty, even though "universities with similar and greater reputations as Rice have actually led the way in race relations in their respective college communities."

The students noted that, of the three Black professors in the spring of 1977 ("yes, only three!"), one was "a part-time lecturer, with full duties at Texas Southern" (Freeman). Another was taking on more administrative responsibilities and reducing time in the classroom (Bell). And the third—a sociologist named Rose Brewer who had taught at Rice since 1974, serving for much of that time as an advisor to the BSU—was planning to leave Rice that summer.

Brewer's impending departure raised the strong possibility that, in the fall of 1977, Rice would once again find itself without any full-time Black professors, a situation that the eight graduating seniors described—"out of concern for our alma mater" and with charitable understatement—as "not adequate."[71]

"Qualified Black faculty do exist, as the Sociology, Psychology, and Religion departments have found out," continued the seniors, "so we are not asking that faculty be hired indiscriminately. But when a University of Rice's stature can only locate 3 Black professors out of a faculty in excess of 300, the obvious conclusions must be drawn." It would remain difficult for Rice to convince prospective Black students that the university had left behind its segregated past, so long as its faculty remained, as Rodrigo Barnes had reportedly described it in 1972, "the only segregated faculty in the state."[72]

At the same time, Rice's record on Black student recruitment and support was making it difficult to convince Black scholars to come and to stay. Brewer, the young sociologist who had first joined Rice as a visiting assistant professor in 1974, was offered a position as a tenure-track assistant professor in 1977, which would have made her the first Black assistant professor to join Rice with the possibility of tenure. A popular teacher and, according to her department's prescient judgment, a rising star in the profession, Brewer did think seriously about remaining in Houston. But on March 30, she instead wrote to Norman Hackerman to turn down the position in favor of a competing offer at Hackerman's former institution, the University of Texas at Austin.[73]

"I think one reason you should be aware of," Brewer explained to Hackerman, "centers on my disappointment with the lack of supportive services offered minority students and minority faculty on campus. This is reflected in the sparsity of culturally diverse activities such as speakers, programs, ethnic studies courses, etc., which appeal to an ethnically mixed student body. The lack of minority input must be seriously questioned. It affects the quality of the university experience offered to the entire Rice student body." As she left for Austin, Brewer continued, it was her "strong hope that the university will move decisively in the direction of helping to create the kind of wider university environment which will complement its fine academic reputation."

In the years ahead, however, even slight gains for Black faculty, staff, and students would come slowly at Rice. There would be no Black associate professors until the 1980s. The appointment of two Black historians to one-year visiting positions in 1986 doubled the number of Black professors then on campus. Ten years later, the *Journal of Blacks in Higher Education* noted that "Blacks still have almost no presence on the Rice faculty," comparing its six Black professors, "slightly more than 1 percent" of the whole faculty, to the 5.1 percent of the faculty who were Black at Emory University, "an institution that did not integrate much sooner than Rice."[74] By the turn of the twenty-first century, the total number of Black tenure-track faculty members still had barely reached double digits at Rice. And even in 2023—eleven years after the university's centennial, sixty years after the Charter Trial, and fifty years after the BSU was born—there were departments and entire schools at Rice University that had yet to tenure a single Black professor, much less two. More than half a century after the university's second founding began, some of the most important work of desegregation remained incomplete.

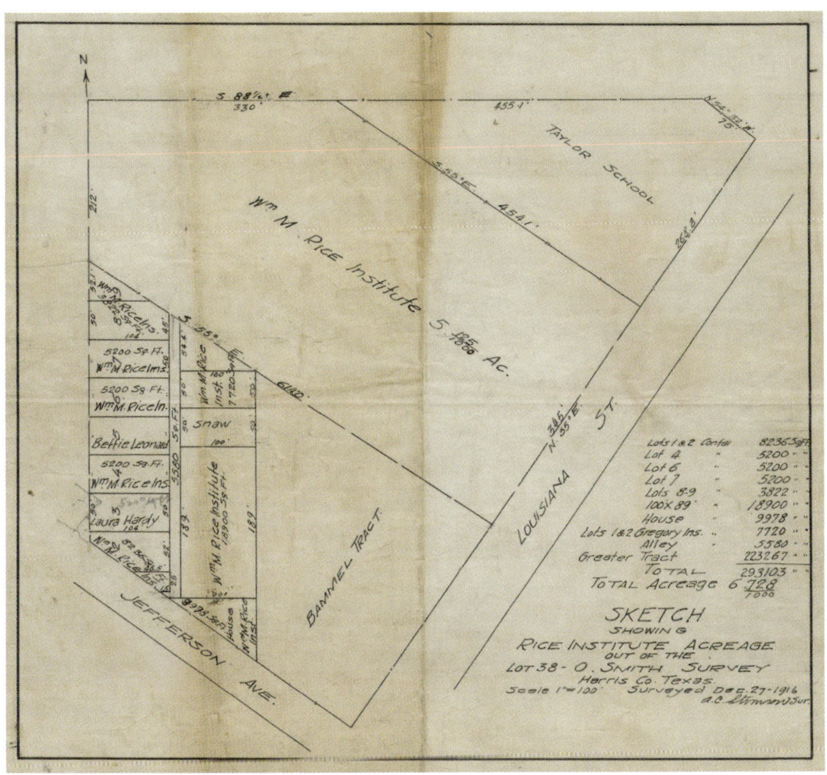

Map of the Louisiana Street Property, 1916, showing adjacent lots from Fredericks Addition still belonging to Black property owners Bettie Leonard, Laura Hardy, and Robert Shaw.

Jack Shelton, 1917, one of the first Black workers at the Rice Institute.

Rice students wearing blackface, ca. 1918.

The Ku Klux Klan of Rice Institute, standing outside the Field House, from the 1922 yearbook.

Jack Shelton (*top row, far left*) with the 1922 football team, also outside the Field House.

A Black waiter (name unknown) photographed in 1937 with faculty club diners, including President Edgar Odell Lovett (seated on the right in the middle of the main table).

HOUSTON, TEXAS, WEDNESDAY, FEB. 12, 1949 — VOLUME THIRTY-SIX — No. THIRTY-THREE

Tuesday Lecture To View World's Food Problems

Professor Merrill Kelly Bennett, of Stanford University, will lecture on "Population and Food Supply" Tuesday evening, February 15, at 8:15, in the Physics Amphitheatre.

Dr. Bennett, who received his master's degree from Harvard and the degree of doctor of philosophy from Stanford, is now Executive Director of the Food Research Institute, Professor of Economic Geography, and Dean of the School of Social Sciences, at Stanford University. He has worked on food problems for many years and has had wide experience. He was Weld Fellow in Economics at Harvard University, 1925-26, and held a Guggenhein Memorial Foundation Fellowship in 1941-42. His connection with the Food Research Institute dates from 1923; it was in 1942 that he became executive director. From Dec. 1941 to June 1942 he was chief statistician in the office of Food Control, Territory of Hawaii. During 1944-45 he was Chief of the Food Allocation Division, Office of Food Programs, Foreign Economis Administration.

Professor Bennett is a fellow of the American Statistics Association, a member of the American Association for the Advancement of Science, the American Economic Association, the American Farm Economic Association, and the American Association of Geographers.

Dr. Bennett has published numerous articles on farm costs in the Unites States; international trade, prices, stocks, production and consumption of wheat and other foodstuffs, and international comparisons of standards of living. He is the author of "Farm Cost Studies in the United States—Their Development, Applications, and Limitations," 1928; "Rice in Monsoon Asia" (with W. D. Wickizer), 1941; "Food for Post-war Europe — What and How Much?", 1944; and also numerous monographs in Wheat Studies of the Food Research Institute.

Dr. Bennett will deal in his lecture with the pressure of population on the world's food supply. Interest in this topic has increased since the war, especially with the appearance of books like **Road to Survival**, by William Vogt. Dr. Bennett's study of the evidence will indicate that the current scare is exaggerated.

—0—

Placement Service Put Bulletin Boards At Three Points

To aid both the students and new Rice Placement Service, sponsored by the Association of Rice Alumni, three new bulletin boards have been placed on the campus.

These bulletin boards will contain nothing but notices coming out of the Placement office—notices about part time employment, about scheduled interviews between graduating seniors and company organizations, about available jobs.

The boards will be placed in three places, in the registrar's office, in the student lounge and in the Placement Office which is in the Faculty Chamber, Lovett Hall.

The Placement Service, instituted January 1, 1949, is planned to aid the students and alumni or Rice in securing jobs for seniors, part time jobs for undergraduates and for alumni who may wish a change of positions. A current file is kept in the Placement Office of available positions. Students are welcome at any time to consult this file. Literature about various organizations seeking employees also may be found there.

No charge is made for placing seniors or undergraduates. The Placement service is financed by the Rice alumni. However, for alumni and for seniors placed arter July of the year they graduate a donation of part of the first month's salary to the Placement Service is customary.

San Carlos College Offers Courses For North Americans

The Summer School of the University of San Carlos of Guatemala has announced plans for presenting its third annual seven-week session, planned primarily for North American students and approved by the Veteran Administration, in Guatemala City from July 1st until August 19th of this year.

A wide variety of courses in the fields of Spanish and Latin American language, literature, and institutions will be offered, while Guatemalan specialties such as Mayan civilization and Guatemalan folklore can be studied by those interested. In the past, credits have been accepted by the major colleges and universities of the United States and Canada, both at the undergraduate and graduate level.

Evaluation of credits should be done in advance of consultation with departmental advisors, so that the choice of electives as well as

(Continued on Page 4)

—0—

NOTICE

The next Forum program, "The Faculty's Reactions to the Instructor Rating Poll," will be held Thursday, February 24 at 8 p.m. in Anderson Hall 110. Speakers selected will represent both the younger and the more experienced faculty members.

Dr. Bullock

Aggies Request Women For Cotton Style Show

The Student Council meeting Thursday considered a request from the Agronomy Society of A. and M. for a Rice girl representative to the 1949 Cotton Style Show and Pageant to be held at A&M on April 29. The council nominated four women students with the provision that more nominations will be accepted until the representative is chosen at the next Council meeting.

Those nominated Thursday were Alpha Reynolds, Nancy Walters, Jo Anne Harwell, and Martha Moore. **An all cotton wardrobe is required for the representative who will model in an afternoon style show and be presented at a pageant the night of the 29th.** The representative who will model in an afternoon style show and be presented at a pageant the night of the 29th. The representative will be escorted by an A&M student, as will the other representatives of the Southwest Conference schools who attend.

—0—

'Mad Magic' Theme for SI Semi-Formal Dance

Tonight Buddy Brock's orchestra will supply the music for an evening of dancing and mad capers, for the S.L.'s will present a semi-formal dance—"Mad Magic." The Armory will be the scene which will combine a setting for Valentine's day and a post final celebration. Couples will be admitted for $2.25 and stags at $2.00. There will be no corsages for the dance which will last from 8 to 12.

Sociologist Says Negro Role Like Individual Emancipation

About ninety people heard Dr. H. A. Bullock, head of the department of sociology at Prairie View A & M College, discuss "The Role of the Negro in the South" at the Forum Thursday night.

Dr. Bullock said that the very nature of the struggle of the Negro in the South, his role in Southern living, was a quest for personal emancipation. He praised "one of the greatest developments of the mind of man, the American creed, that makes the individual the measure of all judgments."

To be judged as an individual, to attain the respect that should be accorded, to approximate the transcendental ideals of the American creed, these are the things that the Southern Negro wants, and expects as part of his heritage as an American citizen, Dr. Bullock said. He sincerely believed that the single greatest characteristic of the American character is the belief in the emancipation of the individual. "It's seen in the Declaration of Independence, in Wilson's Fourteen points, in the Four Freedoms of Franklin Roosevelt," he said.

Dr. Bullock compared this ideal of striving by the Negroes to achieve the dignity of human beings that is the characteristic of the American creed to a drama. He said that like every great drama it had a heroine, weak and timid; and a hero, strong and brave; and a villain, mean and vicious. But in the struggle of the Negro race to reach their goal the villains had sometimes changed, sometimes the background had changed. Sometimes the hero had changed or had been replaced in his dramatic illustration.

At one time, he said, it was the Abolition movement that helped bring about the Civil War and the Emancipation Proclamation, at one time it was the Northern philanthropists who brought their money to the South after the war to help the Negroes educate themselves in the finer aspects of culture. Then, after the Negro had realized that there was no place for a [illegible] educated Negro to exercise his learning, it was the Booker T. Washingtons, who taught that the Negro must learn to work with his hands, must learn to be skilled in some trade.

But even after the founding of Tuskegee Institution upon the sands of Alabama, Dr. Bullock said that the Negro could still not use his training—not because he wasn't just as capable as his white competition, but because he couldn't compete with the economic discrimination that he faced throughout the South.

Dr. Bullock pointed out another villain, entering upon the scene. It was the revenge motif, expressed in escanist literature. Largely the product of Southern Negroes who had moved north and taken their resentment out on the Northern whites, it helped cause the race riots in the big Northern cities during the

(Continued on Page 8)

—0—

Institute Obtains Handbook Telling Of Foreign Schools

For the purpose of promoting international educational interchange among the United Nations and other nations, the United Nations Educational and Cultural Organization, with headquarters in Paris, has made an inquiry into existing programs of fellowships, scholarships, or any other awards which afford opportunities to a national of one country to travel to another country **for study or training for a stated period of time.**

Unesco has prepared a "Fellowship Handbook", which aims at publicizing periodically all possible information of fellowships and related opportunities, at ascertaining their availability and the subject fields covered.

In addition to listing fellowship opportunities, the Handbook contains a chapter summarizing the programs of international fellowships operated by various agencies of the United Nations, together with information on the areas of interest of various agencies' programs which relate to this inquiry.

The inaugural edition of this Handbook is the first of the series, designed to provide details of all available opportunities for transnational study, and organized arrangements in this field.

Any students interested in obtaining information about these fellowships may refer to copies of the Handbook in the registrar's office or in the downstairs library.

Cotton Bowl Ticket Allotment Proposed By A. & M. Students

The "Battalion," student newspaper at Texas A.&M., has taken a stand in favor of proposal by the Student Senate of A.&M. to have Cotton Bowl tickets alloted to all Southwest Conference schools.

In an editorial, the "Battalion said "Theoretically, the Cotton Bowl game on New Year's Day is a conference affair. But heretofore, it has been a winner-take-all proposition as far as the other conference schools were concerened."

The editorial continued to commend the Student Senate for initiating a plan to " . . . give each school in the conference an opportunity to buy a specific number of tickets to the game."

A letter to Tyree Bell, President of the Cotton Bowl Association, included these proposals by the Senate:

"That the student body of each member school of the Southwest Conference be permitted to purchase a number of tickets to the Cotton Bowl game on New Year's Day.

"That the number of tickets be apportioned by a percentage of the school's enrollment. (And.)

"That the tickets be sold at students rates."

Mr. Bell answered the proposals with the assurance that they would be submitted to the Board of the Association.

The "Battalion" editorial concluded with the observations that " . . . The plan is destined for rough sailing when objections are raised by money conscious conference committeemen.

"Football has become a multi-million dollar business in the Southwest. Let us hope that the student bodies of conference schools will not be ungratefully cast aside in the dollar scramble."

Four other conference schools have voiced approval to the plan, the editorial said. It also express the general attitude that the proposals of the Student Senate were valid on the grounds that " . . . Such a policy would increase chances for a growing feeling of unity and sportsmanship among other conference schools."

Marriage to Be Talk Of Emerson Society

At the last meeting of the Emerson Society just prior to finals Sarel Eimerl spoke to the group on "Socialism in England." A period of discussion followed his remarks. The next meeting will be Sunday evening, February 13 at 6:30 p.m. in the Parish house of the First Unitarian Church which is leoted at the corner of Southmore and Fannin. The group will be led in a discussion concerning "Preparation for Marriage" by the vice-president of the Emerson Society, Robert Lindsay. All who may be interested in this subject are cordially invited to participate.

H. A. Bullock, head of the Department of Sociology at Prairie View A&M University, on the front page of the *Rice Thresher*, February 12, 1949.

Hanszen proceeds with deliberate speed

Scene from the 1961 Hanszen College Minstrel in the 1962 yearbook, showing white students in blackface. The caption is a mocking reference to the Supreme Court's desegregation decisions in *Brown v. Board of Education*.

Scene from the 1965 Hanszen College "Non-Minstrel" with a performer wearing blackface at center stage.

Raymond Johnson, ca. 1964, the first Black student admitted to Rice University.

Jacqueline McCauley, one of the first two Black undergraduate students admitted to Rice, as featured on the cover of the *Houston Chronicle* Sunday magazine section in September 1965.

Charles Freeman (*top row, fourth from right*), one of the first two Black undergraduate students admitted to Rice, with part of the 1965–66 Rice Owl Band.

Linda Faye Williams (*middle left*) with Jones College choir in the 1967 yearbook.

John Birotte speaks at a rally in Founder's Court to protest the announcement of William H. Masterson as Rice's next president, February 22, 1969.

Linda Faye Williams's senior page in the yearbook for 1970, the year she became one of the first two Black undergraduates to receive degrees from Rice. Designed by Williams herself, it shows a single bus token on an otherwise empty page.

Another page from the 1970 yearbook. Assembled by student editors from "photo booth" strips submitted by students, the collage shows graduating senior Theodore Henderson in the second column from the right. Students in other columns pose with a watermelon and the Confederate battle flag.

LOU WITT
PHOTOGRAPHY

Rodrigo Barnes, student-athlete and first president of Rice's Black Student Union.

Protesters outside the UT-Rice basketball game, February 12, 1972.

Assistant professor of sociology Rose Brewer, 1974.

THE LIFE OF THE BLACK STUDENT ON THE RICE CAMPUS

What is life like for a Black student attending Rice University? Most of us have been asked this at one time or another, by a variety of people. Often this one question represents several questions, and usually what people really are asking is, "What is it like to be a minority student in a predominantly white institution? What kind of academic pressures are a part of such a competitive atmosphere? and What types of social opportunities exist?" In trying to formulate our feelings about this place, these questions often come to our minds also. Because Rice means different things to different people, however, such answers are not always available in clear-cut statements. For the most part, our real opinions lie somewhere in the gray areas of thought. If we are pushed for an answer though, there are probably several impressions about life here that stick with many of us.

First of all, contrary to rumor, myth, or misinformation, there are Blacks at Rice, even though the population is quite small and increasing at a rather slow rate. Beginning in the mid-60's, Rice had its first Black students—two. Presently, we number about 80. Contrary to another popular myth, there are Black women at Rice (even though the male to female ratio is lopsidedly in favor of the male).

Honestly speaking, life here is a challenge with several problems which are peculiar to our position as minority students in a highly academic, white environment. With many of us coming from predominantly Black situations, adjustment to a predominantly white environment brings about feelings of isolation from the familiar Black culture. Such difficulties have not been insurmountable, however, and it is our hope that an increase in the Black students will help to eliminate some of them. Depending on a student's background and diligence—once he gets here, he may or may not be presented with academic difficulties. Once again, the experience varies with the individual. It might help to add, however, that Black students are coping with these problems when they occur, and in some cases are doing quite well.

A Black student's social life here is usually a result of his own inclinations. Overall, the University's activities are available to all its students, and it is not unusual for Black individuals to participate in these events, as well as those sponsored by the various colleges. Often we plan activities as a group. Football season, for example, is a favorite time of year socially, and we get together after the games for parties. As a group, and as individuals, we often coordinate our activities with the Black Houston community, including the Black students of Texas Southern University and the University of Houston. In the spring of last year, for example, we sponsored a memorial day to Dr. Martin Luther King which included discussions, lectures, an art exhibit, and a concert.

Life here is a highly individualistic experience. It is a challenging one. Sometimes for Blacks, it is a lonely one. If one is willing to work at it, it can be a rewarding experience.

A recruitment brochure created by the Black Student Union, 1972–73. The metal building renovated by the BSU can be seen in the background of several panels.

Unveiling ceremony for the Founder's Memorial, June 8, 1930.

Shifa Rahman, Lovett College Class of 2022.

Velma McAfee Williams, December 2022.

IV

WHITHER THE SECOND FOUNDING?

9 | BLACK STUDENT DEMANDS

Fifty years after Linda Faye Williams and Ted Henderson were awarded their diplomas, and nearly as long since founding members of the BSU had gathered with hand-lettered signs to picket a basketball game on campus, a later group of Rice University students published an online petition, six pages in length, that outlined the urgent need for change at the institution.

"Tangible Ways to Improve the Black Experience, as Demanded by Black Students"—or "The Black Student Demands," as they soon came to be called—had been composed by a largely anonymous "Working Group" whose goal was "to highlight Black voices." But at the end of the six-page remonstration, in the petition's last sentence, two students stepped individually from the Black collectivity whose authorship suffused the document from start to finish, and indicated their names. "We are meeting later," the demands concluded, "to explore how this collaborative group should expand to continue to uplift Black voices." Students who agreed with the mission of the work were invited to get in touch with Kendall Vining or Milkessa Gaga.[1]

The demands were published at 4:46 on the morning of June 19, a date whose importance to the Black freedom struggle in the United States had long been observed in Texas, but whose significance was being recognized far beyond the state in the summer of that year. On May 25, 2020, a month before the publication of the "Black Student Demands," and in the wake of a school year whose second semester had been completely upended by the COVID-19 pandemic, the murder of George Floyd had led unprecedented numbers of people into the streets to protest racial injustice, including in Houston, Floyd's hometown. The arrival of Juneteenth so soon after the murder prompted wide-ranging debates across the nation about the state of the Union, about the deep roots of anti-Black racism in American society, and about the long history of

Black protest that had most recently coalesced around a "Movement for Black Lives." At Rice, meanwhile, the highly charged moment crystallized an opportunity to think about the state of the university's second founding, more than half a century after it began.[2]

Vining's and Gaga's public shepherding of the "Black Student Demands," which insisted that "Inaction is Not an Option," would turn out to be one in a series of actions that would very quickly come to dominate the discourse on race and equity at the university. Nineteen items in length, the demands were public-facing, a kind of open letter, and in the tradition of many such petitions directed to the leadership of the university. At points, however, the authors positioned themselves unmistakably as critical outsiders—as Black students whose full belonging in the university could not be assumed, but had yet to be ascertained. In the document's one-page preamble, the writers maintained an ambiguous distance between themselves and the university they hoped to change. They advocated, for instance, for "the decolonization of Rice University as it specifically pertains to Black Students." Further, in alluding to the changes that the writers hoped to see at the university, their words took form as if offered across an abyss. Thus they hoped to alter "Rice's approach, to their education and curriculum as a whole." It was Rice's approach. Rice's education. Rice's curriculum. Black students, the demands implied, were simply subject to them. That the document was unsigned, except by Gaga and Vining, likewise suggested a distance between the authors and their audience. In order to "protect the anonymity" of members of the community who might not "feel comfortable with their name attached to a stated demand," the working group did not "collect names of Black students who gave suggestions."[3]

Yet the demands themselves, in their range and comprehensiveness, also made clear their origins in a Black community with full purchase on the workings of the university. If the authors wrote as outsiders, they were also very much insiders, carrying forward issues of long-standing concern at the university. Divided into four sections, the list touched upon items related to "access and visibility," "Black community and student well being," "racial bias and sensitivity training" on campus, and "Rice's curriculum." It was an eminently challenging list, including demands familiar to generations of Black students at Rice, touching issues that university leaders at Rice and elsewhere had more recently begun to grapple with in earnest, and highlighting social and political debates brewing in the nation as a whole that the authors thought required local attention as well. The unmistakable message of the 2020 document, no less than the message of the signed petition assembled by the first members of the BSU in 1972, was clear: For the sake of the university's future, and in view of both its present and its past, the moment still needed—still demanded—bold change.[4]

* * *

To be sure, much had changed, both at Rice and in the nation, in the years between 1970 and 2020. At the beginning of that span, it would have been possible, though perhaps not comfortably, for every single Black undergraduate at the university to crowd into the small metal building set aside in 1972 for the use of the BSU. By contrast, two decades into the twenty-first century, attendance at cultural events hosted by Black student organizations, such as the BSA's Soul Night and the Rice African Student Association's Africayé, often tested the capacity of the Grand Hall in the Rice Memorial Center.[5]

By 2020, students had also benefited for thirty years from the leadership, mentorship, and advocacy provided by staff in the university's Office for Minority Affairs (later rechristened the Office of Multicultural Affairs), and a growing Association of Rice University Black Alumni (ARUBA) was making vital contributions to the university. On March 6, 2020, shortly before the COVID-19 pandemic closed the campus and scattered the student community, Black students, faculty, and staff assembled in the Cohen House for the very first Black Excellence Gala to reflect on that year's achievements, to be welcomed by President David Leebron (whose administration had done much to increase the number and diversity of Black students on campus in recent years), and to celebrate the recipients of honors awarded by the Black Student Association (BSA), a successor to the BSU. The gala, now celebrated annually, had roots, in turn, in a series of earlier ceremonies marking the fortieth and then the fiftieth anniversaries of Black students at Rice University—events suggesting the institution's recognition that these milestones warranted pomp and formal celebration, and that they testified to real progress made since desegregation began.[6]

And yet, recent moments of celebration had also sounded dissonant notes, reminders of how long it takes to turn a segregated institution into a desegregating one. In February 2007, the university held an event "commemorating the 40th anniversary," not of the matriculation of the first Black students (whose fortieth anniversaries would have needed to be held in 2004 or 2005), but "of the first black students to enter Rice as undergraduates and earn degrees from the university." At a panel of speakers convened for the event, the then-president of the BSA credited her student organization, and by implication the anniversary event, with helping "put [her] experiences into perspective" as a Black student in 2007. But she also noted that "there are too few black students and faculty at Rice." "It's hard to be a student," she concluded, with a silent *still* implied, "without being taken as a token."[7]

Five years later, amid a year-long celebration of the university's centennial year, a highly produced film about Rice's history would be released and broadcast on local public television. The makers of the film, *Beyond the Hedges*, chose to open it with a powerful observation from the chairman of the Rice Board of Trustees, James W. Crownover: "You can't possibly understand the history of Rice without also understanding the history of Houston, and likewise you can't understand Houston if you don't understand Rice." The entirety of this film's screenplay, however, made no mention of Rice's past as a segregated institution and no mention of the arrival of the first Black students and faculty or the beginnings of integration, much less of the parts of Houston's history that pertained to the city's Black community. A separate documentary by the same filmmakers was commissioned by ARUBA in honor of the centennial and also aired on local public television in early 2013. *Young, Gifted, and Black: Reflections from Black Alumni at Rice* had more to say about subjects not covered in *Beyond the Hedges*. Yet the two films, airing a few months apart, suggested that the university and the larger Houston community to which it belonged were still figuring out how to tell a history of Rice's founding that could incorporate, in the same telling, the lessons of its segregated past and subsequent refounding as a desegregating university.[8]

In some ways, this difficulty was a special instance of a more general problem in the history of the United States. The democratic republic remade by the abolition of slavery and the Thirteenth, Fourteenth, and Fifteenth amendments to the Constitution was fundamentally not the same as the republic envisioned by its founding fathers in 1787. The nation was remade again by the civil rights movement, the Civil Rights Act of 1964, and the Voting Rights Act of 1965. Even so, vestiges of the nation's history with slavery and segregation never disappeared entirely in these refounding moments, complicating efforts to commemorate them as giant leaps forward. The one hundredth anniversary of the Civil War coincided with the final years of *de jure* segregation and the "Second Reconstruction" of the civil rights movement, frustrating the efforts of those who wished to tell a unifying and progressive narrative about the war. The Civil War's sesquicentennial in 2011–15, which also encompassed Rice University's centennial, coincided with the rise of the "Black Lives Matter" movement. And that movement, in turn, responded to a tragic litany of unarmed Black citizens killed in the early twenty-first century, amid a public resurgence of white supremacist violence and political mobilization.[9]

On June 17, 2015, the murder of nine Black worshippers by a white supremacist at the Emanuel African Methodist Episcopal Church in Charleston, South Carolina—two days before the sesquicentennial of Juneteenth, and near the end of the second term for the nation's first Black president—seemed to demonstrate all too clearly the continuing power of slavery's afterlives. One month after the murders at Emanuel, the state of South Carolina finally elected to remove the Confederate battle flag from its capitol building, one and a half centuries after secession. Yet contention over historical symbols and monuments to the Confederacy would continue for years, making this latest major anniversary of the Civil War no easier to synthesize than its centennial had been. Historians had once thought of the war, as Abraham Lincoln did, as the nation's "new birth of freedom." As historian Carole Emberton noted, however, "activists marked the end of the Civil War sesquicentennial not by celebrating the emergence of a nebulous condition that succeeded legal bondage but by indicting the very notion that such a succession was either clear or complete."[10]

University campuses became significant sites of activism and debate in this era, as well as seedbeds for new scholarly inquiries into the roles of higher education institutions in perpetuating slavery and racism over the *longue durée*. Inspired in part by work begun at Brown University in 2004 under the leadership of its then-president Ruth J. Simmons, a movement of universities studying their own histories of racial injustice gained new momentum during and after the Civil War sesquicentennial. The year 2016 saw the formation of the

Universities Studying Slavery consortium at the University of Virginia, an organization that soon comprised more than one hundred schools in twenty states and five countries. At universities from Harvard, Georgetown, and Yale, to the state flagship universities of Mississippi, North Carolina, and Alabama, searching discussions ensued about the histories of white supremacy still visible on campus landscapes, at student social events, or in college archives—as well as the relationship of all of it to the experiences of underrepresented minority groups at elite institutions of higher learning.[11]

Rice University was not insulated from the historic shifts around it. In November 2014, following national protests over the killing of Michael Brown by a white police officer in Ferguson, Missouri, students at Rice mobilized a "die-in" protest around the Founder's Memorial in the Academic Quadrangle and placed a "Black Lives Matter" sign in the lap of the statue of William Marsh Rice. In 2017, following similar decisions at Harvard and Yale, Rice decided to change the titles of residential college "masters" to "magisters." And in early 2019, following reports that Virginia governor Ralph Northam had once appeared in blackface in his medical school yearbook, a series of social media posts about racist images in Rice University's own yearbooks went viral online.[12]

President David Leebron addressed those images with an emailed message to the Rice community on February 10, 2019—one in a series of messages by Leebron to the campus over the coming months concerning (as one later email put it) the "racism that is an unstaunched wound in our national fabric." In the earlier message, the president noted that the "deeply disturbing" imagery in the *Campanile* served as "reminders of the persistence of racial discrimination," adding that it was "appropriate for institutions to take a renewed look at their own histories" and to "acknowledge aspects of that history that are distasteful and painful." Four months later, Leebron joined with Marie Lynn Miranda, then the Howard R. Hughes Provost, in another email to the community, on June 4. It announced their intention to establish the Task Force on Slavery, Segregation, and Racial Injustice. Its steering committee of faculty, students, staff, alumni, and trustees later met for the first time near the end of 2019.[13]

These events clearly owed much to a larger historical context "beyond the hedges." Yet it would be a mistake to locate their origins wholly outside the university's prior history. In the nation as a whole, so also at Rice, twenty-first-century protests about the afterlives of slavery and segregation did not spring suddenly into existence in the 2010s. They were connected to longer histories of struggle. Indeed, in every decade of the university's history since integration began, there had been student, faculty, alumni, and staff voices calling attention to the still unfinished work of desegregation at Rice.[14]

Those on-campus voices again surely contributed to the immediate causes of Rice's new effort to examine its history. The task force created by President Leebron and Provost Miranda was no hothouse flower; it was the offshoot of earlier seedlings. And likewise, in the early morning hours of Juneteenth in 2020, when students Kendall Vining and Milkessa Gaga made public their community-generated list of demands—a list that, according to the petition, had been almost a year in the making—they amplified several demands that had been germinating for decades on the Rice University campus, while also adding to that history in ways that reflected their particular moment in time.

* * *

Undergraduate campus life figured prominently in the work of the "Black Student Demands." The demands called for the recruitment and admission of a greater number of Black students as a firmer foundation of Black community life at Rice. The university's total Black student body had certainly grown with the university, but the view from within the residential colleges, the absolute center of undergraduate life at the university, could conceal that growth, always dividing a growing number of Black students among a growing number of residential colleges—thus reducing visibility and hindering, the demands suggested, the building of Black community.

Other demands built on this first one, and also focused on residential life at the university. Black students new to Rice, the ninth demand made plain, should be able to request a Black roommate. Staff and student leaders of the university's Orientation Week, or O-Week, when new students were introduced to their residential colleges, must continuously develop ways to bring Black students together from across the campus during this important first week at Rice (but also beyond this first week) in order to facilitate and encourage a whole campus life that, if left unaddressed by the colleges, necessarily truncated Black community at the university. The authors of the demands wanted greater attention to the composition of the student leaders who facilitated new student orientation in the colleges—noting that too many colleges had too few Black students serving in such roles, and alluding to the recent fact that it was not unknown for a college to have no Black students serving in such roles. None. The creation of meeting and programming space on campus, especially designed with the needs of Black cultural organizations and Black students in mind—a "Black House"—would also be helpful in this area. The fifth demand made exactly this case.

The demands focused particular attention on the university curriculum and the composition of staff and faculty. Along these lines, the authors called for the creation of a course for new students designed to sensitize incoming Owls to pressing issues related to racial inequality and how such issues played out on global and local scales—all with an eye toward mitigating bias on campus. They expressed concern about the preparation students received in international research-and-development programs, calling for semester-long training in ethical international engagement as a prerequisite for such work. The demands pressed for an increase in the number of Black staff and faculty—especially tenured professors. Seeing so few Black students on campus was "already an isolating experience." Seeing so few Black professors at the front of university classrooms, and few Black staff in key positions across the university, exacerbated an already isolating experience. Students desired greater opportunities to study African and African diasporic languages, and more attention to developing study-away programs where such languages were spoken.

A number of the demands aligned with persistent issues then being debated across the campus and the nation: an item seeking the eventual abolition of the Rice University Police Department, another calling for greater attention to and investment in the historically Black Third Ward of the city (this related to the university's development of an off-campus innovation district and its potential impact on nearby neighborhoods), and a call that "Rice University remove Willy's statue." Willy referred to a common name for the university's namesake. And the call for the removal of his statue from the university's main Academic Quadrangle resonated with then-heightened debates, in the aftermath of George Floyd's murder, about the removal of Confederate monuments and other iconography from public spaces, especially in the South.[15] Only days before the publication of the "Demands," the city of Houston had taken down the two Confederate statues still standing on city property, including a monument that had long stood in a corner of Hermann Park not far from the Rice campus.

Pointedly, the authors of the "Demands" did not indicate that they believed action along all of these lines would definitively or finally improve the Black experience at Rice. They thought it might. In contrast, the breadth, seriousness, and long-standing intractability of many of the issues raised in the "Black Student Demands" were clear indeed. And so were next steps. Two days after the "Demands" began circulating across the Rice community and beyond, a student campaign focused on amplifying the sixth demand took hold online. Gabrielle Falcon launched a petition decrying the monument to William Marsh Rice as a constant reminder "to Black students of the barriers to their success that existed then and now." Quickly thereafter, nearly twenty-three hundred had registered their agreement, calling on the university to remove "Rice's statue and his likeness from all of Rice's branding and marketing materials."[16]

President Leebron and Provost DesRoches addressed the "Demands" in an email to the Rice community on June 23, paying special attention to the "call to remove the statue of William Marsh Rice from the academic quadrangle." Two weeks later, an editorial in the *Rice Thresher* treated the demands in total. It likewise paid particular attention to the matter of the Founder's Memorial, strongly arguing that the sentiments of Black students on campus concerning the statue deserved greater attention, and noting that the long struggle for Black "equity, inclusion, and justice" at Rice had been much too long, especially given gains made in so many other areas across the university.[17]

When the academic year got underway several weeks later, the summer movement showed no signs of abating. And by the second week of classes, it gained even greater energy when Lovett College junior Shifa Rahman began organizing daily sit-ins at the statue, manifesting the issues raised in the "Demands" at the center of the university in new ways. The authors of the "Black Student Demands," members of the community who signed the Falcon petition, the editorial board of the *Thresher*, the president and provost, and the students who now daily protested at the statue were all raising the question of whether the second founding of Rice University was yet complete, and also of how its history might yet be told.[18]

10 | THE FOUNDER'S MEMORIAL

From the moment that Shifa Rahman and others first gathered at the Founder's Memorial to demand its removal, to the afternoon that the Rice University Board of Trustees issued a communication indicating that Willy's Statue would indeed be moved, one year, four months, and twenty-five days passed.[1]

In that span of time, eventually, the authors of the "Black Student Demands"; the protesters who daily gathered at the statue after their publication; the Steering Committee of the Task Force on Slavery, Segregation, and Racial Injustice; the Student Association; and the university's trustees all came to a broad agreement. The university could and should begin to tell a different, a fuller, a truer story about itself than it had ever attempted or managed to tell in the quad, and the historic center of the university could and should better represent the place that Rice hoped to be.

In June 2020, the authors of the "Black Student Demands" were convinced that there were "numerous better options to represent the heart of our university and acknowledge Rice's racist past." Rahman and others daily concurred. By June 2021, the task force agreed. In late November, every voting member of the Student Association supported a "Resolution to Relocate the Founder's Memorial from the Central Academic Quadrangle." And in January of 2022, the trustees of the university unanimously announced a similar position. The "Academic Quadrangle," they wrote, "can be reimagined to be more welcoming, to be an active heart of the university, and more completely represent our history, our achievements and our values." Not all who had followed the debates and protests of the preceding months agreed, of course. Yet an impressive swath of the Rice community had come to a kind of consensus about the need for change.[2]

An important part of the work of coming to this much agreement about the quad involved gaining greater purchase on the development and history of the space itself, and especially on the Founder's Memorial. As far as the memorial was concerned, student protesters, university leadership, and Rice trustees all agreed that the community should be guided by history. But what history? And what would it mean to be so guided? Gabrielle Falcon had pressed in this direction early on when she pushed back against arguments that moving the memorial was tantamount to repudiating the history of the university. The quad, she argued, neglected so much about the history of the university. "So when people say they want to preserve history, I have to ask," Falcon stressed, "whose history are you referring to?"[3]

In communications to university stakeholders following the publication of the "Black Student Demands," and again after the start of the sit-ins, President Leebron and Provost DesRoches leaned into the key charges of the task force in order to make a similar point, in a different way, about what would be necessary in order to come to a conclusion about the disposition of the statue. Even before the publication of the "Demands" or the beginning of the sit-ins in the quad, the task force had been charged with undertaking the work of "discovering, documenting, acknowledging, and disseminating Rice's past with respect to slavery, segregation, and racial injustice." The task force had also been charged, the president and provost made plain, to identify steps that should be taken in order to "more fully realize our aspirations for a diverse and inclusive university." What, then, would the history of the memorial reveal?[4]

Salve Aeternum Aeternumque Salve

For ninety years after its dedication in June 1930, the elevated statue of William Marsh Rice had commanded the university's Academic Courtyard (later the Academic Quadrangle). Cast in bronze at greater than life-sized and set atop nearly eight feet of pink Texas granite, the Founder's Memorial (the name given to it when it was conceived) or Willy's Statue (as it later came to be called by generations of university students) served for almost a century as the dominant feature of the university's historic center. Like nearly everything else at a university whose architecture was long seen as an integral part of its mission for the advancement of "Literature, Science and Art," this was by design. In the years leading up to 1930, the president of the university, the architects in charge of shaping and imagining the still unfolding campus, the family of the founder, members of the university's board, and the artist charged with creating Rice's likeness all thought carefully about how to use the monument to inspire passers-by, to tell a certain story, and to achieve a kind of mastery in and over its surroundings.

Though understood from the beginning as the memorial's primary audience, students too have long had designs on the statue. When the memorial was an inkling in the minds of the university's friends and officers, but not yet a reality, Rice sophomore Max Jacobs penned a letter to the *Thresher* in February 1924 proposing the need for exactly such a thing, and highlighting the necessity that it be largely a student-organized affair. "Such a memorial," wrote Jacobs, "should be erected, not only by popular subscription among friends of the Institute, but by the students themselves, for it is they who are benefiting by the philanthropy and confidence of Mr. Rice." Jacobs laid out a plan for funding the memorial, and offered an idea on where it should go. It "should be a work of art, preferably a statue of Mr. Rice himself, to be executed in bronze and placed in the large court in front of the Administration building." Thus situated, reasoned Jacobs, "all who enter the gates of the Institute will see first of all a splendid tribute to the man who made possible the university represented by the buildings beyond." Jacob's proposal was suffused by an appreciation of symbolism, a firm grasp of the creative and intentional use of space at the university, and a deep gratitude for Rice's philanthropy and the importance of recognizing it. In his view, Rice deserved for those entering the campus "to see expressed in tangible form the atmosphere that the munificence" of the founder had made possible.[5]

Jacobs understood as well the social consequences that thinking about the memorial project and bringing it to fruition could accomplish, at present and well into the future:

> The memorial should be erected by the students of the Rice Institute, by alumni, and by the ex-students. . . . Each present student of the Institute should be asked to contribute one dollar. . . . Every Freshman that enters the Institute in the future should be told of the plan. . . . The details should be placed in the hands of a committee of five students. . . . The present student body . . . should

> decide the form of the memorial, and leave to students of the future only the details incident to the completion of the plan. . . . The entire plan should be submitted to the vote of the students . . . in order that the movement, if adopted, should be an expression of the student's regard for Mr. Rice. . . . The name of each student . . . who contributes to the memorial should be placed in a permanent record.

The memorial, in other words, would be another unifying force at this boundless university on the edge of Houston still excitedly figuring out who its men and women would become.[6]

The trustees and friends of the university who strived to realize a memorial worked with a similar, careful attention to the symbolic power of space. Where the memorial sat mattered. In the spring of 1924, Jacobs thought that placing it in front of the Administration Building offered the best prospects. But in 1922, when a subcommittee of trustees took up the charge of what to do with Rice's remains (he had been cremated four days after his demise in 1900 and his remains subsequently stored in a vault), they settled on but did not immediately advance the idea of entombing the "ashes" in a monument to be built in the middle of the Academic Courtyard. And in 1923, while attempting to forward plans on a magnificent president's house (a plan that in various forms had been batted around for more than a decade), the university's architect returned to the idea of a memorial to the founder as a part of the residence. In this proposal, a statue of the founder was to be placed in a courtyard of the president's home, adding substance to the notion that the entire baronial project could also be understood as a kind of "Founder's House."[7]

A president's house of any sort was not realized on campus for another twenty-five years. In 1925, however, the idea articulated by members of the board a few years earlier, that a memorial to the founder should also serve as the final resting place for Rice's remains, gained traction with the Institute's leaders. The result was the memorial that was finally erected and unveiled in 1930. Interesting minutia of all kinds populated the period between the board's new attention to making the memorial a reality and its actual dedication. More than ever, though, as the memorial moved from notion to thing, its creators lingered over its symbolic importance.

Who made the monument, for instance, was vitally important—and not simply for the skill of the selected artist. Would the board succumb to a base Americanism and reject the suggestion of an English-born sculptor? The university's architect thought John Angel, a prominent British-born artist then working and living in the United States, would be a fine candidate for the work. President Lovett fretted, though, that the suggestion would have to subvert prejudices among the board against any but American-born artists. If such biases had to be overcome, they were, for Angel ultimately secured a contract, "For making and completing a Seated Portrait Statue of William M. Rice, Founder, in Bronze in connection with Monument and Tomb."[8]

Initial thinking about the substance of the work revealed concerns about cost, but these soon gave way to other priorities: a focus on quality of material and workmanship, fitting the monument into the overall design of the present Institute and how it would evolve, and deciding on the narrative to which the overall work would give voice. Every detail of the evolving monument was full of intended meaning. Tennessee marble, for instance, was initially proposed as a possible way to economize on the monument's massive base, but planners reconsidered the idea in light of their other aims. Achieving an elemental congruence with the columns supporting the arcade beside the Administration Building was ideal, and so ultimately the conversation begun at the Administration Building in pink Texas granite would be carried into the Courtyard of Hedges.[9]

A deep concern with workmanship and quality of materials quickly displaced ideas about economy. That the statue portrait be done in the "best quality bronze," that it be "made and finished in the best manner known to the statuary art," and that "All materials and labor be first class in every respect" were critical criteria. Also critical was the requirement that the base be completed exactly according to the "drawings, general conditions, and specifications as prepared by the architects." The fundamental materiality, massing, and craftsmanship of the monument were meant to speak through an attention to quality.[10]

And then the monument was made to say more and to say it more directly. This was especially true of the massive granite base designed both to hold up the bronze statue and to contain Rice's remains. The east-facing side of the pedestal served as a kind of tombstone etched with "the full name of the founder, the years of his birth and death, and the following inscription: 'Salve aeternum aeternumque salve.'" The academic seal of the Institute and two torches completed the monument's front. The north-facing side of the pedestal held the state seal of Rice's adopted home along with "the phrase 'Imperium in imperio,'" or, an empire within an empire—lines chosen "in the absence of any state motto for Texas." Inscribed on the west-facing side of the monument was the seal of the United States and the nation's then de facto motto: "E pluribus unum." Finally, walking counter-clockwise around the monument, the south-facing side of the base gestured to the state of Rice's birth and thus held "the shield of Massachusetts" along with its motto: "Ense petit placidam sub libertate quietem."[11]

When the president of the Institute wrote to the founder's namesake nephew and Institute board member for approval of the memorial's compact narrative turns, he revealed both his hopes and his apprehensions for this part of the work. "Pray do not think that I have run wild on Latin," wrote Lovett to William Marsh Rice Jr., "but I honestly think the 'E pluribus unum' should stand, and if so, I think it better to have all four in the same tongue." This presentation of what Lovett understood to be the most important of the monument's inscriptions likely gestures to what the president saw as a central lesson of Rice's life. The monument's sides illustrated Rice's Yankee birth and southern fortune, but then employed the motto of the United States—which translates to "from many one"—in a way that could not help but allude to a reconciliation between two sections of the nation, especially since Angel's sculpture of Rice as a youthful man, rather than as the older philanthropist who endowed the Rice Institute, would be seen as "representative at once of the period in which Mr. Rice attained his maturity and of his person in the prime of his powers." In other words, it depicted the man who had lived during the Civil War era.[12]

"All monuments tell a story," as historian David Blight has noted, "some more precisely and purposefully than others." That Lovett intended the Founder's Memorial in part to tell a story of sectional reconciliation is easier to imagine, however, when it is placed within its historical context. Many white Americans since the conclusion of the Civil War had preached that combatants on both sides should forgive and forget the causes of strife between the North and the South, for the good (they thought) of the nation. As early as 1867, a popular poem first published in the *Atlantic Monthly*, "The Blue and the Gray," had used the image of a cemetery with Union and Confederate graves to suggest that postwar Americans should mourn both sides equally: "Love and tears for the Blue; / Tears and love for the Gray." Yet that impulse gained new strength in 1915 (as the nation marked the semicentennial of the Civil War's conclusion) and new urgency in 1917 (as American entry into the First World War fueled a burst of wartime patriotism).[13]

Not by coincidence, several leading American institutions of higher education chose this moment to inscribe reconciliationist sentiments permanently onto their campus landscapes. In 1915, Yale University unveiled Memorial Hall, which paired a listing of Yale alumni who had died in the Civil War with an inscription to "the bonds which now unite the land." A stone carving on the floor of the hall's main corridor reproduced the final verse of the 1867 poem "The Blue and the Gray." Princeton University's memorial atrium in Nassau Hall followed in the 1920s with a stone inscription that listed alumni who had died in the Civil War alphabetically by name, without regard to or any indication of the side for which they fought. These early efforts at uniting the nation represented an attempt at reconciliation without truth-telling.[14]

As a well-traveled educator with personal and professional connections in the Northeast, Lovett was surely aware of such developments, especially at Princeton; that was where Lovett had previously taught and William Marsh Rice Jr., board member and nephew of the founder, had studied. But replicating similar Civil War memorials would have been difficult to imagine at the Rice Institute in 1915 or the 1920s. This was not only because of the institution's youthful age, but also because of its location within the former Confederacy (where Lost Cause myths about the righteousness of the rebellion remained strong) and more particularly in a part of the South—Texas—with its own early and often ritually embellished history as the Lone Star republic. The cornerstone of the Administration Building (later Lovett Hall) was formally dedicated in 1911 on Texas Independence Day, and while Princeton was beginning work on the Nassau Hall memorial, the Rice Institute welcomed Confederate veterans to campus during their 1920 reunion in Houston, the same reunion at which the Sam Houston Chapter of the Ku Klux Klan made its first public appearance downtown.[15]

Still, in the various ceremonies and decisions surrounding the establishment of the Rice Institute, it was also possible to hear undertones of sectional reconciliation. In "Texas: A Democratic Ode," an inaugural poem written by Henry van Dyke for Rice's formal opening ceremonies, the Civil War was remembered as a time when "brother fought with brother, each for his country's cause." Van Dyke, a northerner and Princetonian who had also composed an ode for Princeton's sesquicentennial in 1896, alluded briefly to the war's most important result: "Washing away with a rain of blood and tears the dust of slavery." But like the earlier author of "The Blue and the Gray," the inaugural poet avoided assigning moral blame to any section:

> Oh, who shall measure the praise or blame in a strife so vast?
> 	And who shall speak of traitors or tyrants when all were true?
> We lift our eyes to the sky, and rejoice that the storm is past,
> 	And we thank the God of all that the Union shines in the blue.

Such sentiments were less explicitly, but no less clearly, echoed in Lovett's selection around the same time of the new school's colors as blue and gray—"a blue still deeper than Oxford blue, and the gray of the Confederate days."[16] The colors recalled the "War between the States" (as Lovett called it), and they alluded as well to his continued hopes for the aftermath of that war—the further and full development of the South, and the place of this new university in particular in the region's continued growth. For at least a generation, Lovett believed, the region's prospects had been dim, but now across the entire nation, across the whole of the formerly fractured country, the New South shone with promise. "Go South, young man! is the slogan in one section," said Lovett in 1912, quoting the widely reprinted title of an address given to Yale University alumni by a New South booster and railroad tycoon in 1890. "Stay South, young man!" continued Lovett, "is the answering call of opportunity in the other."[17]

An unsigned 1920 *Thresher* article, headlined "Blue and Gray—The Unison," likewise used the school's colors to make a point about sectional reconciliation. "The gray," argued the author, "is the semblance of the Confederacy, the heroic sons and daughters of our beloved Southland who under the leadership of Robert E. Lee, stood firmly for what they considered right." A little more reservedly, the writer continued, "The blue, on the other hand, stands for our Northern brothers, and their chosen emblem." The conclusion went exactly where Lovett pointed with his selection of the university's colors: "How fitting that Rice, a university that was builded by a philanthropist from the North, who made his fortune in the South, should choose colors that are a combination of these two elements of our native land. How fitting that the gray and the blue, after the scars of those who wore them have been healed over, should be reunited in such perfect union, in America's coming university." Eight years later, with the inscriptions he proposed to place on the Founder's Memorial pedestal, Lovett seemed to envision, in the life and peregrinations and philanthropy of William Marsh Rice, another powerful symbol of national reunion and healing.[18]

There is, of course, a perilous, tragic, even violent silence in the reconciliation between North and South suggested by these visions. As scholars of this period have shown, the reconciliationist memory of the Civil War favored by many white Americans depended on forgetting or downplaying slavery as the central cause of that war, and it depended as well on the quite literal "re-subjugation of many of those people whom the war had freed from centuries of bondage." Lovett had remarked at the opening of the university that the "mild climate" of the South "keeps men constantly human and neighborly and friendly in ways of living whose democracy recognizes no inequalities." Further, he continued, Texas was "a State which can know no provincialism, because it has lived under seven flags." This was boosterism, and so must be approached as such. Even so, it spoke profoundly to what many in Lovett's Houston took for granted as far as democracy and equality were concerned. In overlooking the era's racial hierarchies, which belied the nation's claim to treat all its citizens equally, the mainline narrative of the Founder's Memorial included an interstitial, unvoiced history of the Jim Crow era in which it was conceived and produced.[19]

Indeed, the culture of sectional reconciliation—whether advanced in the service of pragmatism, nostalgia, local boosterism, or some combination of all these aims—never required a negation of the Lost Cause. For if "all were true" in the Civil War, as Van Dyke poetically proposed at the Institute's opening, then none were wrong, not even the chief southern rebels. The rise of reconciliationism went hand in hand with widespread veneration of Confederate heroes such as Stonewall Jackson and Robert E. Lee alongside Union heroes like Ulysses S. Grant. Thus, in 1924, when Rice Institute professor of German Lindsey Blayney was invited to deliver the commencement address at Washington and Lee University, where Lee's tomb occupied center stage in the campus chapel, Blayney told the *Thresher* that, "Whether one is a Southerner or not, one must appreciate the privilege of being permitted to speak so near to the mortal remains of that great general, great citizen, and great man." The next year, in an address to white clubwomen in Austin, Edgar Odell Lovett echoed the sentiment in his own speech on Lee, whom Lovett described as "a great patriot, a great Virginian, a great American, a great Christian," and also—for his role in leading Washington and Lee from 1865 until his death—a great college president, worthy of being classed with other departed educational leaders such as Yale's Timothy Dwight and Princeton's Woodrow Wilson. "That Robert E. Lee has been received into their fellowship," Lovett concluded, "I have not the slightest doubt."[20]

Such reflections about legacies, history, and the place of both the South and its universities in the nation as a whole were not far in the past in 1928, as Lovett turned to the developing plans for a memorial to William Marsh Rice. Yet even with its state and national seals and mottos, Lovett's conscious aims for that monument were concerned, most of all, with the literal and symbolic elevation of the Institute's own founder as another model citizen and philanthropist. And if the president's desires concerning the back and flanks of the pedestal were more implied than proclaimed, he very precisely voiced his hopes for its front and its inscription: *Salve aeternum aeternumque salve.* The text, wrote Lovett, was "a slight modification of a line of Virgil, and never to my knowledge used in such a connection as this before." As rendered by Lovett, it meant: "Hail forever, and forever hail."[21]

Here, then, was Lovett's greatest wish for the entirety of the memorial project—that it would make the founder a central presence on campus and a permanent interlocutor with future faculty and students, and in so doing that it would help inform a familiarity with and enthusiastic appreciation for Rice. Ultimately, it would bind the affections of students as much to the founder as to the city, state, and region to which he both owed and had devoted his wealth. "I can think of nothing," wrote Lovett, "that would seem to hold the founder himself quite so intimately and permanently in the midst of the local life of the institution on campus as this, 'Hail forever, and forever hail,' whether you regard it as a greeting from us to him or from him to us."[22]

The Unveiling

But from where on the still-young campus would the figure of Rice greet the university's students and be saluted in return? This had actually been decided before the details of the base were fully worked out. The sculptor, John Angel, thus had the advantage of having a particular site in mind and committed to photographs, even as he started work on his part of the monument and tomb.

Three options had been considered for the location. The first was "in the large open circulation in front of the Administration Building," the place now known as the Founder's Court. The monument would face toward Main Street with its back toward the Sallyport. This would have pleased Max Jacobs, the Rice sophomore from years before, as it was precisely the position he had recommended himself as an ideal location for visitors to the campus and perhaps passersby to very nearly immediately encounter the founder upon encountering the university. But what Jacobs had left unsaid in his earlier imagining of a memorial, William Ward Watkin (a member of the faculty and the Institute's supervising architect) did not leave out when faced with the task of evaluating the best spot for a monument: The large area in front of the Administration Building, save a small garden of hedges and other plantings, was pretty much a parking lot. And if anything, as the university grew, it made sense that the garden would be rooted out and the whole area "given over to a method of controlled parking of automobiles."[23]

The second option was a greener space within the "Academic Court at the end of the hedges nearest to the sally porte," but this spot presented several challenges. If placed here along the main east-west axis through the center of the quad, the president desired that the memorial face the Administration Building. Watkin thought that view "a bit peculiar"—given the significant area of the quad to the west and the substantial foot traffic around the Administration Building. When Watkin thought about the memorial, he had in mind the direction and the frequency from whence it would be approached. He thought it better for the majority of people moving about the Academic Court at any moment to see the front of the monument instead of its back. There were tough spatial issues with this second option, but the differences between the preferences of the university president and Watkin's own ideas about what direction the monument should face may have ultimately doomed the proposal.[24]

A third option allowed for the president's opinion concerning where the memorial faced, but also satisfied Watkin's ideas about placing the monument according to circulation in the court and the current and future plan of the university. Situating the monument farther west on the same axis as the second option "but just beyond Road #3 in the second court of hedges" offered several advantages. The monument "would have the court consisting of the Physics Building, the Administration Building, and the Alumni Building when it is built, all in front of it." (As early as 1927, President Lovett and the university architects had considered erecting a three-story classroom building on the Academic Courtyard opposite of the Physics Building, where Sewell Hall now stands. In 1928 the Association of Rice Alumni, in raising money for the project, sought to make the building a memorial to the founder.) Additional development also recommended the spot. "It would have toward the left," Watkin continued, "the laboratory of biology when it is built and toward the right some future academic building."

This placement, then, was ideal as far out as Watkin thought it reasonable to look: "Practically all approach for that length of time and 75% of all future approach would be in front of this statue rather than from the rear." And lastly, to leave no aspect unexamined, the architect imagined it all in its entirety one more time. This exercise led Watkin to imagine whether the memorial could actually and satisfactorily occupy the whole space of the quad as presently conceived and how it was slated to develop. "The figure and its pedestal," Watkin concluded, "are of quite adequate dimension to have good scale in this position."[25]

Ralph Adams Cram, the chief architect to whom Watkin had been addressing all of this thinking about the memorial, responded enthusiastically and unequivocally concerning the choices put before him. He had "no hesitation whatever in saying that the third position is the one that seems to me by far the best of all. . . . I really think there can be no question in this matter."[26]

On where the monument would be placed, there were no further questions that mattered, and so in the spring of 1930 the university announced the memorial publicly. The *Thresher* informed its readers in February that a "Statue of William Marsh Rice Will Be Erected on Campus: Unveiling to Take Place During Commencement Week." Within a month, clear evidence of the coming addition to the Grand Court was plain to see. "The hole for the foundation, which puzzled so many students," was by then a foundation and now ready for "the complete figure." Within two months of the foundation being laid, Arthur B. Cohn, the Institute's business manager, placed Rice's cremated remains within the memorial itself. So as the "'grand cramming' season" and the university's fifteenth commencement approached, everything was going, more or less, according to plan.[27]

A series of campus events framed the unveiling and dedication of the Founder's Memorial, most of them accentuating and extending ideas that had shaped the monument's creation over the previous eight years. The program for the dedication of the memorial itself was remarkably simple. Slated to last no more than thirty minutes on June 8, 1930, it featured the actual unveiling, a brief paean to Rice as a worthy subject, remarks on the artist John Angel and the place of sculpture in the university's larger architectural program, a rendition of "For Rice's Honor," and a "concluding prayer and benediction" by the morning's baccalaureate speaker.[28]

The public ceremony teemed with students in the audience, but it also featured students in the program—namely, two current student leaders, a member of the first graduating class, who was now head of the alumni association, and the grand niece of William Marsh Rice, who was at the moment a rising senior at the Institute. Each pulled cords that released a large flowing drape that had covered the entire statue and pedestal preceding the ceremony. The subsequent singing of the school song by the university's largest-ever graduating class—led by the Rice Band and another graduating senior—convinced *Thresher* headline writers to remark on the "Prominent Part" taken by the Institute's undergraduates in the entire morning ceremony.[29]

Then came time for remarks. Two of the three speakers at the Sunday dedication were standing in for others—prime movers in the making of the memorial who nevertheless could not or did not attend the public unveiling. First,

Benjamin Botts Rice spoke for William Marsh Rice Jr., who was "unavoidably absent from home" but who had prepared remarks in advance that he gave to his younger brother. (Both were sons of Frederick A. Rice and members of the board of trustees.) Then, Ralph Adams Cram, the 1930 commencement speaker and the original architect who designed the general campus plan, stood in for the sculptor John Angel, "whose engagements regrettably prevented his presence."[30]

Taken together, the remarks of the speakers mostly burnished ideas that had already been applied to the monument. Rice Junior's thoughts for the morning, read by his brother Benjamin Botts Rice, were concise and direct. In fewer than two hundred words, every image and idea presented his uncle in heroic and patriotic tones while managing to communicate too a sense of the family's loss:

> The donor of the Rice Institute was born in the old Bay State in 1816—of old Colonial stock—his grandfather was one of the Minutemen at the Battle of Lexington. He came to Houston in the Republic of Texas in 1838, bringing with him a small stock of merchandise and a heart of oak.
>
> By self-sacrifice and an energy that knew little rest he built up a business that made him the first merchant in the city of his adoption. As he grew in financial strength he assisted in many enterprises among them being the building of transportation lines, first stage lines, and then the railroads.
>
> He was a man of high ideals, charitable without ostentation, appreciative of the wonderful possibilities in a rapidly growing country, and always adding to his store of knowledge. He lived a useful life, fought a good fight, and dying left the fruits of his labor for the young women and young men who are to be the beneficiaries of the Rice Institute for all time.[31]

It is worth lingering on these comments enough to notice both what they did say and what they did not say. At its start, briefly and subtly, Rice Junior's panegyric reinforced Lovett's past efforts to present the university as a site of postbellum white sectional healing. The image of Rice's birth in Massachusetts, his father's fighting at the inaugural battles of the American Revolution, Rice's antebellum journey to Texas, and his dying gift of the university all underlined the point. Rice Junior evoked the Battle of Lexington but passed over the Civil War, choosing instead to emphasize his uncle's entrepreneurial "energy" and appreciation for "the wonderful possibilities in a rapidly growing country." As in many public encomiums to civic leaders at the time, not so much as an allusion to the place of African Americans in that growing country slipped through. The founder's wealth became the "fruits of his labor" alone.

Glancing backward and forward in time from the unveiling ceremony reveals that the story of William Marsh Rice was not always so separated from depictions of African Americans or the Civil War era in the ritual and pageantry surrounding the early Rice Institute. In 1933, the "Legend of Houston" pageant at the City Auditorium, a big event in which Rice Institute students and trustees played roles alongside a cast of hundreds of other Houstonians, featured a kind of dramatic tableaux of the Founder's Memorial. In a part of the pageant depicting the story of William Marsh Rice, William Marsh Rice Jr. portrayed his uncle's effigy by sitting in a chair on stage, with a painting of the campus quadrangle serving as backdrop. "A blue gauze curtain separated the audience from the scene," reported the *Thresher* of the spectacle. "Students with their grey caps and gowns marched slowly down the hedged pathway to the painted sallyport." The scene evoked a commencement ceremony tinged with the school's unifying colors. But the very next scene in the pageant, leaping back in time, depicted "Plantation Days" and featured a group of "Negro singers" performing "negro spirituals" on a set depicting a cotton field. The sponsors and planners of the pageant had included the episode, according to the Houston *Post,* because "no record of a Southern city is complete without some allusion to the negroes, especially the old mammies who nursed the children and the darkies who tilled the soil and cared for the 'white folks.'"[32]

Such events are reminders that the public announcement of the Rice memorial, its construction, and its early years on campus took place in a period in which major aspects of student life and civic culture articulated quite clearly the impossibility of thinking of the South in which the founder had "built up a business" and founded an Institute without also thinking about slavery. Those same activities articulated as well a general belief in the superiority of white people, and of the white South (and, often more specifically, of Rice students), over African Americans, whom students sometimes actually encountered but more often conjured up, drawing on racist stereotypes prevalent at the time.

In the weeks immediately leading up to the dedication of the memorial in June 1930, for instance, the Institute's May Fete—an annual spring festival on campus that later became Rondolet—provided a vivid performance of what Rice students understood as the southern ideal, and the place of Black men and women within it. "This year," the *Thresher* reminded readers in its issue of May 2, 1930, "a Southern theme has been chosen for the fete and the tall oaks and spacious lawns of the campus will form a beautiful background" for the event's main set piece, "a colonial mansion with massive pillars and deep verandah." As if to stress the gentility of the affair, the *Thresher* maintained that, "In keeping with the theme, a note of simplicity will be maintained through the entire ceremony." The subsequent descriptions of how the women would be attired, and the nature of their entrances, reinforced a nostalgic ideal of southern elegance—even if one student had been selected, incongruously, to serve as "Court Jester."[33] Yet that court jester, it turned out, was central to and not at all inconsistent with the festival's theme. As the *Campanile* reported in its recapping of the event, "the jester . . . was in the garb of a pickaninny." There could be no southern-themed May Fete without imagined slaves—in this case a Rice undergraduate offering his idea of an enslaved Black child.[34]

The "pickaninny" at the 1930 May Fete was far from an aberration. Neither was it ubiquitous. Nevertheless, humiliating and debased ideas of Black people and Black life surfaced enough in the cultural and social life of the Institute and its segregated surroundings to indicate the fundamental normality of such ideas across campus. Racist images surfaced often enough to indicate that the thinking and unthinking degradation of African Americans was central, at the very least, to early students' understanding of what it meant to play, to grow into adulthood, and to imagine and to decide whether and how to practice what it was to be white in the Jim Crow South. This was also, after all, a period in which the university's young men and women persistently, proudly, and with a sense of what they understood to be friendship and high regard, referred to Jack Shelton as "Nigger Jack."

Black Houstonians, of course, challenged such distorted pictures of Black lives and southern history at the time. In the weeks before the "Legend of Houston" pageant in 1933, the Houston *Informer and Texas Freeman*, the successor to C. F. Richardson's *Informer*, noted that a segregated section had been set aside for the event and reported that tickets could be purchased at the headquarters of the Colored Young Women's Christian Association. The paper also listed—by name—the fourteen Black Houstonians who would be singing on stage, thereby promising to represent the "colored race" and the "laudable part" it had played in Houston's history. After the pageant, however, an editorial in the *Informer* suggested that the performance of "Plantation Days" had done more harm than good, calling particular attention to the *Post*'s commentary about "mammies" and "darkies." "This expression is not representative of the contribution which Negroes have made to the forward march of progress in Houston," retorted the *Informer*, which advised the city's Black community in the future "to give more careful consideration to these special Negro parts which are offered us by our well-meaning friends in the white community."[35]

Such comments spotlighted the barriers that Jim Crow maintained between Houston's Black community and even their most "well-meaning friends," not to mention those elements of the white community who made no pretense of friendship across the color line. Three years before, when C. F. Richardson was still in the editor's chair at the *Informer*, the Black journalist had not remarked at all on events at the Rice Institute in the weeks stretching from the May Fete on May 2, 1930, to the unveiling of the Founder's Memorial on June 8, 1930. In those weeks, the paper was occupied instead by reports about the savage lynching of a jailed African American farmer named George Hughes on May 9, 1930, in Sherman, Texas, north of Dallas, where a white mob had poured gasoline all over the county courthouse, burned it to the ground, and then used an automobile to drag Hughes's smoldering body from the ruins to a nearby Black neighborhood, where his corpse was hung from a tree across from a local Black store. "Where have we drifted to in this reputed civilized and Christian country," asked Richardson on May 17, "when maddened mobs can trample the law under their profane and unholy feet," giving the lie to pretensions about white "superiority" and the supposed obliteration of "sectional lines" after the Civil War. Knowing that Sherman was renowned at the time for its high density of white educational institutions, including Austin College, Richardson also noted reports that local students had joined the mob and asked, "are our white institutions of learning maintaining courses in lynching, arson, anarchy and treason in their collegiate curricula?"[36]

Richardson's provocative question—what *were* segregated colleges teaching or not teaching their students about Black neighbors?—still hung in the humid Houston air three weeks later, as the Rice Institute community gathered to celebrate its latest graduates and dedicate a monument to its founder. In the remarks made at the unveiling of the Founder's Memorial, there would be no inflammatory race-baiting, no pickaninny, no pointed valorization of the former Confederacy (much less any discussion of what roles Rice had played in the Civil War), and no marked nostalgia for the antebellum South. There was none of that in the personal and powerful remembrance that Benjamin Botts Rice read in place of his brother at its dedication. But barely a month after the "colonial" May Fete, and only weeks after the lynching in Sherman was followed by another in Honey Grove, Texas, there could be no question about the price at which the sectional peace toward which Rice Junior and the memorial gestured had been purchased. At least two more lynchings of Black Texans would follow that June.[37]

Still, if Benjamin Botts Rice took even two minutes to deliver his brother's words on June 8, he spent as much of that time making a case for the essential modernity of their uncle's efforts as he did evoking his life as a balm for postbellum white American sectional politics. In a quick speech, both points were quickly dispensed with. The majority of the address, like the inscription Lovett had chosen for the monument's front panel, drew on and attempted to further impart to its listeners an esteem and gratitude for the founder's work and for his subsequent choices. Because Rice Junior's words were eulogistic, of course, there was much missing and much papered over (from the vantage point of today, no doubt, but from the vantage of 1930 as well). And one small change from Rice Junior's draft is also worth noting. In draft form, the last line of the memorial had read, "and dying left the fruits of his labors to help the young men and young women of Texas for all time," as opposed to how Botts Rice concluded that morning, "and dying left the fruits of his labor for the young women and young men who are to be the beneficiaries of the Rice Institute for all time."[38]

The changed final clause that made it into the program had been written out in longhand on one of Rice Junior's envelopes that accompanied a typed and corrected draft of the brief comments. The change is worth reflecting on for the slightly different view it took of the Institute's students. In one iteration, they were more clearly the charges of the school. In the final version, though, Rice Junior's words cast the students in the audience and their successors as agents, a subtle change more in line with the active, protagonistic bent that Rice himself occupied in the just uttered remembrances. In that last line, Rice Junior intimated that the students were, ideally, not simply wards of his uncle's—or of the Institute's—generosity and good will. They were also brimming with potential themselves—beneficiaries worthy of the rights and privileges of the Institute.[39]

Rice Junior's remarks, read by his brother, were then followed by Ralph Adams Cram, standing in for John Angel. In the context of the morning, Cram's remarks were not terribly longer than Rice Junior's, but they may have very well *felt* prolonged. The architect first took a circuitous and highly embellished route to saying what the Houston papers had put much more succinctly in their own coverage of the dedication: John Angel was a remarkable and highly accomplished artist. "A great deal of Mr. Angel's best known work in this country," the Houston *Post-Dispatch* informed its readers, "appears in the cathedral of St. John the Divine in New York, and some of it in the new chapel of Princeton university." Cram himself went much further in his own remarks. "I have no hesitation in saying," he intoned, "that in my opinion, and this opinion is endorsed by many others of the highest authority, Mr. Angel is a sculptor of such preeminent ability that he finds hardly any rival during the past three centuries." Cram had recommended Angel for the Rice commission and worked with him in New York in Cram's capacity as a principal architect for the Cathedral of St. John the Divine.[40]

But Cram also strove to make an additional point—one that had dominated private conversation and correspondence on the statue but that he desired to make publicly that morning. The unfolding architecture of the campus was an integral part of the whole vision of the university, and the statue was meant to be a deeply considered expression of that architectural program as it presently stood. Cram remarked at the start that "Architecture by itself and without the cooperation of the other arts is almost helpless." Very closely following on this point, he then opined, "This is notably true of sculpture which, of course, is almost the first art on which the architect relies." Toward his conclusion, Cram then brought these points to bear on the campus of the university, saying, "We, the architects, who for so many years have been striving to put into visible form the high ideal of William Marsh Rice, now find here in this 'counterfeit presentment' that supreme personification of the man himself which gives the crowning quality to our endeavors." Indeed, though it was difficult to see, given the statue's elevation, Angel himself had carved an homage to the work of campus architects into his sculpture of the founder. The seated figure held a scroll in his left hand depicting the original campus plan for the Rice Institute.[41]

The dedication program for the memorial—succinct and measured—did not break much new ground on thinking about the monument, or the founder, or the university; the half-hour dedication was more a tightly wound summary of the relationship between all three.[42]

However, the baccalaureate sermon that immediately followed the dedication, by the Reverend James Gordon Gilkey, and the commencement address which followed the next day, by Cram, did add new ideas to the earliest words spoken around the memorial. Both post-dedication speeches, delivered by men who were not from the South, recapitulated many of the notions central to the statue's making and unveiling. But Gilkey and Cram also gave voice to views of the world that complicated the brief ceremony in which they had just participated. In particular, their remarks introduced ways of thinking about the monument (or thinking near it) that very subtly troubled the host of reverent notions that had just brought it into existence.

From the commencement stand in the Academic Quadrangle on June 9, 1930, for example, Ralph Adams Cram gave a speech that assailed "The K.K.K., fundamentalism, and the Scopes Trial." He had no use for the Eighteenth Amendment or the Methodist Board of Temperance, Prohibition, and Public Morals that had helped to bring it about. The extremes of the "evangelical denominations" came in for special opprobrium. He took aim at a press that expected much too little of its readers, and "the medical fakes and psychological superstitions that flourish on popular support." For Cram, "the October orgies of the New York stock exchange"—the 1929 crash and "the alarming menace of unemployment" that followed—were of a piece with these other calamities. Elsewhere, he railed against the "mob psychology" that appeared to motivate too much of human political action, from the Sack of Constantinople through more recent terrors in the aftermath of the Russian Revolution. Cram also trained his ire on the revival of the Ku Klux Klan in the preceding decade, and he carried this questioning of the humanity of humanity toward current racial sensibilities by highlighting a range of modern mass killings: "the extermination of the Indian tribes in America, the record of the Congo and of the islands of the West Indies." Cram said nothing explicitly about the wave of lynchings that had recently dominated headlines in Texas, but it would be no surprise if the minds of some in the audience drifted to stories from Sherman or Honey Grove as the architect railed against "mob-insanity that is worse than the frenzied panic of a herd of wild beasts" and "the mob-action that puts even war to shame."[43]

The New England architect made these remarks primarily to explore what he called "The Limits of Democracy"—an address which the speaker filled with such seemingly forward-looking notions as those recounted above but that he mainly meant as a lament of the passing of wise rule by great men. The speech roundly criticized the evils of modernity, which Cram took to be boundless (but not necessarily harmless) technological and industrial innovation married to a surfeit of democracy that actually amounted to rule by the passion of fools. The combination, he thought, invited cataclysm. The masses were not innocent in all of this, but Cram did not hold them especially responsible. He thought failures of leadership particularly at fault. Ultimately he charged the graduates and the university as a whole with redressing those failures.

Although Cram's view of the world, as presented at commencement, evinced his distrust of democracy and his pessimism concerning the possibilities of humankind, in some ways it also ended up challenging some of the memorial's obfuscations. His anti-populism very nearly led him to speak out against some of the excesses of white supremacy (though he would not have called it that, and if he could have brought himself to speak out against the excesses of white supremacy, it is far from clear that he would have spoken out against its foundations). Still, parts of what Cram offered in the wake of the monument's dedication unsettled the worshipful approach to the founder of the university at which Cram was both a guest and cocreator. Rice Junior had chosen to focus his own brief remarks at the Founder's Memorial on William Marsh Rice's efforts as a confederate of industrialists if not an industrialist himself. (Given his age, railroad investments were the part of his uncle's work with which he would have been most familiar.) Yet in Cram's remarks, it was faith in industrialism and in industrialists that needed to be shaken. "There is to me," he offered, "something fantastic in the orgy of optimism, publicly displayed . . . over the manifest destiny of industrialism to recover from its occasional reverses, and especially the one in process today, and to go on, along the same road, to even higher achievement."[44]

Cram's position on the Great Depression and on the worst of the capitalists and others who were at the helm when all had gone wrong encouraged a piercing criticism: "They are undisciplined children possessed of a vast number of mechanical toys. They do not break them in sheer wantonness, to be sure, but they use them recklessly and without discretion for their own selfish purposes and with no more sense of social values and social ends than the Bandar-log of Kipling's tales." Industrialism had "raised up out of the lower average the present leaders of men and the controllers of physical forces within the field of technological civilization and all that this implies." The result was a "triumphant materialism" and amoral will to power.[45]

"Educator Links Up Dry Law With Methodist Board and Ku Klux Klan" was the headline later given Cram's speech by the Houston *Post-Dispatch*, which made sure to call out the most sensational claims. The *Post-Dispatch* also gave over nearly a complete page of the newspaper to reproduce the entirety of Cram's remarks. He had indeed done what the paper announced. But he had also made room for challenging the kind of thinking that went into the creation of Rice's memorial, and the general celebration of men like Rice—even if Cram did not take up the challenge explicitly, and did not mean to take it up, and did not mean for others to take it up.[46]

The day before, at the baccalaureate sermon given as part of commencement, the Reverend Gilkey, a prominent American preacher hailing from Rice's Massachusetts hometown, had tread similar ground. He did not believe in Great Men, or in the imperatives of success, or in merit in the ways that Cram so obviously did. Greatness, for Gilkey, was an imposter. It is difficult to imagine a more profoundly different set of remarks than the two major addresses that framed the 1930 commencement. But even as Gilkey, contra Cram, argued that one's position in life was neither a true measure of one's "ability or his deserts," and that many were the number who had been "caught up and lifted into positions of comfort and eminence by forces which they neither created nor foresaw," he also lamented along with the university's architect that, "If all of us count money and fame the greatest things in life and then set our hearts on winning them at any cost, most of us are headed for disappointment and heartache, and the civilization we are building is headed for disaster."[47]

It was not a condemnation of the age's magnates. It was an opening, though, to question them. If the earliest planners of the Founder's Memorial had sometimes spoken as if they intended for its viewers to pass by or linger about the monument filled with mute appreciation, what they had also evidently wrought was something along the lines of most of the other decisions they had made in founding the Institute. They had also created a potential site of contestation over values and ideas.

Hail Forever?

"I think the campus of a university is one of these things which has a great influence upon the minds of students." So wrote the sculptor John Angel to Edgar Odell Lovett in the aftermath of the dedication of his statue of William Marsh Rice. Angel hoped that it could become one of the students' "special corners." "Nothing would please me so much as for them to use the seat around the statue [to] rest & talk & study. And I like to feel there is a spirit existing in a statue itself which makes itself felt. I tried hard to make that spirit strong—quiet and effective. I tried to express what Mr. Rice was and what he meant to the students—even more than what he looks like."

Angel hoped that some of Lovett's most affecting aspirations for the monument would be realized too. Recalling a former trip to Houston, he informed Lovett, "I remember when we walked through the campus together you said you could imagine how the silhouette of the statue would look there in the evening." "I hope," Angel continued, "it looks as well as you had envisioned it."[48]

There is good evidence that much of Lovett's, and Angel's, and even Max Jacobs's desires for the Founder's Memorial did indeed come true. By the end of the university's first century, few were the students or faculty who could translate on the fly *salve aeternum aeternumque salve*, but the memorial's common name across the university—Willy's statue—testified to the amicable warmth with which many at Rice regarded the founder and his memorial. And there can be no doubt that the statue evolved into a center of social and cultural activity at the university. In 1988, a group of Rice engineering students added to the memorial's lore by successfully rotating the statue on its pedestal so that Willy faced Fondren Library, a prank that was creatively commemorated at an eightieth-anniversary celebration for the Founder's Memorial in 2010. As celebrants cut into an elaborate birthday cake, decorated so as to look like the quadrangle, an edible likeness of Rice's statue spun around 180 degrees, to the delight of a crowd that had gathered at the monument's base.[49]

But it is also true that not everyone felt the same warmth towards Willy as they passed the Founder's Memorial. One of the university's early Black faculty members, Professor Thomas Freeman, expressed somewhat different feelings about the founder in a 2012 interview. "You see, for a long time Blacks didn't go to Rice. Not because they didn't want to, but the charter stated that no Blacks would be ever admitted to Rice—for Rice was for white, and white only. . . . Now William Marsh contributed millions, and this was his wish and desire that no Blacks would *ever* attend Rice," much less teach there. "Marsh," the professor completed his thought while thinking of his earliest walks across campus, "must have been turning over in his grave."[50]

Meanwhile, by the time Professor Freeman arrived on campus, and with some regularity thereafter, the statue had also become what Cram and Gilkey had implicitly modeled on the weekend of its unveiling: a site for debate, free expression, even protest. It was there, "at the statue of William Marsh Rice in the academic quadrangle," that the Student Action Committee staged a demonstration in December 1968 about its report on minority student recruitment, *Who Enters Rice?* There, too, faculty and students had addressed a crowd protesting the treatment of Charlie Freeman's case for readmission in 1969. There, in the quadrangle, members of the Rice community gathered nearly fifty years later to speak out about the killings of unarmed Black citizens in the wake of Michael Brown's death in Ferguson, Missouri. And these were only three in a long list of examples of community members gathering around or near the statue to express opinions and contend over issues large and small, from war and peace or the marginalization of LGBTQ+ students to more quotidian concerns.[51]

In 1973, for example, Houston mayor Louie Welch came to the memorial to gather student opinions about the city's mass transit system. And some thirty years later, about twenty students, faculty, and staff gathered at the statue to protest a new campus parking plan. It was one of at least two such rallies over that issue in the spring of 2002, which drew the faculty chairman of the University's Standing Committee on Parking into the quadrangle to parley with student protesters. Though small in number, the protesters amplified their views with a bullhorn and received a commendation from the editorial board of the *Thresher.* "The group of students who met at Willy's Statue last Friday did better than protest," said the *Thresher,* "they discussed, they planned and they decided to be proactive."[52]

At various moments across the university's history, questions about the Founder's Memorial itself and about the appropriate use of the quad also became a focus of discussion and debate. A controversy from 1932 illustrates some students' early inclination to embrace the statue as a site of revelry—in this instance, in ways that others thought contradictory to the monument's function as a tomb. After some members of the sophomore class had instructed members of the freshman class to "clean and shave" the founder, a debate arose about students' preserving the dignity of the memorial.[53] A later controversy during the First Gulf War in 1991 revolved around whether it was permissible for students to hang yellow ribbons around the quad, a statement understood by some as politically neutral support for American troops but by others as political speech. Defenders of the ribbons said they were no different from "the annual ceremony for Dr. Martin Luther King, Jr., which features speakers and a wreath that is laid in front of Willy's statue for a day." Administrators disagreed.[54]

Finally, in 2009, a little more than a decade before "Willy's statue" itself became a subject of protest on campus, a student proposal to alter the symmetrical balance and straight lines of the historic quadrangle sparked a debate about the very meaning of the quad and the memorial at its center. The year before, university leaders had solicited proposals from students for an addition to the campus landscape that would honor the Legacy Society—a group of donors who had given at least $4.6 million (or approximately the same as William Marsh Rice's original endowment) to the university. President David Leebron conceived of a design competition as a way to involve Rice students critically in this important effort; he noted that Maya Lin, who designed the Vietnam War memorial in Washington, DC, had also submitted her winning proposal for a memorial while still in her undergraduate years. And in April 2009, after a competition judged by a blue-ribbon committee that included administrators and trustees, the *Thresher* reported that a student winner had been selected. The winning design proposed to surround the Founder's Memorial with concentric circles of Texas pink granite embedded in the ground, with the names of donors inlaid in bronze in the stones. Radiating out from the statue like the rings of a tree, the circles impressed the judges as subtle yet symbolically powerful. Construction was to begin, said the *Thresher,* in 2012.[55]

Instead, the proposal immediately generated controversy among students and alumni. The next week's *Thresher* included a staff editorial describing the concentric circles in the quad as "disrespectful" to the founder, suggesting that they turned his tomb "into a bullseye." Letters to the editor described the plan as "repulsive and offensive," as well as a threat to the "reputation" of the university and its future ability to raise funds from donors. Some critics worried that the plan risked introducing crass materialism to a space devoted to beauty and learning. "Who knew every sidewalk had a price?" one asked. Yet running through all of the criticisms was a repeated theme: The beauty, symbolism, and symmetry of the quad, "the epicenter of Rice's identity," were too important to be changed in any way, ever. "That quad is Rice. Our Rice," said one group of alumni. Construction of the concentric circles was indefinitely postponed and eventually abandoned altogether.[56]

In retrospect, the episode served to demonstrate yet again how deeply attached some members of the community felt to the historic quadrangle and to the monument they fondly and familiarly recalled as "Willy." And yet the idea for the student design competition—as well as the winning design itself—also continued a long history of active student participation in envisioning the campus landscape, encouraged by faculty and university leaders. From Max Jacobs in 1924 to the debate over the Legacy Society project on the eve of the university's centennial, Rice students had long had designs on the quad. They had also actively participated in making the space a site of open debate about what made Rice Rice and about what the university should become.

Viewed within this long history, then, the sit-ins that began to take place at the base of the Founder's Memorial in the year 2020, as well as the "Demands" and online discourse that quickly began to surround them, continued a long tradition of student claims on the quad and the mission of the university, even as they also represented a new departure in that history.

On the one hand, the reaction to the "concentric circles" in 2009 suggested the kinds of opposition that would be sure to face any proposal to modify the monument or its setting. On the other hand, protesters in 2020 were asking questions few had publicly asked before in this context: Did a statue of the man who had determined to exclude Black people from his Institute, and who had enslaved and profited from enslavement in making his wealth, deserve the singular, central place in the campus landscape that the university's original architects had granted to his effigy? Was the diverse university that Rice had become by the beginning of its second century well served by continuing to hail the founder here, in the center of a quad that many identified as the epicenter of the university itself, and in precisely the same way that it was thought good to honor him in 1930?[57]

If these questions were posed more sharply than ever before, however, and if they were sharpened by a larger national conversation about racial injustice and monumental landscapes in the wake of George Floyd's murder, the decision of students to protest at the monument was a decision not unlike those made by many students before. Like earlier Rice protesters at the site, they discussed, they planned, and they decided to be proactive.

In the same way, as the Steering Committee of the Task Force on Slavery, Segregation, and Racial Injustice listened to and talked about the widening conversation in the Rice community, its work, too, reflected methods by which the university had often advanced difficult conversations: reflection, deliberation, and democratic decision-making. In that spirit, in March 2021, the task force distributed a questionnaire to students, faculty, staff, and alumni that was designed to elicit the Rice community's best thinking about the questions being posed in and of the historic quad. More than twenty-five hundred members of the Rice community submitted responses—evidence that, even as the social distancing and other safety precautions related to the COVID-19 pandemic kept many respondents physically apart, there was a rich, multifaceted, and dynamic conversation happening across the university about the statue. Throughout the 2020–21 school year, the historical research being conducted by the task force about Rice, slavery, and segregation continued. And in the meantime, sit-ins at the statue also continued.[58]

Then, in June 2021, shortly before Juneteenth, the task force published two interim updates on its research to that point. One report focused on what was known and still unknown about William Marsh Rice, slavery, and the Civil War. The other focused on what was known and still unknown about the Founder's Memorial. Both updates made clear that more research was both needed and forthcoming. What had become clear to the task force by then, however, was that the Academic Quadrangle needed "bold change." At the conclusion of its June 2021 update on the memorial, therefore, the task force reported several recommendations that had been reached unanimously by its steering committee.[59]

The task force recommended, first, that the "area extending from the main entrance to campus through the Sallyport to the entrance of Fondren Library, and including Founder's Court, can and must be significantly redesigned to reflect more accurately Rice's values, the history of the university, and the current diversity of the campus, and in a way that clearly and visibly rebukes the institution's segregationist founding and decades of racial exclusion." Members of the task force also believed the university should approach the commissioning of such a redesign with the same careful planning and attention to space and detail that had gone into the design of the original quadrangle. The recommendations noted that a "strong majority" of the task force believed the statue of William Marsh Rice should be removed from the quadrangle, "preferably to another location on campus where it would be properly contextualized with the history of Rice as discovered through the research of the Task Force." Yet an "important smaller group of the task force" believed that "a successful redesign could or should properly contextualize the statue in its location within the quadrangle itself." While these differences pointed to "details that would need to be worked out in an overall design," the recommendations of the task force called, unanimously, "for a bold, creative reimagining" of the quad.[60]

During the remainder of 2021, as members of the task force returned to their research and to the other parts of their charge, other groups at the university took up its recommendations about the quad and continued the conversation. On August 31, the chairman of the board of trustees, Rob Ladd, joined President Leebron in a message to the community. "The conversation with respect to William Marsh Rice is complex," they noted, and related to "a larger set of issues regarding our campus, our community and our programs." The board was committed to taking "a broad perspective in order to determine the best course of action to be taken with regard to the Founder's Memorial, the Academic Quadrangle, and how our aspirations of today are best reflected on our physical campus." Ladd and Leebron also invited the community "to share opinions on how best to respond to the work of the Task Force" through a confidential online portal established by the board. More than twelve hundred respondents shared their views through the portal that fall.[61]

As the semester continued, the Student Association also took up a resolution concerning the Founder's Memorial. Introduced by Shifa Rahman along with three other students, the resolution began by noting Rice University's values—responsibility, integrity, community, and excellence—and citing a passage from Rice's current strategic plan about the importance of creating "an inclusive environment." Over the course of two pages, the preamble to the resolution offered an account of William Marsh Rice's direct participation in slavery, as well as evidence of student opinion on his statue in the quadrangle, presenting all this as evidence to support the SA's conclusion: The Founder's Memorial should be moved "from its current location in the Central Academic Quadrangle," and its new location, which "should not be a place of prominence," should include information about Rice's "full history." The resolution passed unanimously on November 29, 2021.[62]

And then—on January 25, 2022—the board of trustees published a statement reporting their "unanimous decision" about what to do with the Founder's Memorial and the quad, thus bringing to one culmination more than a year of deliberation and debate in the Rice University community.

Changes too innumerable to recount had occurred at the university in the nearly seventeen months that had passed since the "Black Student Demands" were published. One of the authors of the "Demands," Kendall Vining, was now serving as the president of the Student Association. Beyond the hedges, the polarizing aftermath of the 2020 U.S. presidential election and a violent attack on the U.S. Capitol on January 6, 2021, continued to loom over the nation's political life. A deadly coronavirus pandemic had disrupted higher education around the world, requiring creative adaptations in the delivery of courses, student life, faculty research, and campus operations—challenges that tested the capacities of the academy in unprecedented ways. In May 2021, Rice president David Leebron had announced his intention to end his historic eighteen-year tenure as the university's leader in June 2022, and in November 2021, the board of trustees had announced that Provost Reginald DesRoches would succeed him as the university's next president.

Meanwhile, as the board now reported in its January 2022 message, the trustees had also been "engaged in a broad consideration of our university's history and how our aspirations of today, including that Rice be a diverse and inclusive institution, can best be reflected in our campus, our community and our programs." A board working group had been formed to consider both the recommendations of the task force from that summer and the SA resolution from that fall. And in the end, the trustees "embraced the recommendations" for bold change in the quad as well as for the removal of the statue from its present, central position there.[63]

Believing that "the founding gift of William Marsh Rice is an essential landmark in our history and his philanthropy should be recognized," but also that his "entanglement with slavery" must be acknowledged, the trustees outlined their plan for next steps. While they had determined that the statue would remain somewhere in the quadrangle, it would not remain where it was, and they would soon "select a distinguished architect or landscape designer to reenvision" the whole multi-acre space. "The board intends for the new design to have a welcoming space at its center, and sites around the quadrangle for artworks or features that prompt ongoing reflection on and appropriate celebration of our history and aspirations." In this way, they hoped, the quadrangle could better "convey the story of our university, including our rejection of the racial inequities of its beginnings."

To that end, the board also announced that a "new monument of similar prominence in terms of both location and visibility will commemorate the beginning of the integration of the university a half century after its racially exclusionary opening." This part of the announcement, though less noted at the time than the decisions over the disposition of the Founder's Memorial, gestured toward a rethinking of the university's history that was also emerging within the task force as it continued its ongoing work, though it would be almost two more years before its final report would appear. The imagining of other monuments, artworks, and features in the historic center of the university suggested an understanding that the history of the university had more than one founding moment and more than one founding figure, and that its "second founding" demanded its own careful and substantial memorialization within the physical curriculum of the campus.[64]

In short, the board's announcement suggested that, while important aspects of Rice's first founding moment were much to be deplored, the university's desegregation also should be hailed. Yet this suggestion, no less than the protests over the Founder's Memorial that had prompted so much new thinking, raised its own complex questions about the university's past. When and where had the university been founded and refounded, invigorated and reinvigorated, and by whom? As it concerned the newly announced memorial, the Rice trustees meant for the community to once again be guided by history. But what did the history of integration reveal? And what would it mean to be guided by that past?

EPILOGUE

Houston, 2023

Close to sixty years after Velma McAfee Williams had resolutely decided to bury her time at Rice, to do her best to forget the trouble and the heartache, to set aside discussing the joys and the accomplishments that characterized her years at the university—nearly sixty years after this decision, the president of William Marsh Rice University stood firmly behind a podium in the Grand Hall of the Rice Memorial Center (where Mrs. Williams had once taken lunch with colleagues and where the staff had watched her children while she worked), and he recognized her contributions to the university at the school's now signal event for Black undergraduate students, the 2023 Black Excellence Gala.[1]

The theme for the evening was tradition, impact, and excellence. But it was not clear, as the president mentioned her, that Mrs. Williams was yet present. Heads craned. Someone threw a stage light on a back table (it was not her). A brief pause in the president's remarks ensued. Then a voice from a table near the front of the chamber called out and clarified that Mrs. Williams was not yet in the hall.

So the evening went on. Those already acquainted with Mrs. Williams (a few in university leadership, a clutch of Black graduate students, and a small number of others) very likely understood that they could find her as the evening unfolded. For the majority in the Grand Hall, though, it looked as though they would leave as they entered—not quite sure who Mrs. Williams was, though likely persuaded that they should be.

Velma McAfee Williams is a university pioneer. She is one of the first Black students admitted to the university in the mid-1960s. Her name, though, is not often recalled among the constellation of Black students understood to have integrated the university—Raymond Johnson, Jacqueline McCauley, Charles Freeman III, Theodore Henderson, and Linda Faye Williams. But it is also true that the history of Black students at Rice is not very well known—which is another way of saying that critical parts of the modern history of the university remain *deeply* unknown.

Mrs. Williams's story, for the most part, lies in that deep. Telling what we can of her story and grappling with its consequences are also critically important to assessing and coming to terms with the work of the Task Force on Slavery, Segregation, and Racial Injustice. Velma McAfee Williams's story challenges the three-point charge that shaped the efforts of the task force from its beginning in 2019 to its conclusion in 2023. And her story questions the possibilities of what the task force was asked to do, even as it demands that the university do even more of what the task force was tasked with doing.[2]

Further, her story—not unlike the untold, rarely told, or half-told stories of many of Rice's Black pioneers—fundamentally reshapes the history of the university. Recovering Williams's road to South Main, and her experience at Rice, and something of her life afterwards, as well as her continuing journey back to the university, is particularly important to gaining a greater command of the unfolding origins of the university. Mrs. Williams's story highlights the ways that Black students, Black Houstonians, and Black Houston found, and shaped, and, most importantly, refounded the university that was endowed *ad maiorem Dei gloriam* with the fortune amassed in and around Houston and across the Gulf South by William Marsh Rice.

As a way of explicating these points, it is useful to approach Mrs. McAfee Williams's long relationship with and contributions to the university in three phases—her unique preparation for Rice from 1945 to 1965; the period from the fall of 1965 until about 1970, when she was enrolled at the university and pursuing a PhD in mathematics; and a final phase from 1970 until the present, a span containing both the interregnum in which she aimed to forget her Rice experience and the moment when, in the eighth decade of her life, she returned to Rice, committed to helping the university come to terms with what is arguably the most important and least understood phase of its history.

From Marshall

Mrs. Williams is from a storied East Texas family, and she took a rich and storied path to Rice. Born in 1929 in Marshall, Texas, Mrs. Williams's mother and father—he a carpenter and builder, she a homemaker—raised nine children to adulthood, sending all of them to Wiley College, from where their mother had also graduated, and in whose orbit they lived on Beaver Street on the west side of town. Mrs. Williams, the youngest, entered Wiley in 1945, majoring in mathematics, taking cognates in chemistry, biology, and physics, and tacking on a minor in business (then called commerce) as well. She finished Wiley in 1949 with a bachelor of science degree but stayed on in the office of the president for several years.[3]

In the early 1950s, Williams moved to Chicago, where she completed a second degree in mathematics at DePaul University (1954), and from there moved to Argonne National Laboratory where she did work in radiation shielding. After a brief period in Beaumont (her spouse's birthplace), Williams's husband opened a branch of Texas State Optical on Dowling Street in Houston's Third Ward, and Williams returned to Marshall while he established the new business and a new household. She was pregnant at the time and desired the stability of her hometown and being near her mother during this transition. (Her father had died in 1956.)

Williams returned to teaching while in Marshall (she had assisted in the department after graduation as well) and quickly made herself indispensable. As her pregnancy progressed, she met students in her home and continued the practice after the baby's birth—meeting a dozen-person class in the mornings, teaching a smaller group of math majors in the evenings, and keeping a newborn in the hours when there were no Wiley students in the house.

Around 1959, she headed to Houston, where her husband continued the work of getting his new practice on firmer ground. While in the city, she tuned in one day to a local radio show where she heard a speaker complain that there were not very many Black professors in the math and science programs at Texas Southern University.

It might as well have been an advert from the university itself, mailed directly to her. Williams phoned the campus, met with the dean, and secured a position. The work was highly rewarding, and the range of demands and opportunities at TSU set the ground for a remarkable professional opportunity. In addition to new college students with varying levels of exposure to the building blocks of freshman math, the department also worked with secondary teachers from the surrounding area in need of additional preparation to shore up their credentials. (Math education was very much in flux in these years, and many teachers needed to retrain.) Such teachers could be in need of a range of courses—from undergraduate-level work to graduate topics. Further, business majors at TSU required calculus, which Williams leapt at the chance to lead as it allowed her yet another level of practice. During these initial years of her teaching at Texas Southern, the children remained in Marshall, and Williams drove back and forth between Harris and Harrison counties every other week.

Williams had always thought she would pursue a doctorate, as her brother, the physicist Walter Samuel McAfee, had. She intended to work a few years following her master of science and then return to graduate school. Williams began in earnest down this road in 1962, heading back to Chicagoland that summer for postgraduate work at Northwestern. In order to make this work, Williams's son split time in Beaumont and Maud, Texas, with two different uncles, and her two daughters lived with their grandmother back in Marshall.[4]

Two years following Northwestern, in 1964, she took additional work at the University of Wisconsin–Madison as part of an institute for teachers from Historically Black Colleges and Universities (sponsored by the NSF, the Rockefeller Foundation, and the Carnegie Corporation). She carried her three children with her, and recruited a niece to help out as she spent the summer completing a spate of post-master's courses while also arranging for a magical three-month experience for the three Williams children (now ten, seven, and five years old). Williams's work at the 1964 institute led to her being invited back to Madison the following summer for independent study as part of a gateway project toward PhD study.[5]

To this point, Williams had managed, remarkably, a teaching career, the nearly constant continuance of her education, and the raising of a family all pretty much simultaneously. Still, the prospect of entering the PhD program at Madison would present a challenge on a different scale. Would it be possible? When talking through the opportunity and the obstacles with mentors in Madison, the chair of the Mathematics Department in Wisconsin suggested that she consider Rice. She had certainly followed what was going on down on Main Street (not three miles from her home and just a bit farther from TSU's Wheeler Avenue main walk). That summer, the university had admitted two Black undergraduate students, the first ever. Of course, she already knew—everyone in the

TSU Math Department knew—that a Black PhD student was also then enrolled in the Math Department at Rice. He had spent a year as a research associate on campus while the university navigated legal challenges related to its desegregation (everyone knew that as well). So Williams had a lot to ponder.

She did not ponder very long. Williams returned from Madison to Houston in August of 1965. By September, she was enrolled at Rice. Williams thus became the fourth remarkable Black student at the university. She entered, though, unlike the other three, quite without fanfare. There were, of course, other differences too. In a Math Department that had already admitted one Black graduate student, she was the first Black woman. Her stage of life was also different from that of the other students. University life and even graduate school were not at all new to her. It was not her first time at either. Her oldest child was but five years younger than McCauley and Freeman. She arrived with a master's degree, a collection of post-master's course work, and experience at a national laboratory. At Rice, her grasp of the geography of higher education must have been unrivaled. Who else at the university boasted degree and work experience from two HBCUs and a slate of predominantly white institutions as well? While teaching at Wiley, she served on the committee that coauthored *College Business Mathematics* (1960), which appeared as she joined the faculty of TSU. Her hours in the classroom and number of students taught likely equaled the résumés of Rice's youngest math professors. She was also already quite well established in the city—she and her family stalwarts at Trinity United Methodist Church, her children enrolled in local schools, her husband with an optometry practice on Dowling Street, and she already with a university teaching career. Of the four Black students in the vanguard of a desegregating university in 1965, Velma McAfee Williams had arrived at Rice along a most winding and distinctive path.[6]

At Rice

In the fall of 1965 and the spring of 1966, Mrs. Williams began the PhD program by enrolling part-time at the university—taking one course per semester while yet teaching at TSU. Williams's strongest interests were in number theory, and she had hoped to focus her PhD work in this area. Unfortunately, "They did not have number theory at all, and that broke my heart," Williams later recalled. In conversation with the department chair, it was decided that she would focus instead on a secondary interest, real analysis. Williams took topology the first semester, and a course in real analysis the second. Jim Douglas Jr. taught the second course, and Williams found the material stimulating and admired his instruction and guidance. She very much looked forward to taking additional courses with Douglas, but he left Rice soon thereafter.

All told, then, it was an uneven start. There was, for Williams, the palpable intellectual excitement and challenge of embarking on the PhD pathway that she had staked out for many years previously. But the start had not been ideal. At Rice, she would have to set aside the research area that most intrigued her. Further, the initial difficulty of finding a potential mentor, probably a small matter from the standpoint of spring 1966 following Douglas's class, would grow in significance, semester to semester, until the difficulty of tapping into formative intellectual relationships at Rice would go from annoyance to impossibility, and would ultimately come to all but define Williams's time at the university.

In the fall of 1966, however, nothing yet seemed impossible, and there was a great deal to look forward to indeed. In her second year at the university, Williams earned a stipend to go along with her previous tuition waiver. The stipend allowed her to devote herself full-time to her studies at the university—or as much of her time as a wife and a mother of three children could possibly muster in the late 1960s. Additionally, a research note completed by Williams and two of her TSU colleagues had appeared in a recent number of the *American Mathematical Monthly*, "The Relationship Between the Performance of the Texas Southern University Freshmen on the Mathematics Placement Test and Their High School Mathematics Background." The piece highlighted the practical intersection of Williams's teaching and scholarly interests around questions that in the early twenty-first century would come to be captured by such concepts as equitable teaching. The *Monthly* paper joined earlier pedagogical work Williams had previously published years before in *College Business Mathematics* upon her arrival at TSU. Along these lines, William's stipend also meant that she joined other math graduate students in the department grading pool—work that as a long-time instructor at Wiley and at TSU she understood as a fundamental part of the scholarly path she was now on, and neither as drudgery nor as a regrettable necessity. On balance, with the first year at Rice behind her, there was a great deal about which to look forward.[7]

The path to the PhD at Rice unfolded in two phases. In the first phase, prospective scholars took a dozen classes in their areas of study. Students needed to complete this coursework with a yearly average grade of 2.0 or higher. Next, students had to prove their competence in two foreign languages and then complete examinations over the materials covered in their coursework. The successful completion of this qualifying exam marked a student's entrance into a second phase of the program where they became a candidate for the PhD, or, in the parlance of university administrators, were "admitted to candidacy."[8]

At Rice in the late 1960s, the qualifying exam was understood as two separate exams: a set of General Examinations, and a Special Examination. The General Examinations were divided into three topical examinations taken orally, supervised by at least two faculty members, and focused on algebra, analysis, and topology. By the time students reached their second year of graduate study, they were expected to have completed the General Examinations (though they could attempt to complete them earlier). By the third year of study, students were expected to have completed the Special Examination, which was focused on a student's individually chosen field of mathematical study. Once a student had completed this entire gamut, they advanced to candidacy. To move from candidacy to the PhD degree itself, students needed to take an additional two mathematics courses, complete an original thesis, and (as an ultimate demonstration of expertise) pass "a final oral examination on the thesis."

In the Mathematics Department's section of the university's *General Announcements* (*GA*), a structured certainty framed the description of this pathway to the PhD—rather as if students were making their way up a now well-worn trail replete with abundant markings and way finders. The section describing "The Qualifying Examinations" consisted of seven neatly ordered points taking up nearly a full page of the *GA*. And there was more order and certainty where that came from. The final and seventh point on the hike indicated that "There are detailed syllabi for the areas to be covered by the General Examination," and yet still went on to offer a rough guide concerning what students could expect. The algebra exam consisted of the "Contents of Herstein plus Math 470a." The analysis exam, in outline, covered "Differential Equations—Coddington," "Real Variable—Royden," "Complex Variable—Hille," and "Either Math 415a or Math 525a." The topology exam, of course, had its own sketch.

Another section followed this work on the Qualifying Exams and iterated the requirements for the PhD in equally categorical form, though it was divided into but two sections (the first with three subdivisions, the next with four further divisions). At first glance, the point was the same: The pathway to the PhD in mathematics at Rice was clear and obvious.

Still, various levels of certainty and ambiguity characterized these requirements. On the one hand, the text in the *GA* conveyed a measured exactitude: This is done, and then this is done, and then that is done. But it was also true that at key points the faculty meant to acknowledge that some things were out of its control, and at others points it meant to make room for ambiguity—perhaps in order to assert a certain kind of professorial authority. Thus the final requirement for the PhD was the necessarily and conspicuously inexact "Any other conditions required by the general rules of the university." And before that in the *GA*, the math faculty itself inserted several additional indeterminacies. By the spring of 1968, for instance, the department decided to leave unnamed the twelve courses required for candidacy. (In previous years they had listed a series of them.) The department also remained silent on the two additional courses that candidates for the PhD needed to take following the successful completion of their qualifying exams, but *before* being granted the PhD degree. Instead of an outline of classes, the faculty's position was now, simply, that a student's coursework had to be "satisfactory to the department."

The faculty also wished to remind graduate students who were hard at work preparing for exams that the "Ability to simply recite the materials" indicated in the *GA* and expanded upon in the aforementioned syllabi was "no guarantee of success." In short, in the late 1960s, the department invested clear effort into presenting a rationalized and highly ordered pathway to the PhD, a clear curriculum. But it was equally clear, even if not clear in precisely the same way, that there was an unwritten curriculum as well.

The pathway to the PhD, as estimated by the mathematics faculty, was a hike of three or four years. Following her first year of part-time study, Williams leaned into full-time work in the program. Williams had taken Set Theoretical Topology and Real Variable Theory during her year of part-time study. The grind of full-time course work consisted of two or three classes per semester. For Williams, beginning in the fall of 1966, those classes were Differential Geometry, Algebra II, and Functional Analysis. She continued the first and third courses in the spring of 1967 and added Thesis Research that semester too. The following school year, a topics course in Potential Theory and another in Real Variables framed the fall of 1967, while in the spring of 1968 more work in Real Variables and another course on Banach Algebra Analytical Functions rounded out the semester. In her third year at Rice a topics course in Probability coupled with Thesis Research filled out the fall of 1968, and the entirety of the next semester was focused on Thesis Research. As spelled out in the *GA*, PhD graduate students also undertook the three topical exams comprising the General Examinations as they moved into their final years of coursework. So Williams began these exams as well during her first three years at Rice.

Flats, bends, fords, switchbacks, false summits, and taluses characterized this trek through coursework. There was also, of course, the math. But the founding segregation of the university and its later desegregation were not really about math, or any other academic discipline really. Neither the university's segregation nor its later desegregation were, that is, rooted in the disciplines themselves. For as long as the university had been in existence, math as a subject was not subject to segregation per se. At the segregated founding of the university, students at Rice in Houston and at Wiley in Marshall, for instance, studied the very same math, and before Rice's trustees decided to desegregate the university in the mid-1960s, the same was true on Main Street at Rice and on Cleburne Street at Texas Southern University.

The segregation and desegregation of the university were less about differences in what professors could offer students of different races. On this point, for instance, the Jim Crow South was not the Slave South where in places the very act of teaching a Black woman to read was forbidden. Segregation in the Jim Crow South did not quite proceed in this manner. Segregation, rather, often depended on the customs and legal practices bearing on proximity, concerning where folks of different races could actually be in relationship to one another, and how they must have behaved when in proximity to one another. This was not the only quality of Jim Crow, but it was a quality at the heart of school desegregation. Thus Jim Crow custom and practice did not outlaw the teaching of calculus to Black students (though it could make such teaching more difficult). It did quite often, however, insist that Black and white students would not learn calculus side by side. It did quite often result in Black students learning calculus in comparatively poorer settings and with comparatively poorer resources than their white counterparts. And certainly many other aspects of Jim Crow deemed that many Black students would not learn calculus at all.[9]

Thus, to understand the quality and scope of desegregation, the compass and the quality of interaction between formerly segregated peoples matter very much. How Williams and other pioneering Black students experienced their desegregating universities—in the lecture hall, and in the academic quad, and at the lunch table at Rice and places like it—mattered a great deal indeed.

For instance, when George McLaurin was admitted to the University of Oklahoma in 1948, the problem the university president set out to address, quite frankly, was "how could the University of Oklahoma admit an African American student and still maintain segregation?" Officials considered hiring professors that would *only* teach McLaurin; wondered how they might give him access to the library while still maintaining some semblance of separation; and fretted that even if they could figure out the McLaurin problem, they would still have to figure out what to do if and when other Black students were admitted. Ultimately, officials scheduled all of his classes in a single room—one configured in such a way that McLaurin could be sat in an alcove while white students passed to and fro and sat inside the room proper.

McLaurin was also provided a table for his singular use in the library; the same solution held true in the student union; and in both places only McLaurin could make use of these stations. At a lunch spot in the student union, for one hour a day the entire facility was closed to every student at the university save McLaurin. These kinds of differential treatment propelled McLaurin back to federal court, and in 1950 the Supreme Court ruled that the limits placed on McLaurin at the university were unconstitutional.[10]

The nature of Mrs. Williams's experiences at Rice from her arrival to her slowly unwinding departure are important and telling and multidimensional. Her experiences suggest a good deal concerning the human potential of early desegregation efforts at Rice, as they also quite clearly reveal the limitations of those efforts—mainly the impossibility that desegregation, as conceived and enacted by university officials in the mid-1960s, could quickly eradicate or even significantly blunt the continuing force and consequence of the many decades of university segregation that preceded it. McLaurin's situation at Oklahoma was the baldest manifestation, a nearly self-satirizing example, of the actual official design of desegregation at many universities across the South—how to admit Black students while changing as little as possible about the university in the process?

The situation at Rice under such an approach hardly mirrored the arrangements that compelled McLaurin to bring his Supreme Court case. Further, by the time Williams and other Black students began to crisscross the academic quad in the mid-1960s, Rice was not the University of Texas in being desegregated *here* but segregated *there* across swaths of the campus. Nevertheless, at Rice, the question that had motivated University of Oklahoma officials at the admission of George McLaurin yet held power at the Houston campus as well.[11]

To be sure, desegregation was revolutionary. How could it not be? But as provocative and unsettling as the breaking of the color barrier was, it couldn't and needn't fundamentally subvert a range of ideas and practices that had flourished during the long reign of Jim Crow, that had been central to the Jim Crow university, that had been thoroughly shaped by Rice's long segregationist past. Though undoubtedly disruptive, consequently, desegregation did not have to be transformational. Indeed, for many in positions of power at universities across the south, that was the point.[12]

The university's Black student pioneers lived and worked within the cyclically exhilarating and depressing turns of this irony. And so while Velma McAfee Williams's experiences at Rice were hardly interchangeable with McLaurin's at Oklahoma, they were similarly auspicious and similarly tragic. What Black students at schools like Rice accomplished and what happened to them along both of these extremes defined desegregation. Neglecting either is to risk a drastic misunderstanding of the moment.

The powers-that-were at Rice in the late 1960s, of course, quite unlike officials at Oklahoma at the time McLaurin entered, were not trying to maintain the physical separation of Black and white students while ostensibly entering into the moment of desegregation. None of the university's first Black students were sat in antechambers to keep distance between them and their white colleagues. Williams, nonetheless, endured instances of unkindness that in the moment of desegregation were all the more maddening because their genesis was ambiguous or could be easily made to look so.

During her second year at Rice, why did men in one class repeatedly throw their jackets into the seats beside them as if to keep her from sitting? And once the department moved into Herman Brown Hall, why was it that one professor many times over entered the office she shared with one official office mate and one unofficial office mate, but never uttered a word to her while there (even when Mrs. Williams addressed the professor herself while all four were stuffed in the room)?

There were, of course, kindnesses, collegiality, and accomplishments as well. Williams's relationships with the two Taiwanese students with whom she shared an office were copacetic. During her second year, she struck up a fortifying alliance with a fellow graduate student from Utah who was also married with children. They sometimes took coffee breaks together in Sammy's at the RMC, where they discussed work and life in the department—a scene some found interesting enough to photograph, an act over which Williams puzzled then and still. She noted other women graduate students who passed through the department during her time, though the two she remembered most did not stay long at all, both in residence one year and gone soon after. The staff at the RMC were lifesavers. Many a day and many an hour they kept an eye on a Williams child while their mother worked and studied.

There were professors who encouraged or inspired. Jim Douglas was a bright light early on (but did not stay long following her enrollment). The Mathematics Department chair upon Williams's arrival was forthright and thoughtful. The professor who supervised the part of the grading pool in which she worked appreciated her pedagogical talents and demonstrated an interest in her development. These were bright spots.[13]

Williams recalled one moment in particular when this last professor publicly pointed up her strengths. In the part of the grading pool in which Williams worked, it was the practice of graders to move through a set number of assigned questions from each student. So a grader might attend to the third question from all of the exams in a class, while another grader might take all of the first questions. After one particular exam the professor in question, a very caring and careful teacher in Williams's eyes, took umbrage at the quality of the work the graders had done on the last exam. He upbraided them all for the shoddiness of their work and very clearly informed them that they were going to regrade the papers, and that they were going to do much better jobs this time around. He upbraided them all, it turned out, except for Williams, because he ended his reproach by indicating that Williams was the only one in the pool who had properly tackled the task at hand. In the quiet of her own mind, Williams couldn't help but agree. *As long as I've been teaching,* she thought to herself, *I surely know how to correct an exam.* But that was her most confident self. A parallel interior monologue anxiously wondered what this professor was trying to do to her by appending his compliment to the tail end of his admonishment of her colleagues. She was unnerved. In any case, the professor excused Williams, though not before asking her to come by his office on tomorrow. He then indicated to the others that they would now be getting back to work.

The next day Williams had a pleasant conversation with the professor who supervised her part of the grading pool. He asked her to recount her professional career and her interests (rather like an oral history, she later recalled). The professor seemed particularly taken both by the long, steady march of her career and by the regular parentheses in her work. Williams remembers that her story made plain to him how an aspiring mathematician who was also a wife and mother necessarily made a go of things in quite different ways than he himself and most of his colleagues had. The professor advised Williams on what the road ahead would or could look like, and appeared to take an interest in her work. This was heartening because, to this point, it was quite unclear whether Williams had a PhD advisor at all—which in graduate school is a kind of uncertainty that puts a student's progress very much at risk. Williams left the meeting with a sense that she had indeed found a mentor.

She had previously spoken to the chair about nailing down a dissertation advisor, and he had recommended a professor with expertise in real analysis. Williams went to speak with him, and he appeared amenable to guiding her future work but communicated at the same time that he did not know for certain how long he would remain in the department. His mother was ill, and he was applying for positions back in Singapore so that he could return home. A few weeks after that conversation, the professor in question informed Williams that he had indeed secured a position in Singapore and would not be available to supervise her work.

Having already lost at least two prospective advisors at this point in her career, Williams was encouraged by the interest shown in her by the professor who supervised the grading pool. But this prospect did not last either, as news was soon circulating among the graduate students that the professor in question would be leaving Rice as well. Among the PhD students there were whispers that he did not jump but rather was pushed. Of course, the intricacies of departmental affairs are not always easily or accurately interpreted beyond the department. What *was* certain, however, was that another prospective advisor for Williams was not to be.

So Williams remained rather stuck as far as this important aspect of her progress was concerned. She had trudged this far—completing several years of coursework, being well prepared now for her language exams in French and German, and with several constituent parts of her General Examinations behind her, those in algebra and topology—but the summit seemed no closer. And then, not long after word spread about the departing professor who had previously announced himself amenable to supervising Williams, she suddenly received notice from a newly arrived math professor, who had since taken on significant administrative duties, that the department was ready to examine her in analysis, the final aspect of her Qualifying Exams.

Velma McAfee Williams did not belong at Rice. This was Williams's assessment of the thinking that animated the professor who sent notice of the exam. Why else would he behave as if she did not exist when he entered her office to speak with the two other graduate students with whom she shared the space? The sentiment was confirmed for her during one such conversation, when she repeated for the professor, so he could understand it clearly, a word that he was struggling to make out that held the key to the meaning of a sentence being uttered by one of her office mates. When the professor dexterously gathered up the word and carried on with new understanding, but all still without acknowledging that Williams was in the room and had just handed him the means to continue the discussion, a sense of Williams's utter invisibility (and vulnerability?) became painfully acute.

The last component of Williams's qualifying exam went just about as well. As Williams recalled the exam decades later, the scene unfolded as if from a nightmare. The professor who scheduled the exam was there. So too was another faculty person from the department. But he, puzzlingly, had a child close by whom he later clarified was ill—a fact which explained his apparent impatience. Just at the doorway was a third math professor who never fully entered the room, but whose presence was felt throughout. Within this atypical scene, Williams recalled a patronizing start as the presiding professor began with a question that would not have been out of place in an undergraduate college math classroom. As the questions became more apt, the professor who had brought a child to the exam abruptly announced that he had to leave (and indeed left) and the presiding professor began closing the examination, now attempting to include, Williams recalled, the ubiquitous third professor who had never really been a part of the proceedings. The confused closing of the exam ended with the presiding professor announcing that the department was prepared to offer Williams a master of arts and Williams responding that she was not seeking an MA as she had been admitted to the university having already earned a master's degree in mathematics from DePaul. And that was that, it seemed, for the day and for the exam.

Williams could not move forward toward candidacy without a pass on the Analysis exam, and so Rice's place in her career and her career at Rice came to an end. Following the close of the Analysis exam, though, this ending rather moved in slow motion. Williams recalls taking and passing her language exams following the Analysis exam. She also raised a complaint about the exam with a former chair of the department who indicated that there was nothing that he could really do about the matter. He could not, he offered, command the presiding professor concerning how to judge the exam.

Williams sat in on another class at the university after having been encouraged by a classmate who indicated to her that doing so might provide another path through the program. The professor in question had been guiding and supporting this graduate student's work following a rough patch when others in the department were ready to force the student out. (The student, Williams recalled, worked at NASA and brought an expertise in computers that the faculty person needed for his work.) Williams asked to attend the course with the idea that the professor would decide afterward whether to serve as her advisor. The professor in question indeed gave her permission to sit in on the course, but then said little to nothing to her over the span of the semester. On the last day of class, Williams held back to speak to the professor alone as it appeared that her efforts in the class had come to nothing. She wondered to him out loud whether he understood what it was like—what it was like to be *her* in her latter years at Rice, and to be so studiously and completely ignored.[14]

He did not reply. Whether it was then or later that Williams decided to do her best to forget her time at Rice is not clear. But she did decide. She decided to live as if her time in the Mathematics Department had never happened. And as much as an institution can be said to have a memory, Rice forgot Williams as well.

"Just Recognition": Remembering Williams's Rice

Williams's youngest daughter, Dr. Yvonne Williams Boyd, recalls when she first felt compelled to delve into her mother's Rice story. It was 2010, and she, her mother, and two church friends were on a day out in Berlin when conversation turned to her mother's education. First Wiley College and then DePaul University were alluded to. Then came mention of Rice, but dolorously and with an ache she had not heard before. This sadness, Williams's daughter recalled, was new and she wanted to know more—all she could about this part of her mother's life and why it pained her. From such a start, momentum gathered in the family—from sibling to sibling, to nieces and nephews, to in-laws, to cousins, to grandchildren—to piece together the entirety of Williams's Rice story for themselves. With this piecing together emerged a desire that Williams's Rice story be remembered by Rice as well.

On April 11, 2013, Williams's daughter wrote to the president of the university, introducing herself, outlining her mother's story as one of the university's pioneers, gesturing toward Mrs. Williams's accomplishments and ordeals at Rice, mentioning Williams's achievements since, and very briefly, but powerfully, situating her mother's story within the stream of her family's history before and since Williams's matriculation at the university in 1965. Dr. Williams Boyd requested that the Rice president examine what she had written about her mother, touch bases with her, and, given the nature of her story and her place in the history of the university, "honor her with just recognition."[15]

Recognition followed. The 2015–16 school year marked the fiftieth anniversary of the first Black undergraduates to enroll at the university. It also marked the fiftieth anniversary of Williams's matriculation into the PhD program (and the hundredth anniversary of the arrival of the very first PhD student at the then Rice Institute). With this in mind, the family of Mrs. Williams in conversation with the dean of the graduate school (and with the support of the provost and the president) agreed and arranged to celebrate Williams's accomplishments at an event that marks the highlight of commencement weekend for many of Rice's PhD students: the annual doctoral convocation and hooding ceremony. Alongside the PhD thesis defense and the official conferral of degrees at commencement itself, the hooding ceremony is probably the most symbolically laden and celebratory of the three most momentous events leading to the awarding of PhD degrees.[16]

The doctoral convocation and hooding ceremony looks rather like a smallish graduation. Various university officials comprise the podium guests, a stage band plays marches and recessionals, the soon-to-be PhD graduates and their mentoring faculty enter together, all in university robes with the students holding their doctoral hoods before them. The year's PhD candidates sit in the front rows of the audience. (In 2016 this was in the Stude Concert Hall of the Shepherd School of Music.)[17]

At a designated moment during the convocation, the dean of the graduate school begins to call the candidates forward. Upon reciting a candidate's name and the name of their sponsoring faculty (and sometimes the title of the student's PhD dissertation), both student and professor approach a small dais near the center of the stage, whereupon the student faces their faculty advisor, hands them their doctoral hood, and then turns to face the audience. At this moment, the advisor places the doctoral hood over the head of the candidate and lays it to rest on the shoulders of their robe. Applause follows, and the time afforded each candidate is something of a small world. In the five or so seconds it takes for candidates to complete this ritual, their posture, stride, facial expressions, brief words, and other communications convey a range of affect—appreciation, pride, joy, exhilaration, forbearance, relief, and more. A profound journey is ending.

Just before the start of the 2016 convocation, the president and provost stood in the stage-left wing of the hall, ready to begin a procession that would ultimately wend for more than ten minutes. These two most senior leaders of the university were positioned beside several rows of seats, and the first seat in the first row was conspicuously empty. "Pomp and Circumstance," of course, officially kicked off the ceremony, cueing the several hundred soon-to-be graduates and their mentors to begin the procession across and then off the stage proper, and finally into several rows of seats saved for them at the front of the auditorium (while honored guests stopped well before this and took seats on the stage itself).

About halfway through the cavalcade, the once-empty first row came to be occupied by a single figure: Velma McAfee Williams in a gray graduation tam, wearing the distinctive doctoral robes of the university—blue gown, gray velvet trim running down the front, three gray velvet bars circling bell-shaped sleeves. Throughout the procession, Williams studied the convocation program, which listed the names and dissertation titles of those then marching by to her right. According to the program, things would begin with bioengineering and a project on "Development of a 'Cytology-on-Chip' Sensor for Monitoring Potentially Malignant Oral Lesions," and the afternoon would wind down with an applied physics PhD on "Gene Network Modeling of Cancer Metabolism." In between, the hard work of four new doctors of mathematics would be recognized. But before any of these graduates with their impressive projects were hooded, the program indicated, there would first be the "Awarding of Honorary Doctoral Regalia" to Mrs. Williams, with the provost doing the honors.

Three officers of the university spoke at the graduate convocation—the dean of graduate and postdoctoral studies, the president, and the provost. Their remarks—as they bore directly and indirectly on Mrs. Williams—and the remarkable responses of those gathered in the hall that day underscore the necessity and the consequence of the kind of recognition (and repair) slated to be undertaken at the head of the day's program.

President David Leebron's remarks cogently emphasized the individual, collective, and institutional achievements represented by the attainment of the PhD. It was, he offered, an extraordinary personal accomplishment but also one made possible by and in community (the contributions and support of family, friends, and others). Additionally, the personal accomplishments that brought everyone to the hall on that day were fundamentally important to Rice.

The candidates' attainments in research, composition, and performance that would soon earn them the highest degree the university could award were fundamental to what made a university a university. Rice's very first PhD student had matriculated one hundred years before and would be awarded the degree two years later in mathematics. Offered the president, "in some ways it was at that moment, we really became a university, even though we were still called the Rice Institute."

The president wound down his appreciation for the assembled PhD candidates with a final set of congratulations before leading into what the program indicated would be the "Awarding of Honorary Doctoral Regalia." "In a few moments," he began, "we will be presenting a very special recognition." And then he moved into what may well have been both the most harrowing and the most promising part of his remarks on that day. Within a span of about twenty seconds he would need to convey a sense of what was about to take place and why it was about to take place, and who would be so honored. Who was Velma McAfee Williams? And what were honorary regalia (at a university that does not offer honorary degrees)?

The president trekked into this uncharted territory by asking the audience to consider both the sweep and specificity of the recognition that was about to take place. The honor unfolding presently, he indicated, was meant to call the audience's attention both to the merit of an individual and to a momentous social transformation—and by implication the significance of the individual in that transformation. "Just over 50 years ago, Rice admitted its first African American students into both the undergraduate and graduate programs. And today we are pleased to have the opportunity to honor one of those first students." The world had changed, the president made clear, and it was the purpose of this occasion to recognize one of those who helped to change it. At that, the dean of graduate and postdoctoral students, Seiichi Matsuda, replaced the president at the podium, and after thanking the president, he resonantly welcomed Mrs. Williams back to Rice and onto the stage to receive her doctoral regalia.

The reaction to that welcome, and to Mrs. Williams's taking the stage, was profound. As she made her first steps forward, the hall stirred with applause and a few cheers. Having welcomed Williams to the stage, the dean drew another breath to continue, but decided otherwise as the applause in the auditorium gained force and volume. Two marshals who had been standing with Williams in the wing paused, focused for a moment completely on her, and beamed. At these first steps forward, Williams took in the din, turned briefly to her left to catch the better part of the more than a thousand who were offering this reception, took in what was happening for a moment more, and smiled in relief, in disbelief, in amazement, in joy. By the time she reached center stage where the provost was standing and waiting for her, everyone else in the hall and on stage was standing as well, in ovation.

As the cheers continued, Williams handed Provost Marie Lynn Miranda her hood, turned to face the audience, and for an instant prepared to be hooded, slightly bending at the knee. The provost began guiding her in that direction with a hand on her right shoulder, but then just as quickly she changed course and with the same hand ushered Williams to stand straight again. It was not time. Provost Miranda whispered something into Mrs. Williams's ear, to which Williams assented. All the while, the applause continued, abating only as Dean Matsuda, by then beaming too at this reception, indicated that there was more to say:

> Mrs. Williams was the first African American woman to enroll in a Rice graduate program in 1965. She performed admirably. In the difficult circumstances faced by African American students in the 1960s, she left without her regalia. She went on to an impressive career as a mathematics educator, and she made a tremendous impact by improving the understanding and love of mathematics in Houston and beyond. She has given knowledge, direction, and inspiration to an enormous number of people. We recognize her trailblazing contributions to Rice University and to the broader academy with this award of honorary doctoral regalia.[18]

At this, the hall erupted once more. Williams bent at the knee. The provost placed the doctoral hood over her head and onto her shoulders. The two embraced before Williams began her exit stage right, pausing to shake hands and exchange words with the president before being met by the university Mace Bearer and accompanied by him back into the audience.

After the spring 2016 doctoral convocation, other recognition and honors followed. Undergraduates don't typically attend the doctoral convocation and hooding, but the more than three thousand students, alumni, and friends of the university who followed the Facebook account of the dean of undergraduates had the opportunity to meet Mrs. Williams that day as the dean featured a photograph of Williams—standing with the president of the university, and with the dean of graduate and postdoctoral studies—and remarked on her time at Rice and on her subsequent leadership in the Houston community.[19]

In the fall of that year, Dean Matsuda along with Black graduate student leaders began planning a series of gatherings designed to help build and strengthen community among Rice's Black PhD and master's degree students, and with Black faculty across the university. A succession of graduate student–faculty mixers and dinners followed, ultimately evolving into the Velma McAfee Williams Community Luncheon (by 2018 a gathering held in the university's faculty club that continues to this day).[20]

Also in 2018, the university mounted an exhibit at the Gregory School Library in the Fourth Ward that was conceived as a continuation of the 2015–16 fiftieth anniversary celebrations. The exhibit, "Blacks at Rice: An Evolving Legacy," featured historical documents, photographs, and essays touching on key moments in the African American history of the university, and speaking as well to the then-current state of Black life at Rice. Notably, among the moments featured at the Gregory School exhibit was Williams's being presented with honorary doctoral regalia two years before. For many friends of the university, the exhibit served as their introduction to Williams and their first snapshot of her Rice story. Running from September 2018 through February of the following year, the exhibit was a phenomenal success, receiving more than six thousand visitors and earning the organizers a Gold Award from the Council for Advancement and Support of Education (CASE). In university publicity recapping the scope and success of the exhibit—published in the print and online newsletter "Rice at Large"—a photograph captures Williams mid-sentence, in all of her power and equanimity, standing before the section of "Blacks at Rice" that addressed her time at Rice and the consequence of her having been there.[21]

The presidential inauguration of Reginald DesRoches in 2022 provided a key recent opportunity for students, staff, faculty, and friends of the university to consider what DesRoches's appointment meant and portended for the history of Black life at Rice. Among the many evocative reflections along these lines made by guests at the university's investiture festivities were the incoming president's own remarks at a celebration put on by the Rice Board of Trustees and the Association of Rice University Black Alumni (ARUBA), which featured Mrs. Williams. The "Celebration for Reginald DesRoches and Paula Gilmer DesRoches in Honor of His Inauguration as the Eighth President of Rice University" took place on the Founder's Court in a building-sized, elegantly appointed structure tent. Mrs. Williams and her party were seated at a table near the dais when the incoming president recalled Williams and other Black pioneers who had helped to clear a way for the present moment. The more than six hundred people in attendance looked to have immediately gathered the meaning of this remembrance—cheering, applauding, and urging Williams to stand in recognition.[22]

There is always a remarkable reception for Mrs. Williams. At the doctoral hooding ceremony in 2016, because that event was itself dotted throughout with small rounds of applause at the calling of each PhD candidate's name, the extraordinary breadth and weight of the approbation offered in response to Mrs. Williams's presence and the snippets told of her story were especially clear. As coherent as every other individual recognition was on the afternoon of the 2016 doctoral hooding, only one acknowledgment commanded the entire hall, only one manifested a qualitatively different volume, density, and tone. Twice that afternoon, those in the Stude Hall left their seats, took to their feet, and cheered Williams's life and work, and her time at Rice. They honored her—and clearly her presence honored those gathered. Such a thing has not happened since in the history of the ceremony, and it is unlikely that it had ever happened before.

Yet even within the sparkling clarity of this moment, there were critical ambiguities. If the event highlighted the importance of exactly the kind of reconciliation underway that afternoon, the program simultaneously gave voice to the stark difficulties of such work. President Leebron's lead into Williams's recognition, for instance, focused on how much things had changed in the fifty years since the admission of Black students to the university, but his remarks did not, on that occasion, map out in detail the distance yet to be traveled. In the concise six-sentence salute that Dean Matsuda offered concerning Mrs. Williams, prior to her hooding by the provost, the second sentence was perfect in highlighting the difficulties of publicly recapitulating a grueling past. That sentence summarized Mrs. Williams's university career: She departed Rice "without. . . ." And the quality of that *without* was made all the more profound by the transition into the next section of the afternoon's program, just following the honoring of Mrs. Williams. "We will now begin," went the segue, "the hooding of our doctoral candidates."

The ovations offered to Mrs. Williams in 2016 and at the Black Excellence Gala in 2023 and at all of the moments in between certainly were meant to honor her past. The nature of ovations is to acknowledge and remember what is done. They are a kind of ending—an apt conclusion, evidence of having seen, and understood, and appreciated what has just passed.

But Mrs. Williams's Rice story, and the larger story of which it is a part, can hardly be said to have concluded. Even with the many ways the university has revisited and observed Williams's Rice experience, it is safe to say that Velma McAfee Williams's story is not yet a central part of how the university understands itself and its history. Though her story originated on campus, it was lost to Rice, carried by Williams into the city, into Black Houston, and held there for decades. And on campus, her presence faded away. What we know about Williams, it is critical to note, we just barely know. In April of 2013 Williams's youngest daughter, Dr. Yvonne Williams Boyd, first wrote to the president's office concerning her mother's time at Rice. In April of 2014, she sent the letter again. In December of the same year, she reached out once more, asking that "the merit of the letter" originally sent in April 2013 be duly considered. In February 2015 the president's office facilitated a meeting between Dr. Williams Boyd, her mother, and Dean Matsuda. The conversation begun then and continued in the weeks and months thereafter ultimately resulted in the recognition at the 2016 Doctoral Convocation and Hooding Ceremony, and most recently at the 2023 Black Excellence Gala as well, and everything in between.[23]

So the integration and reintegration of Williams's story into the annals of the university has been sometimes plodding and uncertain, and at instances urgent and clarion. The nature of this long start is important to consider. We *now* grasp what we do about Williams's experience at Rice, first and foremost, because of Williams herself, and because of the extraordinary efforts and remarkable persistence of her family in recovering her story for themselves and for the university. The university is indebted also to Matsuda and others who listened closely to Williams and to her family—Rice faculty and staff who understood that Williams's individual experience called for close consideration, and who were open to the possibility that her story was a critical part of more fully grasping the history (and the future) of the university. All of this work and movement through all of these years have delivered Williams's story to the enlightening, uneven, engrossing, and yet incomplete state that it stands in now.

Of course, one of the reasons it is this way is because this is exactly how the past, especially the hard past, is properly made sense of in the present—slowly, and with difficulty. With moments of remarkable legibility, and with occasional missteps, and sometimes with apprehension. But it is also this way because Mrs. Williams's story is part of the Black history of the university, and the Black history of the university, in addition to being a difficult history, is a history that is very much in its infancy.

It is, it should be pointed out, a precocious infancy. The staff, undergraduate students, graduate researchers, faculty, and friends of the university who have taken on the task of preserving, chronicling, and interpreting the history of Blacks at Rice have done remarkable and compelling work. It is simultaneously true that the university is, all the same, at a similar place with the entirety of the history of Black Rice as we are with the story of Velma McAfee Williams—very much at the beginning. There is so much that we do not know.[24]

Still, the clues, questions, and themes emergent in what we know (and in what we do not know) are powerfully informative concerning the unfolding history of Black Rice and of the university. Velma McAfee Williams's story—in its sweep, in its evocation, in its present incompleteness—indicates the larger Black history of which it is a part. And so, ending this book with a telling of Williams's story and with an interpretation of its meaning and consequence is a proper place to begin the work that must follow.

What is important about Williams's Rice experience? As a story focused particularly on one student, Williams's circumstance highlights and calls for further attention to the quotidian aspects of desegregation, and especially in Mrs. Williams's case, greater attention to some of the gendered aspects of the work of desegregation. Accomplished, highly educated, professionally experienced women—and wives and mothers too—are hardly the defining images of school desegregation. But the history of the desegregation of the university, of all the things that it is, is also the history of those who desegregated the university. For the history of Rice's desegregation, particular attention to Black women is warranted, which is also to say that particular attention to the notable diversity of Black life and experience on campus—even from the beginning—will be necessary and illuminating. Recovering the history of Black Rice will require the knitting together of many histories of Black Rice.

Centering Mrs. Williams's story in the telling of the university's desegregation also refocuses attention on the early and continuing importance of the graduate program in the university's civil rights era transformation. In the fall of 1965, we now know, there were two Black graduate students (not one) in the Mathematics Department at the university. So when the first two Black undergraduate students arrived at Rice, there were at least two Black graduate students there as well. By the early spring of 1967, when there were four Black undergraduate students at the university, it is very likely that there were just as many Black graduate students. This possibility and its consequences for the history of the desegregation of the university deserve greater attention. It certainly better connects the university to the national history of desegregation—which was across the South very often a graduate and professional school concern. More importantly, it expands and potentially transforms what it meant to be among the first Black students at Rice. The graduate experience, in the early moments of the university's desegregation, was just as important as the undergraduate experience.[25]

Even so, the tenor of Mrs. Williams's story questions the narrative of ascendant progress that sometimes holds sway over histories of desegregation. Williams's story informs an approach to desegregation and to the civil rights period of the 1960s and beyond that is both more beautiful and more terrible (to borrow a phrase from the historian Jeanne Theoharis) than an uncomplicated heroic narrative or a simple morality tale meant to illustrate how far we have come. Mrs. Williams's story is certainly one of progress—made possible by courage and remarkable hard work by her and by many in her circle in Houston and at Rice. Her story is also, in ways that should neither be ignored nor discounted, tragic. Williams's Rice experience was and is both. Keeping all the aspects of her time at Rice before us—as she necessarily had to while a student there—is a way toward telling the truth about her times. As for the university, finding Williams and coming to terms with her story underscore just how fragile the notion of institutional progress can be. This is clear even from a hopeful and propitious view of the university's desegregation as it looked from the Math Department in the fall of 1965 when she first entered Rice. That semester, in 1965, there were two Black graduate students in Rice University's Math Department. *In 1965*. Asking how often the university reproduced that number since is to inquire into the ways the notion of progress can deceive.[26]

Finally, Mrs. Williams's story underlines the early and continuing centrality of Black institutions to the desegregation of the university, and so also situates the history of the desegregation of the university within the Black history of the city and the state. It is self-evident that, without the existence of Black institutions of higher learning, there would have been no practical desegregation of white institutions of higher learning. But it is also true that many histories of desegregation proceed otherwise. Indeed, if the second founding of southern universities can be understood as the moment of their unfolding desegregation, then these subsequent founding stories often unfold quite unlike the stories of their initial founding where a university's institutional origins are made manifestly clear. For Rice, for instance, the importance of Princeton (from which the first president hailed), and the significance of the first president's global excursions to the world's great universities preceding the opening of Rice, loom large. The importance of Texas Southern University and of other Black institutions (of higher education and otherwise) to Rice's second founding remain to be more fully understood.

And this encouragement to understand the university better by paying greater attention to the institutions that helped to make its modern transformation possible is also an explicit recognition of the importance of referring to and understanding the moment of the university's desegregation according to what it actually, eventually, came to be: a second founding. The admission, and arrival, and especially the efforts of Black students to make room for themselves at Rice, and the actions of others who allied with them to also make that room, began the refinement of the university's ideals, refinement to the point of transformation. The university we are all most proud of is rooted in the university's desegregation and in the struggles and achievements, and in work still undone (there is plenty), related to that desegregation.

This second founding is not more important than the university's initial founding. But it does not follow from this that the first is more important than the second. What follows most immediately is how much more we know, and recognize, and honor concerning the first. The university's second founding, and its founders, await their "just recognition."

Appendix A

The Recommendations of the Task Force on Slavery, Segregation, and Racial Injustice

As the stories told in these pages and in the various programs of this task force make clear, there are no quick fixes to Rice University's long and complex history with respect to slavery, segregation, and racial injustice. Only long-term thinking and strategic leadership can create enduring change and take full advantage of the opportunities first opened to the university by its second founding.

The work of the task force has included not only the historical research required by its charge, but also a series of meetings and public events related to the present and future of the university. Taken together, these meetings and our research revealed that there is much work to be done, and on many fronts.

The task force therefore urges the university to adopt the following recommendations. We have organized our recommendations broadly into categories pertaining to staff and faculty, student life, the community, and the institutionalization and continuation of the work we have embarked on over the last four years. But these categories should not be understood as fully separable. All of the parts of the university are related strategically to the whole, and the values and priorities of the whole are reflected in all of its parts.

Staff and Faculty

1. *Expand investments in recruitment and retention of Black staff, while also making general staff development, equity, and career progression major strategic priorities across the university.*

Black Houstonians worked at and for Rice even before it was a university or had a single student. Long before the desegregation of the university's faculty and student body, they performed jobs vital to the university's success in contexts where their work was not always appropriately valued; since desegregation began, many have also performed unrecognized and invaluable work as mentors for Black students.

With this past in view, the university must recommit itself now and into the future to making vigorous efforts to recruit a diverse staff at all ranks, while improving the ways that it acknowledges and rewards the excellence of its diverse workforce. As a major employer in a city with a large African American community, the university should also make substantial new investments across the board in staff wellbeing, with attention to higher compensation packages and more competitive benefits and incentives; campus accessibility and need-sensitive workplace accommodations; more training and advancement opportunities, awards, and recognition for staff; and data-driven methods for creating and sustaining an equitable and inclusive workplace culture.

Moving forward, we must ensure that jobseekers see Rice as one of the best and most inclusive places in Houston to work, and also that outstanding employees see it as a place where they can stay while moving up in their careers.

2. Set and work towards a goal of having at least 80 tenured or tenure-track Black faculty members across the university by 2033.

The low number of Black faculty members at Rice is one of the longest standing problems at the university. While significant gains have been made in the enrollment of Black students in recent years, reaching close to 11 percent of the whole student body, the percentage of tenure-track Black faculty members relative to the whole tenure-track faculty continues to lag far behind that proportion and remains closer to four percent. As the university prepares to add at least 200 faculty members in the near future, it must seize this opportunity and future ones to recruit a professoriate across all schools whose racial composition is more reflective of its growing and racially diverse student body. In the short term, this means working towards a goal of having at least 80 Black tenure-track faculty members by 2033. Simultaneously, the university should set and work towards a goal of significantly increasing the number of Black faculty members holding endowed chairs or University Professorships by 2033. Given the critical contributions that such professors make to the excellence of the university, it is reasonable to expect that at least half of the envisioned complement of eighty Black faculty members should hold such positions by 2033.

University leaders at all levels and in all schools, but especially in those schools that remain without Black faculty representation, will need to commit to aggressive search strategies, competitive offers to finalists, data-driven approaches to increasing pool diversity, and the expansion of schools' and departments' definitions of their research and teaching areas with the greater diversification of the faculty in mind. Innovative cluster hires and predoctoral and postdoctoral programs across disciplines, as well as redoubled commitments within disciplines, must be central parts of this work. All of this work related to the recruitment and retention of Black professors is also critical to the recruitment and retention of Black undergraduate and graduate students to the university. In short, transformational change is needed. When it comes to the diversification of the faculty, doing the same things while expecting different results is to guarantee failure.

3. Commit significant resources to the further growth of the Center for African and African American Studies.

At a moment in which the freedom to study and teach about Black history, culture, and life is under threat in many academic communities, Rice University should work to build up its recently established Center for African and African American Studies into a national leader in the field, as well as a convener of collaborations with related organizations and the local community. The university's own history with respect to slavery, segregation, and Black life demands nothing less.

Examples of significant resources include creating an additional ten tenure-track faculty lines to match the first ten committed to the center at its launch in 2019, creating an attractive set of postdoctoral and graduate student fellowships, hiring more support staff (including a librarian dedicated to building up university collections in African and African American Studies), housing the center in a prominent building on campus with room for growth, and providing significant funding to permit undergraduate and graduate study abroad experiences and research opportunities within Africa and the world of the African Diaspora.

Students

4. Set and work towards measurable increases in applications by prospective students from households with high financial need, while investing in more outreach with historically Black schools and community-based organizations, especially in Houston and Texas.

From its origins, the Rice Institute was committed to providing a world-class education to white students of slender means, especially from Houston and Texas. The university did not begin charging tuition until after it ended racial exclusion in admissions, and in the years since, the cost of higher education has steadily risen. Recent initiatives, most notably the Rice Investment, have underscored the university's commitment to financial aid and admissions without regard to financial need.

Today, as the university plans for significant growth in the size of its student body, Rice must make clear that creating educational opportunities for those with greatest financial need is a core part of our mission, and that first-generation and low-income students are welcome and supported here. We can do this, first, by maintaining a holistic approach to the review of applications that is sensitive to the ways that socioeconomic disparities impact student portfolios. We must regularly review the income ranges and award levels outlined in the Rice Investment to ensure that they are up-to-date. And we must pursue further ways of increasing applications from, and support to, students in households with high financial need.

For example, the university should invest more in outreach with Black community-based organizations and at under-resourced, historically Black schools, especially in Houston and Texas. It should set aggressive goals to increase the number of undergraduate applicants who qualify for federal Pell grants or QuestBridge scholarships. It should thoughtfully re-consider how it calculates the true cost of a Rice education for students with high financial need, and redouble efforts to meet that need on an ongoing basis in areas beyond tuition, room, and board. And the university should closely analyze consequences related to its early decision admission practices, carefully considering the impact of early decision on the diversity of the incoming class and the university's larger commitments to equity and inclusion.

The university must also develop multiple ways to make abundantly clear our commitment to seeking out and welcoming students with high financial need. Currently, even some of our most important recruitment and admission tools—the Rice Investment and need-blind admission, for example—do not convey this about us clearly enough. The distance between our commitments in this area and our ability to effectively reach and communicate them to the students we seek must be closed.

Finally, the university should regard all the other recommendations presented in this report as important to the recruitment of a diverse undergraduate and graduate student body because of what they communicate to prospective students about the university's values and priorities.

5. *Significantly expand investments in student support services while maintaining a vigorous commitment to the wellbeing and success of a diverse student body.*

The Black students who arrived first at the university in the late 1960s encountered a place with only a thin layer of professional support for mental health and student wellbeing. This weakened the university's ability to support the needs of all Rice students equally.

Today, as the student body grows, and in the context of racial disparities in health and education that have been widened by recent national events such as the COVID-19 pandemic, it is essential that the university move well beyond incremental investments in programs and staff working on issues of student success, health, and wellbeing. The university needs strategic investment aimed at transforming the campus landscape and leading the nation in these areas. This can only be accomplished with the commitment of more financial resources to student wellbeing services, college accessibility funds, and student success initiatives. Also important is the articulation of a set of clear principles and measurable outcomes that can drive better education about and accountability to our campus "culture of care."

6. Commission a working group to identify how to improve the residential college system and ensure that it better serves the interests and needs of our diverse undergraduate population.

Undergraduate residential life at Rice, especially as represented in the college system that was founded in 1957, is a central part of the university's excellence. For all of the college system's continued strengths and benefits, it is also true that the shape and character of residential life at Rice has long been at the very center of Black student dissatisfaction with the university. In short, despite many changes and improvements, the current residential college system still is not adequately serving the interests of all students equally.

Today, as the university grows its student body and prepares to build two new residential colleges, it is time to take a critical look at the system as a whole, alongside related areas of student life, with an eye toward enhancing the sense of belonging that all students develop at the university. Areas to be addressed in this re-assessment of the structure and nature of student life should include the following: obstacles to the recruitment of diverse college leadership teams (particularly magisters, resident associates, and college coordinators); the adequacy of student support and staffing levels centered in the colleges; the process around college assignments and transfers; the viability of new opportunities for short- or long-term housing based around cohorts or interests; the efficacy of the conceptualization of colleges only as discrete, undergraduate residential units on campus; and the potential for augmenting and improving the system with other expressions of residential life, both on and off campus.

In addition, the university should explore the development of robust, national study-away pathways designed to offer Rice students more experiences at historically Black colleges and universities, and to provide students from historically Black institutions with study-away opportunities and experiences at Rice.

7. Establish a new Black Cultural Center on campus and invest in physical spaces, staff, and groups, both on and off campus, that are significantly supportive of Black cultural life at Rice.

The establishment of a securely funded Black Cultural Center on campus has been a long-standing goal across several generations of Black students at the university. The time to address its absence is now. Students at many of the university's peer institutions are already well served by robust Black cultural centers—including students at Yale, Duke, Cornell, and Vanderbilt. These centers are based on intentional institutional commitments that prioritized providing space, staff, and resources to support Black cultural life. Rice would also be well-served by such a center, as well as by more support for Black student organizations and cultural programming on campus throughout the academic year. An immediate task for leaders of this new Black Cultural Center would be to bring together students, alumni, faculty, and staff to define its mission, looking to models on other campuses while also determining which model would best support Black cultural life at Rice in particular. Inasmuch as the university has the power to shape commercial life near campus (particularly in Rice Village, the Medical Center, Midtown, and the Ion District), Black cultural life at Rice would also be enhanced by thoughtfully encouraging Black-owned businesses in areas adjacent to Rice that, though technically off campus, have long been central to the social and cultural experiences of Rice students.

8. Make significant financial and institutional investments in engaging, supporting, and connecting Black alumni.

Much of our historical research and story-telling has been through the lens of the Black students who attended Rice over the years. Rice's history with slavery, segregation, and racial injustice is intertwined with the lives of so many students who felt the impact of the university's decisions. Although the recommendations of this task force are primarily focused on improving life within the hedges and the surrounding communities, Black alumni around the world, who have intimately lived this uncovered history at Rice, should specifically be engaged by the university in an effort to hear their stories, concerns, and ideas, while also connecting or reconnecting them to the university. We recommend increasing dedicated funding for programming and outreach efforts to engage Black alumni.

Community

9. Strengthen strategic partnerships with Black community organizations, Black-owned businesses, and historically Black colleges and universities, especially in Texas.

Even prior to the desegregation of the university, Rice University has depended on ideas, human resources, and cultural and social capital generated by Black entrepreneurs and Black-owned businesses, cultivated in historically Black colleges and universities (HBCUs), and rooted within the Black communities of Houston, Texas, and beyond. These connections have not always been strategic and reciprocal, but they should be.

Given the deep investment the university has long made in communities in Houston and Texas with long histories of racial exclusion, Rice should now build thoughtful and equally deep partnerships with the historically Black communities in Texas that the university long neglected, especially in Houston. The university should endeavor to build within these communities the kinds of robust pipelines and exchanges that it has always enjoyed with historically white institutions, neighborhoods, and civil society organizations in the state.

For example, as the recently announced strategic partnership with Texas Southern University takes shape (creating new research collaborations, faculty and student exchanges and visits, and international collaborations between Rice and TSU), Rice should also pursue similar arrangements with other HBCUs, especially in Texas, that work to the mutual benefit of all institutions involved.

Institutes and centers on campus that further the research impact and capacity of the university through collaboration with Black community organizations (e.g., the Office of Multicultural Community Relations, the Kinder Institute, the Center for Engaged Research and Collaborative Learning, and the Center for Civic Leadership) deserve continued and expanded support. Inasmuch as the Glasscock School's collaborative work in Black Houston is impeded by the demands of its place in the financial structure of the university, innovative solutions are needed to unlock the school's full potential as a center for continuing education and professional development throughout the community.

Furthermore, in its selection of vendors, as well as contractors for large capital improvements, the university must develop pathways for increasing the participation of Black-owned businesses in university bidding. Rice should be especially eager to work with excellent partners who also demonstrate substantial commitments to inclusive practices, a diverse workforce, diverse leadership, and equitable investments. The development of vendor and investment management procedures that are more attentive to our suppliers' and partners' commitments on these fronts may be in order. Do the contractors with whom we do the most significant work, in our largest capital projects, demonstrate commitments similar to and beyond the university's when it comes to equitable workforce practices, and diverse, inclusive leadership? The newly created Ion District should likewise include, as an ongoing strategic priority, community resource development and collaboration with Black community organizations and businesses.

Institutional History, Memorialization, and Research

10. *Acknowledge the significance of Black history in the university's history by expanding permanent public art and memorialization on campus and by naming important spaces and buildings, including residential colleges, for Black individuals affiliated with Rice.*

The university's landscape, public art, architecture, and naming practices, along with the artists selected to shape the campus in the short term, all speak powerfully to what the community thinks worthy of honor and contemplation. Yet despite the significant contributions of Black individuals and Black history to the development of the university, the public acknowledgement of that significance across campus is spare to the point of near invisibility.

Without committed programming and effort, such acknowledgement will remain scarce, even after the proposed addition of a work to the Academic Quadrangle to commemorate the beginning of the integration of the university. The planned addition of two new residential colleges and the occasion of their naming represents a chance for the university to seize an important opportunity. Moving forward, the university should also generate policies and procedures around future naming opportunities for physical spaces and buildings on campus that reflect the university's commitment to diversity, inclusion, and equity.

The university's commendable, recent expansion of the campus's public art program to themes and artists that more fully represent the current diversity and aspirations of the university should be redoubled. At the same time, the total absence of permanent figurative art representing non-white figures on campus must be forthrightly and thoughtfully addressed.

11. Invest in further efforts to uncover and share the university's full history, especially but not exclusively with respect to racial injustice.

Institutions that know their own history are improved by that knowledge. As our historical reports make clear, there is still much more to learn about the history of Rice, particularly but not exclusively with respect to racial injustice. In the meantime, the reports of the task force should be widely disseminated and published both online and in print. Sustained efforts are also needed to ensure that historical work like that conducted by the task force continues and expands to include people and themes not discussed comprehensively in our reports and programs, especially the experiences of other marginalized communities.

Future research and reflection should attend, for example, to the experiences of Hispanic students, faculty, and staff; Rice's LGBTQ+ community; and the history of Jewish life at Rice, though this list is not intended to be exhaustive, and there is yet more work to do concerning the history of Black life at Rice, too. Institutional history across multiple dimensions must be an ongoing priority and ever-evolving project for Rice University moving forward, and its importance must be recognized with secure and expanded funding.

In the short term, we recommend the hiring of multiple, simultaneously serving postdoctoral fellows, with terms lasting at least three years each with a possibility of renewal, to assist the newly appointed University Historian and the Woodson Research Center in work such as the following: creating physical and digital exhibits about task force research (including work done by the Racial Geography Project), launching new institutional history projects, and working to identify people directly impacted by the histories uncovered in such work and their descendants.

Work of this nature will also require dedicated funding for administrative staff support to assist the University Historian and affiliated postdoctoral fellows with their work, and it may benefit from a broadly representative standing university committee charged with providing oversight and support to institutional history efforts.

12. *Publish a biennial report on the state of Black life at Rice that should include data on Black students, faculty, and staff. Conduct regular surveys of these groups and of Black alumni to better inform responses to issues related to quality of life, belonging, and Black advancement at the university.*

Especially since the admission of the first Black students to the university, Rice has made great gains related to Black life on campus, and those gains have contributed significantly to the advancement of the university. Over the generations, staff, students, faculty, and friends of Rice have helped to drive the university towards the improvements from which we all now benefit. At the same time, much less energy has been devoted to systemic, transparent, and robust university structures of accountability to measure advancements and more successfully address areas that have been resistant to progress. To take advantage of the benefits to be gained from greater information and wayfinding, the president and provost should commission, fund, and publish, for at least the next twelve years, a biennial report on the state of Black life at Rice, and use its findings to help guide future university advancement.

Appendix B

The Steering Committee of the Task Force

Co-Chairs

Alexander X. Byrd
Vice Provost for Diversity, Equity and Inclusion
Associate Professor of History
Class of 1990

W. Caleb McDaniel
Mary Gibbs Jones Professor of Humanities
Professor of History

Members

Teveia Barnes
Board of Trustees, Emerita
Class of 1975

John B. Boles
William P. Hobby Professor of History, Emeritus
Class of 1965

Donald Bowers
Board of Trustees, Emeritus
Class of 1991

Edward L. Cox
Associate Professor of History, Emeritus

Taylor Crain
Class of 2021

Gabrielle Falcon
Class of 2020

Jeffrey Fleisher
Professor of Anthropology

C. Fred Higgs III
Vice Provost for Academic Affairs
John and Ann Doerr Professor of Mechanical Engineering

Elaine Howard Ecklund
Herbert S. Autrey Chair in Social Sciences
Professor of Sociology

John S. Hutchinson
Professor of Chemistry

Kimberly Jones
PhD Student in History
Class of 2023

William D. Jones
Task Force Postdoctoral Research Fellow
PhD Student in History
Class of 2020

Eden King
Lynette S. Autrey Professor of Psychology
Class of 2001

Fabiola López-Durán
Associate Professor of Art History

Ruth N. López Turley
Professor of Sociology

Akilah Mance
Past President, Association of Rice University Black Alumni
Class of 2005

Allen Matusow
William Gaines Twyman Professor of History, Emeritus

Summar McGee
Class of 2020

Sana Mohamed
Class of 2021

Axel Ntamatungiro
Class of 2021

Anthony B. Pinn
Agnes Cullen Arnold Professor of Humanities
Professor of Religion

Caitlin C. Rosenthal
Class of 2005

Norma Santamaría
Program Administrator for Diversity and Inclusion and Undergraduate Student Engagement
Department of Electrical and Computer Engineering

James Sidbury
Andrew W. Mellon Distinguished Professor of Humanities
Professor of History

Nicole Waligora-Davis
Alan Dugald McKillip Associate Professor of English

Jan West
Assistant Director of Multicultural Community Relations
Class of 1973

Appendix C

William Marsh Rice's 1868 Will

After marrying his second wife, Julia Elizabeth (or Libbie) Baldwin Rice, in 1867, William Marsh Rice moved with her to the North, but he retained many business interests in Houston and visited regularly. His first visit back to Houston after his marriage came in the first half of 1868, according to testimony he later gave in a lawsuit over Elizabeth Baldwin Rice's contested will. It was on that trip, on July 4, 1868, that he drew up this last will and testament, which contains the earliest known reference to an educational institution to be endowed by Rice. It was later supplanted by other wills.

I[,] William M. Rice of the County of Harris and State of Texas revoking and making void all former wills by me at any time made heretofore, do publish and declare this my last will and testament.

I hereby nominate[,] constitute and appoint my brother Frederick A. Rice the sole executor of this my last will, and it is my desire and I so provide that no other action shall be had in the county court in relation to the settlement of my estate than the probate and registration of this my will, and the return of an inventory of my estate, and I direct that no security shall be required of my said executor by the county court.

And after all my debts have been paid which are justly due I give[,] bequeath[,] devise and set over to my brother Fred A. Rice the sum of one hundred and fifty thousand dollars. I give[,] bequeath and set over to my wife Libbie B. Rice the sum of one hundred thousand dollars upon condition she shall receive the amount as a full discharge of all her claim upon my estate, including all property of which I am in possession at my death, whether community property or otherwise, and before receiving the said one hundred thousand dollars she my said wife Libbie B. Rice shall execute a full release and discharge of all further claim upon the entire estate as before stated. Should she prefer to abide by her legal rights, to receiving the said sum of one hundred thousand dollars, then she will do so, but I consider this an ample provision which will fully provide for all her wants in a very liberal manner.

I give[,] bequeath and set over (after the previous amounts are paid) to each of my sisters Louisa R. Blinn, Sally Minerva[1] ——— and Charlotte S. McKee the sum of twenty thousand dollars, this amount to be secured to each of them independent of their husbands, so that they can realise the anual [*sic*] interest, the principal to go to their children. I also direct that each of my nephews and nieces, the children of my brother F. A. Rice and of my sisters above mentioned shall receive, when they shall have arrived at their twenty fifth year, the sum of ten thousand dollars. But should my executor F. A. Rice think it better to secure the amount to them or to any of them, so that they can draw but the interest during their lives, the principal to be paid to their heirs, then he shall have the right to so regulate it.

After the above amounts shall have been settled or deducted from my estate I give and bequeath to the sister of my late wife Mrs Hattie Timpson the sum of ten thousand dollars. I direct that the like sum of ten thousand dollars be secured to the children of the brother of my late wife, Edward L. Bremond, the interest to be paid anually [*sic*] to their father or mother so long as they shall live, after their death the principal to be divided among the said children. After all proceeding provisions have been fully complied with then I direct that from the balance of my estate the sum of three hundred thousand dollars be set apart to endow an institution for the education of the poor white children of Harris County, the principal to be invested as the Trustees shall direct under the approval of my brother F. A. Rice who shall during his life be president of the board of Trustees and have the power to veto any proceeding of theirs of which he may disapprove. He is also charged with the duty of organising the said board of Trustees. I have not the time were I prepared, to arrange all the prominent details, and must leave it to my brother and such gentlemen as he may associate with himself. I do not wish the principal of this bequest to be encroached upon, but to be wisely invested to carry out the desired object, so that the income arising therefrom shall be always ample. Others besides the poor [*interlinear insertion:* "white"] children of Harris County can be admitted at the discretion of the Trustees, but the poor white children of Harris County must have the preference, and then the poor white children of neighbouring counties and others at the discretion of the Trustees. I suggest the following names as Trustees Peter W. Gray, Alfred Richardson, B. A. Botts, George R. Ennis, George Goldthwaite, John Shearn, —— [*sic*] Hill. My idea is to get up buildings with the first year's income after which part of income to open the school & part to make necessary improvements.

From the remaining potion [*sic*] of my estate I give and bequeath to my brother F. A. Rice the sum of one hundred thousand dollars after which I give and bequeath to my fernal [*sic*] cousins the daughters of my mother's brother John Hall the sum of five thousand dollars each. The balance of my estate real personal and mixed I give and bequeath to my brother F. A. Rice to be invested and appropriated at his discretion for the benefit of mankind, in such way as his judgment may dictate.

In Testimony of the foregoing will I have hereunto set my hand and seal using scroll for seal this 4th day of July 1868 AD, W M Rice (Seal) made and declared by W M Rice to be his will and testament and attested by us at his request and in his presence and in presence of each other at Houston this 6th day of July AD 1868

E. H. Cushing
Benj. A. Botts

Notes

Abbreviations

ERI	Early Rice Institute Records
FAR	Frederick Allyn Rice
HHRC	Houston History Research Center, HPL
HPL	Houston Public Library
MS	Manuscript Collection, WRC, Rice University
NARA	National Archives and Records Administration
RT	*Rice Thresher*, student newspaper
TSLAC	Texas State Library and Archives Commission
UA	University Archives, WRC, Rice University
WMR	William Marsh Rice
WRC	Woodson Research Center

Foreword

1. David W. Blight, *Race and Reunion: The Civil War in American Memory* (Cambridge, MA: Harvard University Press, 2001), 133.

Introduction

1. Amanda Sawyer, "A. J. Moore High School," *Waco History*, wacohistory.org/items/show/22. In 1967, thirteen years after the *Brown v. Board of Education* decision, Moore High remained an all-Black public school.

2. See E. W. Rand, *The Journey of Earl Wadsworth Rand: From There to Here, From Then Until Now* (New York: Vantage Press, 1992). Rand also later served as an interim president of Wiley College in Marshall, Texas.

3. Quotes from Rand's speech in this and following paragraphs are from "Seniors at Moore Hear of 'A New Era' Ahead," Waco *News-Tribune*, June 1, 1967, 1. For the prepared text for what appears to be a very similar speech given by Rand in 1987 at a Bishop College commencement, see Rand, *Journey of Earl Wadsworth Rand*, 113–19.

4. Merline Pitre, *Born to Serve: A History of Texas Southern University* (Norman: University of Oklahoma Press, 2018), 61–77; David Ponton III, "Criminalizing Space: Ideological and Institutional Pro-

ductions of Race, Gender, and State-Sanctioned Violence in Houston, 1948–1967," PhD diss., Rice University, 2017, chap. 6.

5. "Seniors at Moore."

6. Oliver's name and picture appeared with coverage of Rand's speech under "Eight Moore Students Graduate with Honors," Waco *News-Tribune*, June 1, 1967, 6. For assistance locating the date of her enrollment at Rice, we thank university registrar David Tenney.

7. See Merline Pitre, *Through Many Dangers, Toils and Snares: The Black Leadership of Texas, 1868–1900*, 3rd ed. (1985; College Station: Texas A&M University Press, 2016), 30–32, 70–76.

8. For "bricks without straw," see E. W. Rand, "Black Colleges in America: Retrospect and Prospect," April 9, 1979, speech at Bishop College, in Rand, *Journey of Earl Wadsworth Rand*, 110–11.

9. Robert Greene II and Tyler D. Parry, eds., *Invisible No More: The African American Experience at the University of South Carolina* (Columbia: University of South Carolina Press, 2021), 3. See also Ellen Schrecker, *The Lost Promise: American Universities in the 1960s* (Chicago: University of Chicago Press, 2021), 265–78.

10. *The 1966 Lion* (Moore High School, Waco, Texas), 64, 105, available in U.S. School Yearbooks, 1900–2016, Ancestry.com; "Eight Moore Students Graduate with Honors"; "Contest Winner," Waco *Tribune-Herald*, May 21, 1967, 39.

11. *Campanile 1968*, 11, 264.

12. *Report of the Academic Affairs Committee of the Rice University Self-Study, 1973–1974* (Houston: Rice University, 1974), 76.

13. "Seniors at Moore."

1. Rice and Slavery

1. "Ranaway," Houston *Weekly Telegraph*, February 27, 1856, 3e. The ad reappeared on March 5, 1856. Both ads contain a typo ("it [*sic*] probably lurking" instead of "is") that is silently corrected here.

2. WMR Application for Special Pardon, August 1865, Case Files of Applications from Former Confederates for Presidential Pardons, RG 94: Records of the Adjutant General's Office, 1762–1984, NARA, Washington, DC, catalog.archives.gov/id/57452487. No biographer appears to have been aware of this document before it was found by Dr. William D. Jones, postdoctoral fellow for the Task Force on Slavery, Segregation, and Racial Injustice.

3. Edgar Odell Lovett, "The Meaning of the New Institution," *Rice University Studies* 1, no. 1 (1915): 46–47; Julian Huxley, "Texas and Academe," *Cornhill Magazine*, July 1918, 54, as well as an undated typescript by Muir describing Rice as "typical Yankee yeoman," both in Andrew Forest Muir Papers, MS 17, box 69, folder 2; J. T. McCants, "84 Years of Capitalism: The Story of William M. Rice," *RT*, April 27, 1972. See also Summer Perritt, "The Evolving Legacy of William Marsh Rice, 1866–2000" (2021), Task Force on Slavery, Segregation and Racial Injustice Records, UA 421, ser. B; Thomas Jefferson Brown, "Education and the State," *Book of the Opening of the Rice Institute* (Houston: Rice Institute, 1914), vol. 1: 117; Fredericka Meiners, *A History of Rice University: The Institute Years, 1907–1963* (Houston: Rice University Studies, 1982), 11; John B. Boles, *A University So Conceived: A Brief History of Rice University*, 4th ed. (Houston: Rice University Office of Public Affairs, 2012), 4–5; David Leebron, "Centennial Address," *Rice Magazine* 15 (2013): 26. Until 2023, a short history of Rice printed in annual commencement programs said only that the founder had "expanded a small merchandising business into a trading empire."

4. On the power of silences in historical narratives, see Michel-Rolph Trouillot, *Silencing the Past:*

Power and the Production of History (Boston: Beacon, 1995); James E. Crisp, *Sleuthing the Alamo: Davy Crockett's Last Stand and Other Mysteries of the Texas Revolution* (New York: Oxford University Press, 2005).

5. Undated typescript, Muir Papers, MS 17, box 69, folder 2; Andrew Forest Muir, "William Marsh Rice, His Life and Death, the History of a Fortune," read before the Harris County Historical Society in Houston, September 6, 1955, Muir Papers, MS 17, box 68, folder 1. Muir's undated typescript originally read that Rice's property holdings "included either no slaves or not more than one or two," but in editing he crossed out "either" and "or not more than one or two."

6. Andrew Forest Muir, "Murder on Madison Avenue: The Rice Case Revisited," *Southwest Review* 44, no. 1 (Winter 1959): 2; undated Muir typescript, Muir Papers, MS 17, box 69, folder 6; "Rice, William Marsh," in Walter Prescott Webb, ed., *The Handbook of Texas* (Austin: Texas State Historical Association, 1952), vol. 2: 467; "Rice, William Marsh," in *The New Handbook of Texas* (Austin: Texas State Historical Association, 1996), vol. 5: 563.

7. Sylvia Stallings Morris, *William Marsh Rice and His Institute: A Biographical Sketch from the Papers and Research Notes of Andrew Forest Muir* (Houston: Rice University, 1972), 30; Randal L. Hall, ed., *William Marsh Rice and His Institute: The Centennial Edition* (College Station: Texas A&M University Press, 2012), 33. In 2019, a published essay by Andrew Maust reported on recent research about Rice's connections to slavery and called for further investigation of the subject. See Maust, "Remembering Rice: How Should the University Acknowledge and Represent Its Founder's Past?" *Rice Historical Review* 4 (Spring 2019): 25–39. For Muir's findings on Rice and slavery, see an undated typescript page in Muir Papers, MS 17, box 69, folder 5.

8. One particularly large collection of relevant papers was discovered in 1979 by a grandson of FAR and then donated to the Houston Public Library. See B. R. Aston, ed., *The Papers of Frederick Allyn Rice, 1838–1869* (Houston: B. R. Aston, 1992). Another important collection apparently not available to either Muir or Morris resides in the Heritage Society of Houston.

9. Morris may have drawn on an undated, typed note in Muir's research papers citing the 1860 slave schedule. The note said that "W. M. Rice owned 15 slaves" and "employed 3 slaves, owners not known," though Morris did not mention those three at all. Careful inspection of the manuscript page shows that only two of the eighteen people listed under Rice's name were bracketed with the note "owners not known." See Muir Papers, MS 17, box 69, folder 2; U.S. Census (Slave Schedule), 1860, City of Houston, p. 23, available on FamilySearch, www.familysearch.org/ark:/61903/3:1:33S7-9BSD-722.

10. For city figures, see Susan Jackson, "Slavery in Houston: The 1850s," *Houston Review* 2 (Summer 1980): 76–78; U.S. Census (Slave Schedule), 1860, City of Houston. For statewide figures, see 1860 historical census table for "Slaveholders by Number of Slaves Held," prepared with Social Explorer, www.socialexplorer.com/tables/Census1860/R12839175.

11. Ralph A. Wooster, "Wealthy Texans, 1860," *Southwestern Historical Quarterly* 71, no. 2 (October 1967): 163–80. The only Texan reported as wealthier than Rice in the 1860 Census was Brazoria County planter John H. Herndon, who was closer to the slaveholding median with around forty enslaved people that year. Cf. Hall, ed., *William Marsh Rice and His Institute*, 28.

12. Hall, ed., *William Marsh Rice and His Institute*, 124.

13. Andrew Torget, *Seeds of Empire: Cotton, Slavery, and the Transformation of the Texas Borderlands, 1800–1850* (Chapel Hill: University of North Carolina Press, 2015); Randolph B. Campbell, *An Empire for Slavery: The Peculiar Institution in Texas, 1821–1865* (Baton Rouge: Louisiana State University Press, 1989), chap. 1.

14. See Brian P. Luskey, "Chasing Capital in Hard Times: Monroe Edwards, Slavery, and Sover-

eignty in the Panicked Atlantic," *Early American Studies* 14, no. 1 (Winter 2016): 82–113; Sean Kelley, "Blackbirders and *Bozales:* African-Born Slaves on the Lower Brazos River of Texas in the Nineteenth Century," *Civil War History* 54, no. 4 (December 2008): 406–23.

15. Quote from Torget, *Seeds of Empire,* 206. For examples of such articles published in Springfield, Rice's hometown, see Muir Papers, MS 17, box 69, folder 2.

16. "Andrews, Stephen Pearl," s.v., *Handbook of Texas Online,* www.tshaonline.org/handbook/entries /andrews-stephen-pearl. See also Luskey, "Chasing Capital in Hard Times," 106–7; Charles Shively, "An Option for Freedom in Texas, 1840–1844," *Journal of Negro History* 50, no. 2 (April 1965), 77–96.

17. Torget, *Seeds of Empire,* 168–71, 270; Campbell, *Empire for Slavery,* 45–47.

18. A copy of Rice's 1839 land grant can be found in Muir Papers, MS 17, box 69, folder 2.

19. Harris County Tax Rolls, 1841, available on FamilySearch.

20. Harris County Tax Rolls, 1844; Houston *Telegraph and Texas Register,* December 25, 1844; September 23, 1846.

21. For representative ads, see Washington *Texas National Register,* July 3, 1845; Houston *Telegraph and Texas Register,* August 13, 1845; Houston *Democratic Telegraph and Texas Register,* July 26, 1847. A shipment of cotton gins to Rice and Nichols is reported in "Manifest of Steamboat Galveston," Galveston *Semi-Weekly Journal,* June 11, 1850. On the larger world of cotton and commerce to which Rice belonged, see Sven Beckert, *Empire of Cotton: A Global History* (New York: Knopf, 2014).

22. Houston *Telegraph and Texas Register,* August 4, 1841; Washington County Tax Rolls, 1841, on FamilySearch.

23. Houston *Telegraph and Texas Register,* September 23, 1846; Houston *Telegraph and Texas Register,* December 2, 1847. For a description of relationships between merchants and planters, see Torget, *Seeds of Empire,* 194–202.

24. WMR to W. G. Rucker, May 6, 1900, WMR Business and Estate Ledgers, UA102, box 25.

25. Ibid. For cotton prices, see "Commercial," Galveston *Semi-Weekly Journal,* December 27, 1850; Torget, *Seeds of Empire,* 273; Brain Schoen, *The Fragile Fabric of Union: Cotton, Federal Politics, and the Global Origins of the Civil War* (Baltimore: Johns Hopkins University Press, 2009), 122–23.

26. Campbell, *Empire for Slavery,* 54–58, 68–75. For "Negro property" accepted as payment for land, see Houston *Telegraph and Texas Register,* December 31, 1845; March 23, 1848; November 2, 1848.

27. Houston *Telegraph and Texas Register,* August 19, 1846; November 9, 1848; March 23, 1848. See also May 25, 1842.

28. Houston *Telegraph and Texas Register,* July 1, 1846. See Anne Schnoebelen, "Benjamin, Sallie, and the Shepherd School of Music," *The Cornerstone: The Newsletter of the Rice Historical Society* 11, no. 3 (Winter–Spring 2007): 1–4; "Shepherd, Benjamin Armistead (1814–1891)," s.v., *Handbook of Texas Online,* www.tshaonline.org/handbook/entries/shepherd-benjamin-armistead.

29. Harris County Deed Book K, p. 27, Harris County Clerk of Court, Houston.

30. Harris County Deed Book L, p. 6. County tax rolls for 1847 show Rice and Nichols in possession of "Negroes" appraised at $1200, possibly referring to John and Tom. See Harris County Tax Rolls, 1847, p. 20.

31. Harris County Deed Book N, p. 443. The year of the transaction is difficult to read in the original and could be 1846 or 1849. *Oxford English Dictionary* online, s.v. "griffe" (accessed July 29, 2024): "Now *historical* and *offensive.* A person who is by descent three-quarters African American and one-quarter white. Also: a person of mixed African American and North American Indigenous ancestry."

32. Harris County Tax Rolls, 1849, p. 28; 1850 U.S. Census (Slave Schedules), Harris County, Texas, www.familysearch.org/ark:/61903/3:1:S3HY-DCNQ-8T9.

33. Because Texas law considered enslaved people to be moveable or personal property, sales and purchases were not required to be recorded in an official deed; buyers and sellers sometimes went before notaries public to record such transactions, but not always. Although McCreary gave Rice a handwritten note to confirm the sale of Ann in 1846 or 1849, the deed was not officially recorded in Harris County until almost a year later, about a month before Rice married Margaret C. Bremond, his first wife.

34. On the dangers faced by enslaved women engaged in domestic work, which could range from verbal abuse to physical violence and sexual assault, see Thavolia Glymph, *Out of the House of Bondage: The Transformation of the Plantation Household* (New York: Cambridge University Press, 2008); Wilma King, "Within the Professional Household: Slave Children in the Antebellum South," *Historian* 59, no. 3 (March 1997): 523–40. On urban slavery, see Paul D. Lack, "Urban Slavery in the Southwest," in *The African American Experience in Texas: An Anthology*, ed. Bruce A. Glasrud and James M. Smallwood (Lubbock: Texas Tech University Press, 2007), 31–56.

35. Ariela J. Gross, *Double Character: Slavery and Mastery in the Antebellum Southern Courtroom* (Princeton, NJ: Princeton University Press, 2000); Daina Ramey Berry, *The Price for Their Pound of Flesh: The Value of the Enslaved, from Womb to Grave, in the Building of a Nation* (Boston: Beacon Press, 2017); Thomas D. Morris, *Southern Slavery and the Law, 1619–1860* (Chapel Hill: University of North Carolina Press, 1996); Bonnie Martin, "Slavery's Invisible Engine: Mortgaging Human Property," *Journal of Southern History* 76, no. 4 (November 2010): 817–66. See also Katelyn Landry, "Indebted: William Marsh Rice's Role in the Financial Regime of Slavery as Examined through Mortgages on Enslaved People" (2021), Task Force Records, UA 421, ser. B.

36. WMR to FAR, March 16, 1887, ERI, UA 101, box 114, folder 9.

37. Harris County Deed Book N, pp. 53–54. Cf. Morris, *William Marsh Rice and His Institute*, 30. On the history of such deeds, which were often conflated with mortgages, see Bonnie Martin, "Silver Buckles and Slaves: Borrowing, Lending, and the Commodification of Slaves in Virginia Communities," in *New Directions in Slavery Studies: Commodification, Community, and Comparison*, ed. Jeff Forret and Christine E. Sears (Baton Rouge: Louisiana State University Press, 2015), 30–52; Morris, *Southern Slavery and the Law*, 121–31.

38. Harris County Deed Book N, pp. 53–54.

39. Harris County Deed Book I, pp. 88–89.

40. In 1841, the Congress of the Republic of Texas had passed a law exempting slaves from forced sale for executing debts, but "the law was repealed within twelve months." An attempt to revive it in 1856 failed. See Campbell, *Empire for Slavery*, 98.

41. Brazoria County Deed Book E, pp. 119–21. On sugar cultivation, see Sean M. Kelley, *Los Brazos de Dios: A Plantation Society in the Texas Borderlands, 1821–1865* (Baton Rouge: Louisiana State University Press, 2010), 114–21.

42. Morris, *Southern Slavery and the Law*, 43–49.

43. Kelley, *Los Brazos de Dios*, 48–56; Kelley, "Blackbirders and *Bozales*"; Luskey, "Chasing Capital in Hard Times." See also James Smith, Brazosport Archaeological Society, "Chenango Plantation," in Rice Research Repository, hdl.handle.net/1911/117659.

44. Rice, Adams, and Company may have paid some of the interest due on that note in order to protect their own interests in the property secured both to them and to Ware.

45. "Albert T. Burnley v. W. M. Rice and Others (1857)," *Reports of Cases Argued and Decided in the Supreme Court of the State of Texas . . .*, vol. 18 (St. Louis, 1882), 434–40. Case file for the suit available in Texas Supreme Court Archives, Texas State Archives, Case M-02771, tsl.access.preservica.com/uncategorized/SO_0d8ebfab-128a-432c-aab8-0129c5efab45.

46. "Uriah S. Cummins vs. Rice and Another (1857)" in *Reports of Cases Argued and Decided in the Supreme Court of the State of Texas . . .* , vol. 19 (Galveston, 1858), 225–26.

47. Ibid. The original case file is no longer extant.

48. Harris County Deed Book N, pp. 53–54. See Hall, ed., *William Marsh Rice and His Institute,* 33. Cf. Morris, *William Marsh Rice and His Institute,* 30. The specific gift of a "half interest" was not noted in either edition of Morris's Rice biography, perhaps because Muir's notes omitted that detail in his transcription of the deed. See Muir Papers, MS 17, box 69, folder 5.

49. E. B. Nichols also divided his interest in another woman and child, Lucy and Evy, and gave one half each to his two sons.

50. Harris County Deed Book N, pp. 53–54.

51. Quoted in Campbell, *Empire for Slavery,* 68; Torget, *Seeds of Empire,* 264. See also Walter L. Buenger, *Secession and the Union in Texas* (Austin: University of Texas Press, 1984), 10–21.

52. Walker County Tax Records, 1861, on FamilySearch. See Kate Sayen Kirkland, *Captain James A. Baker of Houston, 1857–1941* (College Station: Texas A&M University Press, 2012), 13–22.

53. Campbell, *Empire for Slavery,* 50–66; Jackson, "Slavery in Houston."

54. See entries for William Marsh Rice or Wm. M. Rice and Company in Harris County Tax Rolls, 1850–58. Our thanks to Gracey Wallace for research assistance in tabulating these records. On tax assessment undercounting, see Campbell, *Empire for Slavery,* 54.

55. Calvin Schermerhorn, *The Business of Slavery and the Rise of American Capitalism, 1815–1860* (New Haven: Yale University Press, 2015), 226; "Negro Mart," Galveston *Weekly Journal,* February 18, 1853; March 25, 1853; May 6, 1853. See also Gresham's ad in Galveston *Weekly News,* January 3, 1854, 2h. It indicates his place of sale was "at the depot in rear of J. H. Stevens' store, in the city of Houston."

56. Frederick Law Olmsted, *Journey through Texas: A Saddle-Trip on the Southwestern Frontier,* ed. James Howard (Austin: Von Boeckmann-Jones Press, 1962), 227. For examples of Riordan's ads, see Houston *Weekly Telegraph,* March 11, 1857; June 9, 1858. For the location of Rice's store, see Andrew Forest Muir, "William Marsh Rice, Houstonian," *East Texas Historical Journal* 2, no. 1 (1964): 32–39. Slave traders often sought references in order to signal their respectability and to counter some unflattering stereotypes of their business practices. See Steven Deyle, *Carry Me Back: The Domestic Slave Trade in American Life* (New York: Oxford University Press, 2005), 136–38. Edward Riordan also listed references in his later ads, mentioning close partners of Rice's like Cornelius Ennis, William A. Van Alstyne, and Edward W. Taylor. Recent work on slave traders has challenged some older scholarship implying that they were social outcasts. See Joshua D. Rothman, *The Ledger and the Chain: How Domestic Slave Traders Shaped America* (New York: Basic Books, 2021). For Riordan's service with Frederick Rice as Third Ward alderman, see *Houston City Directory, 1877–78,* 25.

57. Houston *Telegraph and Texas Register,* September 2, 1853; entry for WMR in U.S. Census (Slave Schedule), 1860. In 1860, census takers were instructed that, in cases where an enslaved person was found employed or in the charge of a person other than their "proper owner," they should if possible list both "the name of the *bona fide* owner . . . as proprietor, and the name of the person having them in charge as employer." Enumerators were also told to ensure that the enslaved person so listed was not also listed under the *bona fide* owner's household. See Census Office, Department of the Interior, *Eighth Census, United States.–1860 . . . Instructions to U.S. Marshals, Instructions to Assistants* (Washington: Geo. W. Bowman, 1860), 18.

58. WMR Business Ledger, 1859–62, p. 256, UA 102, box 3. See also pp. 38, 163, 532, 556, for references to hiring out, which could often be very profitable and sometimes netted an enslaver a yearly

return of as much as 15 percent of the enslaved person's value. See Campbell, *Empire for Slavery*, 89–90; John J. Zaborney, *Slaves for Hire: Renting Enslaved Laborers in Antebellum Virginia* (Baton Rouge: Louisiana State University Press, 2012), 154–61. On the Rusk House, see Houston *Weekly Telegraph*, April 13, 1859; August 31, 1859; November 13, 1860.

59. *Southwestern Christian Advocate*, May 24, 1877, in Judith Giesberg, ed., "Last Seen: Finding Family After Slavery," informationwanted.org/items/show/1230. Our thanks to William D. Jones for sourcing and drafting these lines about Perry Wilmer.

60. See Lack, "Urban Slavery in the Southwest"; John Garrison Marks, "Community Bonds in the Bayou City: Free Blacks and Local Reputation in Early Houston," *Southwestern Historical Quarterly* 117, no. 3 (January 2014): 266–82; Jackson, "Slavery in Houston," 81–82.

61. "For the Telegraph," Houston *Weekly Telegraph*, April 9, 1856. Cf. Amani T. Marshall, "'They Are Supposed to Be Lurking about the City': Enslaved Women Runaways in Antebellum Charleston," *South Carolina Historical Magazine* 115, no. 3 (July 2014): 188–212. Texas created a formal patrol system in 1846; a patrol could be appointed by the county court for a three-month period of service, and at least half the members of each patrol had to be slave owners. See Campbell, *Empire for Slavery*, 109–10. For Rice's appointment to a patrol, see Minutes of the Harris County Commissioner's Court, August 19, 1851, vol. A, part II, p. 106.

62. "Varioloid," Houston *Telegraph and Texas Register*, March 14, 1851.

63. "Small Pox," Houston *Telegraph and Texas Register*, March 21, 1865. The article also reported that Tom was being closely watched and "is fast recovering." Cf. Hall, ed., *William Marsh Rice and His Institute*, 33.

64. New Orleans *Daily Picayune*, November 25, 1853.

65. Stephanie M. H. Camp, *Closer to Freedom: Enslaved Women and Everyday Resistance in the Plantation South* (Chapel Hill: University of North Carolina Press, 2004).

66. "$50 Reward," Houston *Weekly Telegraph*, January 29, 1861. Based on his age and description, Tom might be the same man who is mentioned in a later runaway advertisement. See "$200 Reward," Houston *Telegraph* (supplement), November 30, 1863. Both advertisements were placed by P. T. Wade; the first mentioned Wm. M. Rice and Company as an address where Tom could be taken for the reward.

67. WMR Business Ledger, 1858–59, p. 335, UA 102, box 2. Archival records do not make clear when the three antebellum ledgers in UA 102, boxes 1–3, arrived in the WRC; neither Muir nor Morris appears to have known about or consulted them. The bound volumes may have been part of a cache of papers found in 1993 in a fruit crate and some "vintage filing cabinets" in the basement of the Allen Center, the university's chief administration building. See the article by Karen Hess Rogers in the newsletter published by the Friends of Fondren Library called *The Flyleaf* 44, no. 2 (Winter 1994): 4–5. The relevance of the ledgers to Rice's history with slavery may not have been obvious to researchers who consulted early finding aids that described the earliest book as containing "Grocery Store Accounts."

68. On Ben, see WMR Business Ledger, 1855–56, pp. 27, 344, 464, UA 102, box 1. For the 1854 example of a "negro" payment without a name, see p. 403. Individual enslaved people were sometimes allowed by their enslavers to arrange work and keep some wages, though their legal status remained unchanged. It is difficult to tell from this account whether Rice's clerks were recording money spent on or by Ben. There are some references to "Negro Ben" in postwar records associated with Rice. See letter to Rice dated July 10, 1866, and a signed check to "Ben," dated April 6, 1867, both in William Marsh Rice Papers, Heritage Society of Houston, box 1. Also see Rice Account with E. R. Wells, 1865–66, UA 101, box 107, folder 2.

69. Rice Business Ledger, 1855–56, pp. 432, 603, 670.

70. Ibid., 341 ("boy Lewis"), 603 ("Henry" and "sundries").

71. Rice Business Ledger, 1858–59, p. 685. Estimate is based on Real Wage/Real Wealth conversion from 1858 to present provided by MeasuringWorth.com. Cf. "Negro Property" account on page 603 in 1855–56 Rice Ledger. On rises in prices, see Campbell, *Empire for Slavery*, 73.

72. Quotations from Harold M. Hyman, "William Marsh Rice's Credit Ratings, 1846–1866," *Houston Review* 6, no. 2 (1984): 91–96. On credit reports, see Scott A. Sandage, *Born Losers: A History of Failure in America* (Cambridge, MA; Harvard University Press, 2005). On the connections between the history of accounting and the history of slavery, see Caitlin Rosenthal, *Accounting for Slavery: Masters and Management* (Cambridge, MA: Harvard University Press, 2018).

73. Hyman, "William Marsh Rice's Credit Ratings," 92; Wooster, "Wealthy Texans," 166.

74. Hyman, "William Marsh Rice's Credit Ratings," 92; Torget, *Seeds of Empire*, 264.

75. "Port of Galveston" section in Galveston *Weekly Journal*, March 19, 1852; May 14, 1852; May 28, 1852; June 4, 1852. See accounts for the *Star State* and for the Navigation Company in Rice Business Ledger, 1855–56, pp. 19, 64, 137. The Galveston *Weekly Journal* for July 2, 1852, listed the price current for middling cotton at 8.5 cents per pound and noted that bales in the last week had sold for $31 to $41 per bale; a typical bale of cotton ran between 400 and 450 pounds. For the contemporary comparison to 2022, see the real price for commodities comparison on MeasuringWorth.com.

76. "Port of Houston" section in Houston *Democratic Telegraph and Texas Register*, January 24, 1851. On average bales per slave, see Campbell, *Empire for Slavery*, 75. On steamboats and the slave trade, see Deyle, *Carry Me Back*, 110–11, 147–48; Schermerhorn, *Business of Slavery*, 204–39, esp. 218–24.

77. See Rice Business Ledger, 1855–56, p. 49; Rice Business Ledger, 1858–59, p. 684. For biographical information on Kyle and Terry, see *Handbook of Texas*. After the Civil War began, Terry would become better known as the commander of Terry's Texas Rangers, a Confederate cavalry group.

78. Hyman, "William Marsh Rice's Credit Ratings," 92, 95.

79. "Editorial Correspondence," Galveston *Weekly News*, September 28, 1858; "Howe's Cotton Harvester," Houston *Weekly Telegraph*, July 30, 1856; Houston *Weekly Telegraph*, March 9, 1859.

80. Buenger, *Secession and the Union in Texas*, 17. See "Texas Legislature: Editorial Correspondence," Galveston *Weekly News*, August 12, 1856; "New Route to the West! The Houston Tap Road!," Houston *Weekly Telegraph*, October 1, 1856. On the Tap and the Buffalo Bayou, Brazos and Colorado, see Andrew Forest Muir, "Railroads Come to Houston, 1857–1861," *Southwestern Historical Quarterly* 64, no. 1 (July 1960): 47–49; "Opening of the Houston Tap Road," Houston *Weekly Telegraph*, April 9, 1856; "An Act to Incorporate the Houston Tap and Brazoria Railway Company," Houston *Weekly Telegraph*, October 8, 1856.

81. On the compress, see Hall, ed., *William Marsh Rice and His Institute*, 30.

82. "Sudden Death of Captain F. A. Rice," Houston *Post*, April 7, 1901; Hall, ed., *William Marsh Rice and His Institute*, 29–30, 104–5, 140, 144. Much of what we now know about enslaved people at the Edge Hill Plantation is thanks to Ben Schachter, "The Rice Brothers, Slavery, and Capitalism in Texas: 1850–1868" (2020), Task Force Records, UA 421, Series B; and Schachter, "Freedom's Archive: Slavery, Emancipation, and Reconstruction in Fort Bend County," undergraduate honors thesis, Rice University (2022), in Rice Research Repository, hdl.handle.net/1911/112431.

83. Fort Bend County Probate Record Books, vol. C, 375–76, available on Ancestry.com.

84. Ibid., vol. D, 77–81.

85. Harris County Tax Rolls, 1855, and Fort Bend County Tax Rolls, 1856, on FamilySearch. To be appointed administrator, Rice had to sign a bond that financially obliged him to carry out his duties,

which required him to petition the county court annually about sales and expenses affecting the estate. His brother William M. Rice and partner Abraham Groesbeeck signed as his securities for the bond.

86. These developments complicate the claim made about WMR in Morris, *William Marsh Rice and His Institute*, 28: "Cannily, he was too shrewd to go into cotton raising himself, subject as it was to the endless uncertainties of labor, soil conditions, unstable markets, and the weather." See also Hall, ed., *William Marsh Rice and His Institute*, 36. For sales of Randon cotton handled by Rice and Company, see Fort Bend County Probate Record Books, vol. F, 499–501.

87. Cf. Rice Business Ledger, 1858–59, pp. 329, 360; Fort Bend County Probate Record Books, vol. E, 585–87.

88. Fort Bend County Probate Record Books, vol. D, 80.

89. Ibid.

90. Ibid., vol. F, 505.

91. Ibid., 495, 498.

92. Ibid., 503–4.

2. Rice and the Rebellion

1. Thomas J. McGee (Hempstead) to William Rice and Frederick Rice (Houston), June 15, 1863, Rice Family Papers, Heritage Society of Houston, box 1. For the penitentiary law, see "An Act Providing for the Disposition of Runaway Slaves (1861)," in H. P. N. Gammel, *The Laws of Texas* (Austin: Gammel Book Co., 1898), vol. 5: 49–51; Thomas Carothers to Board of Directors of the Texas Penitentiary, September 14, 1863, Records Relating to the Penitentiary, TSLAC, box 022–4, folder 15.

2. Fort Bend County Probate Record Books, vol. F, 504, 508.

3. Hall, ed., *William Marsh Rice and His Institute*, 34–40, Rice quoted on 38.

4. B. H. Carroll, *Standard History of Houston, Texas: From a Study of the Original Sources* (Knoxville, TN: H. W. Crew and Co., 1912), 195–97; Muir, "William Marsh Rice, Houstonian," 33 (Muir claimed Rice was "[a] unionist who did not, however, make a nuisance of himself during the secession crisis and the unhappy days of the Confederate States of America"); "Rice, William Marsh," s.v., *Handbook of Texas Online*, www.tshaonline.org/handbook/entries/rice-william-marsh. The quoted line in the *Handbook* was added to the entry in the 1996 print edition. In his talk describing Rice's relationship to the Confederacy as "not entirely clear," Muir cited early Rice history professor R. G. Caldwell's 1941 conclusion that Rice was a "unionist" as evidence in favor of that hypothesis, since Caldwell would have been able to interview Rice's nephew and namesake, William Marsh Rice Jr., during his lifetime. Thus an unsourced entry in a reference work from 1941 may have become the source material for future reference works. See Muir, "William Marsh Rice, His Life and Death," 17; Robert G. Caldwell, "Rice, William Marsh," s.v., *Dictionary of American Biography* (1941), 546–47. See also Kathleen Much, "Rice, William Marsh," s.v., *American National Biography* (Oxford, UK: Oxford University Press, 1999), which claimed that Rice "opposed secession."

5. "A declaration of the causes which impel the State of Texas to secede from the Federal Union," February 2, 1861, TSLAC, www.tsl.texas.gov/ref/abouttx/secession/2feb1861.html.

6. R. J. M. Blackett, *The Captive's Quest for Freedom: Fugitive Slaves, the 1850 Fugitive Slave Law, and the Politics of Slavery* (New York: Cambridge University Press, 2018); Alice L. Baumgartner, *South to Freedom: Runaway Slaves to Mexico and the Road to the Civil War* (New York: Basic Books, 2020).

7. Hall, ed., *William Marsh Rice and His Institute*, 33–34; "Answers to the Interrogatories Drafted

by Mr. Boston to Be Asked of William A. Rice," ERI, Subseries C: *Baldwin vs. Rice*, 1886–1908, UA101, box 43, folder 1.

8. Buenger, *Secession and the Union in Texas*, 1–7.

9. "Cushing, Edward Hopkins," s.v., *Handbook of Texas;* Donald E. Reynolds, *Texas Terror: The Slave Insurrection Panic of 1860 and the Secession of the Lower South* (Baton Rouge: Louisiana State University Press, 2007). Cf. Emory M. Thomas, "Rebel Nationalism: E. H. Cushing and the Confederate Experience," *Southwestern Historical Quarterly* 73, no. 3 (January 1970): 343–55.

10. Dale Baum, *The Shattering of Texas Unionism: Politics in the Lone Star State During the Civil War Era* (Baton Rouge: Louisiana State University Press, 1998), chap. 1.

11. On commercial men's reactions, see Buenger, *Secession and the Union in Texas*, 135–37.

12. "Breckinridge and Lane Club," Houston *Weekly Telegraph*, August 7, 1860. See Buenger, *Secession and the Union in Texas*, 50–52.

13. In "William Marsh Rice, Houstonian," Muir cites an 1845 article in which a list of Houston businessman signed an invitation to Sam Houston to a public dinner in his honor, but this is hardly good evidence of Rice's later views about Houston's course during the Civil War, especially since one of the other men on the 1845 list was Francis Lubbock, future Confederate governor of Texas. See "Gen. Sam Houston," Houston *Telegraph and Texas Register*, November 12, 1845.

14. "What Shall Be Done?" articles by F. S. Stockdale and E. H. Cushing in Houston *Weekly Telegraph*, November 13, 1860. An advertisement for Wm. M. Rice & Co. directly under the masthead says this issue, which was printed a day early, was "forwarded" from Rice's firm, an unusual announcement whose meaning is unclear. It could mean that Rice and Company sponsored the early run of the issue or assisted in getting it into the mail.

15. "Mass Meeting of the People of Harris County," Houston *Weekly Telegraph*, November 20, 1860. See also "Public Meeting," Houston *Weekly Telegraph*, November 13, 1860. Cf. Hall, ed., *William Marsh Rice and His Institute*, 34.

16. "Mass Meeting of the People of Harris County," Houston *Weekly Telegraph*, November 20, 1860. See also "Public Meeting," Houston *Tri-Weekly Telegraph*, November 10, 1860. On Richardson, see Hall, ed., *William Marsh Rice and His Institute*, 143–44; "Richardson, Alfred S.," s.v., *Handbook of Texas*.

17. This seems to be the construction that Muir cautiously placed on this committee's call for Houston to convene the legislature: "If Rice were a unionist, perhaps his support of the measure was intended to obviate what actually happened when Houston refused to call the Legislature together." See Muir, "William Marsh Rice, His Life and Death," 17.

18. William W. Freehling, *The Road to Disunion*, vol. 2: *Secessionists Triumphant, 1854–1861* (New York: Oxford University Press, 2007), 445–52, quoted on 449.

19. "Mass Meeting of Harris County," *Tri-Weekly Telegraph*, December 4, 1860.

20. Ibid. For donations to the committee dated November 15, 1860, see Account Book, F. A. Rice (Trip to Austin), Rice Collection, Heritage Society. The firm and four other donors gave five dollars; eleven others gave smaller amounts.

21. "Now, or Never!" Houston *Weekly Telegraph*, December 18, 1860.

22. Ibid. Speaking of merchants, Cushing added that some in the city "were with us from the first; nearly all are with us now."

23. "Grand Torch-Light Procession" and "Gov. Houston's Speech," Houston *Weekly Telegraph*, December 18, 1860. Cushing's report noted that some of the banners were made by the Southern Rights Association and others by the "K.G.C.," or the Knights of the Golden Circle, a proslavery secret society whose influence was especially strong in Texas. After its founder George Bickley spoke in Houston in

early November, between forty and sixty local men reportedly joined a chapter there. See "K.G.C.," Houston *Weekly Telegraph*, November 6, 1860; also see Cushing's comment at 2a. Roy Sylvan Dunn, "The KGC in Texas, 1860–1861," *Southwestern Historical Quarterly* 70, no. 4 (April 1967): 543–73.

24. "To the People of Harris County," Houston *Weekly Telegraph*, December 18, 1860.

25. The other signatories were P. W. Gray (who gave a public speech rebuffing Houston's), W. P. Rogers, Thomas S. Lubbock, E. W. Taylor, William J. Hutchins, and E. A. Palmer. William McKee had been appointed to the committee on December 1 but no longer appeared. Thomas S. Lubbock was a secessionist and suspected Knight of the Golden Circle who, in the same issue, accepted nomination as the Harris County delegate to the secession convention.

26. Hall, ed., *William Marsh Rice and His Institute*, 34. Both Muir and Morris noted Rice's presence on the Resolutions Committee at the November 14, 1860, meeting but not his involvement in the subsequent meetings detailed here. In a personal letter written in 1897, WMR shared a memory of the last time he saw Sam Houston, recalling that it was in 1863 just before Houston died. He said "the Father of Texas" came to Rice's store to buy some shoes "for his children and said good by. Things looked very blue and he seemed depressed." The letter did not, however, comment on Houston's (or Rice's) politics at the beginning of the war. There were many possible reasons for Houston and Rice to be blue in the middle of 1863 that do not have a direct bearing on whether Rice was a Houston supporter in 1860–61. See WMR to Mary Brewster, October 26, 1897, UA 101, box 103, folder 2.

27. James L. Huston, *Calculating the Value of the Union: Slavery, Property Rights, and the Economic Origins of the Civil War* (Chapel Hill: University of North Carolina, 2003), esp. 27–29. On Lincoln's intentions, see James Oakes, *Freedom National: The Destruction of Slavery in the United States, 1861–1865* (New York: W. W. Norton, 2013), 1–83.

28. James D. Richardson, comp., *The Messages and Papers of Jefferson Davis and the Confederacy, Including Diplomatic Correspondence, 1861–1865*, ed. Allan Nevins (1905; New York: Chelsea House, 1966), vol. 1: 68. See also Schoen, *Fragile Fabric of Union*, esp. 9–10.

29. Vote totals are based on manuscript returns tabulated in Joe T. Timmons, "The Referendum in Texas on the Ordinance of Secession, February 23, 1861: The Vote," *East Texas Historical Journal* 11, no. 2 (October 1973): 12–28. Cf. Dunn, "KGC in Texas," 561–67.

30. Houston *Weekly Telegraph*, April 30, 1861 (Shepherd meeting); "Texas Grays, or Gray Fencibles," July 31, 1861 (Rice and Richardson join a military company); May 7, 1861 (merchant support). Rice and Company also contributed to a fund to support another local military company, the Bayou City Guards. See *Weekly Telegraph*, August 21, 1861.

31. Andrew J. Torget, "The Problem of Slave Flight in Civil War Texas," in *Lone Star Unionism, Dissent, and Resistance: Other Sides of Civil War Texas*, ed. Jesús F. de la Teja (Norman: University of Oklahoma Press, 2016), 43; Oakes, *Freedom National*, 290.

32. Paul A. Levengood, "In the Absence of Scarcity: The Civil War Prosperity of Houston, Texas," *Southwestern Historical Quarterly* 101, no. 4 (April 1998): 401–26. For the purchase of Amanda, see Harris County Deed Book Y, 594–95; Financial Records, 1845–62, William Marsh Rice Papers, MSS0140-b1f04-002, HHRC; "Trustee's Sale," Houston *Weekly Telegraph*, December 18, 1861. For the Thatcher agreement, see Financial Records, Ledgers, 1858–63, William Marsh Rice Papers, box 1, folder 10, HHRC, MSS0140-b1f10-01-09.

33. Levengood, "In the Absence of Scarcity," 405.

34. On the battle of Galveston and defensive preparations in Houston, see Edward T. Cotham Jr., *Battle on the Bay: The Civil War Struggle for Galveston* (Austin: University of Texas Press, 1998); "Our Military Defenses," Houston *Tri-Weekly Telegraph*, October 15, 1862; *Official Records of the Union and*

Confederate Navies in the War of the Rebellion, ser. 1, vol. 19 (Washington, D.C.: Government Printing Office, 1905), 790–800. For Rice and Company's various transactions with Confederate quartermasters, including for "obstructions," see WMR Business Ledger, 1859–62, pp. 529, 530, 536.

35. Henry E. Perkins to the Texas Legislature, February 13, 1863, Correspondence Concerning the Penitentiary, Records Relating to the Penitentiary, Archives and Information Services Division, TSLAC. See also James A. Baker to the Penitentiary Board, January 30, 1864, Records Relation to the Penitentiary, TSLAC, box 022–1, folder 6. Baker Senior had signed up as a private in a company of Confederate volunteers in October 1861 and was stationed in Galveston, leaving his wife to direct the labor of enslaved people on their farm near Huntsville. But in 1862, he would be elected as a district judge. See Kirkland, *Captain James A. Baker*, 27–33.

36. Francis R. Lubbock, *Six Decades in Texas*, ed. C. W. Raines (Austin: Ben C. Jones, 1900), 463–66.

37. Peter Allen to the Legislature of the State of Texas, February 9, 1863, Race and Slavery Petitions Project, University of North Carolina–Greensboro, ser. 1, accession no. 11586302, original in RG 100, Records of the Legislature, Memorials and Petitions, TSLAC; Marks, "Community Bonds in the Bayou City," 275. Men like Allen who worked as "camp slaves" for Confederate officers were not in the Confederate military. See Kevin M. Levin, *Searching for Black Confederates: The Civil War's Most Persistent Myth* (Chapel Hill: University of North Carolina Press, 2019).

38. Vote reported in Houston *Weekly Telegraph*, February 25, 1863. For the legislative debate, see Ninth Texas Legislature (CSA), First Called Session, *House Journal*, 81–83. One of the legislators who voted in favor of Allen, describing his case as an "exception," was Alfred S. Richardson, future charter trustee of the Rice Institute and a state legislator from Harris County at the time. See also Campbell, *Empire for Slavery*, 110–11.

39. On Sabine Pass, see Edward T. Cotham Jr., *Sabine Pass: The Confederacy's Thermopylae* (Austin: University of Texas Press, 2004). On refugees, see Dale Baum, "Slaves Taken to Texas for Safekeeping during the Civil War," in *The Fate of Texas: The Civil War and the Lone Star State*, ed. Charles D. Grear (Fayetteville: University of Arkansas Press, 2008), 83–104; W. Caleb McDaniel, "Involuntary Removals: 'Refugeed Slaves' in Confederate Texas," in De La Teja, ed., *Lone Star Unionism, Dissent, and Resistance*, 60–83.

40. "Wanted to Hire," Houston *Tri-Weekly Telegraph*, December 12, 1862; Robert Colby, "'Negroes Will Bear Fabulous Prices': The Economics of Wartime Slave Commerce and Visions of the Confederate Future," *Journal of the Civil War Era* 10, no. 4 (December 2020): 439–68, qtd. on 445; Houston *Tri-Weekly Telegraph*, July 3, 1863; Houston *Weekly Telegraph*, February 25, 1863.

41. Colby, "'Negroes Will Bear Fabulous Prices,'" 447–53. See also an undated letter to Frederick A. Rice from Jos. O. Wade (Rice Papers, Heritage Society, box 1, folder 2) asking him to send Wade some Confederate notes in exchange for $320 in specie so that Wade can pay for an enslaved person he has arranged to buy.

42. Deed Records of Walker County, Book F, 197–98. See also original copy in Business Documents, William Marsh Rice Family Papers, Heritage Society of Houston, box 1. The enslaved people were named in the deed as Green, Harry, Reese, Anthony or Judge, George, Maria, Sarah, Laura, and Adaline.

43. Mortgage of Thomas W. Mitchell to William M. Rice and Co., April 2, 1863, Book G, pp. 557–59, Deed Records, Fort Bend County Clerk of Court, Richmond, Texas. A manuscript copy of the mortgage is available in William Marsh Rice Papers, box 1, folder 5, MSS0140-b1f05-014, HHRC. See also promissory notes of the same date signed by Mitchell in ERI, UA 101, box 105, folder 43.

44. These wartime notes can be found in the same notebook that contained F. A. Rice's list of donors to the Harris County committee that formed during the secession crisis. It is therefore labeled

Account Book, F. A. Rice (Trip to Austin), in the Rice Papers at the Heritage Society. A few but not all of the names in the notebook also appear to overlap with an undated list of more than fifty enslaved people, also in Frederick A. Rice's script, found on loose-leaf paper in William Marsh Rice Papers, box 1, folder 7, MSS0140-b1f07-066, HHRC, cdm17006.contentdm.oclc.org/digital/collection/p17006c01193/id/1387/rec/352. That list also contained ages and prices beside each name, with the total summed to more than $90,000 in value.

45. Thomas W. Mitchell to William Marsh Rice and Co., October 17, 1863, Financial Records, William Marsh Rice Papers, box 1, folder 5, MSS0140-b1f05-012, HHRC; 1864 Fort Bend County Tax Rolls.

46. Fort Bend County Probate Record Books, vol. H, 123. On "hands," see Camp, *Closer to Freedom*, 64; Walter Johnson, *River of Dark Dreams: Slavery and Empire in the Cotton Kingdom* (Cambridge, MA: Harvard University Press, 2017), 151–54.

47. [WMR] to "Fred" [FAR], May 12, 1863, in Heritage Society Papers. Though unsigned, the brief letter is in the elder Rice's hand. Eight days before, perhaps in preparation for his trip, William Marsh Rice and Company had placed a list of assets—including around $2,500 in bank notes, $15,000 in Texas state bonds, $1,500 in gold and silver, and $4,000 in Confederate bonds—in the hands of an agent in Houston to hold or sell in the interest of the firm. See Memorandum headed "Received from Wm. M. Rice & Co.," Wm. M. Rice & Co., 1853–66, ERI, UA 101, box 105, folder 43.

48. WMR to "Sister Lottie," October 22, 1863, William Marsh Rice Papers, box 1, folder 8, MSS0140-b1f08-010, HHRC.

49. Fredericka Meiners, "The Texas Border Cotton Trade, 1862–1863," *Civil War History* 23, no. 4 (December 1977): 293–306; Ronnie C. Tyler, "Cotton on the Border, 1861–1865," in *Lone Star Blue and Gray: Essays on Texas in the Civil War*, ed. Ralph A. Wooster (Austin: Texas State Historical Association, 1995), 211–32; Robert L. Kerby, *Kirby Smith's Confederacy: The Trans-Mississippi South, 1863–1865* (New York: Columbia University Press, 1972), chap. 4; James W. Daddysman, *The Matamoros Trade: Confederate Commerce, Diplomacy, and Intrigue* (Newark: University of Delaware Press, 1984).

50. "New Advertisements," Houston *Tri-Weekly Telegraph*, June 24, 1863; E. T. Gillespie to W. M. Rice, July 31, 1864, Rice Papers, box 1, folder 5, Heritage Society. On depreciation of the currency, see *Weekly Telegraph*, May 5, 1863. For evidence that Rice and Company did hold some Confederate bills and bonds, see John Bremond to Wm. M. Rice & Co, May 4, 1864, Financial Correspondence, 1860–65, William Marsh Rice Papers, MSS0140-b1f02-009, HHRC; Memorandum headed "Received from Wm. M. Rice & Co."

51. Kerby, *Kirby Smith's Confederacy*, 155–72, Kirby Smith qtd. on 155. See also James L. Nichols, *The Confederate Quartermaster in the Trans-Mississippi* (Austin: University of Texas Press, 1964), chap. 4.

52. Kerby, *Kirby Smith's Confederacy*, 172–78, editor qtd. on 175.

53. Kerby, *Kirby Smith's Confederacy*, 196–207. On the state plan, see also Ralph A. Wooster, "Texas," in *The Confederate Governors*, ed. W. Buck Yearns (Athens: University of Georgia Press, 1985), 211–13; John Moretta, "Pendleton Murrah and States Rights in Civil War Texas," *Civil War History* 45, no. 2 (June 1999): 126–46.

54. Campbell, *Empire for Slavery*, 235–36; Wooster, "Texas," 209. Magruder had previously advocated slave impressment in Virginia, sparking similar controversy there. See Stephanie McCurry, *Confederate Reckoning: Power and Politics in the Civil War South* (Cambridge, MA: Harvard University Press, 2010), 264–70.

55. W. J. Kyle to FAR, December 16, 1862, General Correspondence, 1855–68, William Marsh Rice Papers, box 2, folder 1, MSS0140-b2f01-033, HHRC; file for "Wm. M. Rice" in Confederate Papers Relating to Citizens or Business Firms, on Fold3.com; E. P. Gaines to FAR, December 18, 1863, General

Correspondence, 1855–68, undated, William Marsh Rice Family Papers, HHRC, MSS0140-b2f01-023; WMR Business Ledger, 1859–62, p. 188.

56. "Send Along the Negroes" and "More Negroes Wanted," Houston *Weekly Telegraph*, January 14, 1863.

57. Smith qtd. in Campbell, *Empire for Slavery*, 236.

58. Cushing qtd. in Kerby, *Kirby Smith's Confederacy*, 175 (also "minority opinion").

59. W. Bains to Wm. M. Rice and Co., January 14, 1864, Rice Papers, Heritage Society, box 1, folder 5. See also W. S. Day to Wm. M. Rice and Co., August 4, 1864, Financial Correspondence, 1860–65, Rice Papers, HHRC, box 1, folder 2, MSS0140-b1f02-014.

60. See R. S. Robinson to FAR, November 8, 1864, Heritage Society, box 1, folder 5; A. H. Willie to FAR, August 12, 1864, Heritage Society, box 1, folder 5; Robert C. Campbell to FAR, July 16, 1864, Rice Papers, HHRC, box 2, folder 1, MSS0140-b2f01-027r.

61. For Frederick A. Rice's Confederate service record, see U.S. Compiled Service Records of Confederate General and Staff Officers, and Nonregimental Enlisted Men, 1861–65, NARA, RG 109, Microfilm Publication M331, roll 210; US, Civil War Service Records (CMSR)—Confederate—Texas, 1861–65, RG 109, Microfilm Publication M323 (which also notes his occupation as "farmer with over twenty hands"), Fold3.com. For examples of letters pertaining to his work in the Labor Bureau, see [Frederick A. Rice] to Brig. Gen. J. E. Slaughter, undated, box 1, folder 2, Rice Papers, Heritage Society; James W. Wade, December 5, 1864, Heritage Society, box 1, folder 5; John Pinchback to FAR, August 7, 1864, box 2, folder 3, HHRC, MSS0140-b2f03-002; James W. Wade, July 8, 1864, box 2, folder 1, HHRC, MSS0140-b2f01-029. For his work as an agent for the State Plan and correspondence with Nichols, see Military Board of Texas Records, TSLAC, 2–10/301; R. N. Buxley to F. A. Rice, March 10, 1864, and various other items in Heritage Society, box 1, folders 4–5.

62. Hall, ed., *William Marsh Rice and His Institute*, 38; WMR to FAR, January 23, 1864, William Marsh Rice Papers, box 2, folder 3, HHRC, MSS0140-b2f03-012.

63. WMR Will of 1863, ERI, UA 101, box 21; Memorandum of State Bonds Taken by W. M. Rice, December 6, 1863, Rice Papers, HHRC, MSS0140-b1f05-007b; FAR to WMR, November 11, 1863, Rice Papers, box 1, folder 1, HHRC, MSS0140-b1f01-002a.

64. FAR to WMR, November 11, 1863.

65. Ibid. A few weeks after this letter, Magruder "issued a sweeping order that amounted to an impressment of all the able-bodied male slaves, except one per owner, in Texas." See Campbell, *Empire for Slavery*, 237–38; Cotham, *Sabine Pass*, 77–78.

66. Houston *Tri-Weekly Telegraph*, June 21, 1865.

67. Ibid.; Elizabeth Hayes Turner, "'Three Cheers to Freedom and Equal Rights to All': Juneteenth and the Meaning of Citizenship," in De La Teja, ed., *Lone Star Unionism, Dissent, and Resistance*, 204.

68. Houston *Tri-Weekly Telegraph*, July 4, 1865 (printed July 5); June 21, 1865. The residence referred to was likely the Nichols-Rice-Cherry House which was later moved to its current location in Sam Houston Park.

69. WMR Application for Special Pardon. Frederick A. Rice, officially a prisoner of war due to his Confederate rank when Granger's forces arrived, had already signed an oath in Houston on June 24. See NARA, M331, roll 210, Fold3.com.

70. WMR Application for Special Pardon. While it may be true that Rice did not run the blockade with ships, he worked around it by doing business in Mexico.

71. In one letter to FAR from Mexico, dated November 24, 1864, WMR wrote, "Old Abe is elected and I suppose no body disappointed." He may have meant that Confederates wished to fight on in-

stead of negotiating for peace, as the Democratic Party's presidential candidate might have done had Lincoln lost. But his apparent allusion to Lincoln is as cryptic as it is rare in Rice's surviving papers, which seldom talked politics. WMR to FAR, November 24, 1864, William Marsh Rice Papers, HHRC, MSS0140-b1f11-007a.

72. WMR to FAR, January 23, 1864; E. B. Nichols to WMR, April 10, 1867, box 1, folder 7, Heritage Society, as well as other letters from Nichols in the same folder. See also memorandum about cotton from E. B. Nichols, December 9, 1863, ERI, UA 101, box 107, folder 2; E. B. Nichols to WMR, December 14, 1863, box 1, folder 4, Heritage Society; WMR to Nichols, Early Rice, UA 101, box 103, folder 7; Eugene Bremond to FAR, May 12, 1864, HHRC, MSS0140-b2f01-007. On Armstrong, see Military Board of Texas Records, TSLAC, 2–10/302. How much Nichols was supporting the state, and how much he was contracting with firms on the side to benefit himself and partners, is unclear, but he was eventually suspected by the governor himself of engaging in speculation; see Pendleton Murrah to E. B. Nichols, March 22, 1864, Letterpress Book, Records of Governor Pendleton Murrah, TSLAC; Steven Strom, "Cotton and Profits Across the Border: William Marsh Rice in Mexico, 1863–1865," *Houston Review* 8, no. 2 (1986): 89–96; Dru Sanders, "Texas Cotton, Confederate Tyranny, and Matamoros: William Marsh Rice in the Civil War" (2020), Task Force Records, UA 421, Series B.

73. Hyman, "William Marsh Rice's Credit Ratings," 95; Hall, ed., *William Marsh Rice and His Institute*, 39. The promissory notes documenting credit from New York and Cincinnati are dated November and December 1865, folder 6, box 1, HHRC.

74. Hall, ed., *William Marsh Rice and His Institute*, 41–42, 47–48. On railroads and finance, see Jonathan Levy, *Ages of American Capitalism: A History of the United States* (New York: Random House, 2021), 195–228.

75. Will of WMR, dated July 4, 1868, ERI, UA 101, box 102, folder 5. Also reproduced in appendix C. A few days before, Rice had drawn up a slightly different will (in the same folder) that also set apart funds for an educational institution, but made his wife Elizabeth Baldwin Rice a coexecutor with Frederick and did not mention any trustees or further instructions. This earlier will was not witnessed and was soon supplanted by the July 4 document. Neither will has ever been mentioned in previous scholarship on Rice University, which typically cites Rice's 1882 will, composed in New Jersey, as the earliest in which he had mentioned an institution for the education of white children.

76. Will of WMR, July 4, 1868. For the military company, see "Texas Grays, or Gray Fencibles." Peter W. Gray was the founding partner of the firm that became Baker Botts and represented WMR; Gray's first partner, W. B. Botts, was a friend of George Goldthwaite and the brother of Benjamin A. Botts, who later joined Frederick A. Rice as a director of City Bank of Houston. Botts was also connected to the Confederate unit known as Terry's Texas Rangers; see his obituary in Galveston *Daily News*, September 25, 1885. For more on the networks described here, see J. H. Freeman, *The People of Baker Botts* (Houston: Baker & Botts, 1992); Marguerite Johnston, *A Happy Worldly Abode: Christ Church Cathedral, 1839–1964* (Houston: Gulf Printing Co., 1964).

77. For examples of the difficulty Rice had collecting debts, see Charles Stewart to WMR, July 13, 1866; J. H. Banton to WMR, July 2, 1866; J. H. Banton to WMR, February 20, 1868; W. B. Wood to WMR, June 4, 1867, all in Rice Papers, Heritage Society. For a fuller discussion of Rice's motives for moving to the North, see Task Force on Slavery, Segregation, and Racial Injustice, *Update on Slavery* (June 2021), 62–63.

78. For examples of tenants, see receipts for rents paid by "Blacks" to WMR in 1868, ERI, UA 101, box 107, folder 3; also "Memorandum of Money Collected for Mr. Rice," in Heritage Society Papers. For examples of checks made out by Rice to "Ben," see William Marsh Rice Papers, Financial Records,

1867–69, HPL. One such check has Ben's "X" as a legal mark on the back: cdm17006.contentdm.oclc.org/digital/collection/p17006co1193/id/629/rec/356.

79. Fort Bend County Probate Record Books, vol. H, 126. In 1869, Frederick would eventually lease much of the Edge Hill Plantation to another operator, O. M. Callis. See ERI, UA 101, box 111, folder 8, which also contains a sketch of a map of the plantation.

80. Contract between F. A. Rice and George Wheat et al., January 8, 1867, Richmond, Texas, Register of letters received, December 1866–December 1868, pp. 130–31, Freedmen's Bureau Field Office Records, M1912, roll 25, NARA, accessed on FamilySearch. See also a memorandum of account between FAR and James Blue (whose name appears as "Jim Blue" on the January 8, 1867, contract): ERI, UA 101, box 107, folder 2. For a much fuller analysis of George Wheat's family, see Schachter, "Freedom's Archive."

81. Alton Hornsby Jr., "The Freedmen's Bureau Schools in Texas, 1865–1870," *Southwestern Historical Quarterly* 76, no. 4 (April 1973): 397–417. On the Chenango plantation school, see W. H. Sharpe to William H. Sinclair, March 19, 1866, Records of the Superintendent of Education for the State of Texas, Bureau of Refugees, Freedmen, and Abandoned Lands, 1865–70, Unregistered Letters Received, 1866–67, 1869–70, NARA, Microfilm M822, roll 10, on FamilySearch; monthly report for May 1866 by Ellen Watson, "Sharpe's Plantation," Monthly reports from teachers, 1865–66, January–April 1867, NARA, Microfilm M822, roll 11, on FamilySearch.

82. On the fire, see M. O'Regan to E. M. Wheelock, February 9, 1867, Unregistered Letters Received, 1866–67, 1869–70, NARA, M822, roll 10. See also William L. Richter, *Overreached on All Sides: The Freedmen's Bureau Administrators in Texas, 1865–1868* (College Station: Texas A&M University Press, 1991).

83. *The Constitution, as Amended, and Ordinances of the Convention of 1866, Together with the Proclamation of the Governor declaring the Ratification of the Amendments to the Constitution, and the General Laws of the Regular Session of the Eleventh Legislature of the State of Texas* (Austin: Gazette Office, 1866); Barry A. Crouch, "'All the Vile Passions': The Texas Black Code of 1866," in Crouch, *The Dance of Freedom: Texas African Americans during Reconstruction*, ed. Larry Madaras (Austin: University of Texas Press, 2007), 134–58.

84. Gregory P. Downs, *After Appomattox: Military Occupation and the Ends of War* (Cambridge, MA: Harvard University Press, 2015), 161–210.

85. George Wheat, Fort Bend County, August 8, 1867, in Texas, Voter Records, 1867–1918, on FamilySearch; *Anderson Hall vs. Fred Rice*, January 6, 1868, Registers of Complaints, vol. 2: p. 88, Records of the Field Offices for the State of Texas, Bureau of Refugees, Freedmen, and Abandoned Lands, NARA, microfilm M1912, roll 22, on FamilySearch.

86. W. A. Delespine to WMR, September 4, 1867, William Marsh Rice Papers, HPL, cdm17006.contentdm.oclc.org/digital/collection/p17006co1193/id/1130/rec/483; "Address to the People of Texas," Galveston *Daily News*, January 24, 1868. See also "Proceedings of the Conservative Convention," Galveston *Daily News*, January 23, 1868. On political violence, see Carl H. Moneyhon, "The Democratic Party, the Ku Klux Klan, and the Politics of Fear," in *Still the Arena of Civil War: Violence and Turmoil in Reconstruction Texas, 1865–1874*, ed. Kenneth W. Howell (Denton: University of North Texas Press, 2012), 243–65; William A. Blair, *The Record of Murder and Outrages: Racial Violence and the Fight over Truth at the Dawn of Reconstruction* (Chapel Hill: University of North Carolina Press, 2021), chap. 5.

87. *Depositions: William M. Rice vs. Oran T. Holt, Executor of the Last Will and Testament of Elizabeth B. Rice, deceased. Depositions of William M. Rice and others, on behalf of complainant taken August 1898, before*

Edward C. Manners, Special Examiner, 32–34, 83, 168, in ERI, UA 101, box 2.

88. E. M. Wheelock to E. M. Pease, May 30, 1868, *Journal of the Reconstruction Convention, which Met at Austin, Texas, June 1, A.D., 1868* (Austin: Tracy, Siemering, and Co., 1870), 65–73.

89. Eric Foner, *Reconstruction: America's Unfinished Revolution, 1863–1877* (New York: HarperCollins, 1988), 321–22; Heather Andrea Williams, *Self-Taught: African American Education in Slavery and Freedom* (Chapel Hill: University of North Carolina Press, 2005), 193–94; Tyler D. Parry, "'Irrespective of Race or Color': Examining Desegregation at the Reconstructed University of South Carolina, 1868–1877," in *Invisible No More*, ed. Greene and Parry, 30–50; Adam Harris, *The State Must Provide: Why America's Colleges Have Always Been Unequal, and How to Set Them Right* (New York: Ecco, 2021).

90. "Education," Houston *Weekly Telegraph*, December 10, 1868; "To the Editor of the Telegraph," Houston *Weekly Telegraph*, July 8, 1869. See also "Africanization of Louisiana," Marshall *Texas Republican*, April 4, 1868.

91. "The Condition of the South," *Harrison Flag* (Marshall, TX), October 26, 1867; *State Rights Democrat* (La Grange, TX), November 23, 1866, 2b. See also "Public Meeting," *Texas Republican* (Marshall, TX), May 29, 1868; "Schools," Houston *Weekly Telegraph*, September 17, 1868; "Educational Fragments," Houston *Weekly Telegraph*, August 12, 1869.

92. Hall, ed., *William Marsh Rice and His Institute*, 56–58, 63–68.

93. "Historical Society," Houston *Daily Union*, May 22, 1870. See also Houston *Weekly Telegraph*, June 2 and 9, 1870; "Historical Society Meetings," Houston *Daily Union*, May 25, 1870; "Constitution or Articles of Organization of the Texas Historical Society," Houston *Evening Telegraph*, May 28, 1870. On Lost Cause origins and the Southern Historical Society, see Blight, *Race and Reunion*, 77–84.

94. "Worthy of a Prince: Great Generosity of Mr. W. M. Rice of New York," Galveston *Daily News*, May 19, 1891; "Rice Officially Opened, Address by Pres. Lovett," *RT*, September 24, 1920; "Historical Sketch of Rice Institute, a Gift to Texas Youth," *RT*, November 25, 1920.

95. The undated account, written by Kirby Investment Company manager Edward V. Clark and recalling a story told to him twenty years before Kirby's death in 1940, was found in Clark's papers after his death and mailed to Andrew Forest Muir by lawyer Cooper K. Ragan in 1961. See Muir Papers, box 69, folder 1. Rice's nephews J. S. Rice and WMR Jr. were engaged in the lumber industry and connected to Kirby.

96. "Address of Capt. James A. Baker before Rice Institute Engineers' Society, on the Life of William Marsh Rice, Founder of W. M. Rice Institute, November 13, 1929," in Lovett Papers, UA 014, box 36, folder 3. Cf. James A. Baker, "Reminiscences of the Founder," *Rice Institute Pamphlets* 18, no. 3 (1931).

97. For the 1879 dinner, see Hall, ed., *William Marsh Rice and His Institute*, 55.

98. United Confederate Veterans, *Sponsor Souvenir Album: History and Reunion* (Columbus, OH: Terry Engraving Co., 1895), 24, 30, 58. Cf. "Mrs. Rice's Reception" and "The Floral Parade," Galveston *Daily News*, May 24, 1895. The latter placed Mrs. Rice in the third carriage, instead of the first, but still credited her with the conception and planning of the parade.

3. The Louisiana Street Property

1. Felix Haywood interview in Federal Writers' Project, *Slave Narratives: A Folk History of Slavery in the United States From Interviews with Former Slaves* (Washington, DC: n.p., 1941), vol. 16, part 2: 133; Cary D. Wintz, "Fourth Ward, Houston," *Handbook of Texas Online*; Louise Passey Maxwell, "Freedmantown: The Origins of a Black Neighborhood in Houston, 1865–1880," in *Bricks without Straw: A Compre-*

hensive History of African Americans in Texas, ed. David A. Williams (Austin: Eakin, 1997), 125–52. The Freedmen's Town district is one of a few sites in Houston designated as a UNESCO "site of memory" on the United Nations' international "routes of slavery" project.

2. U.S. Census, 1870, Harris County, Harrisburg, manuscript p. 7. Domestic work was listed as the occupation for both women. For the land purchase, see Harris County Deed Records, vol. 11, p. 474.

3. Marriage License for S. J. Lenord [*sic*] and Betty Weeks [*sic*], February 24, 1876, no. 5125, Texas, U.S., Select County Marriage Records, 1837–1965, on Ancestry.com; "Matrimonial," Houston *Age*, February 26, 1876, 4b; Houston City Directory, 1877–78, 135, 204.

4. J. T. McCants, *Some Information Concerning the Rice Institute* (1955; Houston: Rice University Public Relations, 1971), 16. For the deed transferring the property to the Rice Institute on June 20, 1892, see Early Land Deeds, UA 222, box 60, folder 6.

5. Affidavit by A. B. Cohn, June 21, 1928, Early Land Deeds, UA 222, box 13, folder 17.

6. "Survey of Rice Institute Property West of Louisiana Street, and North of Jefferson Avenue, March 16, 1923," in Early Land Deeds, UA 222, drawer 129, folder 3.

7. See LaDale C. Winling, *Building the Ivory Tower: Universities and Metropolitan Development in the Twentieth Century* (Philadelphia: University of Pennsylvania Press, 2018); LaDale C. Winling and Todd M. Michney, "The Roots of Redlining: Academic, Governmental, and Professional Networks in the Making of the New Deal Lending Regime," *Journal of American History* 108, no. 1 (June 2021): 42–69; Brian Cameron and Andrew Kahrl, "Property and Power," in *After Emancipation: Racism and Resistance at the University of Virginia*, ed. Kirt von Daacke and Andrea Douglas (Charlottesville: University of Virginia Press, 2024), 149–55; Davarian L. Baldwin, *In the Shadow of the Ivory Tower: How Universities are Plundering Our Cities* (New York: Hachette Books, 2021); Michael A. Olivas, "*Brown* and the Desegregative Ideal: Location, Race, and College Attendance Policies," *Cornell Law Review* 90, no. 2 (January 2005): 391–417, esp. 399–404.

8. U.S. Freedmen's Bureau Records, 1865–78: Superintendent of Education, Monthly and Other School Reports, Texas, December 1865–70, Microfilm M803, roll 31, NARA; "Descriptive List of Persons and Articles Employed, . . . April 30, 1869," in Monthly Reports of School Buildings, July 1869–April 1870, and Monthly Reports of Persons and Articles Hired, May 1869–June 1870, M822, roll 17, NARA, both on Ancestry.com.

9. Harris County Deed Records, vol. 6, 617–18; "The Gregory Institute: It Was the Pioneer School House for Colored Children," Houston *Post*, September 15, 1901, 8a.

10. Joseph Welch to O. O. Howard, July 1, 1869, and Welch to C. H. Bering, July 19, 1869, and L. W. Stevenson to J. W. Alvord, June 28, 1870, all in Freedmen's Bureau Records of the Superintendent of Education, Texas, Letters and Endorsements Sent, vol. 2, Microfilm M822, roll 1, NARA, on Ancestry.com; "Gregory Institute–Dedication," Houston *Weekly Telegraph*, January 20, 1870, 5; "Dedication of Gregory Institute," Houston *Daily Union*, January 18, 1870. On Emancipation Park, see Rutherford B. H. Yates and Paul L. Yates, *The Life and Efforts of Jack Yates* (Houston: Texas Southern University Press, 1985), 15, 18–29, 31–34; "Emancipation Park," Houston *Informer*, December 1, 1923, 1a.

11. "Freeman's Demonstration," Houston *Evening Telegraph*, June 21, 1870; "An Act to Incorporate the Gregory Institute of Harris County," in Gammel, *Laws of Texas* 6: 323–24.

12. "The Gregory Institute: It Was the Pioneer School House"; Houston *Times*, January 6, 1870, 4a.

13. Letters from M. E. Davis (sub-assistant commissioner) to Bvt. Capt. C. S. Roberts, dated October 26, November 16, and December 4, 1868, and M. E. Davis, Report for Month Ending November 30, 1868, all in Texas, Freedmen's Bureau Field Office Records, 1865–70, Letters Sent, vol. 5, Microfilm M1912, roll 21, NARA, available on FamilySearch.com.

14. See Joseph Welch to Louis W. Stevenson, July 30 and August 19, 1869, M822, roll 1; and Louis W. Stevenson to Joseph Welch, August 8, 1869 (quote), in Freedmen's Bureau Records of the Superintendent of Education, Texas, Letters Received, S, 1868–70, Microfilm M822, roll 8, NARA. On Allen's building expertise, Pitre, *Through Many Dangers*, 20.

15. "The Gregory Institute: It Was the Pioneer School House for Colored Children." For disbursements to Allen, see E. C. Bartholomew to Richard Allen, October 31 and November 11, 1870, M822, roll 1.

16. Texas Historical Commission historical marker, "Antioch Missionary Baptist Church" (1994).

17. Charles A. Israel, "From Biracial to Segregated Churches: Black and White Protestants in Houston, Texas, 1840–1870," *Southwestern Historical Quarterly* 101, no. 4 (April 1998): 449.

18. Harris County Deed Records, vol. 9B, p. 509; U.S. Census, 1880, Harris County, Enumeration District no. 85, manuscript p. 12.

19. Augustus Koch, *Bird's Eye View of the City of Houston, Texas* (1873), Holcomb Map Collection, GLO 93908.

20. For creation of Fredericks Addition, see Harris County Deed Records, vol. 10, p. 440; vol. 11, p. 832. For lot sales, see vol. 11, p. 474 (Lot 5); vol. 12, p. 76 (Lot 4); vol. 10, p. 954 (Lot 6). For Sallie Wicks and daughter Bettie, see U.S. Census, 1870, Harris County, Harrisburg, manuscript p. 7.

21. Marriage License for S. J. Lenord [*sic*] and Betty Weeks [*sic*], February 24, 1876, no. 5125, Texas, U.S., Select County Marriage Records, 1837–65, on Ancestry.com; "Matrimonial," Houston *Age*, February 26, 1876, 4b; Houston City Directory, 1877–78, 135, 204. For Leonard as an Emancipation Park trustee, see "Report of the Trustees of the Colored People's Park Association, Emancipation Grounds," Houston *Post*, June 29, 1886, 5a; Petition of Colored Emancipation Park Association, March 7, 1892, in Harris Masterson III Papers, MS 470, box 81, folder 4.

22. Henry C. Hardy to Laura F. Shannon, March 4, 1885, Galveston, Texas, County Marriage Index, 1837–1977, on Ancestry.com; Houston City Directory, 1877, p. 164; Harris County Deed Records, vol. 33, p. 391; "Houston Local Items," Galveston *Daily News*, November 8, 1877; Ira B. Bryant Jr., *The Development of the Houston Negro Schools* (Houston: The Informer, [1935]), 10–11.

23. Marriage License for Sandy Parker and Emma McKinney, February 14, 1878, no. 9336, Texas, U.S., Select County Marriage Records, 1837–1965, on Ancestry.com; Houston City Directory, 1887, p. 247; Andrews, Streetman, Logue, & Mobley, "Opinion . . . Re: Title to the Following Tracts of Land Belonging to the Rice Institute," March 16, 1928, p. 11, in Early Land Deeds, UA 222, box 17, folder 26. The "Sandy Parker" who married Emma McKinney was most likely the son or another relative of the Parker who helped to found Antioch; the elder Parker died in 1873. See "Colored Preacher Dead," Houston *Telegraph*, January 9, 1873.

24. Harris County Deed Records, vol. 11, p. 250; "Report of the Trustees of the Colored People's Park Association"; Masterson III Papers, MS 470, box 81, folder 4; Marriage License for Robert Fairchilds and Amanda Williams, April 14, 1868, no. 698, Texas, U.S., Select County Marriage Records, 1837–1965, on Ancestry.com; Robert Childs [*sic*], U.S. Census, 1900, Houston, Harris County, Enumeration District no. 81, sheet 9, family no. 166; "The Bayou City Budget," Galveston *Daily News*, September 14, 1887, 5b (Annie B. Fairchilds teaching at Gregory); "Personal Mention," Houston *Post*, September 14, 1897, 3e (Robert Fairchild Jr. attending Tuskegee); Diana J. Kleiner, "Fairchild, Thornton McNair," *Handbook of Texas Online*.

25. Harris County Deed Records, vol. 119, pp. 273–75; vol. 120, p. 363; vol. 133, p. 627. Andrews, Streetman, Logue, & Mobley, "Opinion . . . Re: Title," pp. 12–13.

26. "The Courts," Galveston *Daily News*, September 22, 1891, 3b; *Bettie Leonard vs. Sam Leonard,*

October 10, 1901, Civil Case File 31267, Harris County District Clerk, Historical Documents Records Center; "Fifty-Fifth Civil District Court," Houston *Post*, June 7, 1899, 6a; Decree File no. 49090, Case no. 24969, entered in Harris County Deed Records, vol. 151, pp. 417–18; Andrews, Streetman, Logue, & Mobley, "Opinion . . . Re: Title."

27. "Republican Senatorial Convention," Houston *Daily Mercury*, October 10, 1873, 4a; "The Gregory Institute: It Was the Pioneer School House"; Ron Bass, "Ancient Order of Pilgrims," *Handbook of Texas Online;* Houston City Directory, 1887, 164; Yates and Yates, *Life and Efforts*, 23.

28. Pitre, *Through Many Dangers*, 29–31; Louis W. Stevenson to J. W. Alvord, June 30, 1870, Freedmen's Bureau Records, M803, roll 31.

29. Stevenson to Alvord, June 30, 1870; Constitution of Texas (1876), article VII, sec. 7.

30. Merline Pitre, "Gregory Institute," *Handbook of Texas Online.*

31. "Colored School Moved," Galveston *Daily News*, April 19, 1893. The high school mentioned later became Booker T. Washington High School. A later iteration of the Gregory eventually reopened at the current location of the African American Library at the Gregory School in Houston. For transfer of land to city for Jefferson Street, see Harris County Deed Records, vol. 80, p. 474.

32. Hall, ed., *William Marsh Rice and His Institute*, 63–65. For Lombardi's oversight of Gregory Institute while with the School Board, see "Colored Teachers Assigned," Galveston *Daily News*, September 13, 1889, 5a. Emanuel Raphael, another of the first Rice Institute trustees, was also a Houston School Board trustee.

33. Hall, ed., *William Marsh Rice and His Institute*, 66–70; Early Land Deeds, UA 222, box 60, folder 6.

34. Rice Institute Board Minutes, vol. 1, pp. 33–34, 44. See also "A Long Council Meeting," Galveston *Daily News*, September 13, 1892; "Houston City Council," Houston *Daily Post*, September 13, 1892.

35. Rice Institute Board Minutes, vol. 1, p. 44 ("under proper regulations"); vol. 1, p. 70 ("keep out trespassers"); vol. 1, pp. 61–63, 213 (fence and trees). Reference to the padlock is later made in A. B. Cohn to James A. Baker, May 4, 1911, Rice Institute Business Manager, UA 353, box 19, folder 3. For copies of the city ordinances granting the board's requests, see ERI, UA 101, box 95, folder 2. For the Rices' own role in selecting and planting trees on the site, see Statement of E. Raphael, ERI, UA 101, box 22, folder 3.

36. Hall, ed., *William Marsh Rice and His Institute*, 74; "The Rice Will Contest," Houston *Daily Post*, March 24, 1897; U.S. Census, 1900, Houston, Harris County, Enumeration District no. 72, sheet 22.

37. Hall, ed., *William Marsh Rice and His Institute*, 75–79.

38. "The Rice Will Contest."

39. Hall, ed., *William Marsh Rice and His Institute*, 87–115.

40. Examination of E. Raphael, December 7, 1899, ERI, UA 101, box 3, folder 3.

41. In 1905, the trustees adopted by-laws to govern their meetings and also sketched out regulations for the Institute's projected library, where admission would be limited "to all white persons over sixteen years of age." William M. Rice Institute for the Advancement of Literature, Science & Art, with Rules and Regulations of the Institute Library, ERI, UA 101, box 95, folder 11.

42. J. J. Pastoriza to Capt. J. A. Baker, October 28, 1905, ERI, UA 101, box 88, folder 8.

43. Rice Institute Board Minutes, vol. 1, p. 196.

44. Andrews, Streetman, Logue, & Mobley, "Opinion . . . Re: Title," p. 14. Records pertaining to Curtin's purchases "for college site purposes" can be found in ERI, UA 101, box 88, folder 8. See also checks conveying money to Curtin for the purchases in Capt. Baker and Rice Institute Papers, UA 200,

box 7, folders 1 and 2. Also see Houston *Chronicle*, June 28, 1905, 3 (Lot 2); *Tom Ewing et al. by Next Friend vs. H. M. Curtin*, 55th District Court, Civil Case File 37760, Harris County District Clerk, Historical Documents Records Center (Lot 7); Houston *Chronicle*, November 27, 1906 (Lots 8 and 9). Pencil sketches showing Curtin's purchases can be found in Early Land Deeds, UA 222, box 59, folder 2.

45. Rice Institute Board Minutes, vol. 2, p. 32; A. B. Cohn to Baker, Botts, Parker & Garwood, March 8, 1909, ERI, UA 101, box 89, folder 6; Houston *Chronicle*, March 16, 1909, 6.

46. For the public record of most of the Curtin purchases, see Rice Institute Board Minutes, vol. 2, p. 105; Harris County Deed Records, vol. 216, pp. 454–59. The board noted that the deeds had not been publicly recorded at first "for obvious reasons."

47. *Bettie Leonard et al. vs H. M. Curtin et al.*, 11th District Court, Civil Case File 48550, Harris County District Clerk, Historical Documents Records Center; Rice Institute Board Minutes, vol. 2, p. 291.

48. Lovett's recollections about his visit, dated July 19, 1944, are in Edgar Odell Lovett Papers, UA 014, box 29, folder 2; Rice Institute Board Minutes, vol. 2, p. 291. See also Letter to Sidney E. Mezes, July 2, 1907, ERI, UA 101, box 88, folder 10; Rice Board to Edgar Odell Lovett, June 11, 1908, UA 101, box 89, folder 3. On Lovett's vision and leadership, see John B. Boles, *University Builder: Edgar Odell Lovett and the Founding of the Rice Institute* (Baton Rouge: Louisiana State University Press, 2007).

49. Dylan Penningroth, *Before the Movement: The Hidden History of Black Civil Rights* (New York: Liveright, 2023).

50. *Leonard et al. vs Curtin et al.*

51. For the opening ceremony, see Meiners, *History of Rice University*, 1–10; Boles, *University Builder*, 100–107.

52. Correspondence and contracts pertaining to shows and circuses on the property can be found in Rice Institute Business Manager Papers, UA 353, box 19, folders 3–5. See also examples of ads for the circus on the "Rice Institute Grounds Back of Baseball Park" (a reference to the adjacent West End Ballpark) in Houston *Post*, September 25, 1910, 43; October 26, 1912, 4.

53. A. B. Cohn to Baker, Botts, Parker & Garwood, March 10, 1913, UA 353, box 19, folder 3. For the pitch, see Adolph Boldt to Capt. James A. Baker, September 9, 1912, Rice Institute Business Manager Papers, UA 353, box 19, folder 3. For notes about the board's discussion, which also mentioned the suit by the "colored people," see writing on Adolph Boldt to E. Raphael, February 19, 1913, UA 353, box 19, folder 3. For a sketch of the proposed playground, see Early Land Deeds, UA 122, drawer 129.

54. For correspondence on the Taylor School and YMCA, as well as proposals from other parties to use the property, see UA 353, box 19; UA 101, box 91, folder 1. Originally the lots purchased by Curtin were considered for the Taylor School, but in the end it was built on the northern part of the property. See Early Rice Land Deeds, UA 222, box 15, folder 21; Rice Institute Board Minutes, vol. 3, p. 89; Early Land Deeds, UA 222, drawer 13, folder 3.

55. Handwritten note by A. B. Cohn to Baker, February 1917, UA 353, box 19, folder 3. The resulting leases with the YMCA appear in folder 5.

56. "Our City," Houston *Chronicle*, November 23, 1923, 1; Casey Greene, "Guardians Against Change: The Ku Klux Klan in Houston and Harris County, 1920–1925," *Houston Review* 10, no. 1 (1988): 3–20. See also Ku Klux Klan in Texas Papers, MS 727.

57. Greene, "Guardians Against Change," 11, 14. On the Klan's political activities in Texas, see Charles C. Alexander, *Crusade for Conformity: The Ku Klux Klan in Texas, 1920–1930* ([Houston?]: Texas Gulf Historical Association, 1962). For Jones's relationship with the Bakers, see Kirkland, *Captain James A. Baker*, 217, 274, 305–7.

58. J. S. Cullinan to Frank Andrews, Chairman, Rice Institute Student Loan Fund, November 1, 1922, box 32, folder 12, Joseph S. Cullinan Papers, University of Houston. The same folder contains the letter from the Student Loan Fund to Cullinan requesting a donation; it lists all the members of the fund committee on letterhead. For Blayney's opposition, see Thomas Lindsey Blayney Papers, MS 064, box 5, folder 9.

59. Newspaper clippings about Autry's funeral are in a scrapbook kept by his sister Allie May Autry, also an alumna, in Alumni Scrapbooks, UA 230; the Klan photo is in Rice *Campanile 1922*. Autry's mother was a prominent donor who had endowed the recently opened Autry House, which served for many years as a student center. For Cullinan's distress about Autry's funeral, see Cullinan to W. W. Moore, September 27, 1922, Cullinan Papers, box 32, folder 12. In an article in *Colonel Mayfield's Weekly*, January 21, 1922, 3, Mayfield described a meeting (possibly fabricated) between himself, Lovett, and Baker to ask why campus construction was stalled. On Mayfield's boosterism for Rice football, which included hosting a dance for the team in 1921, see *RT*, October 7, 1921, 3; November 18, 1921, 1; *Campanile 1924*. References to the Klan publication, some of them critical and parodic, appeared periodically in both the yearbook and the student newspaper. On Munn and Bryan, see Greene, "Guardians Against Change," 9.

60. H. H. Collins to James A. Baker, November 3, 1923, Rice Institute Business Manager Papers, UA 353, box 19, folder 4.

61. Linda Gordon, *The Second Coming of the KKK: The Ku Klux Klan of the 1920s and the American Political Tradition* (New York: Liveright, 2017); Greene, "Guardians Against Change," 11–13. The Klan's letter to Baker also arrived just a week before the group entered a controversial float in the city's annual Armistice Day parade. See "Our City," Houston *Chronicle*, November 12, 1923, 1; Greene, "Guardians Against Change," 8.

62. W. C. Paige to James A. Baker, November 9, 1923, and James A. Baker to A. B. Cohn, November 9, 1923, both in Rice Institute Business Manager Papers, UA 353, box 19, folder 4. The president of the YMCA at the time was Baker's close business associate William A. Wilson. For Abilene, see Jason Fikes, "Jesse P. Sewell, White Supremacy, and the Formative Years of Abilene Christian College," *Restoration Quarterly* 64, no. 3 (2022): 170–81.

63. Business manager A. B. Cohn's initial response to Collins on November 9 told him not to depend on the use of the grounds because several trustees were out of town, and the group would probably not be able to reach a quorum until after he needed an answer. Baker instructed Cohn on the same day that, "if there is to be no meeting [of the trustees] next week, I suggest that you see them individually and advise" the YMCA president on the Institute's position. Cohn was on jury duty that week and passed the file on to an assistant, J. A. Flick. On November 13, Flick was instructed by trustee A. S. Cleveland to contact fellow trustees Benjamin B. Rice and John T. Scott and ask them to meet at Scott's office the next day to discuss the matter. Flick noted being told "that Capt. Baker cannot attend & for me not to call Capt. Baker." (E. A. Peden and WMR Jr. were out of town, while Edgar Odell Lovett was just returning to town.) The trio decided to wait until Rice Junior's return for another conference on the subject. On November 16, a Klan representative wrote Baker again to say they were still waiting on a response; Baker directed the letter to Cohn with a note: "lets answer these people please." Cohn replied that he was waiting to hear back from B. B. Rice, who finally made the call to Murray Jones on the 19th. Rice's message to Jones is recorded in Cohn's handwritten note dated "11/19/23" in Rice Institute Business Manager Papers, UA 353, box 19, folder 4. See also Flick's handwritten note dated "11/13/23"; Cohn's undated "Memorandum in re Application for Use of Rice Institute Grounds on Louisiana Street"; Cohn to H. H. Collins, November 9, 1923; James A. Baker to Cohn, November 9, 1923; and L. A. Hartwig to

James A. Baker, November 16, 1923, all in Rice Institute Business Manager Papers, UA 353, box 19, folder 4. There was no mention of the Klan circus in the official minutes of the board, which met formally on November 28. Another off-the-record meeting of the trustees was apparently held on November 21, because Lovett informed Rice Jr. he would not be able to attend, though the topic of this meeting is unknown. (See Lovett to Rice Jr., November 20, 1923, Lovett Papers, box 35, folder 7.) But in a letter about an unrelated matter that December, Cohn noted the lengths to which trustees usually went to act in concert: "the success of the Institute's financial operations has been in a great measure due to the fact that every transaction is unanimously approved by the Trustees. When there is any objection made to any transaction, regardless of the minority, the business is declined." Cohn to Clarence R. Wharton, December 3, 1923, UA 353, box 22, folder 3.

64. "Huge Crowd at Opening of Klan Circus," Houston *Post*, November 23, 1923, 20. See also "Our City," Houston *Chronicle*, November 27, 1923, 1a–b; "Bring One Friend into the Klan," *Colonel Mayfield's Weekly*, December 8, 1923, 4b. Ads for the circus appeared in the Houston *Post*, November 27, 1923, 18; *Colonel Mayfield's Weekly*, November 17, 1923, 4.

65. Death Certificate for Robert Shaw, January 27, 1917, Texas, U.S., Death Certificates, 1908–82, on Ancestry.com; Andrews, Streetman, Logue, & Mobley, "Opinion . . . Re: Title," pp. 8–9, 12–14; Affidavit by A. B. Cohn, June 21, 1928, Early Land Deeds, UA 222, box 13, folder 17; *Leonard et al. vs. Curtin et al.*; U.S. Census, 1920, Harris County, Houston, Ward 4, Enumeration District no. 69, sheet 7B; Rice Institute Board Minutes, vol. 3, p. 381. The board appropriated the money for "the future purchase" of Leonard's and Shaw's land at the same time, though those purchases were not completed until later.

66. Death Certificate for Bettie Leonard, March 4, 1925, Texas, U.S., Death Certificates, 1908–82, on Ancestry.com; April 10, 1925, Rice Institute Board Minutes, vol. 5, p. 53. The cause of death in Leonard's certificate was pneumonia from "cold & exposure," and Olivewood is listed as the place of burial. Olivewood Cemetery is currently being restored, operated, and maintained by Descendants of Olivewood, a 501(c)3 organization that also maintains a database of burials, only some of which are still marked, at www.descendantsofolivewood.org. The tombstone for Leonard's mother, Sally Wicks, is one of the markers that has survived.

67. Kirkland, *Captain James A. Baker*, 294–304; Stephen Fox, "Public Art and Private Places: Shadyside," *Houston Review* 2 (Winter 1980): 39–60; Stephen Fox, *The Country Houses of John F. Staub* (College Station: Texas A&M University Press, 2007), 1–66; Marguerite Johnston, *Houston: The Unknown City, 1836–1946* (College Station: Texas A&M University Press, 1991), 188–95, 227–33; Sallie Gordon and Penny Jones, *Houston's Courtlandt Place* (Charleston, SC: Arcadia Publishing, 2009); Margaret Culbertson, "Discrete Duplexes: Houston's Sunset Boulevard Double Houses," *Cite* 95 (Fall 2014), hdl.handle.net/1911/117074.

68. David G. McComb, *Houston: The Bayou City* (Austin: University of Texas Press, 1969), 139–41; Kate Sayen Kirkland, *The Hogg Family and Houston: Philanthropy and the Civic Ideal* (Austin: University of Texas Press, 2009), 56–57. On Blayney's role, see "City Planning Commission Is Being Chosen," *RT*, November 3, 1922; "Commission to Plan Houston of Future," Houston *Post*, June 28, 1922. See also "Engineers Meet to Hear Talk on Planning Cities," *RT*, October 10, 1924. On American planners' interest in German cities, see Daniel T. Rodgers, *Atlantic Crossings: Social Politics in a Progressive Age* (Cambridge, MA: Harvard University Press, 1998).

69. Kirkland, *Hogg Family and Houston*, chap. 2; Kirkland, *Captain James A. Baker*, chap. 6; Stephen Fox, "Planning in Houston: A Historic Overview," *Cite* 11 (1985), hdl.handle.net/1911/115801; Archie Henderson, "City Planning in Houston, 1920–1930," *Houston Review* 9, no. 3 (1987): 107–36.

70. *Report of the City Planning Commission, Houston, Texas* (Houston: Forum of Civics, 1929). Physical copies of *Civics for Houston* (1928–29) can be found in WRC. On Ryon's hiring by Hogg's commission, see W. C. Hogg telegram to Edgar Odell Lovett, October 27, 1927, William Clifford Hogg Papers, Briscoe Center for American History, University of Texas at Austin, City Planning, 1927, box 2J299.

71. N. D. B. Connolly, *A World More Concrete: Real Estate and the Remaking of Jim Crow South Florida* (Chicago: University of Chicago Press, 2014); Thomas W. Hanchett, *Sorting Out the New South City: Race, Class, and Urban Development in Charlotte, 1875–1975* (Chapel Hill: University of North Carolina Press, 1998).

72. Arthur Coleman Comey, *Houston: Tentative Plans for its Development* (Boston: George H. Ellis, 1913), 14–17. For the 1924 map, see Hogg Papers, box 2J339.

73. S. Herbert Hare to W. C. Hogg, May 28, 1929, in Hogg Papers, City Planning, 1928–30, box 2J300; W. C. Hogg to S. Herbert Hare, May 25, 1929, Hogg Papers, City Planning, 1928–30, box 2J300; Kirkland, *Hogg Family and Houston*, 64–65.

74. See note to "DMP" in Hogg Papers, City Planning, box 2J299; Ryon to F. W. Turner, June 22, 1929, Hogg Papers, City Planning, 1928–30, box 2J300. On urban planners' turn towards restrictive covenants after court decisions against racial zoning, see David M. P. Freund, *Colored Property: State Policy and White Racial Politics in Suburban America* (Chicago: University of Chicago Press, 2007), chap. 2.

75. *Report of the City Planning Commission* (1929), 25–28. See also letters on maps by L. B. Ryon Jr. in Hogg Papers, City Planning, 1928, box 2J300.

76. Rice Institute Board Minutes, vol. 5, p. 53; Andrews, Streetman, Logue, & Mobley, "Opinion . . . Re: Title," pp. 8–9.

77. For the sale to HISD, see Rice Institute Board Minutes, vol. 5, p. 320; Early Land Deeds, UA 222, box 17, folder 26. On the junior colleges, see also L. B. Ryon Jr., "1836–Houston–1928," in *The Book of Houston, U.S.A., in the Year 1928* ([Houston]: [Lion's Club], 1928?), 7.

78. Pitre, *Born to Serve*, 4–11; Bryant, *Development of the Houston Negro Schools*, 197–218. Before becoming the Houston College for Negroes, the segregated school was also known as the Houston Colored Junior College.

79. See Robert K. Nelson et al., "Mapping Inequality: Redlining in New Deal America," dsl.richmond.edu/panorama/redlining/ (accessed August 22, 2022); Richard Rothstein, *The Color of Law: A Forgotten History of How our Government Segregated America* (New York: Liveright, 2017); Wining and Michney, "Roots of Redlining"; Todd M. Michney, "How the City Survey's Redlining Maps Were Made: A Closer Look at HOLC's Mortgagee Rehabilitation Division," *Journal of Planning History* 21, no. 4 (November 2022): 316–44; Susan Rogers, "Hazardous: The Redlining of Houston Neighborhoods," *Rice Design Alliance*, October 4, 2016, www.ricedesignalliance.org/hazardous-the-redlining-of-houston-neighborhoods.

80. Ponton, "Criminalizing Space."

4. Being Black at the Rice Institute

1. "'Larnin' am a Fine Thing' Declares Old Negro Mammy Who 'Washes De Rice Boys,'" *RT*, November 29, 1923, 3d. More information on Pettit can be found in episode 11 of the Doc Talks podcast produced by the task force. It features research by Giovanna M. Bassi Cendra on Pettit's life and a look at census records about her. Because Pettit's name is spelled with three "t's" in the census, we prefer that spelling here over the one in the *Thresher*.

2. "Sports" section in Rice *Campanile 1926*.

3. "'Larnin' am a Fine Thing.'" The same yearbook that described Shelton as "almost as permanent as the Institute" added that "No one knows exactly when old 'Nigger' first came to Rice." See *Campanile 1926*.

4. "'Larnin' am a Fine Thing'"; "Trainer," Rice *Campanile 1924*.

5. Paul Laurence Dunbar (1872–1906), "We Wear the Mask," poets.org/poem/we-wear-mask.

6. William Ward Watkin to J. T. McCants, December 21, 1918, William Ward Watkin Papers, MS 352, box 9, folder 7; Cohen House Papers, UA 128, box 1 and box 15, folders 3–5; Additions to Cohen House, February 27, 1958, UA 128, drawer 15, item 55.

7. See, from Rice Institute Business Manager Papers, UA 353, box 19: A. B. Cohn to D. D. McClung, April 15, 1912, folder 3; Cohn to C. E. Elliott, June 9, 1911, folder 3; Cohn to City of Houston Water Department, March 8, 1910, folder 10.

8. "Aged Negro Mammy is Claimed by Death," Houston *Post-Dispatch*, June 14, 1928, 7.

9. In February 1921, an African American newspaper, the Houston *Informer*, skewered eulogies similar to Baker's in its regular column called "Cimbee's Ramblings," in which a fictional Black migrant to Houston observes the city, using dialect in this case for satirical effect. Cimbee tells of visiting a Black Baptist church to hear a white preacher: "Lawdy, fokes, dat w'ite man sho' 'spounded de Gospil in grate stile, but sum how er nuther my old mine kep' runnin' back ter fo' de war w'en gospel peddlers useter say ter me an' my feller servants, 'Servants obey yo masters.' An' sho' nuff, fo' he got thru wid dat exerlunt diskose he gin ter minchun his ole 'black mammy,' an' dat jes settled it." See Houston *Informer*, February 26, 1921, 4. For more on "Cimbee's Ramblings," see Tyina L. Steptoe, *Houston Bound: Culture and Color in a Jim Crow City* (Berkeley: University of California Press, 2016), 45–49. Cf. Baker's later eulogy to another Black domestic worker in his household, Mackie Baker: "Long-Time Houston Resident Expires; Paid Lofty Tribute," Houston *Informer*, June 1, 1940, 3. Delivered before a crowd of mourners at Mackie Baker's funeral at Antioch Baptist Church, this later remembrance also referred back to "'Aunt Mary' of blessed memory, whom you knew as Mary King." King's tombstone in College Memorial Park Cemetery was inscribed by her son, John F. B. Johnson, "To My Dear Mother Mrs. Mary King."

10. See Kirkland, *Captain James A. Baker*, 49–55; Olivier Péloquin, "Captain Baker, Rice Institute and the Promise of a 'New Texas': From the Texas Military Institute to the Houston Light Guard" (2021), Task Force Records, UA 421, Series B.

11. John Garland James, *The Southern Student's Hand-Book of Selections for Reading and Oratory* (New Orleans: Lathrop and Wilkins, 1879), 50, 128, 245. See also Rod Andrew Jr., "Soldiers, Christians, and Patriots: The Lost Cause and Southern Military Schools, 1865–1915," *Journal of Southern History* 64, no. 4 (November 1998): 677–710.

12. Kirkland, *Captain James A. Baker*, 57–59. On the Light Guard, see Bruce A. Olson, "The Houston Light Guards: A Case Study of the Texas Militia, 1873–1903," MA thesis, University of Houston, 1985; Olson, "The Houston Light Guards: Elite Cohesion and Social Order in the New South, 1873–1940," PhD diss., University of Houston, 1989.

13. Olson, "The Houston Light Guards: Elite Cohesion and Social Order," 142–46. The tombstone still stands at Sessums's grave in College Memorial Park Cemetery, where a state historical marker was erected to Sessums in 2009.

14. See Micki McElya, *Clinging to Mammy: The Faithful Slave in Twentieth-Century America* (Cambridge, MA: Harvard University Press, 2007); Kimberly Wallace-Sanders, *Mammy: A Century of Race, Gender, and Southern Memory* (Ann Arbor: University of Michigan Press, 2008); Grace Elizabeth Hale, *Making Whiteness: The Culture of Segregation, 1890–1940* (New York: Vintage Books, 1998), chaps. 2 and

3; Donald Yacovone, *Teaching White Supremacy: America's Democratic Ordeal and the Forging of Our National Identity* (New York: Pantheon, 2022).

15. See J. A. Flick to Old Reliable Virginia Minstrels, April 3, 1924, Rice Institute Business Manager Papers, UA 353, box 18, folder 4. On the long tradition of blackface in American popular culture, see Patricia A. Turner, *Ceramic Uncles and Celluloid Mammies: Black Images and Their Influence on Culture* (New York: Anchor Books, 1994); Marilyn Kern-Foxworth, *Aunt Jemima, Uncle Ben, and Rastus: Blacks in Advertising, Yesterday, Today, and Tomorrow* (Westport, CT: Greenwood Press, 1994); Stephen Johnson, ed., *Burnt Cork: Traditions and Legacies of Blackface Minstrelsy* (Amherst: University of Massachusetts Press, 2012); Brian Roberts, *Blackface Nation: Race, Reform, and Identity in American Popular Music, 1812–1925* (Chicago: University of Chicago Press, 2017).

16. "Boat Ride Greatly Enjoyed," *RT*, April 20, 1917; "Sophs Give Annual Boating Down Bayou," *RT*, May 25, 1918; "Society" section, *Campanile 1919*.

17. "Seniors Present Historic Tableaux," *RT*, June 12, 1916; "Holiday Set for Confederate Day," *RT*, October 8, 1920; "Reception of the Confederate Veterans at the Institute at Six O'Clock, Friday Afternoon, October Eighth," Lovett Papers, UA 014, box 14, folder 10; "Reunion Hostesses Meet at Rice and Organize for Duty," Houston *Post*, September 22, 1920; "Michigan Professor to Lecture Tuesday," *RT*, January 28, 1927; Brenham *Banner-Press*, February 8, 1927. Phillips was introduced by Rice history professor and dean R. G. Caldwell. See "Michigan Prof Lectures at Rice," Houston *Post-Dispatch*, February 2, 1927; Announcement Poster, Lovett Papers, UA 014, box 14, folder 10. On Lovett's father-in-law, Henry S. Hale (1836–1922) of Kentucky, note Boles, *University Builder*, 154, 168.

18. "Alpha Rho Dance," *RT*, December 3, 1920; "Alpha Rho Dance," *Campanile 1921;* "Hundreds at First Annual OWLS Dance: Plantation Theme with Rare Lighting Effect Adds Scenic Beauty," *RT*, November 29, 1929. For other examples of racialized dances, see (among others) "Jelly Roll Rogers to Play for PALS Dance Tonight," *RT*, March 31, 1933; "The Archi-Arts Ball," *Campanile 1936*, 144; "Final Plans Made for Bond Dance," *RT*, May 7, 1943; "Guaya-Guayere is Archi-Arts Title This Time," *RT*, April 12, 1945.

19. "Writing Club Meets," *RT*, April 1, 1921; "Writing Club Shows Degeneration; Lack of Manuscripts Felt," *RT*, December 9, 1927. For examples of racist caricatures, see, in general, the *Rice Owl*, a student publication from this period. See also "Monroe's First Trip to the City," *RT*, April 2, 1926, 6b. On colleges and racist performance, see Stephen M. Monroe, *Heritage and Hate: Old South Rhetoric at Southern Universities* (Tuscaloosa: University of Alabama Press, 2021); *After Emancipation*, ed. Von Daacke and Douglas, 35–45.

20. "Rice Senior Girls to Be Honor Guests at College Woman's Minstrel," *RT*, January 28, 1921; "The May Fete," *Campanile 1931;* "Dramatic Club Presentations Great Success," *RT*, February 9, 1923. See also "Junior Minstrels" photograph in *Campanile 1916;* "Tickets for Play are Now on Sale," *RT*, January 26, 1923; "Dramatic Club Gives Plays for the Winter Term," *RT*, January 19, 1923. For more on women and blackface at the Rice Institute, see Emily Lampert, "By Girls and For Girls: Women's Community and Racialized Performance in the Early Years of the Rice Institute," *Southwestern Historical Quarterly* 128, no. 3 (January 2025): 240–61.

21. "Dramatic Club Presents 'Rose of the Southland,'" *RT*, December 1, 1933, 1b; "Is the Civil War Over?" *RT*, November 3, 1933. Cf. Boles, *University Builder*, 198–99. The script for the play shows that "Mammy Evelina" delivered all her lines in a thick dialect common to minstrelsy. See Marion Short, *Rose of the Southland: A Comedy in Three Acts* (New York: Samuel French, 1924).

22. "Dramatic Club Presents 'Rose of the Southland.'"

23. *RI: Rice Institute Magazine* (May 1950), 8.

24. See "The Rack" section, *Campanile 1926;* "Athletimania" on page 16 of "The Nuyjoyle" section, *Campanile 1931.*

25. "Wild Scenes at Pre-Law Banquet," *RT,* November 16, 1928.

26. Ibid.; "Prom Pointers," *RT,* March 2, 1928, 2, 8.

27. "President Edgar O. Lovett's '35 Matriculation Address," *RT,* October 4, 1935, 2–3. Lovett did not regularly make use of racial slurs in his formal public addresses, which were on the whole remarkable for their eloquence, ecumenism, and erudition. But there is also evidence that, like many other orators at the time, he sometimes reached for coarse racial humor or dialect to make points or engage a receptive audience. See Lovett Papers, MS 014, box 49, folder 2; box 53, folders 34 and 39.

28. Beeville *Bee,* December 31, 1897. Historical markers for two Black churches and the Lott-Canada School, started in 1876, were erected in Beeville in the early 2000s. Rice University alumnus Leon Best Jr. (Class of 2001) has traced the genealogy of Shelton's ancestors back to their enslavement on a Goliad plantation owned by Thomas P. C. Lott, who also enslaved Best's own ancestors. Email correspondence from Leon Best to Caleb McDaniel, March 1, 2024.

29. Beeville, Bee County, Texas, U.S. Census, 1900; Arnoldo De León, *They Called Them Greasers: Anglo Attitudes toward Mexicans in Texas, 1821–1900* (Austin: University of Texas Press, 1983), 94–95. On Black migration to Houston, see Bernadette Pruitt, *The Other Great Migration: The Movement of Rural African Americans to Houston, 1900–1941* (College Station: Texas A&M University Press, 2013); Steptoe, *Houston Bound.* Circumstances leading to Shelton's divorce are summarized in *Jack Shelton v. Lula Shelton* (1905), Civil Case no. 36502, Eleventh District Court, Harris County District Clerk, Historical Documents Records Center.

30. Some later accounts of Shelton's time at Rice dated his career to 1912 or 1913, but others, including Shelton himself, told the story of Arbuckle coming to Lunn's after a loss to Texas A&M, which first played Rice in 1914, soundly beating the Institute team. See "Nigger Jack Rests and Remembers," *RT,* April 22, 1932, 4. Dr. Lunn's son later graduated from the Rice Institute in 1920, leaving behind a diary about his student days. See Edwin N. Lunn World War I Diary, MS 283.

31. *RT,* November 15, 1916, 1.

32. Shelton appears in the *Campanile* with the track team in 1916, with the football team in 1918 and 1919, and with the basketball team in 1919 and 1920, along with other appearances in campus photo collages.

33. "Trainer Jack Leaves the Institute," *RT,* January 7, 1921, 1a; *RT,* January 28, 1921, 1a; *Campanile 1921.* On Shelton's working space in the field house, see also "New Field House Nears Completion," *RT,* September 17, 1920, 1c. While the exact nature of the difficulties that led to Shelton's brief resignation is unclear, the *Thresher* seemed to trace them to disputes over Shelton's workload, possibly connected with the new field house. In reporting the settlement of the dispute, the paper noted: "He will serve only as the official rubber and field man now, other help having been secured to assist in the gymnasium." "Disagreements as to his duties" would sometimes return in later years; according to some stories, he protested whenever Tony Martino and his landscaping crew came onto the athletic fields, which Shelton regarded, literally, as his turf.

34. "Coaches" section, *Campanile 1923;* "Football" section, *Campanile 1922.*

35. Houston City Directory, 1912, p. 622; Houston City Directory, 1913, p. 749. Both directories still listed Shelton as an employee at Lunn's sanitarium. Not until 1918 was he identified as a "lab[orer] Rice Inst." See Houston City Directory, 1918, p. 865. Thanks to undergraduate researcher Kennedi Macklin for locating Shelton in these sources.

36. Jack Shelton and Estelle Francis Taylor, February 12, 1917, Texas, U.S., Select County Marriage Records, 1837–1965, on Ancestry.com; "Antioch Auxiliaries," Houston *Informer*, July 26, 1919.

37. *The Red Book of Houston: A Compendium of Social, Professional, Religious, Educational and Industrial Interests of Houston's Colored Population* (Houston: Sotex Publishing Co., 1915).

38. For records of Shelton's salary, which was apparently paid by the Athletic Association, see budgets and notes in Bursar Records, UA 21, box 2, folders 1–4; box 3, folder 4. His annual pay through the 1920s was usually around $1,100. On life for Black Houstonians in the Jim Crow era, see Cary D. Wintz, "Blacks," in *The Ethnic Groups of Houston*, ed. Fred R. von der Mehden (Houston: Rice University Studies, 1984), 19–32; Steptoe, *Houston Bound*.

39. Steptoe, *Houston Bound*, 31–34; Adriane Lentz-Smith, *Freedom Struggles: African Americans and World War I* (Cambridge, MA: Harvard University Press, 2009), 43–79; Adam J. Hodges, "Urban Policing and Race Riots in the Era of World War I and the Red Summer," in *The Routledge History of Police Brutality in America*, ed. Thomas Aiello (New York: Routledge, 2023), 49–60.

40. On the Black soldiers' reception in Houston, see Pruitt, *The Other Great Migration*, 142–44; Chad Williams, *Torchbearers of Democracy: African American Soldiers in the World War I Era* (Chapel Hill: University of North Carolina Press, 2010), 32–33.

41. C. Calvin Smith, "The Houston Riot of 1917, Revisited," *Houston Review* 13, no. 2 (1991): 85–102.

42. W. E. B. Du Bois, *Darkwater: Voices from within the Veil* (1920; New York: Dover, 1999), 138–39; Martha Gruenig, "Houston: An N.A.A.C.P. Investigation," in *Jim Crow: Voices from a Century of Struggle, Part 1: 1876–1919*, ed. Tyina Steptoe (New York: Library of America, 2024), 544. See also Chad Williams, *The Wounded World: W. E. B. Du Bois and the First World War* (New York: Farrar, Straus, and Giroux, 2023).

43. Gruenig, "Houston," 554; Pruitt, *The Other Great Migration*, chap. 4; Steptoe, *Houston Bound*, chap. 1; U.S. Army Public Affairs, "Army Sets Aside Convictions of 110 Black Soldiers Convicted in 1917 Houston Riots," November 13, 2023, www.army.mil/article/271614/ (accessed August 25, 2024). See also "We Apologize for Editorials on Houston's Deadly 1917 Riots (Editorial)," Houston *Chronicle*, December 10, 2023.

44. Jack Shelton, serial no. 1909, order no. 2030, in U.S., World War I Draft Registration Cards, 1917–18, on Ancestry.com. His address in the draft registration is listed as 1014 Howe St., but in the 1918 and 1919 city directories, Shelton is listed as a renter at 1106 Sherman. According to the 1920 Census, he later owned that house. See also a letter by the Rice Bursar to A. B. Cohn, January 23, 1924, UA 353, box 10, folder 7.

45. For a map of the path the marchers took, see Mike Tolson, "The Ugly History of Camp Logan," Houston *Chronicle*, August 19, 2017; Robert V. Haynes, *A Night of Violence: The Houston Riot of 1917* (Baton Rouge: Louisiana State University Press, 1976).

46. *RT*, September 29, 1917, 1d; October 13, 1917, 1d. Rice football played two games against Camp Logan squads the following fall as well.

47. Albert Guérard, *Personal Equation* (New York: W. W. Norton, 1948), 226–33, qtd. on 231. Though Guérard's recollections spent several pages criticizing the racism he had observed in Houston, his memoir also included stereotypical memories of a Black family that had worked in his own house. "The matriarch, old Lou, born in slavery, illiterate, was in bearing, speech and soul a true aristocrat," he said (230). His remembrances of her daughters were far less positive. For more on Guérard, see Boles, *University Builder*, 162–65. For a more recent consideration of American race relations as a caste system, see Isabel Wilkerson, *Caste: The Origins of Our Discontents* (New York: Random House, 2020).

48. These mock elections were sometimes even reported in the city press. See "Jack Shelton to Again Lead Slime Class at Institute," Houston *Chronicle*, September 23, 1919, 5; "Trainer 'Chosen' Freshman Leader," Houston *Chronicle*, September 19, 1920, 46. Shelton was also named the mock editor-in-chief of the *Thresher* for its fake "freshman" issue on April 8, 1920.

49. *Campanile 1926*.

50. Steptoe, *Houston Bound*, 42–43.

51. John A. Kirk, *Winthrop Rockefeller: From New Yorker to Arkansawyer, 1912–1956* (Fayetteville: University of Arkansas Press, 2022), 78–80. Our thanks to John A. Kirk for identifying the professor as Slaughter in email correspondence.

52. "Werlin Writes of 'Democracy, Rice and Chicago University,'" *RT*, February 27, 1925; "P. V. Squad at Game," Houston *Informer*, November 21, 1925; "Convention Rodeo," Houston *Informer*, June 23, 1928.

53. L. B. Ryon Jr. to W. C. Hogg, July 5, 1927, Hogg Papers, City Planning, 1927, box 2J299; Minutes of the Meeting of the Inter-Racial Committee Held at 8:00 P.M. November 10, 1927, and L. B. Ryon Jr. to Will C. Hogg, April 26, 1928, both in Hogg Papers, box 2J399; "The Mirror," Houston *Informer*, December 24, 1927.

54. *Civics for Houston* 1, no. 7 (August 1928).

55. Ibid.; "Houston's Colored Citizens," Houston *Informer*, September 15, 1928.

56. For the Lovett-Washington-Scott correspondence, see Lovett Papers, UA 14, box 4. On Scott, see Maceo C. Dailey, *Emmett J. Scott: Power Broker of the Tuskegee Machine* (Lubbock: Texas Tech University Press, 2023). For quotes from Washington, see "Address at the Atlanta Exposition, September 18, 1895," in *Jim Crow*, ed. Steptoe, 197–201.

57. Pruitt, *The Other Great Migration*, 132–36, 178–80, 356n148; Stephen A. Berrey, *The Jim Crow Routine: Everyday Performances of Race, Civil Rights, and Segregation in Mississippi* (Chapel Hill: University of North Carolina Press, 2015).

58. "Under the X-Ray," Houston *Gargoyle* 2, no. 33 (August 11, 1929), 6, 25. For Richardson's reply, see Houston *Informer*, August 24, 1929, 8. The details of the controversy can be found in the Houston Negro Hospital Digital Collection at the University of Houston, digitalcollections.lib.uh.edu/collections/gx41mk642. See also a potentially related editorial in the June 23, 1929, issue of the *Gargoyle* by Hubert Roussel headlined "Lifting the Rice Taboo." Roussel argued against a frequent perception that the Rice Institute was "aloof" to Houston concerns by pointing to men like Slaughter, Ryon, and Axson. For more on Slaughter, see George Huang, "Eugenicist J. W. Slaughter: His Legacy at the Rice Institute, Houston, and Beyond" (2020), Task Force Records, UA 421.

59. Du Bois, *Darkwater*, 130–31. Line breaks in the original have been removed.

60. "Said The," *RT*, December 7, 1923; *Campanile 1922; Campanile 1923*. The same group may or may not have been responsible for "the little Ku Klux drama" that later took place at the homecoming football game in 1922, which the *Campanile* described as an entertaining stunt that "caused a deal of merriment in the stands." But the *Thresher* report on the stunt at the game attributed it to a group of freshmen, who would not have been present at Rice when the earlier photo was taken. See "Rice Owls Close Football Season in Great Style," *RT*, December 8, 1922. Previous interpreters have sometimes concluded that the 1922 photo of the Rice Ku Klux Klan was a spoof of some sort. Yet the robes worn in the photo appear to be the same as those manufactured by the national Klan at the time. The photo is credited to "A. Klucker," the same signature that appears on contemporary photos taken of large Houston Klan events off campus. Also see discussion of local Klan activity in chapter 3. We thank Fabiola López-Durán for first

identifying the field house as the building in the background of the photo. For similar Klan activities on other campuses in this period, see *The Legacy of Slavery at Harvard: Report and Recommendations of the Presidential Committee* (Cambridge, MA: Harvard University Press, 2022), 95; *After Emancipation*, ed. Von Daacke and Douglas, 65–78; Katherine J. Lennard, "Brother Dixon: College Fraternities and the Ku Klux Klan," *Journal of the Civil War Era* 14, no. 1 (March 2024): 58–89.

61. For "Koo Klucks," see "Kidnappers are Komrades of Koo Klucks," *RT*, November 25, 1921. See also "Girls Had Good Time at P.A.L.'s Circus Tuesday," *RT*, September 30, 1921; "Rice Women Remove Lid Wednesday," *RT*, November 10, 1922. For quote about Shelton, see *Campanile 1924*.

62. "Trainer Jack Leaves the Institute" ("all the gaff"); *RT*, January 28, 1921 ("dusky smile").

63. "Rice Field Turf Best in Conference," *RT*, October 7, 1932, 7c; "'Nigger Jack' Proud of His Well-Kept Football Field," *RT*, October 27, 1923, 3b.

64. "Looking 'Em Over with Lloyd Gregory," Houston *Post-Dispatch*, November 15, 1931.

65. See "Jack Shelton" and "A Student's Tribute," *RT*, October 22, 1937, 2a; "'Nigger Jack's' Death Saddens Owl Gridmen," Houston *Post-Dispatch*, October 16, 1937; "Hundreds of Athletes Saddened by News of 'N–– Jack's' Death," Houston *Chronicle*, October 16, 1937, 10; "Press Box," Houston *Chronicle*, October 17, 1937, 55, and October 31, 1937, 57.

66. Houston *Post-Dispatch*, January 22, 1928, 13, 14. In a photo collage in *Campanile 1936*, a photo of Shelton captioned "Nigger Jack" is placed next to a photo of the band on the football field captioned "Oh, for Rice's Honor!" In 1933, alumni even advocated for the reinstatement of "'Nigger Jack,' one of Rice's few traditional figures," as an athletic trainer, in order to combat what they viewed as a decline in school spirit. See *RT*, December 22, 1933.

67. "Nigger Jack," *RT*, April 26, 1929; "Races Cement Ties at Funeral of Drummer" and "Cimbee's Ramblings," Houston *Informer*, July 14, 1928.

68. "'Nigger Jack' Rice Trainer for 20 Years," Houston *Chronicle*, October 22, 1933, 18; "Jack Shelton," *RT*, October 22, 1937.

69. Kurt Edward Kemper, *College Football and American Culture in the Cold War Era* (Urbana: University of Illinois Press, 2009), 120–22; Monroe, *Heritage and Hate*, 143–54; Evin Demirel, "The Most Loyal Tiger of Them All," *Slate*, November 2, 2018, slate.com/culture/2018/11/wash-randall-lsu-black-trainers-college-football.html (accessed June 2, 2022).

70. Quoted in Demirel, "The Most Loyal Tiger."

71. Paul Hochuli, "His Eulogy Tells the Story of Rice's Beloved 'Nigger Jack,'" Houston *Press*, September 26, 1950, also in Rice Information Files for "'Doctor' Jack Shelton" in WRC.

72. Ibid.

73. Historian Edward Kemper also compares images of Black "rubbers" attached to southern football programs in this period to the image of the "stereotypical antebellum mammy." See Kemper, *College Football and American Culture*, 120–21.

5. Rehearsals for Desegregation

1. "Sociologist Says Negro Role like Individual Emancipation," *RT*, February 12, 1949. See also "Sociologist to Address Forum after Finals," *RT*, January 22, 1949. Bullock spoke in Room 108 of the newly erected Anderson Hall, completed in 1947.

2. "Sociologist Says Negro Role like Individual Emancipation."

3. Darlene Clark Hine, *Black Victory: The Rise and Fall of the White Primary in Texas*, 2nd ed. (Columbia: University of Missouri Press, 2003); Nancy J. Weiss, *Farewell to the Party of Lincoln: Black Politics in*

the Age of FDR (Princeton, NJ: Princeton University Press, 1983); Manning Marable, *Race, Reform, and Rebellion: The Second Reconstruction and Beyond in Black America, 1945–2006*, 3rd ed. (Jackson: University Press of Mississippi, 2007), chap. 1; Joseph A. Abel, "Sunbelt Civil Rights: Race, Labor, and Politics in the Fort Worth Aircraft Industry," PhD diss., Rice University, 2011.

4. Melissa Kean, *Desegregating Private Higher Education in the South: Duke, Emory, Rice, Tulane, and Vanderbilt* (Baton Rouge: Louisiana State University Press, 2008), 10. In 1952, at least four current and emeritus faculty at Rice shared the University of Michigan with Dr. Bullock as the place where they had earned their PhDs. *General Announcements for September, 1952–June, 1954 of the Rice Institute* (Houston: Rice Institute, 1952).

5. Bullock later discussed these cases and others in his monograph, *A History of Negro Education in the South: From 1619 to the Present* (Cambridge, MA: Harvard University Press, 1967), published while he was a professor at Texas Southern University.

6. Kean, *Desegregating Private Higher Education*, 1; "Rice Refuses Stadium Use for Colored," Houston *Informer*, April 13, 1940.

7. Kean, *Desegregating Private Higher Education*, 50–54.

8. For Larkin, see *Campanile 1937*, 124; "Archi-Arts Ball to Be Held Saturday Night," *RT*, February 19, 1937. For Calloway, "Theaters," *RT*, May 13, 1933. For Anderson, "The Front Row," *RT*, April 5, 1945, 4. For a front-page photograph of the "Negro entertainer," who may have been a white comedian wearing blackface, see "Bond Dance Will Feature Minstrel Show," *RT*, May 14, 1943. See also "Sammy Harris' Ork Plays Rice Prom at Rice Hotel," Houston *Informer and Texas Freeman*, June 9, 1945.

9. "Rice Tennis Players Go to Prairie View A&M," *RT*, April 29, 1932; Emmett Brunson, Coach, Rice Institute Track Team, "Spiking through Europe," *Rice Owl* 17, no. 1 (October 1938): 11–13. See also "Bracey Wins Drake Century," *RT*, May 3, 1929; "Nine Man Track Squad Will Go to Regional A.A.U. Meet in San Antonio Friday," *RT*, June 13, 1946; "Around the Track," *RT*, May 1, 1947.

10. "'Mock' in Democracy? Dr. L. S. White Pleads for Better Conditions for Houston Negroes," *RT*, April 30, 1943. White addressed students only two months before "race riots" in several American cities, including nearby Beaumont; the preexisting tensions may well have inspired White's title. Four years later, another minister from the same church came to Autry House for talks on "inter-racial understanding." See "Racial Problems Discussed at M.S.U. by Negro Pastor," *RT*, March 13, 1947; "Talks by Livingston Continued at MSU Weekly Meetings," *RT*, March 20, 1947. For examples of many citywide religious forums on interracial brotherhood involving Rice students or faculty, see "Race Relations Observance is Set for Sunday," Houston *Informer and Texas Freeman*, February 13, 1937; "Interracial Problem Discussion Subject," *RT*, December 6, 1940; "Youth Rally was Sponsored by B'Nai B'rith at A House," *RT*, February 27, 1947.

11. Merline Pitre, *In Struggle Against Jim Crow: Lulu B. White and the NAACP, 1900–1957* (College Station: Texas A&M University Press, 1999); Michael L. Gillette, "Blacks Challenge the White University," *Southwestern Historical Quarterly* 86, no. 2 (October 1982): 321–44; Gary M. Lavergne, *Before Brown: Heman Marion Sweatt, Thurgood Marshall, and the Long Road to Justice* (Austin: University of Texas Press, 2010).

12. On Hudspeth's appointment, see Gillette, "Blacks Challenge the White University," 327; "'Hank' Hudspeth Returns to His Old School as Prof," *RT*, November 20, 1947.

13. "Negro University," *RT*, March 6, 1947.

14. "Students Still Missing at Negro Law School," Fort Worth *Star-Telegram*, March 13, 1947. See also "Sweatt Seeking to End Segregation, Says Daniel," Houston *Post*, March 22, 1947, 1.

15. W. V. Houston to Harry C. Hanszen, January 24, 1947, UA 85, box 2, folder 2. Hudspeth did

briefly comment on the case in a measured law article published by Rice in 1950; he noted only that the outcome was still pending and made no mention of his brief role in the drama. See C. M. Hudspeth, "Judicial Highlights of Civil Rights," *Rice University Studies* 37, no. 1 (1950), 75–108, esp. 94–95.

16. R. O'Hara Lanier to W. V. Houston, August 11, 1948, UA 85, box 3, folder 10. For HBCU invitations, see UA 85, box 21.

17. "YWCA Inter-Racial Conference to be Held Next Month," *RT,* March 19, 1937; "'Y' to Entertain Delegates from Texas Colleges," *RT,* April 9, 1937; "College YM-YW Associations Close Meeting," Houston *Informer and Texas Freeman,* April 17, 1937. See also "YWCA and YMCA Groups to Have Nov. Conference; Autry Meeting Tuesday," *RT,* November 1, 1935.

18. "Student Body Asked to Voice Opinions on Controversial Negro Question Discussed at Meeting of N.S.A.," *RT,* October 9, 1947. See also Tyson's report to the Student Council on the NSA on the issue's front page. On his selection as delegate, see *RT,* May 8, 15, 1947. The NSA's first president, Bill Welsh, hailed from Kentucky's Berea College, a school with a history of interracial education dating to before the Civil War.

19. "Student Body Asked to Voice Opinions."

20. Whaling, "Let Negroes in Rice?," *RT,* October 16, 1947; Foster, "Bill of Rights?" *RT,* October 23, 1947; Davis, "Race Issue Not Dead," *RT,* October 30, 1947.

21. *RT,* November 6, 1947, 1a; "Rice Delegates to NSA Convention in Dallas Offer Plans," *RT,* December 4, 1947; "NSA Delegates Come Back from Regional Meet," *RT,* December 11, 1947.

22. "RI Presents Both Sides: Should Negroes Be Admitted to Rice?," *RI: The Rice Institute Magazine* 2, no. 1 (November 1947): 3, 9–10, 15.

23. Ibid. In later sources, Fance Frank's surname is spelled Franck.

24. "'Disrespectful to Our Maker,' Claims Student Bob King," *RT,* January 12, 1949.

25. "Inter-Racial Forum Meets Tuesday," Houston *Post,* November 14, 1943. See "Charles A. Shaw," in A. W. Jackson, *A Sure Foundation: A Sketch of Negro Life in Texas* (Houston: n.p., [1940?]), 25–27; Ponton, "Criminalizing Space," 127, 315. For other examples of Shaw's activities, see "Plans are Made for Juneteenth Programs Here," Houston *Chronicle,* June 16, 1940; "Negro C. of C. is to Map Activities for Coming Year," Houston *Chronicle,* August 20, 1941; "College of Negroes to Sponsor Program," Houston *Chronicle,* November 13, 1941; "Churches in City to Observe Race Relations Day," Houston *Chronicle,* February 9, 1946; "C. A. Shaw to Address Interracial Meeting," Houston *Post,* January 18, 1948; "18 Negro Houstonians Included in Directory," Houston *Post,* November 1, 1950.

26. "Panel Discussion of Negro Education," Houston *Post,* February 16, 1949; "Brotherhood Program to Be Held by Memorial Chapt. B'nai B'rith," *Jewish Herald-Voice,* February 10, 1949.

27. "We Fall Behind," *RT,* October 2, 1948. For the school articles, see issues for October 30, November 6, and November 20. In his first issue as editor, Tyson published a letter he had sent to South Carolina segregationist Strom Thurmond criticizing race-baiting ads that partisans had run in Houston, along with a reply he received from Thurmond himself. See *RT,* September 16, 1948.

28. "New School in Houston is Center of National Attention: Texas State University for Negroes; A New School with Deep Roots," *RT,* November 20, 1948.

29. "The Case of Heman Sweatt vs. the State of Texas: Struggle Taken to U.S. Supreme Court; Reporter Visits in Sweatt's Home," *RT,* December 4, 1948.

30. "Alumnus Mills Questions Race Attitude of Students," *RT,* December 18, 1948.

31. "Staff Replies to Mills; Answer Three Questions," *RT,* December 18, 1948.

32. "Rice Editor Seeks Admission of Negroes," Houston *Post,* December 21, 1948, in Brady Tyson Papers, UA 030, box 1, folder 3.

33. See Kean, *Desegregating Private Higher Education*, 54–56; Ponton, "Criminalizing Space," 199–214.

34. Lulu B. White to Brady Tyson, December 22, 1948, and Charles A. Shaw to Brady Tyson, January 4, 1949, both in Tyson Papers, UA 030, box 1, folder 1.

35. "Houston Explains Charter Provisions of Rice Institute," *RT*, February 19, 1949. Houston had already made clear in the city press that no action on integration had even been "contemplated" by the Institute. See "Rice Administration is Quiet on Race Question," Houston *Chronicle*, December 21, 1948.

36. "A Battle to Admit Blacks: 'You Have Done More Damage to Rice than Any Student in History,'" *RT*, February 19, 1988. Tyson did not name the senior administrator who approached him, but in January 1949, then dean of students Hugh Scott Cameron brought up Tyson's editorial to the faculty-and-staff Committee for Student Activities. According to the minutes from the meeting, Cameron "pointed out that Mr. Tyson's job as editor of 'The Thresher' is to prepare a newspaper for students and not to use The Thresher as a vehicle to express his own thoughts." See Dean of Students Papers, UA 269, box 16, folder 8. After graduation, Tyson became more active in the civil rights movement, later serving as a board member in the Southern Christian Leadership Conference.

37. "Heman Sweatt Explains Whys and Wherefores of Civil Rights Program," *RT*, April 6, 1949; "Negro University Prexy Speaks to Methodist Students," *RT*, February 24, 1950; "Houston Artists to Speak Here Tonight," *RT*, November 7, 1952; Bill Hobby, "Convention Highlights," *RT*, March 22, 1951. For other examples of contact between Rice and area campuses, see James C. Morehead to W. V. Houston, August 8, 1949, UA 85, box 3, folder 10; "TSU Art Exhibit to Close Sunday; HLT Opens Play," *RT*, May 11, 1951; "Lack of Business About to Put Reporter on Skids," *RT*, November 7, 1952; "Rice Student Council Members Guests at Texas Southern Play," *RT*, April 30, 1954; "Simply a Week," *RT*, February 26, 1960. See also Melissa Kean, "It is rather we who should thank you, 1957," *Rice History Corner* (blog), December 13, 2017, ricehistorycorner.com/2017/12/13/it-is-rather-we-who-should-thank-you-1957/; "Religious Clubs Active," *RT*, September 19, 1959.

38. "TISA Convention Ends on Successful Note," *RT*, March 27, 1953; Kean, *Desegregating Private Higher Education*, 175. On the dance show, see "Spring Follies to Entertain Delegates, Students," *RT*, March 20, 1953.

39. For TSU *Herald* article, see UA 30, box 1, folder 3. The first African American undergraduates in the modern history of Washington University would enroll three years later, in 1952.

40. "At the Mellerdrama," *RT*, January 19, 1949; Hubert E. Mills, "Segregation Vote at Rice Proposed," Houston *Post*, December 25, 1948. See also "Guaya-Guayere is Archi-Arts Title This Time," *RT*, April 12, 1945; "Black Face Show to Be Given by PALS," *RT*, March 18, 1948.

41. Rice Institute Class of 1949 Senior Banquet Program, digitalcollections.rice.edu/Documents/Detail/63648.

42. "Poll Shows Campus Favors Integration," *RT*, March 22, 1957; "First Forum Airs Student Views in Lively Debate," *RT*, November 1, 1957. On the Confederate flag incident at the game, see letters to the editor in *RT*, October 11, 18, and 25, 1957. For the home video, see "Rice Homecoming—The Frank and Carolyn Hathorn Collection," *Texas Archive of the Moving Image*, texasarchive.org/2020_01791?b=533&e=536 (accessed September 2, 2024).

43. "Rice Administration Is Quiet." While a student, Tyson also professed to be a States Rights Democrat who disagreed with Strom Thurmond on segregation but agreed that states should be given the freedom and the responsibility to manage their own reform. He therefore opposed, for example, Truman's civil rights program.

44. Birdelle Ransom to Brady Tyson, December 22, 1948, Brady Tyson Papers, UA 030, box 1, folder 1; Birdelle Ransom, U.S. Census, 1950, Enumeration District no. 263–620A, sheet 4A, on Ancestry.com;

"Birdelle Wycoff Ransom" (obituary), Houston *Chronicle,* July 26, 2000. In her letter to Tyson, Ransom also sounded a more skeptical note about white student interest in schools like TSUN. The letter recounted the story of a "half frightened little student" from the University of Houston who had recently come to the Black student's campus, trying to write a thesis on "The Negroes in Houston" but with "no greater knowledge of the Negro people than she had gained through contact with maids and cooks." Tellingly, when the white student was asked if Black students could make a similar tour of her campus, the response was "OH NO!"

45. "TISA Convention Ends on Successful Note."

6. Charter Trials

1. David D. Medina, "Opening Doors," *Rice Sallyport,* Fall 2004, 26–31, first two quotes on 28; Mike Williams, "Raymond Johnson, Rice's First Black Student, Back as Math Professor," *Rice News,* August 28, 2009 ("desegregated university").

2. "Excerpt, Report to the American People on Civil Rights, 11 June 1963," *John F. Kennedy Presidential Library and Museum,* www.jfklibrary.org/asset-viewer/archives/tnc-262-ex (accessed on September 2, 2024).

3. Medina, "Opening Doors," 28. In a webinar hosted by the task force in 2020, Johnson also reflected on his concern in 1963 that Rice might have been too much like Texas after all. See "Black at Rice: A Conversation with Raymond L. Johnson," December 1, 2020, taskforce.rice.edu/past-events/conversation-raymond-l-johnson; also: www.youtube.com/watch?v=eRn2RicyEJs.

4. Board member H. Malcolm Lovett replied often to those who inquired with his belief that Rice was "the last private university in the South, and probably in the nation, certainly the last of those of comparable standing and aspirations, to obtain authority to eliminate restrictions on admission of students" (Lovett to David C. Gardner, March 17, 1964, Charter Trial Records, UA 275, digitalcollections.rice.edu/Documents/Detail/77533). See also Lovett to Mrs. Daniel W. McKeel, Jr., January 10, 1969, UA 67, box 17, folder 1.

5. Kean, *Desegregating Private Higher Education,* 8–11, 126, 172–73. See also Kerri Gantz, "On the Basis of Merit Alone: Integration, Tuition, Rice University, and the Charter Change Trial, 1963–1966," MA thesis, Rice University, 1991.

6. Kean, *Desegregating Private Higher Education,* 220–21. To some at Rice, the name "institute" had seemed inapt from the beginning. The prominence of vocational schools for Black students like the Tuskegee Institute and the Hampton Institute also gave the term a particular connotation in the South. In 1944, Edgar Odell Lovett recalled noting this in his earliest interviews with the trustees: "The very designation 'institute,' if it did not mean a female seminary, or one for defectives, or one for the colored race, meant an institute of technology. There was some hint of this that night, so I told them that I could not be a party for any such undertaking that would not secure as large a place for pure science as for applied science. It was an entering wedge away from technology and towards the university idea." See Lovett Papers, UA 014, box 29, folder 2. Also see "Why Institute?" in *Campanile 1923; RT,* April 6, 1960, 1.

7. Handwritten note, October 10, 1961, Pitzer Papers, UA 083, box 21, folder 5; "Two Referendums Bring Record Vote," *RT,* January 10, 1962.

8. Louis Galambos, "Why Little Concern Over Integration at Rice?" *RT,* November 17, 1961, 2; "Faculty Series Receives Some Heated Criticism," *RT,* December 8, 1961, 2–3; "Segregation Not Fundamental Issue," *RT,* December 15, 1861, 3. Two other professors rebuked Bourgeois with letters of their own in the December 15 issue, including S. K. Krishnaswami of Biology and A. C. L. Barnard of Physics.

9. "Vote 'For' Desegregation" and "Referendum Vote Monday," both in *RT,* December 15, 1961.

The specific resolution that students were asked to vote "for" or "against" read: "In a university, no restrictions based solely on race should be exercised in admissions policy or in use of facilities." The inclusion of "use of facilities" may also have affected the outcome of the polling by leading students who opposed that step, but favored a change in admissions, to vote against the entire proposition. Viewed as a percentage of the student body as a whole, rather than only those who voted, only about half of the enrolled undergraduates actively endorsed that resolution. In certain colleges, the poll results came closer to that proportion; at Will Rice College, for example, 130 voters favored the resolution compared to 101 who voted against. See Reed Martin to Kenneth S. Pitzer, December 21, 1961, Pitzer Papers, UA 083, box 21, folder 5.

10. On the campus visit by Graves and King, see "Forum to Discuss Integration" and "A Matter of Black and White," both in *RT,* April 29, 1960. On the Houston sit-in movement, see Thomas R. Cole, *No Color Is My Kind: Eldrewey Stearns and the Desegregation of Houston,* 2nd ed. (Austin: University of Texas Press, 2021); "Rice Demonstrators Quizzed on Arrests," *RT,* March 3, 1961. On variation in opinions and the level of involvement at Rice in the Houston sit-ins, see Kean, *Desegregating Private Higher Education,* 226; Gantz, "On the Basis of Merit Alone," 29–31; Nina Nevill, "Student Activism in Houston's Civil Rights Movement: Texas Southern University and Rice Institute Integrate the Bayou City," UA 421, ser. B.

11. Kent Anderson to Kenneth S. Pitzer, November 8, 1961, with promotional college brochure, Pitzer Papers, UA 083, box 29, folder 1; "Hanszen Fills Hamman Hall with Minstrel Show Tonight," *RT,* November 10, 1961; Rice *Campanile 1962,* 99, 255. The Hanszen "Black Edge Minstrel Company" made its debut at homecoming in 1960. The *Campanile* photograph of that event also showed a large group in blackface, over another caption that mockingly alluded to the civil rights movement: "In fact, a sit-in." See "Hanszen Premieres Gala Minstrel," *RT,* November 11, 1960; *Campanile 1961,* 358.

12. "Alum Advocates Fund Restriction," *RT,* October 13, 1961; "Houston to Give First Lecture of Alumni Series," *RT,* February 16, 1962; "Rice Official Explains Alumni Lecture Policy," *RT,* February 23, 1962. Officials claimed afterward that, while it was the administration's policy to admit members of the general public to on-campus lectures, "whether or not they are negroes," the physics lecture was "held under the auspices of the Alumni Association and was an invitation affair only, not open to the public." Invitations had been extended to some University of Houston instructors and to some high school students in the city. English professor Alan Grob, a new faculty member that year, later remembered the incident this way: "the Director of the Development Office at Rice asked a black physicist from Texas Southern to leave a lecture by a former president of Rice who was himself a physicist." See his untitled 1989 speech in Alan Grob Academic Papers, UA 413, box 4, folder 23.

13. Gantz, "On the Basis of Merit Alone," 31–32; M. V. McEnany, Registrar, to James N. Hinga, February 16, 1962, Pitzer Papers, UA 083, box 21, folder 5. Hinga wrote to request an application on January 27, 1962. After graduation from TSU, he pursued graduate study in math there and at the University of Houston. See obituary for James Nyoike Hinga (1934–2022), McCoy & Harrison Funeral Home, www.mccoyandharrison.com/james-hinga-1934-2022/ (accessed August 24, 2022). Pitzer told the *Thresher* that December that the university had received "several 'inquiries' from potential Negro applicants." See "University Forced to Reject Negroes; Courts Approve Tulane Integration," *RT,* December 12, 1962.

14. Kean, *Desegregating Private Higher Education,* 222–23.

15. Ibid., 223; Alan Grob, "Integration at Rice," Alan Grob Papers, UA 413, box 4, folder 30.

16. The clause Pitzer referred to in the charter said that instruction at the Institute was to be "subject to such restrictions only, as in the judgment of the Board of Trustees will conduce to the good order and honor of the said Institute."

17. Transcript of interview of Kenneth S. Pitzer by John B. Boles and Louis J. Marchiafava, March 22, 1994, Rice Oral Histories Collection, UA 310, box 1, folder 3. See also Gantz, "On the Basis of Merit Alone," 40–43.

18. Pitzer later recalled Lovett as a board member who felt "ambivalence" about growing Rice's national profile. Though he realized that his father's original aims were high, his actual experience as a student was in the years when Rice had been small and making do with less money than it would later have. In Pitzer's words, Malcolm Lovett therefore "remained nostalgic for the Rice that he had known in reality as compared to the Rice that his father had contemplated" (Harold M. Hyman interview with Kenneth Pitzer [video], August 1, 1995). See also pages 8–9 and 14–16 in transcript of interview of Kenneth S. Pitzer by John B. Boles and Louis J. Marchiafava, March 22, 1994, both in Rice Oral Histories Collection, UA 310.

19. H. Malcolm Lovett to George R. Brown, September 25, 1961, with attached memorandum, Pitzer Papers, UA 83, box 21, folder 5. On the Girard College decision, see also Kean, *Desegregating Private Higher Education*, 172–73.

20. Undated handwritten letter from Pitzer to Lovett, Pitzer Papers, UA 83, box 21, folder 5; Kean, *Desegregating Private Higher Education*, 217–20, 227–28; Malcolm Lovett to Kenneth Pitzer, December 7, 1962, Pitzer Papers, UA 83, box 21, folder 5. Though the winter letter is undated, it mentions the completion of the Tulane suit from December. Two Rice alumni also wrote a letter to Pitzer after the Tulane decision, arguing that it freed the trustees to act immediately: "I trust that Rice's trustees will take the necessary steps to end racial discrimination on the campus. To do so freely and quickly will contribute to the growing prestige of the University. To hesitate will tarnish its reputation. . . . As in the case of Tulane, the question is now squarely before the Trustees of the University." See John W. Hill and Carol Wheeler Hill to Kenneth S. Pitzer, December 18, 1962, Pitzer Papers, UA 83, box 21, folder 5. Pitzer's reply, dated December 28, said he still did not know exactly when the legal action planned by the board would begin, though around that same time, Rice lawyers wrote the state attorney general to inform his office of their plans.

21. Mike Jaffe to Martin Luther King, February 21, 1963, Pitzer Papers, UA 83, box 21, folder 5; "Forum Cancels All Speakers on Suit to Avoid Prejudice," *RT*, March 11, 1964, which mentions the cancellation of King's visit the year before. On Jordan, see "Republicans Need Organizer, Democrats Push Local Activity," *RT*, November 13, 1963; untitled 1989 speech in Alan Grob Academic Papers, UA 413, box 4, folder 23.

22. Medina, "Opening Doors," 28.

23. "Remarks to Bd of Governors, 1/30/63," handwritten note by Pitzer in Charter Trial Records, UA 275, box 3, folder 9.

24. "Suit Filed to Change Rice Charter; No Tuition Next Year, Pitzer Says," *RT*, February 27, 1963, 1.

25. J. Newton Rayzor to Kenneth S. Pitzer, June 27, 1963, Charter Trial Records, UA 275, box 3, folder 6.

26. Ibid. See also Gantz, "On the Basis of Merit Alone," 107–9. Pitzer later recalled of this incident that "the mathematics department wanted to jump the gun a little bit, and we had to do some pretty sensitive maneuvering there." Transcript of interview of Kenneth S. Pitzer by John B. Boles and Louis J. Marchiafava, March 22, 1994, p. 27, Rice Oral Histories Collection, UA 310.

27. Petition in Intervention by John B. Coffee and Val T. Billups, Case no. 612,668, June 20, 1963, digitalcollections.rice.edu/Documents/Detail/77665. Billups was part of the Class of 1919 but did not graduate, according to *RT*, September 18, 1963. See also "Alumni of Rice Fight Move to Admit Negro Students," New York *Times*, June 21, 1963.

28. Memos by Kenneth Pitzer to Board of Governors, dated October 16, 1963, and January 29, 1964, both in Pitzer Papers, UA 83, box 18, folder 2. See also memo dated September 30, 1963, which reported on a letter in which Coffee himself seemed to concede the Board's ability to act without court approval. The university's lawyers had also acknowledged in their petition to the court that "there have been admitted, since the earliest days of the university, reasonable numbers of out-of-state students, among whom were members of the brown and yellow races. Students at Rice University have never been restricted to 'white persons.'" See Petition in Case no. 612,668, digitalcollections.rice.edu/Documents/Detail/78691.

29. "SMU's Tate Testifies for Trustees in Third Day of Charter Suit Trial," *RT*, February 12, 1964; "Court Decision Favors Trustees but Intervenor Appeals Expected," *RT*, March 11, 1964. For more detailed analysis of the lawsuit, see Steven Harmon Wilson, "The Will to Change: The Legal Battle over the Rice University Endowment," paper presented to Texas State Historical Association, Houston, March 2, 2012, www.law.uh.edu/ihelg/monograph/11–08.pdf; Michael A. Olivas, *The Law and Higher Education: Cases and Materials on Colleges in Court* (Durham, NC: Carolina Academic Press, 2006), 9–17; Gantz, "On the Basis of Merit Alone," chap. 4; Kean, *Desegregating Private Higher Education*, 228–32. See also the Task Force webinar, "The Legal Battle Over Desegregating Rice," November 5, 2020, www.youtube.com/watch?v=BUd7b4DA9mk.

30. For this and the previous few paragraphs, see "Black at Rice: A Conversation with Raymond L. Johnson." See also Noe Perez, "Negro Is Studying at Rice," Houston *Post*, February 5, 1965.

31. President William V. Houston Papers, UA 085, box 4, folder 2. On the persistence of residential segregation after *Shelley v. Kraemer*, see David Ponton III, *Houston and the Permanence of Segregation: An Afropessimist Approach to Urban History* (Austin: University of Texas Press, 2024), 93–129.

32. Medina, "Opening Doors," 31; email from Raymond L. Johnson to Alexander X. Byrd, October 6, 2023, in authors' possession; "Raymond Lewis Johnson: Son of the New Day," Houston *Forward Times*, April 17, 1965. See also Johnson's autobiographical narrative in Raymond Johnson Info File, WRC, www-users.math.umd.edu/~rlj/RJ.html.

33. "Black at Rice: A Conversation with Raymond L. Johnson." On King's speech at TSU, see "King Gives Warning on Civil Rights Bill," Houston *Post*, May 18, 1964. On Rice student involvement in "restaurant testing" during the 1963–64 school year, see "Chronicle's Friedman at ACCORD," *RT*, February 12, 1964; "Rice Area Restaurants, Housing To Be Subject of ACCORD Study," *RT*, May 6, 1964. See also "Students Protest School Policies by Picketing National Convention," *RT*, April 29, 1964.

34. "Court Decision Favors Trustees but Intervenor Appeals Expected," *RT*, March 11, 1964.

35. Handwritten note titled "For George Brown Discussion on 4/17/64," Pitzer Papers, UA 083, box 22, folder 2.

36. Correspondence on ACCORD in Pitzer Papers, UA 083, box 38, folder 9; "Forum Head King Offers Variations from Old Themes," *RT*, May 6, 1964.

37. By that time it was traditional for the homecoming queens of Houston's area universities to be invited to Rondolet, but TSU had never been included.

38. "TSU Honoree Invitation Withdrawn; Board Decides to Approve Action," *RT*, April 29, 1964.

39. "Dr. Pitzer's Statement to the Thresher, 4/30/64," in Pitzer Papers, UA 083, box 40, folder 1; "TSU Honoree Invitation Withdrawn." Alan Grob recalled the gist of the conversation between Lassiter and Williams in his undated 1989 speech, Grob Academic Papers, UA 413, box 4, folder 23.

40. "Hanszen College Budget, 1963–1964," Pitzer Papers, UA 083, box 41, folder 20.

41. *Campanile 1964*, 64–65, 356. See also "Homecoming Returns in Traditional Form," *RT*, November 6, 1963; "Hanszen Slates Minstrel to Spice Aggie Weekend," *RT*, November 14, 1962. The 1963 *Cam-*

panile included a photograph of a blackface performer at the minstrel show with the caption: "Haven't seen a bonfire lak that since Ah was back in Mississippi." That year's show also included a student in blackface with a graduation cap. See *Campanile 1963*, 171.

42. "Black at Rice: A Conversation with Raymond L. Johnson."

43. See memo by Pitzer and correspondence between Gerald MacLane, new chairman of the Math Department, and Dean G. Richter, June 5, 1964, in Pitzer Papers, UA 083, box 9, folder 5.

44. For all of the drafts of Lovett's letter, including one proposed by Rayzor and the one Johnson signed, as well as Pitzer's notes on Davis's position, see Pitzer Papers, UA 083, box 9, folder 6. As late as 1967, Lovett remained concerned to have the record show that Johnson had not been admitted until 1964, which he cited as one example of the trustees' "fine record of having conformed to the provisions of the Trust Indenture" until the litigation to change it concluded. See Gantz, "On the Basis of Merit Alone," 110–11; H. Malcolm Lovett to Kenneth Pitzer, March 16, 1967, UA 275, digitalcollections.rice.edu/Documents/Detail/77537.

45. "Black at Rice: A Conversation with Raymond L. Johnson." A review of the *Thresher* shows that Idaho State played at Rice on December 14, 1966.

46. "Discourteous Owl Basketball Fans Disappoint Maguire," *RT*, December 8, 1966.

47. "Jones Asked to Limit Negro Guests Until Conclusion of Trustees' Suit," *RT*, October 1, 1964.

48. Memo by Pitzer to Members of the Faculty, Administrative Officers, and Student Leaders, October 5, 1964, Pitzer Papers, UA 083, box 40, folder 1.

49. "Of Intellectual Schizophrenia," *RT*, December 3, 1964. See also "'Tired Professor' Rakes Rice Students," November 19, 1964; "Hanszen Delays Minstrel Decision," *RT*, December 10, 1964. Another professor wrote to say that, while he deplored the show, he also deplored Glidden's calls for the university to "censor" it and urged him to see "the world as it is rather than just black and white." See "De Bremaecker Rakes Censorship by Students," *RT*, December 10, 1964. The 1965 *Campanile* reported, with photos of students in blackface, that "the third annual Last Hanszen Minstrel . . . was basically unchanged in format from previous years" (58–59).

50. "Rice and the Negro: The Whited Sepulchre," *RT*, March 4, 1965. Later that month, the *Thresher* included Johnson's name and department in a list of winners of NSF grants at Rice. See "Rice Receives 18 NSF Grants," *RT*, March 25, 1965.

51. For Johnson's letter to Pitzer, dated March 24, 1965, as well as Pitzer's reply, dated March 31, 1965, see Pitzer Papers, UA 083, box 9, folder 6.

7. A Token Start

1. The contents of *Campanile 1970*, which was published as a box with multiple kinds of media, are online at digitalcollections.rice.edu/Documents/Detail/91829. For an early description of the unusual edition, see "Hester Clarifies Proposed Format for Campanile 70," *RT*, December 4, 1969.

2. Linda Faye Williams, *The Constraint of Race: Legacies of White Skin Privilege in America* (University Park: Pennsylvania State University Press, 2003), vii–viii. Williams's book won awards from the American Political Science Association and the National Conference of Black Political Scientists.

3. "Percentage of College Blacks in this Area," Houston *Chronicle*, April 13, 1975. The *Chronicle* report included Rice-provided figures from 1970 through 1974, by which time the percentage of Black students at Rice had risen to 4 percent. The standing ovation was recollected by Charles Szalkowski, Class of 1970, at "Reflections of the Past, Promises for the Future," a panel held February 18, 2016, as

part of a yearlong series of events marking "50 Years of Black Undergraduate Life." See www.youtube.com/watch?v=BD2ciIsOnbo.

4. Scheleen Johnson, "Breaking the Barriers," *Sallyport* 45, no. 1 (Fall 1988): 16–17.

5. Martha Biondi, *The Black Revolution on Campus* (Berkeley: University of California Press, 2012), 16; Tomiko Brown-Nagin, *Courage to Dissent: Atlanta and the Long History of the Civil Rights Movement* (New York: Oxford University Press, 2011), 230.

6. Davidson qtd. in Christopher Dow, "Diversity: That Was Then, This Is Now," *Sallyport* 63, no. 3 (Summer 2007): 24–29.

7. "On Minority Admissions: Grob Discusses Committee's Work," *RT*, January 23, 1969.

8. Suzanne Johnson, "1968–1971: What a Long, Strange Trip It Was," *Sallyport* 45, no. 1 (Fall 1988): 9.

9. M. Yvonne Taylor, "Linda Faye Williams," *Rice Magazine*, Fall 2016, 29; Linda Faye Williams Info File and Linda Faye Williams Application File, WRC.

10. W. C. Williams's essay was provided by his daughter Zandra Williams to Chandler Davidson in January 2007 and is included in the Linda Faye Williams Info File.

11. Linda Faye Williams Application File.

12. Johnson, "Breaking Barriers"; "Campus Activist of '60s in Insurance Now," Houston *Chronicle*, July 26, 1976. Freeman added: "I had a burden placed on my shoulders that I was too young to handle. I was 17 when I first went to Rice."

13. For news clippings on the enrollment and high school backgrounds of McCauley and Freeman, see Rice Students—Minorities Info File, WRC.

14. Nancy Van Cleave, "Rice Plans to Recruit Negroes," Houston *Post*, June 7, 1968.

15. "'Relatively High' Tuition, 'Very Large Fund' for Scholarships in Works at Rice U.," Houston *Chronicle*, March 11, 1964; "She Didn't Enter Rice, At Least Not at Age 8," Houston *Chronicle*, April 25, 1977. Archival sources contain conflicting accounts of how many Black students applied and were accepted in 1965 and 1966. A memo from July 1965 reported that "five were accepted after they applied and two have enrolled," but a report several years later stated that only three were offered admission in 1965. The later report gave three as the number who applied, but that may refer to the number of applicants who were not accepted. Compare memo by Lee Estes, July 14, 1965, in Students—Minorities Info File, with Frank E. Vandiver to Clarence A. Laws, May 29, 1969, box 4, folder 4, Vandiver-Hackerman Papers. For a fuller review of the institutional history of admissions after the Charter Trial, see William D. Jones, "Undergraduate Diversity and Admissions at Rice University, 1965–2004," copy in authors' possession.

16. James Lewis from Corpus Christi, Texas, was one of the students admitted by Rice in 1965, but he also received offers from Brown University and Cornell University. He told the *Wall Street Journal* that "Rice called and sent letters to my parents after I had chosen Cornell." See Paul R. Martin, "Interracial U.: Northern Colleges Seek to Draw More Negroes from Schools in South," *Wall Street Journal*, September 23, 1965.

17. "Major Development in Lawsuit within Ninety Days," *RT*, November 13, 1963; "Rice Plans Tuition, Integration by Fall of 1965, Pitzer Says," *RT*, March 18, 1964.

18. David Medina, "Gifted and Black: Jacqueline McCauley," *Rice Magazine*, Fall 2016, 27.

19. See unsigned typewritten memo, with handwritten notes, in Students—Minorities Info File. A later version of the memo prepared for official filing (and also in the Info File) removed the grades and parenthetical comment.

20. Johnson, "Breaking the Barriers."

21. M. Yvonne Taylor, "Ted Henderson," *Rice Magazine*, Fall 2016, 29. When not studying, Henderson supported himself financially by working at the Faculty Club. See "2 Black Graduates a Milestone for Rice," Houston *Chronicle*, May 24, 1970.

22. Gregory J. Vincent, Virginia A. Cumberbatch, and Leslie A. Blair, *As We Saw It: The Story of Integration at the University of Texas at Austin* (Austin: Tower Books, 2018), x, 31–52, quote from Dorothy Cato on p. 50. Raymond Johnson likewise remembered that, despite the racism he experienced as an undergraduate at UT, he found socializing in the "friendly" environment of his all-Black dorm to be one of the easier parts of his experience. See "Black at Rice: A Conversation with Raymond L. Johnson."

23. Meiners, *History of Rice University*, 178–87, 193; Michael Raphael, ed., *The History of Student Life at Rice University: A Series of Papers* (Houston: Rice University Centennial Celebration Committee, 1990). Before 1957, women students lived off campus.

24. Quotes from *Golden Years* (1962), a film produced by the Association of Rice Alumni in collaboration with the university, Texas Archive of the Moving Image, texasarchive.org/2018_04727.

25. "Playhouse Replaces Minstrel," *Hanszen Voice*, October 21, 1965 (both quotes); *Campanile 1966*, 205. For the faculty quartet, see "Hanszen Premieres Gala Minstrel," *RT*, November 11, 1960. See also Coco Owens and Ross Goldberg, *Hanszen College: A History* (Houston: Hanszen College, 2012), 11–12.

26. Johnson, "Breaking the Barriers." On the Rockwell speech, see "Frossard, Schild Criticize Rice Audience Reaction," *RT*, February 3, 1966. On Stoner, see "Stoner Stands for 'American Way,'" *RT*, February 23, 1967; "Negro Group Breaks Up Racist Speech," Houston *Post*, February 22, 1967; "Sound-Off," Houston *Post*, March 1, 1967.

27. Taylor, "Ted Henderson"; Johnson, "Breaking Barriers"; Students—Minorities Info File; Melissa Kean, "The Tuba Player, 1965," *Rice History Corner* blog, March 28, 2017; *Wiess-Crack*, February 15, 1966, Wiess College Records, UA 079, box 2, folder 5. See also "Rice University Between Decisions: From Co-Education to Integration, 1957–1970," online exhibit from the WRC by Edna Otuomagie, Samhita Sunya, Itohan Idumwonyi, Danni Vasquez, and Matthew Holloway, digitalcollections.rice.edu/online-exhibits/rice-university-between-decisions-from-coeducation-to-desegregation.

28. "J. H. Griffin Speaks at Hanszen," *Hanszen Voice*, February 10, 1966. The article about Griffin in the *Hanszen Voice* included a crude sketch of the author's face, colored in with black ink. See also "Griffin Speaks," *RT*, February 3, 1966; "Griffin Sees Negro Dehumanizing," *RT*, February 10, 1966.

29. "Forman Cites Cause for Racism," *RT*, October 6, 1966; "Gorgeous Cassius: Ali Wows 'Em with Poetry, History," *RT*, February 2, 1967; *Campanile 1967*, 66, 68, 255 ("shock treatment"). Forman spoke at Will Rice College in the spring 1966 semester.

30. *Campanile 1967*, 54, 243; "Pride, Power Seen as Keys to Solving Minority Problems," *RT*, December 8, 1966.

31. Medina, "Gifted and Black: Jacqueline McCauley."

32. "Hafter Cites Active, Geographically Unbiased Admissions," *RT*, May 11, 1967.

33. "Grob Criticizes Token Integration, Urges Mobilization," *RT*, October 19, 1967.

34. "Giles Denies Racial Tokenism Here," *RT*, November 2, 1967. See also "Committees Evaluate Rice Policies," *RT*, November 16, 1967.

35. "Open Forum Emphasizes Necessity for Liberalizing Integration Policies," *RT*, September 19, 1968. See also "Porter Urges Changes in University's Racial Policies," *RT*, April 25, 1968.

36. In a handwritten note addressed to Gordon, who would effectively run the university during a search for his successor, Pitzer said that he "had intended" to form a committee that would include faculty and students, Black and white, to study the issue of minority student admissions. See letters

from F. K. Levy (April 17, 1968) and Gaston V. Rimlinger (April 19, 1968), as well as Pitzer's penciled note to Gordon on the Rimlinger letter, in Vandiver/Hackerman Papers, UA 067, box 78, folder 5.

37. Biondi, *Black Revolution on Campus*, 1–5; Schrecker, *Lost Promise*, 263–86.

38. Allen J. Matusow, *The Unraveling of America: A History of Liberalism in the 1960s*, 2nd ed. (1984; Athens: University of Georgia Press, 2009).

39. "Rice Graduation Speaker Calls for Reconstruction with Intelligence," Houston *Chronicle*, June 2, 1968; "Masterson Shuns Sentiment," *RT*, February 22, 1969. Though it is difficult to reconstruct all of Masterson's arguments from newspaper reports, he also offered, according to the *Chronicle*, a somewhat unusual explanation for the low enrollments of racial minorities at many universities: "Racial and social bitterness are now so intense that thousands of minority groups, however able, are not interested in any college since they regard colleges as part of a system hostile to them and alien to their aspirations."

40. On these events, see "The Masterson Crisis," an exhibit from the WRC by Emma Satterfield, digitalcollections.rice.edu/online-exhibits/a-time-of-protest; Melissa Kean, "Rice's 'Masterson Crisis': 'The Problem Is, What Is the University Going to Be," lecture, September 13, 2011, www.youtube.com/watch?v=2c3ULZg-bOs; Nancy Boothe, "Documenting an Administrative Crisis: Rice's 4-Day Presidency," *Cornerstone* 8, no. 2 (Spring 2003).

41. "Skaaren Asks Senate Commitment," *RT*, September 12, 1968.

42. "Open Forum Emphasizes Necessity for Liberalizing Integration Policies"; Minutes of the Meeting of the Faculty Council, November 6, 1968, Faculty Council Records, UA 106, box 3, folder 3; [Committee on] Minority Admissions, Rice University Ad Hoc and Other Committee Records, UA 306, box 9, folder 1 (hereafter referred to as Grob Ad Hoc Committee folder).

43. Student Committee on University Research of the Rice University Student Action Committee, *Who Enters Rice?* digitalcollections.rice.edu/Documents/Detail/237257; "Who Enters Rice?" *RT*, November 21, 1968. For a fuller discussion of these events, see Jones, "Undergraduate Diversity and Admissions."

44. *Who Enters Rice?* 6–7, 28.

45. "Gwyn Accuses SCOUR of Racism," *RT*, December 5, 1968. Cf. "Streeter Calls Pro-Minority Discrimination an Asset" in the same issue.

46. "SA Reports Work in Crucial Areas; Restructuring of Senate Suggested," *RT*, October 10, 1968; Meeting Agenda, October 10, 1968, Campus Executive Committee Records, UA 238, box 1, folder 3. Quote taken from front matter to *Who Enters Rice?*

47. "SAC Plans a Week of Life," *RT*, October 17, 1968. The title of the week also evoked the title of Norman O. Brown's 1959 book *Life Against Death*, a text that gave some theoretical inspiration to the hippie counterculture. See Matusow, *Unraveling of America*, 277–79.

48. *Campanile 1967*, 255. On the spring 1967 events at TSU, see Pitre, *Born to Serve*, 61–77; Ponton, "Criminalizing Space," chap. 6; Biondi, *Black Revolution on Campus*, 31–32.

49. "Black Against the Wall," *RT*, October 24, 1968.

50. "Charles E. Freeman Goes on Trial for His Life in Victoria," *RT*, October 31, 1968.

51. "Life Week," *RT*, October 24, 1968.

52. Interview with Elaine Frank, May 3, 1969, Masterson Controversy Records, UA 068. After the SAC's "Life Week," one student wrote to the *Thresher* cheekily proposing the formation of a Student Inertia Committee, made up "of Rice students who do not wish to have their education disrupted by a handful of campus radicals. The lesson of Columbia University is not to be shrugged off with 'it can't happen at Rice.' It can, and may, if such organizations as the Students for a Democratic Society are allowed to gain a foothold." See "SIC Embodies Rice Student Apathy," *RT*, November 7, 1968.

53. *RT*, December 5, 1968. The quote was rendered slightly differently, but with the sense intact, in W. E. Gordon, "The State of the University," *Rice University Review* 4, no. 1 (Spring 1969): 3. On San Francisco State, see Biondi, *Black Revolution on Campus*, 43–78.

54. "Two Student Leaders Assail Gordon for His Blocking SCOUR Proposal," *RT*, December 12, 1968. For Birotte's National Achievement Scholar award, see "Seven Negroes Win Merit Scholarships," Houston *Chronicle*, March 6, 1968. The actual number of Black students was still smaller than seventeen.

55. Charles E. Freeman to Committee on Examinations and Standings, November 26, 1968, Charles Freeman Info File, WRC; Minutes of the Meeting of the Committee on Examinations and Standing, December 5, 1968, UA 163, box 2, folder 6. Official minutes for the meeting that approved Freeman's admission, held sometime between December 5 and 17, were apparently not taken or were not preserved, which one member of the Committee on Examinations and Standing (who reported the vote as seven to zero) later found curious. See notes on an April 1969 conversation with Ira Gruber in Chandler Davidson Papers, UA 189, box 5, folder 10.

56. Campus Executive Committee Meeting Minutes, December 17, 1968, UA 238, box 1, folder 5. See Charles E. Freeman and Ruby Freeman to M. V. McEnany, March 27, 1969, Charles Freeman Info File. The Freemans mentioned writing to the university "for the third time in less than a year" and noted that McEnany's communications about where Freeman's case stood had been "verbal and vague."

57. Meeting Minutes for January 6 and 9, 1969, Campus Executive Committee Records, UA 238, box 1, folder 7.

58. See Grob Ad Hoc Committee folder.

59. "Grob Discusses Committee's Work," *RT*, January 23, 1969; Campus Executive Committee Meeting Minutes, January 9, 1969.

60. "Grob Discusses Committee's Work." For an early news report about the UCLA shooting, see "Two Negroes Slain at U.C.L.A. Meeting of Black Students," New York *Times*, January 18, 1969, 1.

61. For the SCOUR postscript (dated January 7, but stamped as received on January 9), see Grob Ad Hoc Committee folder. It was republished in *RT*, January 9, 1969, 2.

62. "Gordon Surveys Admissions Scene" and "Student Cross-Section Represented at Gordon Minority Admission Talk," *RT*, January 16, 1969; "Notes and Notices," *RT*, January 9, 1969. Gordon had formally recommended that Grob's committee review the SCOUR report on January 3. For that letter, and a leaflet from students denouncing Gordon's Will Rice appearance even before it occurred, see Grob Ad Hoc Committee folder.

63. "Shadows of Apocalypse," *RT*, January 16, 1969.

64. Shortly after the New Year, for example, C. M. "Hank" Hudspeth, past president of the Association of Rice Alumni and a future member of the Rice Board of Trustees, sent Gordon an article discussing the complex problem of campus turmoil, written by Franklin L. Ford, a respected Harvard University dean. Ford encouraged administrators not to think of all student dissent as equally destructive or emerging from a single source, and one of the arguments elaborated in the article had to do with specific "interest groups," including Black students. Ford wrote: "We shall continue to engage black students in the search for qualified candidates for admission back in their home communities . . . but we must reject the notion of guaranteed quotas of black students or staff." A cover note by Hudspeth told Gordon that he approved of Ford's main ideas: "(a) the pluralistic approach to student unrest and (b) the purpose of the university." Gordon apparently filed the letter and the article in the folder on the Grob Committee. See Hudspeth to Gordon, undated, in Grob Ad Hoc Committee folder; Franklin L. Ford, "To Live with Complexity: A Problem for Students—And for the Rest of Us," *Harvard Today*, Autumn 1968, 4–12.

65. H. Malcolm Lovett to J. U. Teague, January 14, 1969, in Grob Ad Hoc Committee folder. The other trustee copied was Herbert Allen.

66. Ibid.

67. M. V. McEnany to H. Malcolm Lovett, January 29, 1969, in Grob Ad Hoc Committee folder. Gordon received a carbon copy.

68. Minutes for January 28, 1969, meeting, with enclosures and handwritten notes mentioning the SDS, in Campus Executive Committee Records, UA 238, box 1, folder 7. The *Wall Street Journal* article was marked as being "from LSS," likely referring to treasurer Leo S. Shamblin.

69. Minutes, Faculty, Student, and Alumni Committee of the Board of Governors, February 6, 1969, UA 238, box 1, folder 14. The February 14 date for the board's decision on Masterson was reported in the *Thresher*, February 22, 1969.

70. Minutes, Faculty, Student, and Alumni Committee of the Board of Governors, February 6, 1969.

71. M. V. McEnany to Alan Grob, February 17, 1969, in Grob Ad Hoc Committee folder.

72. *RT*, February 20, 1969.

73. *RT*, February 22, 1969.

74. Interview with Elaine Frank; interview with Alan Grob, both in Masterson Controversy Records, UA 068.

75. Interview with Elaine Frank.

76. Interview with Ira D. Gruber, in Masterson Controversy Records, UA 068.

77. "Group Asks Where the Power Lies in the University," *RT*, February 22, 1969. Many of the signatories joining Birotte on this letter were associated with the SDS, though the letter was not presented as a statement from that group, one of many indications that weekend that SDS students were seeking to join with other students in a unified response to the crisis.

78. Birotte is identified as the speaker in "Masterson Meets Massed Students," *Rice Daily Thresher*, February 24, 1969. For the recording of his question, see "William Masterson Addressing Students," KTRU Rice Radio Archive, UA 011, digitalcollections.rice.edu/Documents/Detail/57232.

79. Interview with Ira D. Gruber

80. "Micheletti Hails Masterson," *RT*, February 22, 1969; interview with Jean De Bremaecker, Masterson Controversy Records, UA 068.

81. The typescript of Williams's research paper, festooned with the professor's penciled comments and questions, still resides in the university's collections. The paper was titled "If Negroes, Latin Americans and Poor Whites Voted at the Same Rate as Affluent Whites, What Would Happen to Texas Politics?" See Chandler Davidson Academic Papers, UA 189, box 2, folder 5. See also Johnson, "Breaking the Barriers"; notes by Davidson, February 26, 2011, in Davidson Papers, box 8, folder 28; "Remarks by Chandler Davidson on Linda Faye Williams," undated, in Linda Faye Williams Info File.

82. Williams, "If Negroes, Latin Americans and Poor Whites Voted." For the joint statement of the Young Republicans and Young Democrats, see *Rice Daily Thresher*, February 25, 1969.

83. Vandiver quoted in "Mass Protest Set at Rice Today," Houston *Chronicle*, April 11, 1969. For the review of the case, see Charles Freeman Info File; Rice University Welfare Committee Records, UA 177, box 2, folder 2; Hackerman/Vandiver Papers, UA 067, box 46, folder 14.

84. "Freeman Outlines Admissions Case," *RT*, March 6, 1969; "Freeman Case Heads SA Agenda," *RT*, March 20, 1969; picture of Freeman speaking in tie in *Campanile 1969*. See also Freeman Info File; *RT*, April 10, 1969.

85. Figures for the two rallies provided in "Vandiver, Rice U. Students Resolve Freeman Hassle," Houston *Chronicle*, April 13, 1969.

86. "Rice Watermelon Deliverers Caught," Houston *Chronicle*, April 18, 1969; *Campanile 1969*. See also *RT*, April 17, 1969; "Freeman Readmission Supporters Ask Help," Houston *Post*, April 15, 1969. Students had also placed watermelons outside the Vandiver home. Another example of SDS students identifying Freeman's cause with theirs occurred on February 26, in the immediate aftermath of the Masterson crisis, when a screening of a documentary film, *The Columbia Revolt*, was held on campus at 8 p.m., with remarks following it by Charles Freeman. See *Rice Daily Thresher*, February 26, 1969.

87. "Campus Activist of '60s in Insurance Now." See letters in Vandiver/Hackerman Papers, UA 067, box 5, folder 6; and box 46, folder 14. Vandiver and the Committee on Examinations and Standings ultimately reached an agreement that Freeman could reapply for admission in the fall after successfully completing some courses for credit at another university over the summer. Freeman did so and returned, briefly, to Rice the following academic year.

88. Interview with Alan Grob, Masterson Controversy Records, UA 068.

89. Interview with Virgil Topazio, Masterson Controversy Records, UA 068.

90. Ibid.

91. Campus Executive Committee Records, UA 238, box 1, folders 8 and 14. For detailed notes from the registrar's review of Black applicants, see Grob Ad Hoc Committee folder. A similar review was conducted in January 1971 of minority students who entered in 1969, plotting their freshman grade point averages relative to the university average on a graph. See Hackerman Papers, UA 067, box 37, folder 5.

92. Attached to a request from Grob to then-president Hackerman in December 1970 is a handwritten note from Russ Pittman: "NH–Last year FEV [Frank Vandiver] tried to give this group some money and Board hit the ceiling. You may wish to check with him before you proceed." See Grob Ad Hoc Committee folder.

93. Minutes of the Meeting of the Faculty Council, February 24, 1969, UA 106, box 3, folder 4. A few weeks after her first meeting with the committee on February 22, Williams received a formal appointment letter from Dean Gordon and sent back a typed and signed reply: "I accept with pleasure membership to the Committee on Minority Admissions." See Grob Ad Hoc Committee folder, which also includes the committee's written report on its activities. According to the interview with Elaine Frank in the Masterson Controversy Records, the students met only one more time with the committee that semester.

94. Johnson, "Breaking the Barriers."

95. Comments by Jan West at "Reflections of the Past, Promises for the Future"; "Room Assignment Questionnaire" for Hanszen College from 1969 in Ira Gruber Academic Papers, UA 204, box 6, folder 1; "Jensen's Study Casts Doubt on Compensatory Education," *RT*, January 15, 1970. On the sordid history of the use of IQ tests to postulate innate racial differences, see Stephen Jay Gould, *The Mismeasure of Man*, rev. ed. (New York: W. W. Norton, 1996).

96. Linda Faye Williams's sister Susan Williams (Brown College, Class of 1977) served as secretary in the Black Students Union in her sophomore year. See "Black Student Union Picks New Leaders," *RT*, March 14, 1974.

8. Black Student Unions

1. *RT*, February 17, 1972. See also "Rice's Linebacker Barnes Protests Lack of Blacks," Houston *Post*, February 13, 1972; "Barnes, Black Students Protest Before Rice-UT Basketball Game," Houston *Chronicle*, February 13, 1972.

2. A report on Black undergraduates enrolled at Rice in November 1972, after twenty-five Black freshmen had matriculated that fall, put their number at seventy-nine. See Hackerman Papers, UA 067, box 69, folder 3.

3. "Black Recruiting Campaign Gets Underway at Rice," *RT*, January 20, 1972.

4. Miles Schulze to Frank Vandiver, August 6, 1969, Vandiver/Hackerman Papers, UA 067, box 4, folder 4. For a fuller accounting of the university's record with respect to faculty hiring, see William D. Jones, "Faculty Diversity at Rice University, 1969–2012," copy in authors' possession. Rice had hired Dr. Kennard Reed Jr., a Black mathematician on the faculty at TSU, as a lecturer at Rice for the fall of 1965, but Reed resigned after one semester, alleging that he had faced harassment and hostility.

5. For the SA-approved constitution, see Student Association Records, UA 252, box 9, folder 11. In documents from the time, the BSU was referred to interchangeably as the "Black Students Union" or the "Black Student Union."

6. The petition, with signatures, can be found in Black Student Association Records, UA 370, box 1, folder 2. See "A Happy Hunter," Houston *Chronicle*, April 1, 1972; "Rice BSU Plans King Observance," Houston *Post*, April 8, 1972.

7. Stefan M. Bradley, *Upending the Ivory Tower: Civil Rights, Black Power, and the Ivy League* (New York: New York University Press, 2018); Biondi, *Black Revolution on Campus*, chaps. 5 to 8; Noliwe M. Rooks, *White Money/Black Power: The Surprising History of African American Studies and the Crisis of Race in Higher Education* (Boston: Beacon Press, 2006); Rose M. Brewer, "Politics and Power: Securing Resources for Black Study," *Black Perspectives*, November 14, 2019, www.aaihs.org.

8. James L. Conyers Jr., "Honoring the UH African American Studies Program's 50th Anniversary," *Houston History* 17, no. 1 (2019): 7–11. In 1969, on the initiative of anthropologist Frederick Gamst, Rice joined a Houston Inter-University African Studies Program that involved faculty at UH, TSU, Rice, and the University of St. Thomas. But the program, limited to joint colloquia and opportunities for graduate students to enroll in courses at other campuses, was short-lived and little utilized at Rice. In making requests for limited funds to administrators, Gamst also took pains to emphasize that the consortium was "not a 'Black studies program,' and is not constituted or administered with reference to the headlines or the academic fashions of the hour." It did "not concern itself with those of African descent and African culture in the New World." See Memorandum from Frederick C. Gamst to Rice Faculty and Administrative Officers, March 17, 1969, Vandiver-Hackerman Papers, UA 067, box 4, folder 7.

9. "Black Students Organize at Rice," *RT*, March 11, 1971. A few later records mention April 1971 as the founding moment for the BSU, suggesting that the group Birotte cochaired was a precursor for the official student organization whose constitution was approved the following year. See Student Association Records, UA 252, box 9, folder 11.

10. "Davidson: Token Integration Won't Satisfy Rice's Need to Progress," *RT*, September 2, 1971. At a homecoming panel the next month, Davidson appeared on a panel with Birotte, Alan Grob, Goldie Domingue, and others that stressed the importance of minority faculty hiring. See *Sallyport*, October–November 1971, 10; Rice University Task Force April 2, 2021, Doc Talk, digitalcollections.rice.edu/Documents/Detail/146610.

11. "Feelings Seconded Re Minorities," *RT*, September 16, 1971. Tapia had previously been a student and faculty member at UCLA and a postdoctoral researcher at the University of Wisconsin. See Richard A. Tapia, *Losing the Precious Few: How America Fails to Educate Its Minorities in Science and Engineering* (Houston: Arte Público, 2022), xv–xxxiv; David D. Medina, "'I Must Help': Richard Tapia's Mission is to Bring More Minority Students into Science, Engineering, and Mathematics Classes," *Sallyport* 50, no. 2

(October–November 1993): 16–21. On the official founding of RAMAS in 1972, when a record number of Mexican American students (seventeen) entered Rice, see "Mexican-Americans Organize at Rice," *High Emprise*, October 1972, 8; Jennifer Evans, "Excellence Comes in Many Flavors," *Sallyport* 59, no. 3 (Spring 2003): 12–13. See also RAMAS to Richard Stabell, May 30, 1972, in UA 067, box 37, folder 5. Although students and faculty from Latin America were not excluded from Rice even in the Institute years, the long and ongoing struggle for equity and respect for Latinx and Latin American students, faculty, and staff on campus needs and deserves much fuller historical study.

12. Minutes of the Meeting of the Faculty Council, April 1, 1971, Faculty Council Records, UA 106, box 4, folder 2. See also presidential staff meeting minutes in Hackerman Papers, UA 067, box 74, folders 11 and 12. In response to concerns raised by the Department of Health, Education, and Welfare to Frank Vandiver in 1969, an advisory Affirmative Action Committee, comprising faculty and staff, had been formed before Hackerman arrived. Yet, as a federal official pointed out, its authority was limited and the committee's initial membership was entirely white, which only underscored the problem it was meant to address. A Black staff scientist in space science, Willie Porter, was added to the committee for 1971–72, along with Spanish and Portuguese professor María Teresa Leal de Martinez, who was described by Vandiver as "Mexican-American" though she was born and raised in Brazil. Porter was succeeded the next year by two other Black staff members, Roosevelt Hodge and Dorris Murray; Martinez was succeeded by Tapia. See Hackerman/Vandiver Papers, UA 067, box 4, folders 4 and 5, and box 42, folder 14; "Rice University: An Equal Opportunity Employer," *High Emprise*, May 1972; Jones, "Faculty Diversity at Rice University."

13. *Sallyport* 26, no. 1 (August 1970): 1; M. V. McEnany to Norman Hackerman, with annotations, December 15, 1970, Ad Hoc Committees, UA 306, box 9, folder 1. The Grob committee appears to have ended as an official university committee in late 1971, though many of its members continued to work on recruiting with the help of funds from outside donors, including Humble Oil and John de Menil. See Faculty Council Minutes, April 1972, Faculty Council Records, UA 106, box 4, folder 3; Ad Hoc Grob Committee folder. Also compare Special Funds, President's Office, Monthly Reports for December 1970 and December 1971, UA 067, box 74, folder 8.

14. See annotations on memo from John L. Margrave to Norman Hackerman, November 29, 1971, Committee on Affirmative Action Records, UA 158, box 1, folder 3; "Black Recruiting Campaign Gets Underway at Rice." For Hackerman's budgetary concerns, see also "What It's Like to Pick a Staff, Black or White," Houston *Post*, April 2, 1972.

15. Rodrigo Barnes, with Christopher Dow, *The Bouncing Football: Life Lessons on the Gridiron* (Meadville, PA: Fulton Books, 2021), 103. While still president at UT-Austin in 1969, President Hackerman had also been approached there by Black students, led by Rodney Griffin, presenting their findings from a survey about their experiences. See Vincent, Cumberbatch, and Blair, eds., *As We Saw It*, 51–53; "Survey Shows Black Students' Problems," *Daily Texan* (UT-Austin), November 21, 1969, 10.

16. "What It's Like to Be Black at Rice," Houston *Post*, April 2, 1972. In the same article, perhaps in reference to his conversations with the president in the gym, Barnes said that "Dr. Hackerman is one of the people who thought we should start a black student union on campus. He did this the first of last year (1970–1971) when he came here."

17. Barnes, *The Bouncing Football*, 24–25.

18. Ibid., 59.

19. Ibid., 59, 61.

20. Ibid., 66, 76, 80.

21. Ibid., 77; speech by Stahlé B. Vincent at Rice University's First Black Student-Athletes Celebration, held at The Ion, Houston, September 16, 2022, manuscript in authors' possession.

22. Barnes, *The Bouncing Football*, 75. For examples of "slave auction" fundraisers at Rice's residential colleges, see *RT*, March 29, 1973; March 17, 1975; March 6, 1980; March 27, 1987; February 12, 1988; September 21, 1990; and December 8, 2000. In 1983, a study at Texas A&M University commissioned by Frank Vandiver, who was by then president on the College Station campus, found that "slave auctions" were among the college traditions that depressed minority student recruitment. See "Committee Finds Racism Rampant in College Town," *RT*, February 11, 1983.

23. Barnes, *The Bouncing Football*, 80–82; speech by Vincent.

24. Barnes, *The Bouncing Football*, 86. The examples mentioned here are drawn from recollections by Barnes and Vincent, as well as from anonymized reports in a speech by Chandler Davidson to the Society of Rice University Women given in spring 1975. Included in those reports was the story of a Black woman who was invited by a group of white students to room with them at a professor's house they were renting for the summer. When the Black woman indicated she would join, the rental offer was rescinded. See also "Survey of Black Population at Rice," a research paper by Gloria Guilford written for Davidson's class in 1974. Both the speech and the paper are in Chandler Davidson Academic Papers, UA 189, box 5, folder 4.

25. Barnes, *The Bouncing Football*, 88–89.

26. "Porter Urges Changes in University's Racial Policies," *RT*, April 25, 1968; Jan F. West comments in "Gifted and Black: The Early Years," *Rice Magazine*, Fall 2016, 30; "Panels Commemorate 40th Anniversary: Discussions Focus on the Past, Present and Future of Blacks at Rice," *RT*, February 23, 2007.

27. Barnes, *The Bouncing Football*, 88.

28. Ibid., 88.

29. Ibid., 87, 100–101.

30. Ibid., 102.

31. "Ex-Rocket McLemore Coaches for Owl Teams," *High Emprise*, April 1972, 1; "What It's Like to Be Black at Rice." See also "Staff Meeting—Minutes, February 28, 1972," Hackerman Papers, UA 067, box 74, folder 12.

32. "Freeman, Thomas F.—Religious Studies, 1972–1992," Past Faculty and Staff Files, UA 008. For Freeman's recollections about the conversation between Hackerman and TSU president Granville Sawyer, see "Dr. Freeman Reflects on His Time at Rice University," Texas Archive of the Moving Image, texasarchive.org/2013_00002.

33. "New Man in Admissions," *High Emprise*, September 1972, and "Assignment: Rice University," *High Emprise*, April 1972. For discussions about hiring a Black admissions counselor, see also M. V. McEnany to John Margrave, March 6, 1972, Hackerman Papers, UA 067, box 37, folder 5.

34. The Pfister profiles are in Hackerman Papers, UA 067, box 61, folder 17.

35. "Stabell Seeks More Personal, Intense Admissions Practices," *High Emprise*, December 1972–January 1973, 1; "Findings of the Subcommittee of the Affirmative Action Committee," Rice University Committee on Affirmative Action Records, UA 158, box 1, folder 5.

36. "Fulfillment Called Student Goal," Houston *Post*, September 30, 1973. See also "Bell, Robert L, Jr.—Psychology, 1973–1981," Past Faculty and Staff Files, UA 008. As an undergraduate, Bell had studied with Thomas Freeman at TSU, where he was a member of the debate team. As a graduate student at UT-Austin, he had participated in civil rights protests alongside Chandler Davidson, who was then an

undergraduate in Austin. See Doug Rossinow, *The Politics of Authenticity: Liberalism, Christianity, and the New Left in America* (New York: Columbia University Press, 1998), 121–32.

37. See the course listings in *General Announcements* for these years; research by Indya Porter, Class of 2022, "Student Research Showcase," episode 2 of the Task Force Doc Talks Podcast, September 18, 2020.

38. Pfister profiles in Hackerman Papers, UA 067, box 61, folder 17.

39. Ibid.; "What It's Like to Be Black at Rice."

40. Curtis Davis to Norman Hackerman, March 16, 1972, Black Student Association Records, UA 370, box 1, folder 2.

41. Black Student Association Records, UA 370, box 1, folder 2; "What It's Like to Be Black at Rice."

42. See memo by F. A. Wierum in Black Student Association Records, UA 370, box 1, folder 3.

43. Virgil W. Topazio, "Education Here and Abroad," *Sallyport* 26, no. 1 (August 1970): 4. See also Schrecker, *Lost Promise*, 389–90, 410–11.

44. "Davis Urges Black Student Center," *RT*, April 13, 1972. Davis's editorial also explained why he disagreed with the "proposals" that some on campus had made (though he did not say who) "for the establishment of a minorities student center instead of a Black Student's Union Center."

45. "BSU Planning King Memorial Day," *RT*, April 13, 1972.

46. Curtis Davis to Dr. Norman Hackerman, May 9, 1972, Hackerman Papers, UA 067, box 63, folder 9; M. V. McEnany to Curtis Davis, [June 7, 1972], Hackerman Papers, UA 067, box 63, folder 9. The same folder contains a memo (dated May 11) on the reasons why the ROTC building had been condemned, as well as a handwritten note by presidential assistant Carl MacDowell asking Hackerman if he wanted to explore alternative sites, such as the Rice Media Center, that might provide "limited use for black studies" or "cultural, sociological activities." Next to the question, Hackerman scrawled only a question mark, and a few days later MacDowell directed a secretary to file the Davis correspondence "as appropriate," noting "no action" was taken.

47. "Rice University Campus, Houston, Texas," map in *General Announcements for the Academic Year, 1973–1974* (Houston: Rice University, 1973), 2. See "Referendum is Big Issue in Senate," *RT*, October 5, 1972, which described the BSU's "'new' headquarters" as "an old fine arts building which they are sharing with the athletic Dept." The same rectangle is labeled "Fine Arts" on previous campus maps. On its past use as an art studio, see Melissa Kean, "The First Studio Art Building, 1966," *Rice History Corner* blog, March 19, 2019. For Hackerman's commitment of $2,000 in funding to the Black Students Union, see Monthly Report for December 1972, in UA 067, box 74, folder 8. The building, which still stands today surrounded by thick overgrowth, is now used for storage by Buildings and Grounds. Though it has been slightly modified and repainted, the rust-orange panels visible from inside the building confirm it to be the same steel shed seen in historical images. For one view of the building as it looked at the time, see *Campanile 1975*, 471, in the background of the bottom photograph.

48. For the $13,000 estimate, see "Referendum is Big Issue in Senate." For the Art Department's use of the space, see Bill Camfield to V. W. Topazio, September 7, 1971, UA 067, box 86, folder 5. See also Buildings and Grounds Department Capital Improvements, Special Maintenance, and Renovations Budget, 1973–74 Fiscal Year, UA 067, box 19, folder 6. That budget projected costs of $2,200 to "Replace 12 game table chairs and two easy chairs in lounge" at Wiess College, $2,000 to resurface the floor in Student Health Services with vinyl tile and some carpeting, plus drapes for the windows, and $2,000 to replace or repair chairs in three physics classrooms.

49. "Treasurer's Report, September 1972–1973," and "Proposal for Raffle," both in Student Association Records, UA 252, box 9, folder 11; "Referendum is Big Issue in Senate."

50. Gloria Guilford to Norman Hackerman, April 30, 1973, Hackerman Papers, UA 067, box 65, folder 14; "Treasurer's Report, September 1972–1973"; Black Students Union Proposal, April 22, 1974, Black Student Association Records, UA 370, box 1, folder 6.

51. Guilford to Hackerman, April 30, 1973, with attached note dated May 10, 1973, UA 067, box 64, folder 14. In addition to Guilford's presidency, women held all of the officer positions that year. See "New Leaders, Plans for BSU," *RT*, March 29, 1973.

52. Gloria Guilford to the Student Association of Rice University, April 30, 1973, and Douglass Appling to Gloria Guilford, May 31, 1973, Student Association Records, UA 252, box 9, folder 11.

53. "BSU and KTRU Vie for Profitable Xerox Concession," *RT*, September 13, 1973.

54. Ibid. See also Gloria Guilford to Ed Barnum, September 4, 1973, UA 252, box 9, folder 11.

55. "SA Awards Concession to BSU, Approves Chess Club," *RT*, September 20, 1973. After the BSU received the Xerox concession again, at least one of the colleges that had voted to direct $100 to the BSU rescinded the donation. See Will Rice Diet Meeting no. 8, September 18, 1973, UA 067, box 79, folder 6.

56. "Telephone Message from Dr. Akers, 2/15/74," Hackerman Papers, UA 067, box 11, folder 6; Black Student Association Records, UA 370, box 1, folder 3; Guilford to Richard Stabell, January 16, 1974, UA 067, box 11, folder 6.

57. The idea was initially raised before the SA in February. See "Senate Hears BSU Request for Share of College Money," *RT*, February 7, 1974. For the proposal to the masters and presidents, with mention of the history volumes, see Black Students Union Proposal, April 22, 1974, Black Student Association Records, UA 370, box 1, folder 6. On the TexPIRG arrangement, see Richard Bost, "TexPIRG at Rice," *Rice University Review*, Spring 1975, 9–13.

58. Memo from Katherine Brown to President Hackerman on Black Students Union, in Black Student Association Records, UA 370, box 1, folder 6.

59. Ibid. See UA 067, box 37, folder 8; Craig Leonard Jackson, "Black Studies Should Be Included at Rice," *RT*, February 6, 1975.

60. "Admissions Policies and Procedures," *Faculty Club Forum*, April 4, 1973. On the freshman week reception, see UA 067, box 46, folder 15. For examples of Black students working on admissions issues, see University Standing Committees, 1973–74, Committee on Admissions, UA 067, box 2, folder 1; "SCOAP Wants People to Sell Rice," *RT*, December 7, 1972.

61. Staff Meeting—Minutes, September 9, 1974, Hackerman Papers, UA 067, box 74, folder 15; notes on memo by Wierum and Hackerman in UA 067, box 37, folder 8. Hackerman's objection remained ten years later. See "Minority Groups Denied Funding," *RT*, September 21, 1984.

62. Details on this arrangement can be found in Student Association Records, UA 252, box 9, folder 48.

63. Report of the Minority Organization Funding Committee, UA 252, box 9, folder 48; "Minority Groups Get Chance at Blanket Tax," *RT*, October 30, 1975; "BSU Leaders Urge Approval of Minorities Blanket Tax," *RT*, November 3, 1975; "Blanket Tax Defeated in Student Vote," *RT*, November 13, 1975; "Senate Opposes Brown's Plan to Alter Funding," *RT*, April 15, 1976. The "blanket tax" was defeated by a vote of 809 students against, to 371 in favor.

64. Gloria Guilford to Bonnie Hellums, August 30, 1974, in Black Student Association Records, UA 370, box 1, folder 3.

65. Minutes of the Meeting of the Committee on Examinations and Standing, December 5, 1974, UA 163, box 3, folder 2.

66. *Campanile 1975*, 290. See also Guilford's independent research paper, written for Chandler Davidson in the fall of 1974, on a survey of Black students at Rice, in UA 189, box 5, folder 4. Cf. quote

from Paul Guillory in *Rice University Report of the President 1976* (Houston: Rice University, 1976), 12; senior pages by Frederick Brancha Foston in *Campanile 1973* and Craig Leonard Jackson in *Campanile 1977*.

67. *Rice University General Announcements, 1977–1978* (Houston: Rice University, 1977), 2. The building was still labeled on the map in *Campanile 1977*, inside the back cover.

68. For the Bubbha Thomas and the Lightmen concert, see Rice University KTRU Radio Records, Audio Recordings, 1976–77, box 7; "Music and Discussion Mark Black History Week," *RT*, February 10, 1977; "Pub Hosts Lightmen's First Gig," *RT*, February 17, 1977.

69. Mission quoted from the BSU Constitution in UA 252, box 9, folder 11.

70. "Vandiver Warns of Private Schools' Problems" and "Minority Staff Called Tokenism," *RT*, October 31, 1974; "Rice is 'Playing Games' with Affirmative Action," *RT*, November 14, 1974. Both Tapia and Bell soon thereafter resigned from the university's Affirmative Action Committee, citing internal polarization and the lack of any real power afforded to the group to recruit minority faculty and staff. See Affirmative Action Committee Records, UA 158, box 1, folder 5. The worry that affirmative action hiring risked "sacrificing quality" apparently had at least some adherents even on the Affirmative Action Committee. See "Report to the Rice University Self-Study Committee, May 14, 1973," item 12, in UA 067, box 4, folder 5.

71. "Faculty Should Contain More Blacks," *RT*, April 28, 1977.

72. Ibid.; "Rice's Linebacker Barnes Protests Lack of Blacks," Houston *Post*, February 13, 1972.

73. The Sociology Department had been lobbying for a permanent appointment for Brewer since at least 1975, on the strength of her already strong academic record. See Chad Gordon to Norman Hackerman, July 14, 1975, Hackerman Papers, UA 067, box 94, folder 1.

74. Rose Brewer to Norman Hackerman, March 30, 1977, in Past Faculty and Staff Files, UA 008, box 2, folder 1; "Black Culture, Women's Studies Programs Now at Rice," *RT*, April 25, 1986; "The Short History of Race-Based Affirmative Action at Rice University," *Journal of Blacks in Higher Education* 13 (Autumn 1996): 36–38.

9. Black Student Demands

1. "Tangible Ways to Improve the Black Experience, as Demanded by Black Students: Inaction is Not an Option," drive.google.com/file/d/1gi27qlhNjILkzvM-lzpdovnfVK6kkjkl/view (accessed September 29, 2024), copy in authors' possession. For more on the context around the petition, see Riya Misra, "'Read the Room, Willy': Students, Alumni Retrace the Down with Willy Movement," *RT*, November 29, 2023.

2. For early responses by students to this historic moment, see "Black at Rice: 'It Feels Like We're Mourning All the Time,'" *RT*, June 4, 2020. For an early statement by university leadership, see "Message to the Rice Community from President Leebron and Provost DesRoches" (email), June 16, 2020.

3. "Tangible Ways to Improve."

4. Ibid.

5. "Soul Night at Rice University," March 12, 2012, www.youtube.com/watch?v=VPkP-uJFFoo; "Afrofuturism–Africayé 2019," February 18, 2019, www.youtube.com/watch?v=92IxAq3mo4Q; "'We're All We've Got': BSA and RASA Celebrate Shared Identities," *RT*, February 16, 2022.

6. Katharine Shilcutt, "Black Excellence Gala Celebrates Black Life at Rice," *Rice News*, March 9, 2020. The inaugural gala was preceded in 2016 by the "ARUBA Blueprint for Excellence Gala: Celebrating 50 Years of Undergraduate Life at Rice," which honored six award winners, including early Black

students Rodrigo Barnes, Class of 1973, and Janis Scott, Class of 1974. See David Medina, "6 Honored at Blueprint for Excellence Gala," *Rice News*, October 3, 2016; Kendall Schoemann, "The State of Black Life at Rice," *Rice News*, October 3, 2016.

7. "Panels Commemorate 40th Anniversary: Discussions Focus on the Past, Present, and Future of Blacks at Rice," *RT*, February 23, 2007.

8. Both films are available in the collections of the WRC and were produced by Mouth Watering Media in collaboration with Rice University.

9. Eric Foner, *The Second Founding: How the Civil War and Reconstruction Remade the Constitution* (New York: W. W. Norton, 2019); Robert J. Cook, *Troubled Commemoration: The American Civil War Centennial, 1961–1965* (Baton Rouge: Louisiana State University Press, 2007); Peniel E. Joseph, *The Third Reconstruction: America's Struggle for Racial Justice in the Twenty-First Century* (New York: Basic Books, 2022).

10. Carole Emberton, "Unwriting the Freedom Narrative: A Review Essay," *Journal of Southern History* 82, no. 2 (May 2016): 377–94.

11. One of the earliest books to take stock of this wide-ranging movement on campuses was Leslie M. Harris, James T. Campbell, and Alfred L. Brophy, eds., *Slavery and the University: Histories and Legacies* (Athens: University of Georgia Press, 2019). See also Craig Steven Wilder, *Ebony and Ivy: Race, Slavery, and the Troubled History of America's Universities* (New York: Bloomsbury, 2013).

12. See "Rice University Students Engaged in a Black Lives Matter Protest on Campus" (photo), WRC Digital Collections, digitalcollections.rice.edu/Documents/Detail/70322; "Rice Considers Changes to 'Master' Title," *RT*, March 23, 2016; "Echoes of Slave-Owning Past Bring Change to Rice's College Masters" (online), Houston *Chronicle*, April 11, 2017; Lisa Gray, "At Rice, a Tweet-Storm Sets Off Discussion of the University's Racist Past" (online), Houston *Chronicle*, February 12, 2019.

13. Quotes are taken from emailed messages by President David Leebron to the Rice community on February 10, 2019, and May 30, 2020.

14. See, for example, from the *RT*: "Welcome to Rice, Maybe," April 18, 1980; "Blacks at Rice: Views of the Black Experience," September 25, 1980; "Chance for Minorities," March 12, 1981; "Barnes Defends Blanket Tax for Minorities," March 26, 1981; "Blacks Meet Constant Challenges at Rice and Elsewhere," February 17, 1984; "Rupp Speaks to Minority Students at Rice," May 15, 1987; "BSU Forum Raises Awareness of Hurdles Facing Blacks at Rice," February 16, 1990; "Rice Remembers MLK," January 25, 1991; "Institutionalized Riceism," February 8, 1991; "Rupp's Faux Pas Symbolizes Rice's Ambivalence about Black Culture," February 21, 1992; "Rice's 'Atmosphere' for African-American Students Needs Work," March 12, 1993; "Students Say Race Relations Far from Perfect," March 11, 1994; "Campus Practices Closet Racism," January 24, 1997; "Students Push for Ethnic Studies Major," April 12, 2002; "College System Can Alienate Minorities," November 7, 2003; "Gillis, Students Remember Martin Luther King, Jr. at Vigil," January 23, 2004; "Student Association," April 16, 2004; "Campus Reacts to Fallout from Incidents at Sid," February 1, 2008; "Value Marginalized Voices in Our Colleges" and "Students of Color Should Apply to Advise," February 24, 2016; "The Silenced Experience at Rice," March 5, 2019; "How Can Rice Be More Accommodating to Black Students?," January 11, 2022.

15. Quotes in this and the preceding paragraphs come from "Tangible Ways to Improve."

16. "Remove William Marsh Rice's Statue from the Rice University Academic Quad," June 21, 2020, *Change.org*, www.change.org/p/rice-university-administration-remove-william-marsh-rice-s-statue-from-the-rice-university-academic-quad. See also Misra, "Read the Room, Willy."

17. Email from President David Leebron and Provost Reginald DesRoches to Rice community,

June 23, 2020; Thresher Editorial Board, "Demands, not suggestions: When it comes to anti-racism on campus, the administration must listen to Black students," *RT*, July 6, 2020.

18. Talha Arif and Serene Lee, "Students sit-in at Founders Memorial to push for removal of statue," *RT*, September 15, 2020.

10. The Founder's Memorial

1. Arif and Lee, "Students sit-in at Founders Memorial to push for removal of statue"; Savannah Kuchar, "The Statue Dilemma: Students Are Leading a Daily Protest at the Founder's Statue," Winter 2021, *Rice Magazine*, issuu.com/riceuniversity/docs/ricemag_winter21_final; and Rice University Board of Trustees, "Board Statement Regarding the Academic Quadrangle and the Founder's Memorial," January 25, 2022, boardfeedback.rice.edu/board-statement-academic-quad-founders-memorial.

2. "Tangible Ways to Improve"; *On the Founder's Memorial* (Task Force on Slavery, Segregation and Racial Injustice, June 16, 2021), digitalcollections.rice.edu/Documents/Detail/297307; Talha Arif, "SA Unanimously Passes Resolution to Relocate Founder's Statue" (online), *RT*, November 30, 2021; Rice University Board of Trustees, "Board Statement."

3. Rynd Morgan, "Students push for removal of Founder's Memorial from academic quad, administration responds," *RT*, June 24, 2020.

4. Email from President David Leebron and Provost Reginald DesRoches to Rice community, June 23, 2020; "The Charge of the Task Force on Slavery, Segregation and Racial Injustice at Rice University," taskforce.rice.edu/charge (accessed October 5, 2024); and Anna Ta, "With Barely a Break for a Tropical Storm, Rice Students Continue to Protest Willy's Statue," Houston *Press*, September 28, 2020, www.houstonpress.com/news/rice-students-continue-to-call-for-removal-of-willys-statue-11498079.

5. "Student Proposes Memorial to William Marsh Rice," *RT*, February 29, 1924.

6. Ibid.

7. Meiners, *History of Rice University*, 125–26; Minutes of the Rice University Board of Trustees, May 24, 1922, vol. 4, Board of Trustees Minute Books, UA062; Stephen Fox, *The General Plan of the William M. Rice Institute and Its Architectural Development* (Houston: Rice University, 1980), 56–58, 65–66, plates 70–71.

8. Assistant Secretary of Rice Institute to John Angel, December 1, 1928, Rice University Early Land Deeds, Contracts, and Related Records, UA222, box 44, folder 6; Fox, *General Plan*, 70.

9. Alexander E. Hoyle to William Ward Watkin, February 28, 1927, William Ward Watkin Papers, MS 352, box 3, folder 3.

10. Contract with John Angel, New York, NY, for making and completing a Seated Portrait Statue of William M. Rice, Founder, in Bronze in connection with erection of Monument and Tomb, November 20, 1928, Early Land Deeds, Contracts and Related Records UA222, box 44, folder 6.

11. Edgar Odell Lovett to William M. Rice Jr., November 30, 1928, Lovett Papers UA 014, box 45, folder 6.

12. Ibid.; "Unveiling of the Statue of the Founder," *Rice Institute Pamphlets* 17, no. 3 (1930): 157.

13. F. M. Finch, "The Blue and the Gray," *Atlantic Monthly*, September 1867, www.theatlantic.com/magazine/archive/1867/09/blue-and-gray/590320/; David W. Blight, with the Yale and Slavery Research Project, *Yale and Slavery: A History* (New Haven, CT: Yale University Press, 2024), 307.

14. Blight, *Yale and Slavery*, 307–8; Richard Anderson, "Princeton's Civil War Memorial," *The Princeton and Slavery Project*, slavery.princeton.edu/stories/civil-war-memorial (accessed September 18, 2024).

15. Boles, *University Builder*, 90. For the reunion, see chapter 4 above.

16. Lovett, "Meaning of the New Institution," 87. Lovett mentioned the school's colors in two passages from this essay. In the second, briefer passage, he admitted, "The choice of colors was rather more difficult [than designing the university's shield], and it is a long story" (89). The first mention of the school's colors, quoted above, is full of symbology meant to evoke "the memories and traditions of the South, and all the moving inspiration in the promise and adventure of the West." While imagining the memories students would make for themselves at the university, Lovett said: "Under the Lone Star of Texas and the Owls of Rice, under the Blue and Gray floating from their standards—a blue still deeper than Oxford blue, and the gray of the Confederate days warmed into life by a tinge of lavender—they shall sing their songs; sing of jasmine, magnolias, and roses, poinsettia and violets blue; they shall cheer their teams and their heroes for the deeds of valor they do in field or forum or class-room; for Rice and for Houston and Texas they shall cheer and sing." For Van Dyke's poem, see hdl.handle.net/1911/8575.

17. Lovett, "Meaning of the New Institution," 49, 125. For the Yale alumni address by Chauncey Depew, see Blight, *Yale and Slavery*, 297–98. For a more extended analysis of Lovett's views about the South, which warrant further research and examination, see Task Force on Slavery, Segregation, and Racial Injustice, *Update on the Founder's Memorial, June 2021* ([Houston: Rice University], 2021), 7n10.

18. "Blue and Gray—The Unison," *RT*, September 17, 1920. An article in the *Thresher* from 1923 on the upcoming Rice-TCU football game contained a similar reflection on Rice's colors: "The war of the 60s saw fighting between the gray and the blue, but the North and South is cemented now more strongly than ever before. Blue and Gray now suggest unity." "Rice Topics," *RT*, November 29, 1923.

19. Blight, *Race and Reunion*, 3 (quote). See also Thavolia Glymph, "'Liberty Dearly Bought': The Making of Civil War Memory in Afro-American Communities in the South," in *Time Longer than Rope: A Century of African American Activism, 1850–1950*, ed. Charles M. Payne and Adam Green (New York: NYU Press, 2003), 111–39; W. Fitzhugh Brundage, *The Southern Past: A Clash of Race and Memory* (Cambridge, MA: Harvard University Press, 2005).

20. "Dr. Blayney to Deliver Commencement Address at Washington and Lee," *RT*, May 17, 1924; Edgar Odell Lovett, "Robert E. Lee: Address at the 'Southern Dinner' of the Twenty-eighth Annual Convention of the Texas Federation of Women's Clubs, Austin, Texas, 11 November 1925," in Lovett Papers, UA 014, box 51, folder 25. In another speech, "Southern Idealism," delivered in 1926 to the Southern Memorial Association, Blayney argued "that there is such a thing as a right-minded, constructive sectionalism" (Blayney Papers, MS 064, box 5, folder 2). See also "U.D.C. Will Honor Jackson and Lee at Exercises Today," Houston *Chronicle*, January 18, 1920; "Veterans Honor Doctor Blayney," Houston *Chronicle*, January 18, 1920; Thomas L. Connelly, *The Marble Man: Robert E. Lee and His Image in American Society* (New York: Knopf, 1977).

21. Edgar Odell Lovett to William M. Rice Jr., November 30, 1928, Lovett Papers, UA 014, box 45, folder 6. In late 1989, a professor of classics responded to a query from the office of then-university president George Rupp, asking for "Translations of the Latin Inscriptions on Willy's Statue." The lines on the side of the monument facing Lovett Hall, responded the professor, were "based on Virgil, *Aeneid* 11.97, salve aeternum . . . aeternumque vale: Hail forever . . . and forever farewell." As varied for the memorial, the meaning had been slightly changed to replace "farewell" with a second "hail." Harvey Yunis to George Rupp, December 2, 1989, Founder's Statue Information File, WRC; Edgar Odell Lovett to William M. Rice Jr., November 30, 1928, Lovett Papers, UA 014, box 45, folder 6.

22. Lovett to Rice Jr., November 30, 1928.

23. William Ward Watkin to Ralph Adams Cram, June 18, 1928, Watkin Papers, MS 352, box 3, folder 3.

24. Ibid.

25. Ibid. On the Alumni Building, see Fox, *General Plan*, 67–68.

26. Ralph Adams Cram to William Ward Watkin, July 2, 1928, William Ward Watkin Papers, MS 352, box 3, folder 3.

27. "Statue of William Marsh Rice Will Be Erected on Campus," *RT*, February 21, 1930; "Memorial to Rice Founder to be Erected," Houston *Post-Dispatch*, February 22, 1930, 15; "Watkin Tells Plan of W. M. Rice Statue," *RT*, March 21, 1930; Board Minutes, May 28, 1930 (for the placing of the remains); "Seniors to Hear Ralph Adams Cram," *RT*, May 2, 1930 ("cramming season"). For more on the construction process, see Task Force, *Update on the Founder's Memorial*, 13n20.

28. "Unveiling of the Statue," 158.

29. Ibid.; "Students Take Prominent Part in Unveiling of Rice Statue on June Eighth," and "Largest Class in History Will Be Graduated," *RT*, May 23, 1930.

30. "Unveiling of the Statue," 158; William Marsh Rice Jr. to Edgar Odell Lovett, May 21, 1930, Lovett Papers, UA014, box 36, folder 10.

31. William M. Rice Jr., "The Founder," *Rice Institute Pamphlet* 17, no. 3 (1930): 159.

32. "Students to Participate in Pageant," *RT*, May 5, 1933; "Legend of Houston is Applauded," *RT*, May 15, 1933; "Colorful Pageant Depicting History of Houston Will Be Staged at Auditorium Today," Houston *Post*, May 13, 1933; "5000 Applaud Presentation of Legend Here: History of Houston is Beautifully Depicted in Production," Houston *Post*, May 14, 1933. See also "Negro Singers in City Legend: Plantation Day Episode Arranged for Production Sunday," Houston *Post*, May 10, 1933 (quote). For a treatment of this kind of racialized white nostalgia in another southern city, see Stephanie E. Yuhl, *A Golden Haze of Memory: The Making of Historic Charleston* (Chapel Hill: University of North Carolina Press, 2005), esp. chaps. 2 and 4.

33. "Co-Eds Perfect Plans for May Fete at Mass Meeting," *RT*, March 28, 1930; and "Scene of Southern Splendor Set for Colorful Ceremony," *RT*, May 2, 1930.

34. "The May Fete," *Campanile 1931*, 162. That same year *Thresher* editors filled space with the following ditty: "L'il pickaninny / Looks just like his poppy, / Don't know what to call him. / 'Less its' carbon copy." "Carbon Copy," *RT*, March 28, 1930.

35. "Negroes to Depict Plantation Days in the 'Legend of Houston,'" Houston *Informer and Texas Freeman*, May 13, 1933; "These Special Negro Parts," Houston *Informer and Texas Freeman*, May 20, 1933.

36. See "The Mirror," "Folks, Just Leave it to Texas," and "Indictment against the South," Houston *Informer*, May 17, 1930. See also "Sherman Mob Burns Court House Cremating Negro Attack Suspect," Houston *Post-Dispatch*, May 9, 1930; Dustin Crawford, "The Lynching of George Hughes," *East Texas History*, easttexashistory.org/items/show/367; Sydney Trent, "In Texas, a struggle to memorialize a brutal lynching as resistance grows to teaching historical racism," Washington *Post*, June 3, 2021.

37. See "Crowd Burns Body of Negro Slayer," Houston *Post-Dispatch*, May 17, 1930, 1; "Body of Slain Negro Found Near Bryan," Houston *Post-Dispatch*, June 19, 1930; "Negro Gunman Slain by Posse," Houston *Post-Dispatch*, June 29, 1930, 1.

38. "The Founder," draft manuscript in Lovett Papers, UA 014, box 36, folder 10. This draft was likely enclosed with a letter from William Marsh Rice Jr. to Edgar Odell Lovett, December 3, 1928, found in the same folder.

39. Ibid. It isn't perfectly clear who rewrote that final line, but it was likely Rice Junior. In addition to the correction having been written on one of his stationary sets, idiosyncrasies of the handwriting in Rice Junior's December 3 note to Lovett also appear in the handwritten revision to the brief remarks on the founder—namely the cursive "R" in "Rice" and the "I" in "Institute." On the subtleties of Rice

Junior's choice of "beneficiaries" to describe the Institute's students, see *A Dictionary of Greek and Roman Antiquities*, comp. William Smith, William Wayte, and George Eden Marindin (Ann Arbor, MI: J. Murray, 1901), s.v. beneficium, and on the ways the change also fit into a certain Rice ideal about its colleges, and the relationship of the university to society, see "Rice Students and Alumni Should Be Proud of School," *RT*, May 5, 1933; and Lovett, "Meaning of the New Institution," 76–86, 108–26, and *passim*. The switch from "the young men and women of Texas" to "the beneficiaries of the Rice Institute" raises other issues worthy of consideration. The first draft may have seemed at once too broad (it did not take into account the charter's racial bar, for instance) and too geographically narrow for the Institute's ambitions, under Lovett's leadership, to be a university that would benefit not just Texas, but the nation and the world. Also worthy of further reflection is the fact that Rice Junior transposed the order in which he mentioned the men and women of the Institute for the final version of his remarks—giving primacy of place to the Institute's women students as a daughter of the family who was also then a student at the university looked on and listened.

40. "Memorial to Rice Founder to be Erected," Houston *Post-Dispatch*, February 22, 1930; "Statue of William Marsh Rice Will be Erected on Campus," *RT*, February 21, 1930; and "The Sculptor," *Rice Institute Pamphlet* 17, no. 3 (1930): 160.

41. "The Sculptor," 160–61.

42. We do not presently know the nature or content of the prayer that concluded the brief ceremony.

43. Ralph Adams Cram, "The Limitations of Democracy," *Rice Institute Pamphlet* 17, no. 3 (1930): 194, 178.

44. Cram, "The Limitations of Democracy," 185–86.

45. Cram, "The Limitations of Democracy," 187–88, 197.

46. "Cram Pictures Man's Decline Through the Ages: Educator Links Up Dry Law With Methodist Board and Ku Klux Klan," Houston *Post-Dispatch*, June 10, 1930.

47. James Gordon Gilkey, "Getting a Perspective on Success," *Rice Institute Pamphlet* 17, no. 3 (1930): 168–69, 172.

48. John Angel to Edgar Odell Lovett, June 14, 1930, Lovett Papers, UA 014, box 14, folder 9.

49. "Willy's Statue Celebrates a Birthday," March 19, 2010, www.youtube.com/watch?v=YEi7EjXlseg. See also "'Willy Revolutionaries' Return to Rice for 20th Anniversary of Prank," *RT*, April 18, 2008. Opening any yearbook since 1931 provides ample evidence of the monument's growing centrality on campus. Also see "Centennial Video Series: Willy's Statue," September 7, 2012, www.youtube.com/watch?v=xGE5B-dQsJo; and Melissa Kean, "there are always special corners," *Rice History Corner* blog, February 6, 2021, ricehistorycorner.com/2017/02/06/there-are-always-special-corners-1930/.

50. "Dr. Freeman Reflects on His Time at Rice University," Texas Archive of the Moving Image, texasarchive.org/2013_00002. See also Rice University Task Force, November 6, 2020, Doc Talk, digitalcollections.rice.edu/Documents/Detail/146601.

51. "20 Percent of Student Body Cheer, Jeer [Richard] Nixon Appearance," *RT*, September 12, 1968; "Reaction to Abbie [Hoffman] Precipitates Crisis at Rice," *RT*, April 16, 1970; "Anti-War Willy," *RT*, March 7, 2003, 1; "Rice Gay/Lesbian Support Group," *Campanile 1983*, 89; "KTRU Off the Air Pending 'Reorganization,'" *RT*, December 1, 2000, 1.

52. "Making a Plan, Proving a Point," *RT*, April 26, 2002. See also "Students Design Parking Proposal" in the same issue, with a photograph of the rally on page 7. For Welch, see "Rice People's Calendar," *RT*, March 22, 1973.

53. "Scott Quits Sophomore Class Post: Resignation is Submitted After Resolution Concerning

Rice Statue is Made," *RT*, October 28, 1932; "Rice Sophomores Called to Meet in Effort to Settle Official Tangle," Houston *Chronicle*, November 4, 1932; "Sophomores Will Settle Class Issue: Group Will Meet Wednesday—Letters On Situation are Turned In," *RT*, November 4, 1932; Meiners, *History of Rice University*, 126–27. Also see "To Protect a Tomb," *RT*, October 18, 1935.

54. "Administration Disallows Yellow Ribbons," "Ribbon Rabblerouser Reprimanded," and "Ribbons as Worthy as King Wreath," all in *RT*, February 22, 1991. Debate over the administration policy continued in subsequent letters to the editors; one writer who opposed the ribbon policy as "political correctness" run amok suggested, as a kind of *reductio ad absurdum*, that perhaps the statue of William Marsh Rice himself should be removed, since he "founded this university exclusively for white male [*sic*] residents of the city of Houston." See *RT*, March 8, 1991, 3.

55. "Art Around Willy's Statue to Honor Donors," *RT*, April 10, 2009.

56. Editorial page of *RT*, April 17, 2009. See also "Leebron Q&A," *RT*, May 15, 2009; "Student Association Minutes," *RT*, March 12, 2010; "Decision to Postpone Willy's Rings Sensible," *RT*, February 5, 2010.

57. For more examples of student participation in this debate, see "Replace Willy's Statue with Johnson," *RT*, June 22, 2020; "Remembering Rice," *RT*, July 20, 2020; "William Rice's Statue Can Stand for His Achievements Despite his Moral Flaws," *RT*, August 3, 2020; "Say Something: Administration Should Respond to Willy's Statue Sit-Ins," *RT*, September 23, 2020; "An Open Letter to the Board of Trustees: When are You Taking the Statue Down?" *RT*, September 30, 2020; "It's Black History Month. Let's Listen to our Black Students," *RT*, February 2, 2021; "Enough Deliberation: Down With Willy," *RT*, March 2, 2021; "Letter to the Editor: An Old Alum Joins the Statue Debate," *RT*, March 24, 2021; "The Statue is Only a Starting Point," *RT*, March 27, 2021; "Willy Week No More: Students have the Power to Distance from William Marsh Rice," *RT*, April 7, 2021; "Dear Tex: Willy's Statue Should be Removed," *RT*, April 21, 2021.

58. For sample responses from the community questionnaire, see "Community questionnaire on Founder's Memorial, Rice University," digitalcollections.rice.edu/Documents/Detail/374165.

59. See Rice University Task Force on Slavery, Segregation, and Racial Injustice, *Update: June 2021, on Research about Slavery* (Houston: Rice University, 2021), digitalcollections.rice.edu/Documents/Detail/297308; *Update: June 2021, on the Founder's Memorial* (Houston: Rice University 2021), digitalcollections.rice.edu/Documents/Detail/297307.

60. Rice University Task Force, *Update . . . on the Founder's Memorial*, 30.

61. "Message from the Chairman of the Board and the President," email, August 31, 2021.

62. "SA Unanimously Passes Resolution to Relocate Founder's Statue," online, *RT*, November 30, 2021.

63. "Board Statement Regarding the Academic Quadrangle and the Founder's Memorial," email, January 25, 2022, boardfeedback.rice.edu/board-statement-academic-quad-founders-memorial.

64. Ibid. In February 2023, the university announced the selection of a new design for the quad produced by landscape architecture firm Nelson Byrd Woltz (NBW). That fall, the quad closed for the construction of the NBW design, which included the relocation of the William Marsh Rice statue to a corner within the quad. The redesigned space reopened with a ribbon-cutting ceremony on September 12, 2024.

Epilogue

1. Rice University Black Student Association (@ricebsa), "Ticket Form is due today!! Get your tickets before it's too late!!" Instagram, February 2023, www.instagram.com/p/CpD2dkYuVcl/; BSA Officers' email message to BSA Black Excellence Gala Guests, March 4, 2023.

2. The details of Velma McAfee Williams's Rice story, as captured here, are based on three phone conversations (two individual discussions with Mrs. Williams, and one with her youngest daughter, Dr. Yvonne Williams Boyd); two video-recorded interviews with Mrs. Williams, with Dr. Williams Boyd contributing; and one additional follow-up conversation with Mrs. Williams and Dr. Williams Boyd. The telephone conversations took place on October 26, October 27, and November 3, 2022. The recorded interviews transpired on December 2, 2022, and on January 18, 2023. The final follow-up conversation occurred on August 1, 2023.

3. Texas Department of Health–Bureau of Vital Statistics, State File no. 63214, January 5, 1956 (corrected), Velma Bernice McAfee, on Ancestry.com.

4. Williams's elder brother, Walter Samuel McAfee, was a part of the U.S. Army Signal Corps team that pioneered critical radar astronomy experiments, called Project Diana, in the late 1940s. He earned a PhD in physics from Cornell University in 1949. "Project Diana Scientist Gets GS-16 Promotion," *Army Research and Development: Monthly Newsmagazine of the Office of the Chief Research, Research and Development* 12, no. 1 (January–February 1971): 1, 10; Office of the Deputy Chief of Staff for Operations and Plans, U.S. Army CECOM, *A History of Army Communications and Electronics at Fort Monmouth, New Jersey, 1917–2007* (Fort Monmouth, NJ, 2008), 29, 35, 37–38; 165 Cong. Rec. E1110 (Extension of Remarks, September 9, 2019, statement of Hon. Christopher H. Smith); BlackPast.org, s.v. "Walter Samuel McAfee," by Christopher Kinson (accessed August 28, 2023); *Wikipedia*, s.v., "Walter Samuel McAfee," last modified June 13, 2023, en.wikipedia.org/wiki/Walter_McAfee/.

5. "6 TSU Profs to Attend Institutes," Houston *Chronicle*, May 6, 1964; National Science Foundation, *14th Annual Report* (Washington, DC, 1965), 69–75; *Carnegie Corporation of New York, Annual Report: For the Fiscal Year Ended September 30, 1965* (New York, 1965), 31; Rockefeller Foundation, *Annual Report for 1965* (New York, 1965), 61.

6. Committee on Business Mathematics, *College Business Mathematics* (New York: Pitman Publishing Corp., 1960). Of those on the Rice faculty in the fall of 1965, Kennard W. Reed Jr.'s experience in U.S. higher education approached Williams's in breadth. Reed, the university's first Black faculty member, was visiting assistant professor in the Mathematics Department upon Williams's arrival. He held an undergraduate degree from Fisk University and a PhD from New York University, had previously taught at Dartmouth College, and while teaching at Rice was on leave from an appointment at Texas Southern University. See Morton L. Curtis to Kennard Reed, March 17, 1965, Rice University Past Faculty and Staff Records, UA 008, folder 98; R. O. Wells Jr. to Norman Hackerman, "Re: Black Faculty Members," April 2, 1972, UA 067, box 90, folder 1; "First Negro to Serve on Rice Faculty," Houston *Post*, June 17, 1965; "It's Not News In a Just Society, but . . . ," Houston *Chronicle*, June 18, 1965; "What Ever Happened to . . . Rice's First Black Professor," Houston *Post*, May 25, 1981. Reed is featured in the trailblazing online exhibit "Rice University Between Decisions: From Co-Education to Integration, 1957–1970," digitalcollections.rice.edu/online-exhibits/rice-university-between-decisions-from-coeducation-to-desegregation.

7. L. K. Bradley, C. R. Newell, and V. M. Williams, "The Relationship Between the Performance of the Texas Southern University Freshmen on the Mathematics Placement Test and Their High School Mathematics Background," *American Mathematical Monthly* 73, no. 2 (1966): 188–90.

8. The following treatment of the pathway to the PhD in mathematics is drawn from *Rice University General Announcements*, 1964–70, digitalcollections.rice.edu/rice-publications/rice-university-general-announcements.

9. On the nuances and complexities related to the articulation of Jim Crow education in the United States, classic work by Anna Julia Cooper, W. E. B. Du Bois, and Carter G. Woodson offer excellent starting points: Anna Julia Cooper, *A Voice from The South: By a Black Woman of the South* (Xennia, OH: Aldine Printing House, 1892), esp. 48–79; Carter G. Woodson, *The Mis-Education of the Negro* (Washington, DC: Associated Publishers, 1933); W. E. B. Du Bois, "Does the Negro Need Separate Schools?" *Journal of Negro Education* 4, no. 3 (1935): 328–35. For background on the shape, nature, and continuing dismantling of segregated education in the United States, particularly in the South, see James D. Anderson, *The Education of Blacks in the South, 1860–1935* (Chapel Hill: University of North Carolina Press, 1988); Jarvis R. Givens, *Fugitive Pedagogy: Carter G. Woodson and the Art of Black Teaching* (Cambridge, MA: Harvard University Press, 2021); Richard Kluger, *Simple Justice: The History of Brown v. Board of Education and Black America's Struggle for Equality* (New York: Vintage Press, 2004); Adam Fairclough, *A Class of Their Own: Black Teachers in the Segregated South* (Cambridge, MA: Belknap Press, 2007); Vanessa Siddle Walker, *The Lost Education of Horace Tate: Uncovering the Hidden Heroes Who Fought for Justice in Schools* (New York: New Press, 2018); Raymond Gavins, *The Perils and Prospects of Southern Black Leadership: Gordan Blaine Hancock, 1884–1970* (Durham, NC: Duke University Press, 2012); and Pitre, *Born to Serve*.

10. In David W. Levy's recounting of George McLaurin's enrolling at the University of Oklahoma, the chapter focused on McLaurin's initial classroom experiences is called "Twenty-One Months of Hell." Levy, *Breaking Down Barriers: George McLaurin and the Struggle to End Segregated Education* (Norman: University of Oklahoma Press, 2020), 85–114 (quote from 85).

11. The same Supreme Court heard the cases that resulted in the desegregation of the University of Oklahoma and the University of Texas. Still, when the first Black undergraduates entered UT in the mid 1950s, the consequences of Jim Crow persisted. Accordingly, the desegregation of the undergraduate student body at Texas did not at first include the provision of desegregated undergraduate housing or other facilities. *Sweatt v. Painter*, 339 U.S. 629 (1950); *McLaurin v. Oklahoma State Regents*, 339 U.S. 637 (1950); Vincent, Cumberbatch, and Blair, eds., *As We Saw It*, 33–34, 63–67; and Dwonna Goldstone, *Integrating the 40 Acres: The Fifty-Year Struggle for Racial Equality at the University of Texas* (Athens: University of Georgia Press, 2012).

12. Kean, *Desegregating Private Higher Education*, esp. chap. 5.

13. Jim Douglas Jr., also a Rice PhD, was a faculty member in the Mathematics Department from 1957 to 1968. Among his more than forty PhD students—from Rice, the University of Chicago, and Purdue University—was Raymond Johnson. Mathematics Genealogy Project, s.v. "Jim Douglas, Jr." (accessed August 31, 2023).

14. From fall 1964 through spring 1968, the *General Announcements* outlined a provision for retaking qualifying exams in mathematics. From the fall of 1968 through the spring of 1970, however, there was no such provision. The provision in question returned in the fall of 1970. As best as we can tell, Mrs. Williams's exam took place sometime between the fall of 1968 and the spring of 1969. See *Rice University General Announcements*, 1964, 162; 1965, 179; 1966, 192; 1967, 204; 1968, 218–19; 1969, 232–33; 1970, 248–49.

15. Yvonne Williams Boyd to David W. Leebron, n.d. [April 11, 2013], copy in authors' possession.

16. For a sense of the scope and nature of the 2016 recognition, see "Fifty Years of Black Undergraduate Life," *Rice Magazine*, Fall 2016, rice-magazine.com/tag/50-years-of-black-undergraduate-life/.

17. The description that follows depends on a video recording of the 2016 ceremony and on a program from the event. Rice University Class of 2016 Doctoral Convocation program, May 13, 2016, Rice University Commencement Files, UA 342; vimeo.com/861298473.

18. The scope and consequence of Mrs. Williams's "impressive career," alluded to in Dean Matsuda's remarks, were expansive. Of course, before enrolling at Rice for graduate school, and for a short time while enrolled at Rice, she served in the Mathematics Department at Texas Southern University. Following Rice, Williams taught math at the University of St. Thomas and later at the fledgling High School for Health Professions (now the Michael E. DeBakey High School for Health Professions). As during her higher education, she continuously balanced pressing professional and personal demands. Williams accepted a position at Texas Instruments while teaching at the University of St. Thomas, but she ultimately did not take up the post because her mother became ill around the same time. Thereafter Mrs. Williams focused on caring for her mother, as well as on community work.

19. John Hutchinson (Dean Hutch): "Today, Velma McAfee Williams was honored with the presentation of the doctoral academic regalia at the doctoral hooding ceremony, part of Rice's 103rd Commencement," Facebook, May 13, 2016, www.facebook.com/photo/?fbid=10203263546877780.

20. Seiichi Matsuda, email message to selected faculty, September 6, 2016; Black Graduate Student Association Officers, email message to selected students, staff, and faculty, December 2, 2016; Matsuda, email message to selected faculty, August 11, 2018; Rice Black Graduate Student Association (@bgsarice), "Friendly reminder to our graduate students to grab a bite and hang out with your fellow colleagues," Instagram, February 16, 2019, www.instagram.com/p/B2ek468ABgE/.

21. Kendall Schoemann, "Tracing the History of Blacks at Rice," *Rice at Large* (Rice University Office of Public Affairs), Winter 2016, ral.rice.edu/stories/2019/winter/tracing-history-blacks-rice/; Jan West, "A Golden Moment for Public Affairs," *Rice at Large*, Spring 2019, ral.rice.edu/stories/2019/spring/golden-moment-public-affairs/.

22. Randal L. Hall, *The Inauguration of Reginald DesRoches: The Beginning of His Presidency at Rice University* (Houston: Rice University, 2023), 44; Arie Wilson Passwaters, "Black Alumni Celebrate New President," *Rice News*, October 24, 2022, news.rice.edu/news/2022/black-alumni-celebrate-new-president/; Rice University, "The Inauguration of President DesRoches," November 14, 2022, vimeo.com/770810741/, at 4:13.

23. Williams's story faded away on campus, but it did not disappear completely. Traces remained in the archives. For instance, two of the pages in a folder collecting materials on minority students at Rice list Williams among eight Black students enrolled at the university in the late 1960s. Both lists were evidently composed in the 1960s. See Students—Minorities Info File, WRC.

24. The work of Black students, staff, and faculty—who thoughtfully advocated for, recorded, and reflected on their experiences in multiple forms and fora—laid the archival foundations for the history of Black life at Rice. Among the recent examples are a series of compelling student profiles in the *RT* under the headlines "Black at Rice" and "Black Art at Rice." Additionally, Black alumni have played a leading role in collecting, analyzing, and contributing to knowledge about Black Rice. While a history PhD student at the university in 1996, Rice undergraduate alumna Karen Kossie-Chernyshev helped to create a sense of historical urgency and imagination around analyzing the Black experience on campus; she delivered a speech in the Duncan Recital Room at Alice Pratt Brown Hall titled "Africana Students at Rice: A Collection of Memories, a Work in Progress" and conducted an early survey of Black alumni about their experiences. The activities of ARUBA and its precursors have also been crucial. The Office of Multicultural Community Relations, often through the work of David Medina (who wrote an early

profile of Raymond Johnson for the *Rice Sallyport* in 2004) and Jan West, has been fundamental to nurturing and expanding consciousness of the importance of Black history to the history of the university. The office's 2016 exhibit is one key example; the 2012 documentary *Young, Gifted and Black* is another. The published and unpublished work of undergraduate and graduate researchers, examples of which are cited in other areas of this report and listed in the appendix, round out an advantageous starting place for a fuller history of the university and of Blacks at Rice.

25. In addition to naming Raymond Johnson and Velma McAfee Williams as Black graduate students in the late 1960s, contemporary documents in the Students—Minorities Info File indicate that James E. McLeod (misspelled as "McCloud" in the file) was a PhD student in Germanics, and that N. C. Mogbo was pursuing a doctorate in civil engineering. For more on McLeod, see Susan Killenberg McGinn, "James E. McLeod, 67," *The Record* (Washington University in St. Louis), September 7, 2011, source.wustl.edu/2011/09/james-e-mcleod-67/; Rebecca S. Rivas, "Jim McLeod, Pioneering Washington University Dean, Passes at 67," St. Louis *American*, September 9, 2011; Gerald Early, "Remembering James McLeod and the Rise of Black Studies at Washington University," 10th Annual James E. McLeod Memorial Lecture, Center for the Humanities, Washington University in St. Louis, September 30, 2021, humanities.wustl.edu/news/remembering-james-mcleod-and-rise-black-studies-washington-university/. For more on Mogbo, see Nathan C. I. Mogbo, "Torsional Behavior of Spandrel Beams," MS thesis, Rice University, 1968, hdl.handle.net/1911/89263; Nathan Chidozie Ikpeazu Mogbo, "Effect of Concrete Coating on the Behavior of Line-Pipe," PhD diss., Rice University, 1970, hdl.handle.net/1911/14646; "Ford Engineer and Son of Nigerian Village Chief," May 26, 2012, on Ancestry.com, www.ancestry.com/mediaui-viewer/collection/1030/tree/26157324/person/12585770632/media/2b3db466-cc7a-4fad-b36d-c77796dee291/, copy in authors' possession. So by 1970, when the first two Black undergraduate students were graduated from the university, two Black PhD students had been graduated from Rice as well: Raymond Johnson and Nathan C. I. Mogbo.

26. Jeanne Theoharis, *A More Beautiful and Terrible History: The Uses and Misuses of Civil Rights History* (Boston: Beacon Press, 2018).

Appendix C

1. The full maiden name of Rice's younger sister, Minerva Rice Olds, whose married name was omitted in the blank space of this will, was Sally (or Sallie) Minerva Rice. She married Amos Olds in 1846. See B. Rice Aston, *The Promiscuous Breed* (Houston: [B. Rice Aston], 2005), 13; Andrew Forest Muir Papers, MS 17, box 69, folder 5.

Index